Certificate Stage

Module D

Tax Framework
(Finance Act 1998)

ACCA Textbook

7768/J98

British Library Cataloguing-in-Publication Data

A catalogue record for this book is available from the British Library.

Published by AT Foulks Lynch Ltd
Number 4
The Griffin Centre
Staines Road
Feltham
Middlesex
TW14 0HS

ISBN 0 7483 3776 8

© AT Foulks Lynch Ltd, 1998

Printed in Great Britain by Ashford Colour Press, Gosport, Hants.

Acknowledgements

We are grateful to the Association of Chartered Certified Accountants, the Chartered Institute of Management Accountants and the Institute of Chartered Accountants in England and Wales for permission to reproduce past examination questions. The answers have been prepared by AT Foulks Lynch Ltd.

CONTENTS

September 99.

October 99

November

PREFACE

This Textbook is the ACCA's official text for paper 7, Tax Framework, and is part of the ACCA's official series produced for students taking the ACCA examinations.

It has been produced with direct guidance from the examiner specifically for paper 7, and covers the syllabus in great detail giving appropriate weighting to the various topics. It is fully up-to-date for the Finance Act 1998, which is examinable in June 1999. This book is not suitable for candidates for the December 1998 exam for whom a separate textbook is available.

This Textbook is, however, very different from a reference book or a more traditional style textbook. It is targeted very closely on the examinations and is written in a way that will help you assimilate the information easily and give you plenty of practice at the various techniques involved.

Particular attention has been paid to producing an interactive text that will maintain your interest with a series of carefully designed features.

- **Activities**. The text involves you in the learning process with a series of activities designed to arrest your attention and make you concentrate and respond.

- **Definitions**. The text clearly defines key words or concepts. The purpose of including these definitions is **not** that you should learn them - rote learning is not required and is positively harmful. The definitions are included to focus your attention on the point being covered.

- **Conclusions**. Where helpful, the text includes conclusions that summarise important points as you read through the chapter rather than leaving the conclusion to the chapter end. The purpose of this is to summarise concisely the key material that has just been covered so that you can constantly monitor your understanding of the material as you read it.

- **Self test questions**. At the end of each chapter there is a series of self test questions. The purpose of these is to help you revise some of the key elements of the chapter. The answer to each is a paragraph reference, encouraging you to go back and re-read and revise that point.

- **End of chapter questions**. At the end of each chapter we include examination style questions. These will give you a very good idea of the sort of thing the examiner will ask and will test your understanding of what has been covered.

Complementary Revision Series

The ACCA Revision Series contains all the new syllabus exams from June 1994 to December 1997 with the examiner's own official answers. The edition of the Revision Series updated for the Finance Act 1998 will be published in late 1998 or early 1999.

What better way to revise for your exams than to read and study the examiner's own answers!

FORMAT OF THE EXAMINATION

	Number of marks
Section A: 3 compulsory questions	67
Section B: 3 (out of 5) questions of 11 marks each	33
	100

Time allowed: 3 hours

Tax rates and allowances will be given in the paper.

Section A will contain questions on Income Tax, Corporation Tax and Capital Gains Tax.

With regard to business taxation, students sitting paper 7 should note the following:

(a) **The preceding year basis (PYB)**

The PYB rules are not examinable.

(b) **The transitional rules**

The transitional rules are not examinable.

(c) **The new current year basis (CYB)**

This covers the rules for profits, capital allowances and losses both on commencement, on a continuing basis and on cessation.

CYB rules are examinable in full.

(d) **Self assessment**

Self assessment is examinable in full.

The old system of administration applicable to income tax and CGT is no longer examinable.

(e) **Change of accounting date**

The rules applicable to a change of accounting date are examinable.

Following the Finance Act 1997 (No. 2), a corporation tax question will not be set:

- Involving the carry back of losses incurred in an accounting period commencing prior to 2 July 1997.

- On s.242 ICTA 1988 loss relief.

SYLLABUS

Certificate stage - Module D Paper 7: THE TAX FRAMEWORK

Chapter reference

(1)   OVERVIEW OF THE TAX SYSTEM

(a)	Structure and procedures of Inland Revenue and Customs & Excise.	1, 25
(b)	Duties and powers of the Inspector of Taxes and VAT offices.	1, 26
(c)	Returns.	1, 26
(d)	Schedular system of Income Tax.	2
(e)	Assessments, due dates, interest on overdue tax, repayment supplement.	1
(f)	Sources of information - statute, case law, statements of practice, VAT leaflets, extra-statutory concessions.	1, 25

(2)   INCOME TAX ON EMPLOYEES AND UNINCORPORATED BUSINESSES

(a)	Basis of assessment under Schedule E (including emoluments of office and pension).	7
(b)	Benefits in kind.	8
(c)	Lump sum receipts.	7
(d)	PAYE system.	1
(e)	Employees' incentive schemes.	7
(f)	Principles and scope of Cases I and II of Schedule D.	9, 13
(g)	Rules basis and application of Cases I and II.	9, 13
(h)	Other sources including	
	(i) Schedule A	3
	(ii) Schedule D Cases III and VI.	4
(i)	Calculating tax liability.	2
(j)	Minimising/deferring tax liability.	5, 10, 11, 12

(3)   TAXATION OF CORPORATE BUSINESSES

The impact of Corporation Tax on the transactions and other activities of corporate taxpayers

(a)	Principles and scope of Corporation Tax.	22
(b)	Rules basis and application of Corporation Tax.	22, 23

THE OFFICIAL ACCA TEACHING GUIDE

Paper 7 - Tax Framework

*Syllabus
Reference*

Session 1   Income Tax - Introduction

♦   organisation of Inland Revenue   1
♦   income liable to Income Tax
♦   schedular system
♦   returns, assessments and appeals
♦   Special and General Commissioners and later appeal courts
♦   introduction to personal computations

Session 2   Income Tax - Schedule D Case I

♦   meaning of trade   2
♦   badges of trade
♦   income assessable under Schedule D Case I or Schedule E
♦   self employment and employment

Session 3   Income Tax - Schedule D Case I

♦   computation of assessable profit   2, 5, 6
♦   pre-trading expenditure
♦   National Insurance and Social Security aspects

Session 4   Income Tax - Schedule D Case I

♦   basis of assessment   2
♦   basis of assessment in opening and closing years with alternative bases
♦   farmers' averaging claims

Session 5   Income Tax - Capital Allowances

♦   basis periods in opening and closing years with alternative bases   2
♦   plant and machinery allowances including writing-down allowances,
     first-year allowances, short-life assets and assets with private use by the
     proprietor

Session 6   Income Tax - Capital Allowances

♦   definition of industrial building   2
♦   industrial buildings allowance including temporary disuse and non-
     industrial use
♦   agricultural buildings allowance
♦   patents
♦   scientific research
♦   know-how

Session 7   Income Tax - Losses

♦   early years   2
♦   carry-forward
♦   set-off against other income relief for S350 assessments
♦   terminal loss relief
♦   relief for losses on shares in unquoted trading companies

List of Excluded Topics

NATIONAL INSURANCE
- The calculation of directors NIC on a month by month basis.
- For the purposes of class 4 NIC: the offset of trading losses against non-trading income.

INCOME TAX
- Loan interest - £30,000 per person relief for main residence.
- Foreign income, non-residents and double tax relief.
- Anti-avoidance legislation.
- Detailed computations in respect of share options, share incentives, profit sharing and profit related pay. An employee share ownership plan (ESOP) will not be examined in its own right.
- A detailed knowledge of the conditions which must be met to obtain Inland Revenue approval for an occupational pension scheme.
- Commercial woodlands.

CAPITAL GAINS TAX
- Settlements and period of administration after death.
- Groups of companies and consortia.
- Anti-avoidance legislation.
- The rules applicable to assets held on 6 April 1965.
- The grant of a lease or sub-lease out of either a freehold, long lease or short lease.

A question would not be set in respect of a principal private residence where the tax-payer was not in occupation on 31 March 1982.

VALUE ADDED TAX
- Second-hand goods scheme.
- The capital goods scheme.
- In respect of property and land; leases, do-it-yourself builders and demolition.
- A detailed knowledge of penalties, apart from the default surcharge, serious misdeclarations and default interest.

CORPORATION TAX
- Close companies.
- Controlled foreign companies.
- Investment companies.
- Groups of companies and consortia.
- Foreign income, non-resident companies, double tax relief and other overseas aspects.
- Companies in receivership and liquidation.
- Anti-avoidance legislation.
- A detailed computational question on S242 ICTA 1988 loss relief.
- Demergers and reconstructions.

RATES AND ALLOWANCES (up to and including Finance Act 1998)

(A) INCOME TAX

(1) Rates

Rate %	1997/98 Band of income £	Cumulative tax £	Rate %	1998/99 Band of income £	Cumulative tax £
20	1 - 4,100	820	20	1 - 4,300	860
23	4,101 - 26,100	5,060	23	4,301 - 27,100	5,244
		5,880			6,104
40	26,101 -		40	27,100 -	

(2) Personal allowances and reliefs

	1997/98 £	1998/99 £
Personal allowance	4,045	4,195
Married couple's allowance	1,830*	1,900*
Age allowance (65 - 74)		
personal	5,220	5,410
married couple's	3,185*	3,305*
income limit	15,600	16,200
Age allowance (75 or over)		
personal	5,400	5,600
married couple's	3,225*	3,345*
income limit	15,600	16,200
Additional personal allowance	1,830*	1,900*
Widow's bereavement allowance -ONLY 2 YEARS.	1,830*	1,900*
Blind person's allowance	1,280	1,330

* Relief restricted to 15%

(3) Pension contribution limits

Age at start of tax year	Personal pension schemes (%)
35 or less	17½
36 - 45	20
46 - 50	25
51 - 55	30
56 - 60	35
61 and over	40

(4) Daily apportionment calendar

Month	No of days	Month	No of days
January	31	July	31
February	28	August	31
March	31	September	30
April	30	October	31
May	31	November	30
June	30	December	31

(5) **First year allowance rates**

Date expenditure incurred on plant and machinery	*FYA rate*
2 July 1997 - 1 July 1998	50%
2 July 1998 - 1 July 1999	40%

(B)   CORPORATION TAX

	FY 1994	FY 1995	FY 1996	FY 1997	FY 1998	FY 1999
Rate	33%	33%	33%	31%	31%	30%
Small companies rate (up to £300,000)	25%	25%	24%	21%	21%	20%

Section 13(2) ICTA 1988 relief

$(M-P) \times \frac{1}{P} \times$ fraction

where M is £1,500,000

	FY 1994	FY 1995	FY 1996	FY 1997	FY 1998	FY 1999
Fraction	$\frac{1}{50}$	$\frac{1}{50}$	$\frac{9}{400}$	$\frac{1}{40}$	$\frac{1}{40}$	$\frac{1}{40}$
Advance corporation tax	$\frac{20}{80}$	$\frac{20}{80}$	$\frac{20}{80}$	$\frac{20}{80}$	$\frac{20}{80}$	N/A

The amounts of dividends received or paid represent the actual amounts without any adjustment for tax credits or advance corporation tax.

(C)   CAPITAL GAINS TAX

(1)   **Annual exemption**

	£
1993/94	5,800
1994/95	5,800
1995/96	6,000
1996/97	6,300
1997/98	6,500
1998/99	6,800

(2)   **Retail price index** (RPI)

	1982	1983	1984	1985
January	-	82.61	86.84	91.20
February	-	82.97	87.20	91.94
March	79.44	83.12	87.48	92.80
April	81.04	84.28	88.64	94.78
May	81.62	84.64	88.97	95.21
June	81.85	84.84	89.20	95.41
July	81.88	85.30	89.10	95.23
August	81.90	85.68	89.94	95.49
September	81.85	86.06	90.11	95.44
October	82.26	86.36	90.67	95.59
November	82.66	86.67	90.95	95.92
December	82.51	86.89	90.87	96.05

	1986	1987	1988	1989	1990	1991
January	96.25	100.0	103.3	111.0	119.5	130.2
February	96.60	100.4	103.7	111.8	120.2	130.9
March	96.73	100.6	104.1	112.3	121.4	131.4
April	97.67	101.8	105.8	114.3	125.1	133.1
May	97.85	101.9	106.2	115.0	126.2	133.5
June	97.79	101.9	106.6	115.4	126.7	134.1
July	97.52	101.8	106.7	115.5	126.8	133.8
August	97.82	102.1	107.9	115.8	128.1	134.1
September	98.30	102.4	108.4	116.6	129.3	134.6
October	98.45	102.9	109.5	117.5	130.3	135.1
November	99.29	103.4	110.0	118.5	130.0	135.6
December	99.62	103.3	110.3	118.8	129.9	135.7

	1992	1993	1994	1995	1996	1997	1998	1999
January	135.6	137.9	141.3	146.0	150.2	154.4	159.5	e164.8
February	136.3	138.8	142.1	146.9	150.9	155.0	160.3	e165.1
March	136.7	139.3	142.5	147.5	151.5	155.4	e160.7	e165.3
April	138.8	140.6	144.2	149.0	152.6	156.3	e161.2	e165.7
May	139.3	141.1	144.7	149.6	152.9	156.9	e161.3	
June	139.3	141.0	144.7	149.8	153.0	157.5	e161.8	
July	138.8	140.7	144.0	149.1	152.4	157.5	e162.6	
August	138.9	141.3	144.7	149.9	153.1	158.5	e162.2	
September	139.4	141.9	145.0	150.6	153.8	159.3	e163.3	
October	139.9	141.8	145.2	149.8	153.8	159.5	e163.8	
November	139.7	141.6	145.3	149.8	153.9	159.6	e163.9	
December	139.2	141.9	146.0	150.7	154.4	160.0	e164.1	

e - estimated

(3)   **Lease percentages**

Years	Percentage	Years	Percentage	Years	Percentage
50 or more	100.000	33	90.280	16	64.116
49	99.657	32	89.354	15	61.617
48	99.289	31	88.371	14	58.971
47	98.902	30	87.330	13	56.167
46	98.490	29	86.226	12	53.191
45	98.059	28	85.053	11	50.038
44	97.595	27	83.816	10	46.695
43	97.107	26	82.496	9	43.154
42	96.593	25	81.100	8	39.399
41	96.041	24	79.622	7	35.414
40	95.457	23	78.055	6	31.195
39	94.842	22	76.399	5	26.722
38	94.189	21	74.635	4	21.983
37	93.497	20	72.770	3	16.959
36	92.761	19	70.791	2	11.629
35	91.981	18	68.697	1	5.983
34	91.156	17	66.470	0	0.000

(4)   Taper Relief

Number of complete years after 5/4/98 for which asset held	Percentage of Gain chargeable	
	Business Assets	*Non-business Assets*
0	100	100
1	92.5	100
2	85	100
3	77.5	95
4	70	90
5	62.5	85
6	55	80
7	47.5	75
8	40	70
9	32.5	65
10 or more	25	60

(D)   CAR AND FUEL BENEFITS

(1)   Car scale benefit

35% of list price when new including accessories, delivery charges and VAT (subject to £80,000 maximum). Reductions in the charge are as follows:

Business mileage 2,500 to 17,999 pa	⅓
18,000 or more pa	⅔
Then, cars 4 years old and over at end of tax year	⅓
Second car 18,000 or more pa	⅓

Cars over 15 years old at tax year end with an open market value of more than £15,000 (which is also higher than the original list price) taxed by reference to the open market value.

(2)   Van scale benefit

Vans (under 3.5 tonnes) including fuel	*Under 4 years*	*4 years and over*
	£	£
1998/99	500	350
1997/98	500	350
1996/97	500	350

(3)   **Car fuel benefit (petrol)**

	1997/98 £	1998/99 £
Cylinder capacity		
Up to 1400 cc	800	1,010
1401 - 2000 cc	1,010	1,280
over 2000 cc	1,490	1,890

(E)   INHERITANCE TAX

(1)   **The nil rate band**

6 April 1991 to March 1992:	£140,000
10 March 1992 to 5 April 1995:	£150,000
6 April 1995 to 5 April 1996:	£154,000
6 April 1996 to 5 April 1997	£200,000
6 April 1997 to 5 April 1998	£215,000
6 April 1998 onwards	£223,000

(2)   **Tax rates**

	Rate on gross transfer	Rate on net transfer
Transfers on death	40%	$\frac{2}{3}$
Chargeable lifetime transfers	20%	$\frac{1}{4}$

(F)   NATIONAL INSURANCE CONTRIBUTIONS 1998/99

(1)   **Class 1 employed**   From 6 April 1998

Employee
£ per week earnings

	Contracted in	Contracted out
Up to £63.99	Nil	Nil

Rates for earnings between
£64.00 and £485.00

		Contracted in	Contracted out
(a) plus	on first £64.00	2%	2%
(b)	£64.01 to £485.00	10%	8.4%

Employer
£ per week earnings

Select earnings band	Contracted in	Contracted out First £64	Contracted out Balance
Up to £63.99	Nil	Nil	Nil
£64.00 to £109.99	3%	3%	Nil
£110.00 to £154.99	5%	5%	2%
£155.00 to £209.99	7%	7%	4%
£210.00 to £485.00	10%	10%	7%
Over £485.00	10%	£35.87 plus on excess over £485.00	10%

(2)   **Class 2 Self-employed**

Weekly rate £6.35

Small earnings exemption £3,590 pa

(3)   **Class 3 Voluntary**

Weekly rate £6.25

(4)   **Class 4 Self-employed**

6% on annual profits £7,310 – £25,220

1 ADMINISTRATION OF TAX

INTRODUCTION

This chapter brings together the main rules regarding the administration of the tax system and the methods and dates of payment. It will give you an understanding of the mechanism by which the UK tax system operates.

---

1   THE PRINCIPLES OF REVENUE LAW

1.1   Scope

Taxation is the raising of money by the State from the general public. The principal taxes in the UK which are examinable in Paper 7 are:

Tax	Nature	Suffered by	Impact	Administered by
Income tax	Annual	Individuals Partnerships Trusts	Direct	Board of Inland Revenue
Corporation tax	Annual	UK Companies	Direct	Board of Inland Revenue
Capital gains tax	Annual	Individuals Trusts Companies (which pay corporation tax on their capital gains)	Direct	Board of Inland Revenue
Value added tax	Permanent	Anyone who is liable to register	Indirect	Commissioners of Customs & Excise

1.2   Statute law

(a)   The main statutes relating to tax are:

   Income and Corporation Taxes Act 1988 (ICTA 88)
   The Taxation of Chargeable Gains Act 1992 (TCGA 92)
   Capital Allowances Act 1990 (CAA 90)
   Taxes Management Act 1970 (TMA 70)
   Annual Finance Acts
   Value Added Tax Act 1994 (VATA 94).

(b)   The *ICTA 88* is a consolidation of the tax legislation relating to income tax and corporation tax up to April 1988. Since then amendments have been added by the *Finance Acts 1988 to 1998.*

(c)   A similar consolidation has been enacted by means of the *TCGA 92* and this Act contains the body of the law on Capital Gains Tax together with the amendments implemented by subsequent Finance Acts.

(d)   The *CAA 90* sets out the main reliefs for capital expenditure given by means of the capital allowance system.

(e)   The *TMA 70* contains the law relating to the administration of income tax, corporation tax and capital gains tax.

(f)   Amendments and additions to the law are given effect by means of the annual Finance Act. Each Finance Act is the vehicle by which the annual taxes are reimposed and each provides that it shall be construed as one with all previous legislation so that the total body of tax law is brought into force each year.

1.3   Statutory instruments

The statutory legislation often empowers the Treasury or The Board to make orders or regulations to give effect to the legislation; these are usually made by means of Statutory Instruments.

1.4   The European Union

The Council of Ministers, representing the member states of the European Union, is the main decision-making body. The legally binding acts of the Council comprise

(a)   **regulations** – these are community laws binding on member states which take effect without the need for any action by member states

(b)   **directives** – these are as binding as regulations but it is left to the governments of member states to take the necessary action on implementation. For example: Art 99 of the Treaty of Rome makes harmonisation of VAT throughout member states mandatory. The main method of implementation is via the 'Sixth Directive' with the *VATA 94* being the UK's method of taking action.

1.5   Case law

Judges cannot make law relating to taxation as is possible in Common Law cases. They can only be required to interpret the law which applies to the circumstances of the particular case. When reading reports of decided cases, care must be taken to distinguish between the *ratio decidendi* (binding decisions) and the *obiter dicta* (comments which do not provide precedent).

A considerable body of case law has been built up around taxation and many of the decisions are embodied in the text of this manual. The syllabus does not require identification of specific cases or a detailed knowledge of the judgements, although a knowledge of the principles derived from the leading cases is expected.

1.6   Extra statutory concessions

In cases where there is doubt as to the meaning of the law and no case law precedent is available, or where a strict application of the law produces an unacceptable result, the Inland Revenue do not always seek to apply the law strictly but instead make an **extra-statutory concession**. The concessions are numbered and published and are available from the Revenue.   For example: ESC A2 exempts luncheon vouchers up to 15p per day from charge as a benefit for employees.

1.7   Inland Revenue Statements of Practice

These are public announcements of the Revenue's interpretation of the legislation; they have no legal force and do not remove the taxpayer's right of appeal. Each statement is published under an identifying reference number, for example: SP D24 permits initial repair expenditure which is disallowed for Schedule A purposes to be allowed as part of the base cost for capital gains tax. Statements are currently numbered according to the year of issue, for example SP 3/98 is the third SP issued in 1998.

2   PAYMENT OF INCOME TAX

2.1   Introduction

Wherever possible tax is deducted at source (eg, interest on building society deposit accounts is paid net of 20% income tax). However, deduction at source does not satisfy a taxpayer's higher rate liability. There are also situations where deduction at source is impractical (eg, on business profits or rents.)

Up to and including 1995/96 the Revenue raised assessments to collect income tax on income received gross or on income which had suffered insufficient tax deduction at source.

For 1996/97 onwards a new system called 'self-assessment' applies under which the responsibility for calculating and accounting for income tax has been shifted from the Revenue to the individual taxpayer. This does not alter the existing system of deducting tax at source. In fact the average taxpayer with a salary taxed under PAYE and small amounts of investment income taxed at source is unlikely to be affected by the change to self-assessment as his tax liability will continue to be settled in full at source.

Only the new self assessment system will be tested.

2.2   The due date of payment under self assessment

An individual taxpayer pays tax on his income received gross as follows:

31 January in the tax year:	First payment on account
31 July following the tax year:	Second payment on account
31 January following the tax year:	Final payment

The payments on account are estimated from the previous years' tax liabilities. The final payment is the difference between the total tax liability for the year and the tax already paid either by deduction at source or on the payments on account.

3   SELF ASSESSMENT

3.1   Introduction

Self assessment puts the onus on the taxpayer to calculate his or her own tax liability. Each year the taxpayer will be sent a self assessment tax return. This must be completed and submitted by 31 January following the tax year. This is also the due date for the payment of the year's income tax, Class 4 NIC and CGT liability, although interim payments on account may be required on 31 January in the tax year and 31 July following the tax year.

3.2   The self assessment tax return

(a)   The return for 1998-99 must be submitted by 31 January 2000. If the return is issued late, then the due date will be three months after the issue of the return should this be later.

(b)   The return should contain all information required to calculate the taxpayer's taxable income (from all sources) and any chargeable gains for the tax year concerned. Reliefs and allowances will also be claimed in the return.

(c)   For self-employed people, the return includes a section for standardised accounts information. Therefore, the information contained in a taxpayer's financial accounts has to be submitted in a standardised format. However, separate accounts may have to be submitted if the business is large or complex.

(d)   For employees who pay their tax liability under PAYE, a self assessment tax return will often not be required because they will have no further tax liability.

(e)   Although partners are dealt with individually, a partnership return will have to be completed to aid self assessment on the individual partners. This will give details of the partners, and a partnership statement detailing the partnership's tax adjusted income and how this is allocated between the partners.

3.3   Calculating the tax liability

(a)   The return includes a section for the taxpayer to calculate his or her own tax liability (hence the term 'self assessment'). This self assessment is required even if the tax due is nil or if a repayment is due.

(b)   The Inland Revenue will calculate the tax liability on behalf of the taxpayer if the return is submitted by 30 September following the tax year (rather than 31 January). The calculation by the Inland Revenue is treated as a self assessment on behalf of the taxpayer. The Inland Revenue will not make any judgement of the accuracy of the figures included in the return, but will merely calculate the tax liability based on the information submitted.

(c)   The Inland Revenue may correct any obvious errors or mistakes within nine months of the date that the return is filed with them. For example, they will correct arithmetical errors or errors of principle. This process of repair does not mean that the Inland Revenue has necessarily accepted the return as accurate.

(d)   The taxpayer can amend the return within twelve months of the filing date. For 1998-99, amendments must therefore be made by 31 January 2001.

If an error is discovered at a later date then the taxpayer can make an error or mistake claim (see later) to recover any tax overpaid.

(e)   The Revenue normally communicate with the taxpayer by issuing a statement of account. This shows the self-assessed tax charges and any charges of interest or surcharges (see later) and shows any payments made by the taxpayer - much in the style of a credit card statement. The statement is not a notice to pay but merely a reminder of the taxpayer's indebtedness. Statements are issued as appropriate.

3.4   Notification of chargeability

(a)   Taxpayers who do not receive a return are required to notify the Inland Revenue if they have income or chargeable gains on which tax is due.

(b)   The time limit for notifying the Inland Revenue of chargeability is six months from the end of the tax year in which the liability arises.

(c)   Notification is not necessary if there is no actual tax liability. For example, if the income or chargeable gain is covered by allowances or exemptions .

3.5   Penalties for failure to submit a return

(a)   The initial penalty for not filing a return by the due date is £100.

(b)   A daily penalty of up to £60 per day can be imposed provided leave is given by the General or Special Commissioners (see later).

(c)   If a daily penalty has not been imposed within six months of the filing date, and the return is not submitted by this date, then there is a further penalty of £100.

(d)   The fixed penalties of £100 cannot exceed the amount of tax due.

(e)   If the failure to file a return continues for more than twelve months after the filing date, then a tax geared penalty may be imposed. The tax geared penalty is in addition to the fixed and daily penalties, although it cannot exceed the tax liability for the tax year in question.

3.6   Example: Penalties

A taxpayer does not submit his return for 1998-99 (which was issued during April 1999) until 10 October 2000. The tax due is £175.

Solution

Two fixed penalties of £100 will be due as the return is submitted more than six months after the filing date of 31 January 2000. The penalties will be reduced to the tax due of £175.

If a daily penalty was imposed, then this would run from the date when the Commissioners make a direction to 10 October 2000. The second fixed penalty of £100 will not be due if the daily penalties commenced before 31 July 2000 (six months after the filing date).

3.7   Determination of tax due if no return is filed

(a)   Where a self assessment tax return is not filed by the filing date, the Inland Revenue may determine the amount of tax due. This determination is treated as a self assessment by the taxpayer, and will be replaced by the actual self assessment when it is submitted by the taxpayer.

(b)   There is no appeal against a determination. Instead, the taxpayer should displace it with the actual self-assessment.

(c)   A determination can be made at any time within five years of the filing date.

3.8   Records

(a)   Taxpayers are required to keep and preserve records necessary to make a correct and complete return. For a business (including the letting of property), the records that must be kept include records of:

•   All receipts and expenses.

•   All goods purchased and sold

- All supporting documents relating to the transactions of the business, such as accounts, books, contracts, vouchers and receipts.

Other taxpayers should keep evidence of income received such as dividend vouchers, P60s, copies of PllDs and bank statements.

(b)   For taxpayers with a business (ie the self employed), all their records (not just those relating to the business) must be retained until five years after the filing date. For 1998-99 records must therefore be retained until 31 January 2005.

(c)   For other taxpayers, records must be retained until the later of:

- Twelve months after the filing date (31 January 2001 for 1998-99).

- The date on which an enquiry into the return is completed (see later).

- The date on which it becomes impossible for an enquiry to be started.

(d)   A penalty of up to £3,000 may be charged for failure to keep or retain adequate records. The maximum penalty is only likely to be imposed in the most serious cases such as where a taxpayer deliberately destroys his records in order to obstruct an Inland Revenue enquiry.

4   PAYMENT OF TAX

4.1   Payments on account

(a)   Payments on account are required if the taxpayer had an income tax liability in the previous year in excess of any tax deducted at source.

(b)   The due dates for payments on account for 1998-99 are:

- First payment on account - 31 January 1999
- Second payment on account - 31 July 1999

(c)   No payments on account are ever required for CGT.

(d)   For self-employed taxpayers each payment on account will include a payment on account of the Class 4 NIC liability due for the year.

(e)   Payments on account are based on the previous year's tax liability, so the payments on account for 1998-99 are based on the tax liability for 1997-98.

The tax liability used for calculating payments on account excludes tax that was deducted at source - eg, PAYE, tax deducted from bank and building society interest, and tax credits on dividends.

The tax liability for the previous year, net of tax deducted at source, is known as the relevant amount.

(f)   Each payment on account is 50% of the relevant amount of income tax and Class 4 NIC, if appropriate.

4.2   Payments on account not required

(a)   Payments on account are not required if:

- The relevant amount for the previous year is less than £500.

- More than 80% of the income tax liability for the previous year was met by deduction of tax at source. This will mean that most employed people will not have to make payments on account, since at least 80% of their tax liability is paid through PAYE.

(b)   Payments on account are also not required if there is no relevant amount in the previous year. A taxpayer who commences self-employment on 1 May 1998 will not have to make payments on account for 1998-99, since he or she will not have a relevant amount for 1997 -98.

4.3   Example: Payments on account

A taxpayer's tax liability for 1997-98 was as follows:

	£
Income tax	9,400
Less: Tax deducted at source	2,100
	7,300
Class 4 NIC	700
CGT	3,500
	11,500

Solution

The relevant amount for income tax is £7,300.

The relevant amount for Class 4 NIC is £700.

Payments on account will be due for 1998-99 as follows:

31 January 1999 (£7,300 + £700 = £8,000/2)	£4,000
31 July 1999	£4,000

4.4   Claims to reduce payments on account

(a)   At any time before 31 January following the tax year, a taxpayer can claim to reduce the payments on account.

In the above example, the taxpayer would claim to reduce the payments on account if he expected his actual income tax and Class 4 NIC liability (net of tax deducted at source) for 1998-99 to be less than £8,000.

(b)   The claim must state the grounds for making the claim.

(c)   Following a claim, the payments on account will be reduced. Each payment on account will be for half the reduced amount, unless the taxpayer claims that there is no tax liability at all.

If payments on account are paid before a claim is made, then the Inland Revenue will refund the overpayment.

(d)   In certain circumstances, the relevant amount may alter as a result of an amendment to the self assessment for the previous year. Such an amendment will automatically result in a corresponding increase or decrease in the payments on account due for the current year.

4.5   Incorrect claims

(a)   A taxpayer should only claim to reduce payments on account if the tax liability (net of tax deducted at source) for the current year is expected to be less than the payments on account.

(b)   Where a claim is made and the actual tax liability for the current year turns out to be higher than the original payments on account, then interest will be charged on the tax underpaid (see later).

(c)   In addition, a penalty will be charged if a taxpayer fraudulently or negligently claims to reduce payments on account. The maximum penalty is the difference between the amounts actually paid on account, and the amounts that should have been paid.

(d)   A penalty will not be sought in cases of innocent error. The aim is to penalise taxpayers who claim large reductions in payments on account without any foundation to the claim.

4.6   Balancing payments

(a)   The balancing payment is due on 31 January following the tax year. For 1998-99 this will be 31 January 2000.

(b)   The balancing payment will be the total tax liability for the year (income tax, Class 4 NIC and CGT), less amounts deducted at source and less payments made on account.

It is possible that a balancing repayment will be due, in which case the Inland Revenue will repay the amount of tax overpaid.

(c)   Where the amount of tax due changes as a result of an amendment to the self assessment (by either the taxpayer or the Inland Revenue), any additional tax due must be paid within 30 days of the notice of amendment if this is later than the normal due date.

4.7   Example: Balancing payment

Continuing with example 4.3, suppose that the taxpayer's tax liability for 1998-99 is as follows:

	£
Income tax	10,800
Less: Tax deducted at source	2,500
	8,300
Class 4 NIC	800
CGT	4,600
	13,700

Solution

The balancing payment for 1998-99 due on 31 January 2000 will be as follows:

	£
Total tax liability as above	13,700
Less: Payments on account	8,000
Balancing payment due 31 January 2000	5,700

5 INTEREST AND SURCHARGES

5.1 Interest on tax paid late

(a) Interest will automatically be charged if tax is paid late (whether it is income tax, Class 4 NIC or CGT).

Interest can arise in respect of payments on account, balancing payments, any tax payable following an amendment to a self assessment, and any tax payable following a discovery assessment (see later).

(b) For payments on account, interest runs from the due date of 31 January in the tax year or 31 July following the tax year.

(c) In other instances, interest runs from 31 January following the tax year to the date of payment. This is the case even if the tax was not actually due until a later date (ie following the amendment of the self assessment).

The only exception to this is where the return was issued late, in which case the due date will be three months after the issue of the return should this be later.

(d) Interest is charged on penalties from the date they become due to the date that they are paid.

5.2 Example: Interest on tax paid late

A taxpayer pays his 1998-99 payments on account on 15 March 1999 and 10 August 1999. The balancing payment is paid on 15 April 2000.

Solution

Interest will be charged as follows:

- First payment on account from 1 February 1999 to 14 March 1999.

- Second payment on account from 1 August 1999 to 9 August 1999

- Balancing payment from 1 February 2000 to 14 April 2000

5.3 Interest on incorrect claims to reduce payments on account

(a) Interest is charged where an excessive claim is made to reduce payments on account.

(b) The charge is based on the difference between the amounts actually paid and the amounts that should have been paid. The amount that should have been paid is the lower of:

- The original payments on account based on the relevant amount for the previous year, and

- 50% of the final tax liability (excluding CGT, and net of tax deducted at source) for the current year

(c)   Interest runs from the due dates of 31 January in the tax year and 31 July following the tax year to the date of payment. The date of payment will be 31 January following the tax year when the balancing payment is due, unless the balancing payment is made late.

5.4   Example: Interest on incorrect claim to reduce payments on account

A taxpayer's relevant amount for 1997-98 is £5,000 (payments on account are therefore £2,500), but a claim is made to reduce the payments on account to £1,000 each. These payments are made on time.

The actual tax liability (net of tax deducted at source) for 1998-99 is £4,500. This is paid on 31 January 2000.

Solution

Payments on account should have been reduced to £2,250 (£4,500/2) rather than £1,000. Interest will therefore be charged as follows:

- On £1,250 from 1 February 1999 to 30 January 2000.
- On £1,250 from 1 August 1999 to 30 January 2000.

5.5   Interest paid on overpayments of tax

(a)   Interest is paid by the Inland Revenue on any overpayment of tax.

(b)   Interest runs from the date of actual payment to the date of repayment.

(c)   Interest is only paid on the amount of tax that should have been paid (ie, deliberate overpayments will not attract interest).

(d)   Tax deducted at source (eg, PAYE) is deemed to have been paid on 31 January following the tax year for the purpose of calculating interest on overpayments.

5.6   Surcharge on unpaid tax

(a)   Interest on tax paid late is not a penalty, since it merely compensates for the advantage of paying late. Therefore, to further encourage compliance, surcharges can also be imposed where income tax, Class 4 NIC or CGT is paid late.

(b)   The surcharge does not apply to payments on account.

(c)   Where a balancing payment is not paid until more than 28 days after the due date (31 January following the tax year), a surcharge equal to 5% of the tax unpaid is imposed.

(d)   A further 5% surcharge arises if the tax is still unpaid after six months.

(e)   Where additional tax becomes due as a result of an amendment to a self assessment, a surcharge is only imposed if the additional tax is not paid within 28 days of the due date, which is 30 days after the amendment. This differs from interest which runs from the 31 January following the tax year.

(f)   Interest is charged if a surcharge is not paid within 30 days of the date that it is imposed.

(g)   A surcharge may be mitigated by the Inland Revenue, for example if there is a reasonable excuse for the non-payment of the tax. Insufficiency of funds is not a reasonable excuse.

5.7   Example: Surcharge on unpaid tax

A taxpayer's balancing payment due for 1998-99 is £5,000. Only £1,200 of this was paid on 31 January 2000.

Solution

Interest will be charged on £3,800 from 1 February 2000 to the date of payment.

A surcharge of £190 (£3,800 at 5%) will be due if the tax of £3,800 is not paid by 28 February 2000.

A further surcharge of £190 will be due if the tax is not paid by 31 July 2000.

6   APPEAL TRIBUNALS

6.1   Introduction

Disputes that cannot be settled between the Inspector and taxpayer, are usually adjudicated by either the General or Special Commissioners, which are bodies set up for this purpose.

The Commissioners will hear the appeal at which the Inspector and the taxpayer (or his representative, ie, his accountant) present their cases. The Commissioners then adjudicate on the dispute.

Their findings are conclusive on a point of **fact**, but disputes on points of **law** (ie, interpretation of the Taxes Acts) may be continued through the High Court - Chancery Division, the Court of Appeal and finally to the House of Lords.

6.2   The Commissioners

(a)   **The General Commissioners**

These are **lay** persons appointed by the Lord Chancellor (in a similar manner to magistrates) who have no special legal or taxation qualifications. The appointments are honorary and part-time. They function as follows

- The meet periodically to hear appeals for a specified local area known as a division.

  All appeals are heard by them automatically, unless an election is made for the appeal to be determined by the Special Commissioners. This election, however, is not available unless the General Commissioners direct that they are satisfied that the case should be heard by the Special Commissioners. Also, the General Commissioners are able to transfer appeals to the Special Commissioners subject only to obtaining their agreement. They are likely to do this because of the complexity of the appeal or the length of time likely to be required for hearing it.

- They appoint a Clerk to the Commissioners, who will be a legally qualified expert in tax law, to advise them.

(b)   **The Special Commissioners**

These are full-time paid officials who are appointed by the Lord Chancellor. They have no connection with the Inland Revenue. Special Commissioners must be persons who are barristers, advocates or solicitors of not less than ten years standing.

They hear all appeals where an election has been made for them to do so.

They may agree to hear appeals transferred to them by the General Commissioners.

Certain appeals on special points **must** be heard by the Special Commissioners - normally those involved with complex interpretations of the Taxes Acts, eg, patent and copyright royalties; anti-avoidance rules on share transactions.

Generally, hearings will be held before a **single** Special Commissioner except where the presiding Special Commissioner directs otherwise.

Certain appeals from decisions of the Special Commissioners may be referred direct to the Court of Appeal, rather than via the High Court.

6.3   General points on appeals

Assuming that a decision is made to go beyond the District Inspector, the taxpayer will in many cases have a choice as to whether the General or Special Commissioners hear the appeal.

As a general rule, if one's case is considered to be good in equity, the General Commissioners should be chosen. Being experienced laymen they will be able to give a fair decision in equity.

Conversely, if one's case turns on a point of law - especially a strict or controversial interpretation - the case should be put before the more expert Special Commissioners.

At the Commissioners' stage of appeal, both sides will normally meet their own costs although the Special Commissioners can award costs against a party that has acted unreasonably in bringing or persisting with the case. Special Commissioner cases are published where the decision is likely to be of interest to other taxpayers.

Before requesting the Commissioners to state a case for the High Court, the taxpayer should carefully consider the costs involved against the potential tax savings. The costs of appeal incurred by the taxpayer are not allowable expenses for tax purposes.

6.4   Further points

(a)   Even after a self-assessment has been finally agreed, if an inspector then **discovers** that income which should have been assessed has not, he may raise a further assessment.

(b)   Where a self-assessment is excessive due to some **error or mistake** in the tax payer's return or other information supplied by him, he can claim relief within five years of 31 January following the end of the relevant tax year.

7   PAYE

7.1   Introduction

PAYE is a system of collection of income tax at source from the emoluments of employed individuals.

All payments of emoluments assessable under Schedule E are subject to deduction of tax under the PAYE system. A formal self-assessment may be required each year to equate deductions with true liability and any overpayments are refunded by a payment order are usually issued at the same time as the notice of assessment, while underpayments are usually collected in the next following year by coding adjustments.

Formal self-assessments need not be made in cases where both coding and deduction of tax under it are correct.

All employers making payments of such emoluments are required to deduct the appropriate amount of tax from each payment (or repay over-deductions) by reference to PAYE Tax Tables, which are so constructed that, as near as may be, tax deducted from payments to date corresponds with the correct time proportion to date of the net total tax liability (after allowances and reliefs) of the recipient on those emoluments for the year.

7.2   Coding notice

From the information supplied in his tax return, each employee is sent a coding notice (P2) which sets out the total reliefs and allowances available to him for the year. The last digit is removed to arrive at the code **number** shown. Thus, allowances of £3,099 become 309. The employer will be notified of the code number, but is not given details of its make up. Using this code number and a set of tax tables the employer will be able to calculate the correct amount of tax each week or month.

Most code numbers issued to the employer (on form P6) will carry a suffix of which the most usual are H or L. The letter H denotes that the married couples allowance has been given, and L that just the ordinary personal allowance has been given. These letters are added to simplify the revision of codes, eg when the personal allowance was increased from £4,045 to £4,195 for all code numbers with the suffix L were increased by 15 by the employers, thus obviating the need to issue every employee with a new coding notice.

Some code numbers carry a K prefix. This indicates that the deductions to be made from allowances actually exceed the allowances. The code number is effectively 'negative'.

Where an employee has not been allocated a code number (perhaps because no return of income has been submitted, or the individual was previously assessed under Schedule D), the employer must deduct tax under PAYE in accordance with an *emergency code* which reflects only the personal allowance (ie Code 419L).

This code is applied until the correct code number is supplied by the Revenue.

7.3   Example: Notice of coding

Albert is a married man employed as a purchasing manager of Fellows Ltd. He is paid a monthly salary of £1,150 (gross). He is provided with a 1600 cc company car costing £14,250 in 1996 and pays for all private fuel. His business mileage in 1998/99 is expected to be 12,000. He pays 3% of his gross salary to a pension scheme run by his company and approved by the Inland Revenue, and a professional subscription of £50. He pays mortgage interest of £1,650 under MIRAS on a mortgage of £25,000 on his home. He receives £166 of National Savings Bank (ordinary account) interest assessable in 1998/99. His wife is employed at a salary of £15,000 pa.

Show Albert's notice of coding for 1998/99.

7.4   Solution

NOTICE OF CODING – YEAR TO 5 APRIL 1999

YOUR ALLOWANCES		£	£
Expenses (eg professional subscriptions)			50
Building society interest payable (see note (a))			-
Loan etc interest payable			-
Personal			4,195
Married couple's			1,900
Age (estimated total income £)			-

TOTAL ALLOWANCES			6,145
Less:	Allowances given against other income		-
	Restriction of relief for married couple's allowance (note (f))	661	
	Untaxed interest (the £70 exemption is given)(note (e))	96	
	National Insurance benefits	-	
	Car benefit £14,250 × 35% × ⅔ (see note (b))	3,325	4,082
NET ALLOWANCES			2,063
Less:	Underpayments from previous years)		-
Add:	Overpayments from previous years) (see note (c))		
ALLOWANCES GIVEN AGAINST PAY			2,063
Code			206H

Notes:

(a)   Loan interest in respect of a mortgage upon the taxpayer's principal private residence is usually dealt with under the MIRAS scheme. No amount of interest relief is therefore included in the coding notice.

(b)   The taxable value of most **recurring benefits-in-kind** are usually subject to tax under PAYE. Car benefits are an important example and their taxable value reduces the total of allowances set against total pay for Schedule E purposes. You should refer to the chapter on benefits in kind for the detail as to how the benefit is computed.

(c)   Where tax deducted by employers under Schedule E for previous years is either under- or over deducted, and the amounts involved are small – certainly under £1,000 – the tax may be recovered or refunded through an **adjustment** to **next** year's coding. The adjustment will be a grossed-up amount of the tax; the grossing up being at the highest marginal rate of tax that the employee is expected to pay in the current fiscal year. Thus, a £100 deduction in 1998/99 from allowances for a basic rate taxpayer would denote that he owed £23 in tax from a previous year.

(d)   No relief in the coding is given for the allowable pension contributions made by the employee to occupational pension funds. Employers deal with pension contributions under the **net pay scheme** (ie the contributions are deducted from total pay, the net pay forming total pay for PAYE purposes).

(e)   Small amounts of investment income, that have not been subjected to tax at source, are usually assessed by using an appropriate amount of PAYE allowances to cover them. This obviates the need for a formal self-assessment. The NSB interest is a good example of how this is done.

(f)   Note that the married couple's allowance is not deducted in arriving at taxable income. Instead, relief is given via a tax credit against income tax liability. However, relief will be given through the PAYE code with a restriction depending on the employee's likely marginal tax rate to give an effective rate at 15%. For example, as above, $(1,900 - 661) \times 23\% = £285$; just as relief is restricted to $£1,900 \times 15\% = £285$.

7.5   Action required to set-up PAYE scheme and commence deductions

Initial action is to write to the Inspector of Taxes in whose district the employer is operating requesting that a PAYE scheme be set-up and a PAYE reference number allocated.

The Inspector will then supply

- Employers' Guide to PAYE

- Employers' Guide to National Insurance Contributions

- the necessary documentation to establish the scheme with instructions on how to calculate and make deductions.

The following documents/records are necessary in order to commence operating the system.

- Detailed records of each employee's wages, salary, expenses and benefits-in-kind.
- Tax deduction working sheets (P11) – one for each employee.
- Notice of PAYE coding for each employee (P6).
- Tax and national insurance deduction tables.
- Documents for employees joining or leaving the company – P45, P46 and P15.

Operation of the system depends upon having a PAYE coding for each employee, therefore for each new employee/director request production of Form P45. This will have been completed by the previous employer and will show amongst other things

- PAYE reference and national insurance number

- employee's name and the date he left old employment

- PAYE coding at the date he left old employment

- the last entries on the old tax deductions working sheet showing week/month number last paid and total pay and tax deducted to that time.

The form is in four parts (1, 1A, 2 and 3). Parts 2 and 3 only should be received. Part 2 is retained by the new employer as authority to make PAYE deductions using the coding on the form. After completing the details as new employer on Part 3 this is sent to the Inspector. (This will enable the Inspector to obtain the employee's PAYE file from the old Inspector.)

Where Form P45 cannot be produced the employee must be asked to complete Form P46. This involves:

- the employee ticking statement A on the form if this is the first full time job. The employee can then be allocated the personal allowance PAYE Coding (419L for 1998/99) on a **full cumulative basis**.

- the employee ticking statement B if this is the employee's main employment. The emergency code procedure will be put into operation provided the employee has not ticked statement C, but the emergency Code (419L) will be allocated and operated on a **non-cumulative** basis.

If the employee has ticked statement C, that he receives a pension, or no statement has been ticked because his main employment is elsewhere, then Code BR (deducting basic rate tax on the full amount of remuneration) should be allocated and used.

If none of the statements have been ticked the employee should complete the bottom of the form P46 with details of other employments etc. This will enable the correct PAYE code to be allocated by the Inspector and subsequently notified to the employer on Form P6.

If the employee is paid below the PAYE threshold (see tax tables) and this is the main employment then the P46 should be retained until the threshold is exceeded.

7.6   Calculation of deductions

The calculation of PAYE is done on the tax deductions working sheets (P11) and, other than in exceptional cases, is done on a cumulative basis using the tax tables provided

The tax tables are as follows

TABLE A	– Pay adjustment table – use PAYE code number with this table.
TABLES LR and B-D	– Taxable pay tables at all rates.

The tax is calculated for any given pay week or month on a cumulative basis, ie the tax for, say month 5, is the difference between the cumulative total tax due at the end of month 5 compared with the cumulative total due at the end of month 4. Each month's calculation is made by deducting the total free pay to date, or adding total additional pay for K codes, (per Table A) from the total pay to date to arrive at total taxable pay to date. Tax on cumulative taxable pay to date is then calculated by reference to Tables LR and B-D.

Since PAYE deductions for any week or month depend upon the amount of emoluments received to date, it is essential that the time that earnings are received is governed by statute.

Note.   Employers may use their own forms in place of the official 'workings sheets' provided the Inspector approves.

7.7   Payments to Collector of Taxes

The amounts of tax and national insurance that the employer was *liable* to deduct during each tax month ending on the 5th are due for payment to the Collector of Taxes not later than 14 days after the month ends, ie by the 19th of each month.

The employer is supplied with a book of remittance advices and a payment record. Each payment is accompanied by a remittance advice and the record kept as proof of payments.

Employers whose average monthly payments of PAYE and NICs are less than £600 in total are allowed to make quarterly, rather than monthly, payments. Payments are due by the 19th of the month following the quarters ending 5 July, 5 October, 5 January and 5 April.

7.8   Interest on PAYE unpaid by employer

Regulations enable the Revenue to charge interest on amounts of PAYE that have not been paid by the employer in circumstances where the amount due has had to be formally determined by the Inspector.

Interest will be charged on PAYE which remains unpaid more than 14 days after the end of the year of assessment for which the amount was due.

7.9   Procedure to be adopted when employee leaves

When an employee leaves an employment the PAYE system is interrupted. A form P45 must be completed for each employee in order that either

- a new employer can carry on making deductions using the appropriate code and cumulative totals from the last employment or

- the employee can claim a tax repayment and/or unemployment benefit.

The form is in four parts – part 1 is sent by the old employer to his PAYE office; part 1A is retained by the employee for his own records; parts 2 and 3 are given to the employee, who then gives them to either his next employer or the Job centre, or sends them to the Inland Revenue to obtain a repayment.

7.10   End of year procedure

The following returns will need to be completed at the end of each tax year.

P35 – Employer's Annual Statement, Declaration and Certificate (to be submitted by 19 May).

The P35 performs four functions. These are to provide

- an overall summary of tax and NIC deducted by the employer for the year

- a statement of the number of deduction working sheets prepared but not used because the respective employees did not pay tax. This would apply to part-time employees, for example

- a questionnaire to ensure compliance with PAYE arrangements

- a declaration and certificate signed by the employer confirming that all year-end returns have been completed and submitted and that other post- year returns will be despatched (eg Form P11D).

P11D – a form P11D must be submitted for each employee by 6 July if the employee is in receipt of expense allowances or reimbursed expenses, or is provided with benefits-in-kind and

- either he or she is an employee, whether or not a director receiving gross emoluments at the rate of £8,500 or more per annum or

- is a director who is not earning as above, unless such director has no material interest (5% of ordinary share capital) *and* is a full-time working director of the company or the company is non-profit making or a charity.

P9D – a form P9D must be completed by 6 July for any employee who is not a P11D employee where that employee received in a fiscal year expenses and benefits which are assessable because they represent a reward for services. That is benefits in .

- money or capable of being converted into money (ie money's worth) or
- the satisfaction by the employer of a liability incurred by the employee or
- any other benefit which is assessable on employees regardless of their status.

P14–P60 – Certificate of Pay and Tax Deducted

P14 Not later than 19 May the employer must send the first two copies (P14) of this three-part form to the Collector of Taxes, showing for each employee

- personal details
- total emoluments for the year
- final PAYE code
- total net tax deducted for the year
- total national insurance contributions.

P60 – this third part of the form, which must show in addition to the above the employer's name and address and the employee's national insurance number, is given to each employee.

7.11   Other provisions

The Revenue has power to conduct a PAYE audit and inspect wages books, workings sheets and other records to ensure that the PAYE regulations are being complied with.

(a) **Employee dying**. Employer must forthwith send all parts of the P45 to the Inspector, together with the name and address of the deceased's personal representatives.

(b) **Employee retiring on pension**. The employer must, within 14 days, notify the Inspector on form P160, and continue to operate PAYE on pension payments using the latest Code on a Week 1/Month 1 non-cumulative basis.

(c) **National Insurance Retirement Pensioners**. Where the **state pension** exceeds the personal allowances, the tax attributable to the excess will be collected through the normal self-assessment system. Where a pensioner has a **steady source of income to which PAYE can be applied**, a special code with the prefix K will enable the tax on the excess pension to be recovered through the PAYE system, but the taxpayer has the option to continue to pay by self-assessment.

(d) **Jobseeker's allowance** is taxable – as earned income under Schedule E. The taxable amount includes the flat rate benefit and any addition for adult dependants, but not additions in respect of children, housing or special needs.

No income tax is deducted by the Department of Employment or DSS benefit office issuing the payment and no income tax repayment can normally be made to the taxpayer while he is drawing benefit. If the taxpayer has paid too much tax a refund may be made to him with his final payment of benefit or after the end of a fiscal year if he still remains unemployed after 5 April. In other cases the refund may be made soon after the taxpayer starts work again.

If too little tax has been paid by the taxpayer the amount owed to the Revenue will usually be included in his coding for a later year, so that he pays extra tax on his earnings later on.

8   DEDUCTION OF TAX IN THE CONSTRUCTION INDUSTRY

8.1   Introduction

A system of tax deduction at source operates in the construction industry because it was found that there was formerly widespread tax evasion. Unless a subcontractor holds a valid exemption certificate, anyone making payments to him is obliged to deduct basic rate tax.

8.2   Administration

The scheme is based largely on the administrative mechanics of the PAYE system. Contractors are obliged to record payments made to subcontractors, and deduct basic rate tax from them (other than reimbursement of the cost of materials). The contractor then has to account monthly to the Revenue in respect of amounts deducted (or, like PAYE, quarterly where the average monthly liability is less than £600).

8.3   Exemption

(a)   A subcontractor can avoid having tax deducted from payments made to him if he has been issued with an exemption certificate (which must be valid when payment is made).

(b)   Exemption certificates are issued only to bona fide businesses. In particular applicants must satisfy the Revenue that:

- the business operates mainly through a bank account (not on a cash basis);
- proper business records are kept; and
- the business is carried on from business premises with proper equipment and stock.

(c)   In addition, applicants must demonstrate a period of three years (in the previous six) during which they have been employed or self-employed and have discharged all tax-related obligations.

9   ORGANISATION OF THE INLAND REVENUE

9.1   Overview

The **Treasury** is the ministry responsible, under the Chancellor of the Exchequer, for the imposition and collection of taxation. The Treasury appoint permanent civil servants, as the **Board of Inland Revenue**, to administer the UK's direct taxation system; they are responsible for income tax, corporation tax, capital gains tax, inheritance tax and stamp duty.

For the purposes of administrative control the UK is divided into regions, with each region sub-divided into **districts**. There are between 600–700 districts, each under the control of a **district inspector**, assisted by other inspectors, tax officers and clerical grade civil servants. An inspector is more formally described as Her Majesty's Inspector of Taxes, or HMIT.

9.2   The Inspector of Taxes

The Board of Inland Revenue appoint the Inspectors of Taxes. The Inspectors' main duties are to:

- issue tax returns;
- examine returns and accounts of individuals, businesses and companies;
- calculate the amount of tax due; and
- advise the taxpayer of the amount of tax due by sending him a statement of account.

Under self-assessment the tax calculation task has generally been replaced by the taxpayer self-assessing although the inspector can still be requested to do the calculation.

9.3   The Collector of Taxes

The Board of Inland Revenue also appoint the Collectors of Taxes. Their responsibility is to collect tax which is:

- shown in a self-assessment;
- due under the PAYE system; and
- due from companies under the quarterly return system.

Following recent changes in Revenue administration there is less separation between the Inspector and Collector roles - each being referred to as an 'officer of the Board'.

9.4   Organisation of the Inland Revenue (simplified)

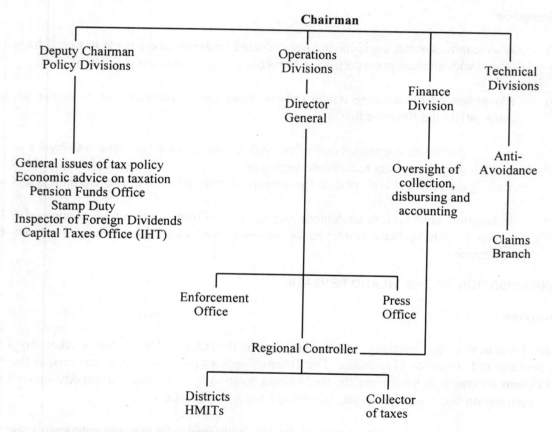

9.5   Special departmental responsibilities

(a)   **Enforcement Office**

Responsible for gathering arrears of tax which have not been recovered through the normal machinery and for authorising legal proceedings for recovery through the Solicitor's Office.

(b)   **Inspector of Foreign Dividends**

Deals with

- claims by non-residents **for exemption**
- relief under double taxation agreements
- assessment of income tax on foreign dividends paid in the UK.

(c)   **Pension Funds Office**

- Examines and approves applications for approval of superannuation funds, retirement benefit schemes, personal pension schemes etc
- Deals with claims for relief in respect of the income of pension funds.

(d)   **Claims Branch**

Deals with

- claims by non-residents **for personal reliefs**
- claims for exemption by charities, scientific research associations, etc.

(e)   **Investigation Units**

There are four specialist units which operate, in addition to district inspectors, to counter tax evasion. These are as follows.

- **Investigation Office**: also investigates fraud, but operates mainly in the area of the construction industry.

- **Special Compliance Offices**: deal with cases outside the ability or experience of the district inspector, eg those involving trusts and with cases of serious fraud.

- **Special Investigations Section**: monitors and attacks avoidance schemes which give rise to serious evasion of tax and which have far reaching implications.

- **PAYE Audit Units**: monitor operation of PAYE and investigate irregularities.

10   ADMINISTRATION OF NATIONAL INSURANCE

10.1   Departmental responsibility

The Department of Social Security (DSS) is the government department responsible for the administration of National Insurance. The head of the DSS is the Secretary of State for Social Services. The Contributions Agency is the executive agency of the DSS responsible for the collection and recording of National Insurance Contributions (NICs).

10.2   DSS organisation

Local offices are the point of contact between the DSS and the public. Each local office is controlled by a Manager answerable to his regional office. Under the manager are a number of DSS Inspectors and Officers.

The main function of the DSS Inspectors is to monitor and enforce compliance with the various laws and rules on contributions.

(**Note**: The **Social Security Acts** make no provision for appeals in connection with matters relating to contributions, nor do the appellate bodies have any jurisdiction regarding contributions.)

10.3   National Insurance Number

(a)   **Automatic issue**

A national insurance number is allocated to a person within the year preceding the 16th birthday. It is notified on a plastic national insurance number card and given to the person shortly before leaving school.

(b)   **Purpose**

It is by means of the national insurance number, which appears on all documentation relevant to national insurance, that each person's contribution record is maintained and updated – thus providing evidence of entitlement to benefits.

Moreover, national insurance numbers are to be used as reference numbers in the Inland Revenue's computerised PAYE system when this is fully operational.

(c)   **Application**

Any person resident or present in the UK and over the age of 16, who has not been notified of a number as above, **must**, if an employed or self-employed person, apply to the Secretary of State (through the Local DSS office) for a national insurance number.

Any person who has a national insurance number **must** supply it to any other person who is liable to pay earnings-related contributions in his respect.

11   PAYMENT OF CORPORATION TAX

11.1   The due date of payment

The general rule is that mainstream corporation tax is payable nine months after the end of the accounting period regardless of whether a notice of assessment has been issued.

11.2   Payment by instalments

For accounting periods ending on or after 1 July 1999, 'large' companies must pay their corporation tax liabilities in four quarterly instalments. The instalments will be due on the 14th of the month, in months 7 and 10 in the accounting period, and in months 1 and 4 of the following accounting period.

These provisions are being phased in, so that in the first year 60% of the liability will be payable in instalments, with the balance being due nine months after the end of the accounting period. The percentage payable by instalments rises to 72% in the second year, 88% in the third and 100% in the fourth year.

Since the instalments of corporation tax will be payable before the actual liability is calculated, the company must make its best estimate of the amount due, revising the estimate each quarter.

For these purposes a 'large' company is one whose profits are in excess of £1.5 million (the small companies upper limit).

11.3   Length of accounting period

There is nothing to prevent a company from preparing accounts for periods other than 12 months. An obvious method of delaying the payment of tax would be to prepare accounts for, say, 18 months. The legislators foresaw this situation, so that where a company prepares accounts for a period exceeding 12 months this period of account (ie period for which accounts are prepared) is divided into two successive accounting periods, ie

- first of 12 months
- then a balance of (say) 6 months.

Separate corporation tax liabilities must be computed for each accounting period and each liability will fall due for payment nine months from the end of that accounting period.

11.4   The Pay and File scheme for corporation tax

This scheme is aimed at streamlining the administration of corporation tax. The object is to eliminate the costly and time-wasting process of: an estimated assessment; appeal by the company; application for postponement; final submission of accounts; agreement and final settlement of liability – all triggered by the company's accounts not being received in time to agree the liability before payment is due.

The scheme comprises

(a)   **The Pay element**

The company is required to pay its mainstream CT liability on a fixed date (9 months after the end of the accounting period) without any need for an assessment to be made. Large companies are moving to a system of paying by quarterly instalments, again without the need for an assessment.

Interest will run from the due date on any tax paid late, or on any repayment made by the Revenue. The interest rate charged on under paid tax is greater than the interest rate paid on overpaid tax.

(b)   **The File element**

The Inspector will issue a formal notice requiring the company to make a corporation tax return on the official form (CT 200) or on an approved substitute.

The company is required generally to supply its return and accounts within 12 months after the end of the accounting period (there are special rules for long periods of account) or if later, three months after the date of issue of the notice.

The company must not only complete the return form but must submit with it

- a copy of the relevant accounts for the period covered by the return, and
- computations showing how figures in the return have been derived from the accounts.

If any boxes on the return are not completed or amounts are estimated or marked 'information to follow' the return is not completed and penalties may ensue. However, provided a full explanation is given as to the reason for the omissions and provided such outstanding information is notified to the Inspector as soon as it becomes available, the Revenue have indicated that penalties would not be invoked.

It is, therefore, not just a matter of filing the return within one year after the accounting period end but also filing the accounts and tax computations!

If the company fails to file within the specified time, then, unless it can show reasonable excuse, an automatic fixed penalty arises.

11.5   Table of pay and file penalties

Return overdue by	*Penalty*	
	First and second consecutive offences	*Third (or more) consecutive offence*
Up to 3 months	£100	£500
3 to 6 months	£200	£1,000
Over 6 months	£200 plus 10% unpaid tax	£1,000 plus 10% unpaid tax
Over 12 months	£200 plus 20% unpaid tax	£1,000 plus 20% unpaid tax

Unpaid tax is the tax due but not paid as at 18 months after the end of the return period (6 months after the date when the return was due), deducting advance corporation tax carried back from periods ending within 2 years (but no later) of the relevant return period.

The penalties will be recovered by assessment as tax due 30 days from the date of issue of the notice of assessment. The company has the right of appeal against the assessment.

11.6   Self assessment for companies

Self assessment is to apply to companies for accounting periods ending on or after 1 July 1999. In practice many of the requirements of self-assessment have already been incorporated in the pay and file system, but self-assessment formalises the procedures for:

- amending the return (by the company)
- correcting obvious errors and omissions (by the Revenue)
- keeping records
- raising enquiries
- making claims
- determining the corporation tax payable where no return has been filed.

12   CAPITAL GAINS TAX

12.1   General administration

Individuals 'self-assess' their net capital gains. Companies include net capital gains as part of their chargeable profits and are assessed by reference to accounting periods.

12.2   Returns

Details of chargeable assets disposed of during a fiscal year, must be given on the annual tax return issued to taxpayers soon after the commencement of the following fiscal year.

Where the chargeable gains of an individual for a year of assessment do not exceed the annual exemption (£6,800 for 1998/99) and the total consideration for the disposal of chargeable assets does not exceed twice that amount (£13,600 for 1998/99), a statement by the taxpayer to this effect is all that is necessary by way of return.

A chargeable person, who has not already made a statutory annual return, or has not received a notice requiring such a return, must, within 6 months after the end of the fiscal year, or accounting period for companies, notify the Inspector of the chargeability.

12.3   The due date of payment

Tax is payable on 31 January following the year of assessment. Companies pay tax on their chargeable gains as part of the normal mainstream corporation tax.

12.4   Payment by instalments

Where the consideration for a disposal is receivable by an individual in instalments over a period exceeding 18 months, the liability may be paid by instalments at the taxpayer's option. The Board of Inland Revenue can allow what instalments it considers appropriate over a period not exceeding eight years. Tax on gifts of certain other specified assets can be paid in 10 equal annual instalments.

13   PENALTIES

When a taxpayer

- fails to make a return; or
- omits information from a return; or
- includes false information in a return,

a penalty of 100% of the additional tax may be charged.

When anyone (eg, a professional adviser) assists someone in making a false declaration or return, there is a £3,000 penalty.

14   BACK DUTY

14.1   General considerations

Back duty claims are made by the Board of Inland Revenue where they consider tax has been lost due to **fraudulent or negligent conduct** by the taxpayer.

In such cases

- normal time limits for assessment are extended and
- interest is charged on the understated tax and
- penalties are imposed (which the Board may mitigate).

Fraudulent conduct consists of making false statements, known to be false or made recklessly, whereas negligent conduct is omitting to do what a prudent and reasonable person might be expected to do.

14.2   Extended time limits

Normal time limit for 'discovery' assessments is five years after 31 January following the end of the year of assessment concerned.

However, an assessment to recover tax lost through fraudulent or negligent conduct may be made at any time not later than 20 years after the end of the chargeable period to which it relates.

14.3   Interest

Where a back duty assessment is raised, interest is charged from the date the tax ought to have been paid to the date of actual payment, if an Inspector or the Board so determines.

14.4   Penalties

The maximum penalty applied in addition to the requirement to pay the lost tax, is an amount equivalent to the underpaid tax. The taxpayer guilty of fraudulent or negligent conduct can, therefore, have to pay

- the tax underpaid (including Class 4 NIC where appropriate);
- interest on the underpayment; and

- a penalty equal to the underpaid tax.

The interest and penalty element is determined by an officer of the Board (eg an Inspector) subject to the taxpayer's right of appeal.

The normal procedure is to invite the taxpayer to make an offer in consideration of the Board not formally proceeding with assessments and penalties.

The offer will have to be for an amount at least equal to the underpaid tax and the interest. How much above this amount proves acceptable will depend upon the circumstances of the offence and the degree of co-operation by the taxpayer.

14.5   Investigatory powers

The Inspector, with the Board's authority and the Commissioner's consent, may require production of all relevant documents by the taxpayer and any other person.

The Inspector, with the Board's authority and consent of the Court, may require a convicted tax accountant to produce documents relating to a client's affairs.

Where there is reasonable suspicion of fraud, the Board may apply to the Court for a warrant to enter premises to search for and seize any relevant evidence.

15   CHAPTER SUMMARY

This chapter has dealt with the general administration of the UK tax system and the payment of tax.

The following areas were covered:

- the payment of income tax;
- self assessment;
- tax appeals;
- the organisation of the Inland Revenue;
- payment of mainstream corporation tax; and
- the administration and payment of capital gains tax.

16   SELF TEST QUESTIONS

16.1   When should a tax return be submitted? (3.2)

16.2   How are payments on account calculated? (4.1)

16.3   What are the consequences of late payment of the balancing payment? (5.1 and 5.6)

16.4   What are the two bodies of appeal commissioners and what is their function? (6.2)

16.5   What is the significance of an employee's code number and how does it operate? (7.2)

16.6   When an employee leaves employment, what PAYE procedure must be adopted? (7.9)

16.7   How is the Inland Revenue organised? (9.1)

16.8   What is the pay and file scheme for corporation tax? (11.4)

16.9   What is the due date of payment of capital gains tax? (12.3)

16.10   When are back duty claims made? (14.1)

2 AN OUTLINE OF INCOME TAX

INTRODUCTION

This chapter gives an outline of income tax, and looks at different types of income and how they are dealt with, within the tax system.

1 THE PRINCIPLES OF INCOME TAX

1.1 Introduction

Liability to income tax is computed by reference to income for a fiscal year (also known as a tax year). This is a year ended on 5 April and is labelled by the calendar years it straddles. Thus the year from 6 April 1998 to 5 April 1999 is referred to as the fiscal year 1998/99.

1.2 The income tax return

Every fiscal year each taxpayer is required to complete an income tax return and submit it to the appropriate district inspector of taxes. Using separate working sheets (which need not be submitted) the taxpayer calculates his own income tax and capital gains tax liabilities for the year just ended based on the information included in the return. These liabilities shown on the return constitute a 'self-assessment' which the inspector uses in preparing the taxpayer's statement of account. Tax is payable whether or not a statement is issued. If the return is submitted by 30 September after the tax year, the Inspector will calculate the taxpayers liability based on the information in the return. This is purely a mechanical calculation and is still referred to as a 'self-assessment'. Returns are not usually required from non-tax payers (eg, children) or those who are fully taxed at source (eg, employees).

1.3 Basic rules for charging tax

Two rules can be established for charging UK income tax on an individual's income. These are

- **UK resident's rule** – an individual who is resident in the UK is liable to UK income tax on his income arising throughout the world

- **UK income rule** – a person not resident in the UK is only liable to UK tax on income arising in the UK.

There is no statutory definition of the term 'residence'. An individual is generally considered to be resident in the UK if he satisfies either of the following tests:

- he is physically present in the UK for six months (183 days) or more in any fiscal year;

- he makes regular visits to the UK so that these visits become habitual (visits become habitual after four successive years) and substantial (an average visit of three months a year is substantial).

1.4   The rates of income tax

The charge to income tax for 1998/99 comprises three tiers:

- A lower rate of 20%;
- A basic rate of 23%;
- A higher rate of tax of 40%.

The upper limits of the lower rate band and the basic rate band of taxable income can be found in the tax tables at the front of this manual – find them now.

Note that for 1996/97 and 1997/98 the basic rate of income tax was 24% and 23% respectively.

1.5   Independent taxation

Individual taxpayers, married or single, male or female, are taxed separately on their own income.

Each individual is separately responsible for

- making a tax return, and
- declaring all their income to the Inspector of Taxes, and
- claiming their own allowances and reliefs, and
- paying any tax due on their own income (and capital gains) or receiving any repayments due.

Married men are not responsible for their wives' tax affairs.

1.6   Collection of income tax

Income tax may be collected either by deduction from the income at source, or by the taxpayer making payments of his 'self-assessed' liability.

(a)   **Deduction at source**

Where possible, the Inland Revenue collect income tax at source – that is immediately the income arises. This avoids the necessity of collecting the tax subsequently from each individual taxpayer receiving the income. The payer of the income acts, effectively, as an agent for the Revenue, deducting income tax usually either at the basic rate or lower rate and paying over that tax to the Revenue. The recipient will, therefore, receive only the net income.

It is vital to realise that deduction at source is a method of collection and not necessarily the final liability of the recipient. Thus the gross income must be brought into the taxpayer's computation, and once his total liability has been calculated the amount of income tax already deducted at source is offset against that total liability. Any overpayment may be reclaimed from the Revenue.

The most widely-known method of deduction at source is the Pay As You Earn (PAYE) system applied to income from employment.   Under this system the employer is liable to account to the Revenue for the tax deducted at the lower, basic and higher rates.

In the following cases, where deduction at source applies, only lower rate tax is deducted.

- bank interest;
- building society interest;
- loan and debenture interest received from UK resident companies; and
- interest paid on UK government in certain situations and local authority securities.

Dividends received from UK resident companies are treated as if lower rate tax had been deducted at source.

(b)   **Self-assessment**

Under self-assessment the tax liability on income not taxed (or not taxed sufficiently) at source is payable through two payments on account, one due on 31 January in the tax year and one due on 31 July following the tax year, with a final (or balancing) payment due on 31 January following the tax year. (See chapter 1 for details.)

2   THE SCHEDULAR SYSTEM OF INCOME TAX

2.1   Schedular System

Income is classified for income tax purposes according to its nature and source. The classifications into which the income falls are known as Schedules. There are four Schedules and, in Schedules D and E, there are further subdivisions called Cases. The type of income to be included in each Schedule and Case is laid down by statute (Schedules B and C have been abolished).

According to the statutory rules of each Schedule and Case the income will be assessable on either an actual or a current year basis (ie the assessable amount will be the actual income arising in the year of assessment or the profits of an accounting period ending in the current year of assessment). The Schedules and Cases are summarised below

Schedule		Nature of income	Normal basis of assessment
A		Income from land and buildings in the UK	Actual
D	Case I	Profits of a trade	Current year
	Case II	Profits of a profession or vocation	Current year
	Case III	Interest received from UK sources	Actual
	Case IV*	Interest on foreign securities (eg, debentures)	Actual
	Case V*	Income from foreign possessions (eg, foreign dividends, rents, business profits and pensions)	Actual
	Case VI	Any taxable income not assessed under another Schedule or Case	Actual
E**		Emoluments and benefits derived from an office or employment (including all UK pensions)	Actual
F		Dividends received (plus related tax credits) from UK resident companies	Actual

*   Not examinable

**   The cases of Schedule E concern 'foreign element' which is not examinable for paper 7.

2.2   Income taxed at source

Examples of income received by a taxpayer under deduction of tax at source include interest from banks or building societies (Schedule D Case III), dividends received from UK resident companies (Schedule F), and emoluments of employment (Schedule E).

Income taxed at source is always assessable on an actual basis and the gross equivalent is included in the computation. The grossing up is usually at the lower rate (ie, 100/80) as most deduction at source is at the lower rate.

Income from a life interest trust is either received net of 20% tax (if derived from interest or dividends) or net of 23% tax (if derived from other sources) and grossed up at $^{100}/_{80}$ or $^{100}/_{77}$ respectively. Income passing through a life interest trust retains its original Schedule/Case labels.

Income from a discretionary trust is received net of 34% (and grossed up at $^{100}/_{66}$) regardless of the underlying source of income. The income received by the beneficiary is technically labelled as Schedule D Case VI income.

Interest on UK government stocks purchased after 5 April 1998 is paid gross. For stocks purchased before 6 April 1998 interest continues to be paid net (of lower rate tax) but recipients can elect to be paid gross. Whether such interest is received net or gross it is still Schedule D Case III income and is subject to the 'savings income' treatment - see beyond. Some care is needed in exam questions to ensure that net received interest is grossed up (at $^{100}/_{80}$) but gross received interest is left unaltered.

3   EXEMPTIONS

3.1   Exempt income

The following income is exempt from income tax

(a)   interest on National Savings Certificates

(b)   interest on SAYE savings schemes

(c)   interest on repayment of overpaid tax

(d)   redundancy payments under *Employment Protection Act 1978*

(e)   scholarship income and bursaries

(f)   wages in lieu of notice (except where there is a contractural entitlement)

(g)   insurance benefits paid in the event of accident, sickness, disability, infirmity or unemployment

(h)   interest and dividends received in a personal equity plan (PEP) (see chapter 4)

(i)   interest on Tax Exempt Special Savings Accounts (TESSAs)

- **General Principle.** An individual aged 18 or over can hold ONE TESSA, with a bank or building society.

- **Exemption.** Provided the capital is left in the account throughout the 5 year life of the TESSA, the interest is tax free.

- **The investment.** Up to £3,000 can be invested in the first year and up to £1,800 pa thereafter, with a maximum total investment of £9,000. Interest is credited gross but can be withdrawn net of notional lower rate tax as it arises. Any withdrawal in excess of this will result in termination of the exempt status and all interest credited up to that point would become assessable. The account will cease to be tax exempt after 5 years.

- **Reinvestment.** When a TESSA matures after five years, the investor may open a second account with the full amount of **capital** (not interest) deposited in their first TESSA. This allows the investor to continue receiving tax-free interest on up to £9,000, provided they leave the capital untouched for a further five years. The reinvestment must take place within 6 months of the first account maturing. If less than £9,000 is invested in the first year of the second TESSA, further investments may be made over the next 4 years within the usual limits of £1,800 for each year.

  All TESSAs remain subject to an overall investment limit of £9,000.

- **Interaction with ISAs.** A new form of tax efficient saving - Individual Savings Accounts (ISAs) - becomes available from 6 April 1999 with the intention of replacing TESSAs and PEPs. Therefore no new or reinvestment TESSAs can be taken out after 5 April 1999 but the saver can continue to invest in his TESSA already taken out. When an existing TESSA matures after 5 April 1999 the capital (not interest) can be transferred into an ISA.

(j)   income arising in an Individual Savings Account (ISA) - available from 6 April 1999 onwards. (See chapter 4).

3.2 Exempt persons

The following persons are exempt from income tax

(a)   charities
(b)   approved pension funds and personal pension schemes
(c)   local authorities
(d)   scientific research associations
(e)   members of visiting armed forces and foreign diplomatic staff (on their salaries and expense allowances).

4   FORMAT OF THE INCOME TAX COMPUTATION

4.1   Basic computation

An individual's income tax liability for a year of assessment is determined by

(a)   computing statutory total income (STI) – income from all sources less allowable outgoings therefrom, and then deducting

(b)   the reliefs and allowances (eg personal allowance) to which there is an entitlement in the current year of assessment.

The resultant figure is known as taxable income, the first £4,300 of which is charged to income tax at the lower rate of 20%; the next £22,800 is charged at the basic rate of 23% and any excess over £27,100 at the higher rate of 40%.

4.2   Example: Income tax computation

Tony, who is single, has statutory total income of £9,265 in 1998/99.

The personal allowance is £4,195. What is Tony's income tax liability for 1998/99?

4.3   Solution

Step 1   Calculate Tony's taxable income:

	£
Statutory total income	9,265
Less: Personal allowance	4,195
Taxable income	5,070

Step 2   Calculate Tony's income tax liability:

£	£
4,300 at 20%	860
770 at 23%	177
5,070	1,037

4.4   Activity

Teresa, who is single has statutory total income of £38,195 in 1998/99.

What is Teresa's income tax liability for 1998/99?

4.5   Activity solution

			£
Statutory total income			38,195
Less: Personal allowance			4,195
Taxable income			34,000

Income tax liability

	£	%	£
At lower rate	4,300	at 20	860
At basic rate	22,800	at 23	5,244
At higher rate	6,900	at 40	2,760
Income tax liability on	34,000	is	8,864

4.6   Statutory total income

This may be broken down into three constituent parts

- net earned income plus
- unearned income less
- allowable outgoings (called **charges on income**).

4.7   Earned income

It is necessary to separate earned from unearned income in income tax computations because certain deductions relevant to provisions for retirement are allowable against earned income only.

The following are the **main** sources of earned income

(a)   **Schedule A** rents from the commercial letting of furnished holiday accommodation.

(b)   **Schedule D Cases I and II** profits of a trade, profession or vocation

(c)   **Schedule D Case VI** casual freelance earnings

(d)   **Schedule E** emoluments from an individual's office or employment including

- wages and salaries
- assessed benefits in kind (eg the use of a company car)
- bonuses, commissions and expense allowances
- pensions arising from past employment.

4.8   Net earned income

In order to arrive at this figure it is necessary to deduct from the earned income the following:

- allowable expenses of employment, give-as-you-earn (GAYE) charitable contributions, professional subscriptions and occupational pension contributions – deducted from Schedule E income

- allowable personal pension plan contributions paid by the self-employed or people in employments where either no occupational pension is provided by the employer, or where personal provision for a pension has been opted for rather than entry into an employer's scheme.

4.9   Unearned income

Unearned income includes all taxable income other than earned income. It may be classified broadly as

- income already taxed by deduction at source – although taxed already, the gross amount of such income must be included in the computation on an actual year basis.

- income received gross and taxable by self-assessment – for example income assessable under Schedule A, and Schedule D Cases III–VI (where not earned income as above).

For the purposes of calculating tax borne, unearned income in the form of interest or dividends should be classified separately and referred to as 'savings income'. The special tax rules on savings income are explained in a later chapter and are not mentioned further in this chapter.

4.10   Allowable outgoings: charges on income

Certain payments made by an individual are allowable deductions for income tax purposes. Some, like those mentioned above, are deductible from specific source(s) of income; others, referred to as charges on income, are deductible from **total** income (earned and unearned). The most common example is a charitable deed of covenant. Relief is given in a fiscal year for payments made in that same year.

4.11   Revision of the main points

In order to compute an individual's income tax liability it is first necessary to determine his statutory total income. This comprises

- income from all sources, some of which may have been received under deduction of tax at source, classified as appropriate under a relevant Schedule or Case and assessed on actual or current year basis; less

- charges on income paid (always dealt with on an actual year basis).

4.12   Layout of a personal tax computation

An example of a personal tax computation follows. Pay attention to the way it is set out. Much of the terminology is explained in later chapters.

Mr White: Income tax computation 1998/99

	£	£	£
Earned income			
Schedule D Case I			X
Schedule E Salary/bonus		X	
Benefits in kind		X	
		—	
		X	
Less: Expenses	X		
Occupational pension scheme contributions	X		
GAYE payments	X		
	—		
		(X)	
		—	
			X
			—
			X
Less: Personal pension premiums			(X)
			—
			X

Unearned income

Assessable income, Schedules A and D (Cases III to VI)		X
Taxed investment income		
Schedule F:	UK dividends (including tax credit)	X
Schedule D Case III:	Building society interest (including tax credit)	X
	Bank interest (including tax credit)	X
Trust income (including tax credit), Schedule		
	A and D (Cases III to VI)	X
		X
Less:	Charges on income (gross)	(X)

		X
Statutory total income		X
Less:	Personal allowance	(X)
Taxable income		X

Tax liability

	£
At lower rate (20%)	X
At basic rate (23%)	X
At higher rate (40%)	X
	X

Less:	Relief for maintenance payments (@ 15%)	(X)
	Tax credit for mortgage interest (@ 10%)	
	(where not paid under MIRAS)	(X)
	Tax credit on personal allowances (eg, MCA)	
	(where tax relief is restricted to 15%)	(X)

Income tax borne on taxable income		X
Add:	Basic rate tax retained on charges	X

Income tax liability			X
Less:	PAYE		(X)
	Tax suffered on:	dividends	(X)
		bank interest	(X)
		building society interest	(X)
		trust income	(X)
		other taxed income	(X)
	Tax paid in two payments on account(31.1.99 and 31.7.99)		(X)

Final income tax due on 31.1.2000	X

5   SOCIAL SECURITY BENEFITS

5.1   General considerations

Social security benefits can be classified into two main groups. These are as follows.

(a)   Benefits which are payable out of the National Insurance Fund (contributory benefits). For example:

- state retirement pension
- jobseekers' allowance.

(b)   Those benefits which are paid out of funds provided by the Exchequer (non-contributory benefits). For example:

- Payable as a right

    (1)   child benefit
    (2)   invalid care allowance
    (3)   severe disablement benefit.

- Means-tested benefits

    (1)   family credit
    (2)   income support.

There is a wide range of 'benefits' available from sources other than the DSS, for example:

(a)   'benefits' paid by employers (eg, statutory sick pay);

(b)   assistance with training and job-seeking (eg enterprise allowance scheme) available through local job centres.

5.2   Benefits taxable

The amount of the benefits is irrelevant, since this information is always given.

The following are the principal tax-free benefits:

(a)   family credit
(b)   incapacity benefit (initial period only)
(c)   child benefit
(d)   lump sum widow's payment.

5.3   Benefits paid by employers

There are three 'benefits' which are only available to employees since the law requires payment to be made by the employer. In each case the employer may be able to reclaim a proportion of the payment from the State. These payments are:

(a)   **Statutory sick pay (SSP)**

No payment is made for the first three days of sickness (the qualifying period) and the maximum entitlement is for 28 weeks in the period of incapacity for work. (Strictly 28 times the weekly rate of SSP.)

(b)   **Statutory maternity pay (SMP)**

SMP is liable to income tax under PAYE and Class 1 NI contributions.

Benefit is paid by the employer - an earnings related element equivalent to 90% of earnings for 6 weeks, followed by a flat rate payment for a further 12 weeks; a maximum period of 18 weeks.

(c)   **Statutory redundancy payments**

Under the provisions of the *Employment Protection (Consolidation) Act 1978* an employee is entitled to a statutory redundancy payment since if he loses his job through redundancy the fault is not his own.

The amount of the payment is computed according to the method laid down in the Act and is payable by the employer as a lump sum. The amount is a multiple of the employee's normal weekly gross pay depending upon the length of continuous service and the age of the employee. However, the amount is subject to an overriding maximum, so that the maximum redundancy payment will be less than £6,000. Most employers are entitled to recover 35% of the amount from the Department of Employment.

The lump sum is not liable to income tax under the normal rules of Schedule E and, although technically chargeable under the rules dealing with lump sum payments on termination of employment, it will not in fact give rise to a charge since it will fall within the £30,000 exemption limit given under those rules.

5.4   Job-seeking, training and employment

There are a number of specific types of benefit or state assistance which relate to job-seeking, training and employment.

These are available through the nationwide network of Job Centres which are the main contact with the public.

(a)   **Enterprise Allowance Scheme**

This scheme provides a flat-rate weekly allowance for the first year of a new approved business venture set up by an unemployed person who is between the ages of 18 and 65.

Applicants must work full-time in the business and invest £1,000 of their own capital. They must also have been unemployed for at least 8 weeks and be in receipt of either jobseeker's allowance or income support. While receiving the allowance a person will not be entitled to other social security benefits.

(b)   **Youth Training Scheme (YTS)**

The Scheme provides up to 2 years training in work-related skills for 16 year old school leavers and disabled students under 21, and for 1 year for 17 year olds.

Young people are either employed, and are paid a taxable wage under a contract of employment, or are taken on as non-employed trainees, in which case a weekly tax-free (NIC free) allowance is received. A non-employed trainee cannot be paid any overtime or bonus, but these are, of course, payable to employed YTS persons.

5.5   Children

(a)   **Child benefit** - this is the principal benefit payable to people with the care and responsibility for children. It is a non-contributory tax-free benefit with an additional amount paid to a single parent.

(b)   **Family credit** - family credit is a tax-free income-related benefit paid to eligible persons who are responsible for one or more children of school age. The benefit is paid weekly for an initial period of 26 weeks after which a further award must be claimed.

6   SELF TEST QUESTIONS

6.1   What is a fiscal year (also known as a tax year)? (1.1)

6.2   Which individuals are liable to UK income tax? (1.3)

6.3   What Schedules and Cases is income classified into for the purposes of income tax? (2.1)

6.4   What type of income is included in each Schedule and Case? (2.1)

6.5   What is the normal basis of assessment for each Schedule and Case? (2.1)

6.6   What income is exempt from tax? (3.1)

6.7   How is an individual's income tax liability determined for a year of assessment? (4.1)

6.8   What are the main sources of earned income? (4.7)

6.9   What deductions may be made from earned income in order to arrive at the net earned income figure? (4.8)

7   EXAMINATION TYPE QUESTION

7.1   Kate

Kate, a single person, has the following income, outgoings and allowances for the year ended 5 April 1999.

Year ended 5 April	1999 £
Salary	32,000
Benefits in kind by reason of employment (BUPA)	875
Allowable expenses of employment	(95)
Taxed investment income - bank interest (gross)	520
- building society interest (gross)	890
Rents from UK unfurnished lettings	1,890
Personal allowance	4,195
Allowable charge on income paid (gross)	2,160

Calculate the income tax borne for 1998/99.

8   ANSWER TO EXAMINATION TYPE QUESTION

8.1   Kate

Income tax computation 1998/99

	£	£
Earned income		
Schedule E		
Salary		32,000
Benefit in kind - BUPA		875
		32,875
Less: Allowable expenses		(95)
		32,780

Unearned income

Schedule D Case III	- bank interest	520	
	- building society interest	890	
Schedule A	- unfurnished lettings	1,890	
			3,300
			36,080
Less: Charge on income (gross)			(2,160)
Statutory total income			33,920
Less: Personal allowance			(4,195)
Taxable income			29,725

Income tax

	£	%	£
Lower rate	4,300	20	860
Basic rate	22,800	23	5,244
Higher rate	2,625	40	1,050
Income tax borne			7,154

3 INCOME FROM LAND AND BUILDINGS

INTRODUCTION & LEARNING OBJECTIVES

All UK income from land and buildings is taxed under Schedule A for individuals and companies, although special rules apply to furnished holiday lettings.

The rules for individuals are dealt with in this chapter, whilst the modifications to these rules as they apply for companies are dealt with in the corporation tax chapters.

When you have studied this chapter you should have learned the following:

- How Schedule A income is assessed, and the relief available for Schedule A losses.
- How premiums for the grant of leases are dealt with.
- The special treatment of furnished holiday accommodation.
- Rent a room relief.

1 SCHEDULE A

1.1 Income liable

The following income is liable to assessment under Schedule A

(a)   rents under any lease or tenancy agreement
(b)   premium received on grant of a short lease (this is covered in the next section).

1.2 Basis of assessment

The income from land and buildings is computed as if the letting of the property were a business, and the amount assessable under Schedule A will be the rental business profits of the year of assessment. If the landlord lets more than one property, the different lettings all form one single business, so that the assessable amount is the aggregate of the profits and losses from each separate property.

The due dates for payment of the rent, the date of actual receipt of the rent, and the date of payment of the expenses are irrelevant since business accounts should be drawn up on the accruals basis. Thus the assessable income for 1998/99 is the rent due for the period 6 April 1998 to 5 April 1999, less the expenses payable for the same period.

Note that although the computation is made as if the letting were a business, the net income is still generally assessable under Schedule A, and the letting is not treated as an actual business. This principle also applies to furnished holiday lettings (see beyond) although it is treated as a business separate from normal lettings and enjoys certain 'trade' advantages not available on normal lettings. Occasionally the letting may constitute an actual trade, for example where lodgers are taken in, in which case the net income will be assessable under Schedule D Case I.

1.3   Activity

Hembery owns a property which was let for the first time on 1 July 1998. The rent of £5,000 pa is paid alternatively (i) quarterly in advance; (ii) quarterly in arrears; (iii) annually in advance. Hembery paid allowable expenses of £200 in December 1998 (related to redecoration following a burst pipe), and £400 in May 1999 for repairs completed in March 1999.

Compute the rent assessable for 1998/99 in each case.

1.4   Activity solution

The rent assessable in each case is the rent due for the period 1 July 1998 to 5 April 1999. Expenses relating to the same period are deductible.

	£	£
*Rent due 9/12 × £5,000		3,750
Expenses		
Redecoration	200	
Repairs	400	
		(600)
Schedule A amount for 1998/99		3,150

* Should be on a daily basis

1.5   Allowable deductions

The expenses allowable against the rental income are computed under the normal rules for businesses. These are discussed fully in the chapter on Schedule D Case I, but the main rules are given below.

(a)   To be allowable, the expenses must have been incurred wholly and exclusively in connection with the business.

This covers items such as:

- insurance;
- agents fees;
- other management expenses;
- repairs;
- interest on a loan to acquire or improve the property.

Where property is not let at a full rent (eg, to an aged relative) the Revenue are likely to disallow a portion of the expenses as not being wholly and exclusively incurred for the business. For example, if rent charged is £250 pa but a commercial rent would be £1,000 pa, only 25% of expenses are likely to be allowed.

(b)   Capital expenditure is not allowable.

The main distinction between capital and revenue expenditure is between improvements and repairs. Repairs are allowable expenses, whilst improvements are not. In some cases a repair will include an element of improvement, in which case it is necessary to apportion the expenditure between capital and revenue.

Depreciation may be charged in accounts as a means of writing off the cost of capital expenditure over the life of an asset. It is not an allowable deduction, but capital allowances may be claimed instead for expenditure on plant and machinery used for the purposes of the letting (see Capital Allowances chapter).

Chapter 3   Income from land and buildings   41

For furnished lettings, capital allowances are generally replaced by a 'wear and tear' allowance, which is calculated as 10% of the rent. If the landlord pays the council tax on the property, the wear and tear allowance is calculated as 10% of the rent net of the council tax.

(c)   Specific bad debts are allowable, whilst a general provision for bad debts is not allowable. If a tenant leaves without paying the outstanding rent, the amount owed can be deducted as an expense. However the landlord could not make a general deduction of (say) 5% of rent due in case a tenant should default.

(d)   Relief is available for any expenditure incurred before letting commenced, under the normal pretrading expenditure rules.

1.6   Activity

Giles owns a cottage which he lets out furnished at an annual rent of £3,600, payable monthly in advance. During 1998/99 he incurs the following expenditure:

May 1998	Replacement of windows with new UVPC double glazed units (it is estimated that the improvement element in the expenditure was £1,500)	£2,000
June 1998	Insurance for year from 5 July (previous year - £420)	£480
November 1998	Drain clearance	£380
May 1999	Redecoration (work completed in March 1999)	£750

The tenant had vacated the property during June 1998 without having paid the rent due for June. Giles was unable to trace the defaulting tenant, but managed to let the property to new tenants from 1 July 1998.

Calculate the income assessable under Schedule A for 1998/99 assuming Giles claims the 10% wear and tear allowance.

1.7   Activity solution

	£	£
Rent due £300 × 12		3,600
Expenses		
Bad debt - June 1998 rent	300	
Window repairs £(2,000 − 1,500)	500	
Insurance 3/12 × £420 + 9/12 × £480	465	
Drain clearance	380	
Redecoration	750	
Wear and tear 10% × £(3,600 − 300)	330	
		(2,725)
Schedule A amount for 1998/99		875

[handwritten: because June 98 was not received]

[handwritten: Rent received]

1.8   Schedule A losses

If the landlord owns more than one property, the profits and losses on all the properties are aggregated to calculate the Schedule A assessable income for the year. Effectively this allows the loss arising on one property to be set against the profits arising on other properties.

This set off applies irrespective of the nature of the underlying lease, and thus enables losses made where a property is let at less than the market rental to be relieved.

If there is an overall Schedule A loss, the assessable income for the year will be nil. The loss is carried forward, and set against the Schedule A assessable income for the following year. If the income in the following year is insufficient to relieve the loss, the unrelieved balance is carried forward against future Schedule A income.

1.9   Activity

Sheila owns three properties which were rented out. Her assessable income and allowable expenses for the two years to 5 April 1999 were:

	Property		
	1	2	3
	£	£	£
Income			
1997/98	1,200	450	3,150
1998/99	800	1,750	2,550
Expenses			
1997/98	1,850	600	2,800
1998/99	900	950	2,700

What are Sheila's Schedule A assessable amounts for 1997/98 and 1998/99?

1.10   Activity solution

	Property		
	1	2	3
	£	£	£
1997/98			
Income	1,200	450	3,150
Less: Expenses	1,850	600	2,800
	(650)	(150)	350
Total			(450)
Schedule A assessable (loss c/f £450)			Nil
1998/99			
Income	800	1,750	2,550
Less: Expenses	900	950	2,700
	(100)	800	(150)
Total			550
Less: Schedule A loss b/f			(450)
Schedule A assessable			100

2   PREMIUMS RECEIVED ON THE GRANT OF A SHORT LEASE

2.1   Premiums

A premium is a lump sum payment made by the tenant to the landlord in consideration of the granting of a lease. Since the payment is in the nature of rent (a higher annual rent would be charged if no premium were paid) the landlord is assessed under Schedule A on the premium received, **unless the premium is for a long lease (exceeding 50 years).** (Premiums on long leases are treated as capital receipts and are dealt with only under the capital gains legislation.)

A premium received on the grant of a short lease (for 50 years or less) is treated as rent assessed under Schedule A in the fiscal year in which the lease is granted.

The amount assessable is

(a)   the amount of the premium *less*
(b)   2% of the premium for each complete year of the lease (other than the first).

This can be calculated as follows:

	£
Premium	X
less: 2% × (n − 1) × premium	(X)
	X

where n is the duration of the lease in years.

This rule does not apply if a lease is being assigned (ie, where the entire interest in a property is sold).

2.2   Activity

A 21 years 11 months lease is granted for a premium of £10,000 in 1998/99.
What is the amount assessable under Schedule A for 1998/99?

2.3   Activity solution

Assessable under Schedule A for 1998/99.

	£
Premium	10,000
less: 2% (21 − 1) × 10,000	(4,000)
	6,000

Note: the remaining £4,000 is subject to the capital gains tax rules.

2.4   Leases determinable at intervals

In order to avoid income tax it would be a simple matter to grant a lease for over 50 years, but to give the landlord the right to determine (ie end) the lease before the expiration of 50 years.

Anti-avoidance legislation provides that where the lease can be terminated at some date during the lease, the period of the lease is taken to extend only to the earliest date on which the lease may be terminated, where the premium payable is obviously less than market value for a longer lease.

2.5   Example: Duration of a lease

Arnold grants a 99-year lease on property in Kensington for a premium of £4,000. The agreement states that the lessor may terminate the lease at the end of the fifth year. The current market value of a 99-year lease on a similar property in that area is £180,000.

What will be taken as the period of the lease, and what amount, if any is assessable under Schedule A?

2.6   Solution

In this case it is patently obvious that the landlord intends to terminate the lease after five years and that the premium charged relates only to that period and not 99 years. Thus the duration of the lease for Schedule A purposes will be five years and the computation will be:

Assessable under Schedule A

	£
Premium	4,000
less: 2% (5 − 1) × 4,000	(320)
	3,680

2.7   Premiums paid by traders

A proportion of a premium paid for the grant of a short lease (not exceeding 50 years) of business premises is deductible each year from business profits.

The amount allowable each year is computed by dividing the sum assessable on the landlord under Schedule A by the number of years of the lease.

2.8   Example: Premiums paid by traders

Rodney granted a 21-year lease of business premises to Charles on 1 July 1998 for a premium of £10,500. Charles uses the premises for his trade as a restaurateur.

What are the income tax consequences on Rodney and Charles?

2.9   Solution

The amount assessable under Schedule A on Rodney for 1998/99 is

	£
Premium	10,500
less: 2% (21 − 1) × 10,500	(4,200)
	6,300

The **annual** deduction given to Charles, the payer of the premium, in his Schedule D Case 1 computation is

$$\frac{\text{Amount assessable as income on recipient}}{\text{Duration of lease}} \quad \text{ie,} \quad \frac{£6,300}{21} = £300 \text{ pa for 21 years..}$$

If Charles prepares accounts to 30 September each year only a 3 months portion of the annual amount ie, £75 (3/12 × 300) will be allowed in the year ended 30 September 1998.

2.10   Premiums for granting subleases

If a tenant sublets his property and grants a lease to a subtenant, any premium he charges to the subtenant will be assessable under Schedule A under the normal rules for granting leases. However, if the tenant originally paid a premium on his own lease (known as the head lease) relief is given as follows:

$$\text{Taxable premium for head lease} \times \frac{\text{duration of sublease}}{\text{duration of headlease}}.$$

2.11   Example: Grant of a sublease

Victor granted a lease to Alec on 1 August 1992 for a period of 20 years. Alec paid a premium of £20,000.

On 1 August 1998 Alec granted a sublease to Max for a period of 5 years. Max paid a premium of £24,000.

Calculate the amount assessable under Schedule A on Alec for 1998/99 for the premium received from Max.

2.12   Solution

Step 1   Calculate the taxable premium for the head lease

	£
Premium	20,000
less: 2% (20 − 1) × 20,000	(7,600)
	12,400

Step 2   Calculate Alec's Schedule A income for 1998/99.

	£
Premium received	24,000
less: 2% (5 − 1) × 24,000	(1,920)
	22,080
Less: Relief for premium paid	
$£12,400 \times \dfrac{5}{20}$	(3,100)
	18,980

3   FURNISHED HOLIDAY ACCOMMODATION

3.1   Introduction

Profits arising from the commercial letting of furnished holiday accommodation are treated as **earned** income arising from the operation of a single and separate trade, even though still assessable under Schedule A.

3.2   Furnished holiday accommodation

The letting will only be treated as furnished holiday accommodation if it is furnished, let on a commercial basis with a view to the realisation of profits, and satisfies the following conditions.

(a)   It is **available** for commercial letting, to the public generally, as holiday accommodation for not less than 140 days a year;

(b)   the accommodation is **actually let** for at least 70 days in that 140 day period;

(c)   for at least seven months out of the twelve months qualifying period, the property must not normally be occupied by the same person continuously for more than 31 days.

3.3   Tax treatment of furnished holiday lettings

Any profits from commercially let furnished holiday accommodation remain assessable under Schedule A computed as if the letting were a business. Note, however, the following.

The profits deriving from all the qualifying holiday accommodation will be treated as earned income arising from a single trade carried on by the landlord. The following advantages and reliefs thereby become available.

(a)   The profits are relevant earnings for the purposes of relief for personal pension scheme contributions.

(b)   Relief may be claimed for any losses sustained as if they were trading losses (see chapter on trading losses).

(c)   Capital gains tax roll-over relief and retirement relief are available where appropriate.

> [Conclusion]   Profits from furnished holiday lettings, although assessable according to the Schedule A rules are treated as earned income. From an exam point of view the most important of the tax treatments listed are:
>
> •   profits treated as relevant earnings for personal pension premium purposes; and
>
> •   any loss may be relieved as if it were a trading loss.

4   RENT A ROOM RELIEF

4.1   Introduction

If an individual lets furnished accommodation in his main residence, and the income is liable to tax under Schedule A or Schedule D Case I a special exemption applies.

If the gross annual receipts (before expenses or capital allowances) are £4,250 or below, they will be exempt from tax.

4.2   The rent a room scheme

The detailed rules for the rent a room scheme are as follows:

(a)   The individual's limit of £4,250 is reduced by half to £2,125 if, during a particular tax year any other person(s) also received income from letting accommodation in the property while the property was the first person's main residence.

This rule allows a married couple taking in lodgers to either have all the rent paid to one spouse (who will then have the full limit of £4,250) or to have the rent divided between the spouses (and each spouse will then have a limit of £2,125).

(b)   An individual may elect to ignore the exemption for a particular year (for example if a loss is incurred when taking account of expenses).

(c)   If the gross annual receipts are more than £4,250, an individual may choose between:

   •   paying tax on the excess of his gross rent over £4,250 (without relief for expenses); or
   •   being taxed in the ordinary way on their profit from letting (rent less expenses).

Conclusion   Gross annual income from renting furnished accommodation in an individual's only main residence is exempt from tax if it amounts to £4,250 or less.

5   CHAPTER SUMMARY

This chapter has dealt with income from land and buildings. The following areas were covered:

   •   income from land and property. The rent due in a tax year for a landlord subject to income tax is assessable under Schedule A. Note how the losses are relieved;

   •   furnished holiday accommodation. This income is treated as earned income, although still assessable under Schedule A. Note the tax treatment of income from furnished holiday accommodation

   •   rent a room relief. Where an individual receives gross annual receipts of £4,250 or less from renting furnished accommodation in his main residence, it will be exempt from tax.

6   SELF TEST QUESTIONS

6.1   What is the basis of assessment for income assessed under Schedule A? (1.2)   *Accrued Basis*

6.2   What deductions are allowable from income assessed under Schedule A? (1.5)

6.3   How are premiums which are received in consideration of granting a lease taxed? (1.7)

6.4   What deduction is available for depreciation from income from furnished lettings? (2.2)

6.5   What relief is available for Schedule A losses? (1.19)

6.6   What are the conditions for lettings to be treated as furnished holiday accommodation? (3.2)

6.7   What is the tax treatment of furnished holiday lettings? (3.3)

6.8   What exemption applies if an individual lets furnished accommodation in his own residence? (4.1)

6.9   If gross rents from the letting of furnished accommodation in an individual's main residence exceed £4,250, how will the income be taxed? (4.2)

7   EXAMINATION TYPE QUESTION

7.1   Tom Jones

For many years Tom Jones has owned six houses in Upland Avenue which are available for letting unfurnished. He is responsible for the repairs to numbers 21, 23, 25 and 67. The tenants are responsible for the repairs to numbers 38 and 40.

Tom's mother lives at number 67. The rent she pays is about 25% of a commercial rate.

The following details have been provided by the client.

	Property number					
	21	23	25	38	40	67
	£	£	£	£	£	£
Rent due for y/e 5.4.99	2,080	1,820	2,340	1,300	1,300	520
Insurance due for y/e 5.4.99	280	220	340	150	150	140

(1)   Tom employs a gardener to look after all the properties and pays him £1,200 a year. There are also accountancy charges of £480 a year; both of these costs are allocated equally to each property.

(2)   Numbers 23 and 40 had new tenancies in the year. The cost of advertising for tenants was £50 in respect of number 23 and £100 for number 40. The new tenant at number 23 took over immediately the old tenant moved out. Unfortunately, the old tenant at No 40 defaulted on rent of £350 due before the new tenant moved in.

(3)   During the year Tom had to replace the boiler in number 40 at a cost of £800. During the year he also had to replace the water tank at number 21 at a cost of £100 and a new roof for number 25 cost him £5,000.

(4)   Tom has loans outstanding on each of the six properties and pays interest of £500 per year on each loan.

You are required:

(a)   to compute the amount assessable under Schedule A for 1998/99

(b)   to explain how relief can be obtained for any losses.

8   ANSWER TO EXAMINATION TYPE QUESTION

8.1   Tom Jones

Schedule A assessable for 1998/99

Upland Avenue No	21	23	25	38	40	67
	£	£	£	£	£	£
Rent due for y/e 5.4.99	2,080	1,820	2,340	1,300	1,300	520
Expenses payable						
Insurance	280	220	340	150	150	35
Gardener	200	200	200	200	200	50
Accountancy	80	80	80	80	80	20
Advertising		50			100	
Repairs	100		5,000		800	
Bad debt					350	
Interest	500	500	500	500	500	125
	1,160	1,050	6,120	930	2,180	230
Net amounts	920	770	(3,780)	370	(880)	290

Summary

	£
No 21	920
No 23	770
No 25	(3,780)
No 38	370
No 40	(880)
No 67	290
	(2,310)
Amount assessable under Schedule A for 1998/99	Nil
Loss carried forward for offset against future Schedule A profits	£2,310

(*Note:* Although the question refers to a new roof for No 25 it is reasonable to assume that there was one there already and the expenditure is essentially on a repair or replacement.

As it is not necessary to consider profits and losses on each property individually the accounts could be drawn up to show the total rents etc for all the properties, instead of property by property. Care has to be taken to disallow a portion of expenses relating to the non-commercial letting.

4 FINANCIAL INVESTMENTS AND SUNDRY INCOME

INTRODUCTION & LEARNING OBJECTIVES

Funds may be invested in banks, building societies or stocks and shares; income received from such investments may be paid gross, paid under deduction of tax or be tax free. It is important to know how the various types of income are dealt with.

Individuals may pay premiums into a pension fund, which is a very tax effective way of investing. The provisions relating to pension premiums are quite complicated, but nevertheless, important for exam purposes.

When you have studied this chapter you should have learned the following:

- Investments that are tax-free
- The special rules applying to 'savings' income
- What constitutes Schedule D Case III income
- The types of income received under deduction of tax
- The scope of Schedule D Case VI income
- How trust income is taxed
- The tax relief given by a personal equity plan (PEP)
- The rules for holding an individual savings account (ISA)
- Relief for investment in pension funds.

1 TAX-FREE INVESTMENTS

1.1 Introduction

The following investment income is tax-free

- Proceeds of National Savings Certificates

- Save As You Earn scheme interest and bonuses

- Premium Bond winnings

- First £70pa of interest from an NSB (National Savings Bank) ordinary account

- Interest and bonuses on a TESSA

- Income and gains from a personal equity plan

- Income and gains from an individual savings account (ISA)

2   DIVIDENDS

2.1   Introduction

Dividends received from a company resident in the UK are charged to income tax. The actual basis applies. For example, dividends accompanied by dividend vouchers dated between 6 April 1998 and 5 April 1999 inclusive are assessable in 1998/99.

2.2   Tax credit

(a)   A dividend received carries with it a tax credit which may be set against the recipient's total tax liability. Where the amount of the credit exceeds the total liability the taxpayer may reclaim the balance from the Revenue. It is the gross dividends (ie, dividend received plus the tax credit) received in the actual fiscal year which are assessable.

(b)   The tax credit is 20/80 of the dividend received (or 20% of the gross dividend). Thus if an individual received a dividend of £160 on 1 August 1998, the tax credit is £160 × 20/80 ie, £40, and the amount assessable in 1998/99 is £200 (£160 + £40).

2.3   Taxation of dividends

Special rules apply to the income taxation of dividends. These special rules also apply to the taxation of interest (see later in this chapter). Interest and dividends are normally labelled as 'savings income' in the computation to signify that such sources are subject to the special rules.

Dividends received by an individual from a UK resident company are taxable only at the lower rate of 20% or the higher rate of 40%. No part of the dividend is taxable at the basic rate of 23%.

The reason for this treatment is that dividends only carry a 20% tax credit so that if dividends were to be taxed at 23% it would mean an additional charge on basic rate taxpayers.

Dividends are taken to be the highest part of an individual's income, so that when the amount of a gross dividend takes an individual's taxable income over the higher rate threshold of £27,100, at least part of the dividend will be taxed at 40%.

As dividends (and interest) receive a special tax treatment, it is useful to include two extra columns in the standard taxable income layout to analyse between dividend and non-dividend income. Where interest is also taxable, the labels to use are 'savings' and 'non-savings' income.

2.4   Example: Taxation of dividends - basic rate taxpayer

Jeremy, a single person, received a salary of £14,000 (PAYE deducted: £2,126) and net dividends of £6,000 in 1998/99.

Calculate the income tax due.

2.5   Solution

The dividends are treated as the highest part of Jeremy's income. As he is only a basic rate taxpayer, all the dividends (grossed up) will be taxed at the lower rate of 20%.

	£	£	Non-dividend £	Dividend £
Schedule E		14,000	14,000	-
Dividends	6,000			
Tax credit (6,000 × 20/80)	1,500			
		7,500	-	7,500
		21,500	14,000	7,500
Less: Personal allowance		4,195	4,195	-
Taxable income		17,305	9,805	7,500

	£
Income tax liability	
Taxable at lower rate (Sch E) £4,300 × 20%	860
Taxable at basic rate (Sch E) (9,805 − 4,300) = 5,505 × 23%	1,266
Taxable at lower rate (dividend plus tax credit) £7,500 × 20%	1,500
	3,626
Less: Tax credit on dividends £7,500 × 20%	(1,500)
PAYE	(2,126)
Income tax liability remaining	Nil

Note that the personal allowance is set first against the non-dividend income. PAYE has clearly collected the correct amount of tax on employment income.

2.6   Example - Taxation of dividends - higher rate taxpayer

Jacob, a single person, received a salary of £22,000 (PAYE deducted: £3,966) and net dividends of £14,000 in 1998/99.

Calculate the income tax due.

2.7   Solution

	£	£	Non-dividend £	Dividend £
Schedule E		22,000	22,000	-
Dividends	14,000			
Tax credit (14,000 × 20/80)	3,500			
		17,500	–	17,500
		39,500	22,000	17,500
Less: Personal allowance		4,195	4,195	–
Taxable income		35,305	17,805	17,500

The dividends are treated as the highest part of Jacob's income. The first £9,295 (£27,100 − 17,805) of the gross dividend falls into the basic rate band, and will be taxed at the lower rate of 20%, the remaining £8,205 (17,500 − 9,295) falls into the higher rate band and will be taxed at the higher rate of 40%.

	£
Income tax liability	
Taxable at lower rate (Sch E) £4,300 × 20%	860
Taxable at basic rate (Sch E) (17,805 − 4,300) = £13,505 × 23%	3,106
Taxable at lower rate (dividend) £9,295 × 20%	1,859
Taxable at higher rate (balance of dividend) £8,205 × 40%	3,282
	9,107
Less: Tax credit on dividends £17,500 × 20%	(3,500)
PAYE	(3,966)
Income tax liability remaining for self-assessment	1,641

Conclusion   Dividends received by an individual are taxable only at the lower rate or the higher rate. They are treated as the highest part of an individual's taxable income for the purpose of calculating the tax liability.

3   BANK AND BUILDING SOCIETY INTEREST

3.1   Introduction

Banks and building societies pay interest net of lower rate tax (20%). Thus if a building society pays interest of 6% net of lower rate income tax, an individual with an investment of £100 will actually receive £6 interest.

3.2   Basis of assessment

(a)   An individual is taxable under Schedule D Case III on the grossed up amount of the actual interest received in a tax year (ie, the amount credited to the account by the bank or building society during the tax year regardless of when the individual has his passbook written up). He will receive a lower rate tax credit for the lower rate suffered at source, or a repayment where tax is overpaid. Thus if an individual receives interest of £240, he will be taxed on £240 × 100/80 ie, £300 and has a tax credit of £60 (£300 × 20%).

(b)   Bank or building society interest is taxed at the lower rate (20%) to the extent that it falls in the basic rate band and 40% to the extent that it falls in the higher rate band in the same way as dividends are taxed (ie, as 'savings income'). Thus bank or building society interest and dividends are treated as the top slice of income.

(c)   Banks and building societies may pay interest gross to an individual who has supplied a certificate of non-liability to income tax. If it transpires that the individual is liable to income tax after all, then the gross interest is still assessable under Schedule D Case III. Interest paid by the National Savings Bank is always paid gross and assessable under Schedule D Case III (see below).

4   INTEREST RECEIVED GROSS

4.1   Income assessable

UK interest received gross is assessable under Schedule D Case III.

The main examples of sources which pay interest gross are:

- National Savings Bank accounts;

- holdings of 3½% War Loan;   *examiners favourite*

- UK government securities either acquired after 5 April 1998 or where an election to receive gross interest has been made;

- loans between individuals;

- certificates of tax deposit; and

- National Savings Income Bonds.

4.2   National Savings Bank interest

(a)   The first £70pa interest from an **ordinary** account with the NSB is exempt from tax.

(b)   Interest from an **investment** account with the NSB is taxable in full.

4.3   Basis of assessment

The current year basis of assessment applies. The income assessable is the interest arising (ie **received** or **credited** to the account) during the fiscal year.

No account is taken of accrued interest under the income tax rules, ie interest arises when it is received.

Whether interest is received net or gross it is still subject to the special 'savings income' rules.

Conclusion   Interest received gross is assessable under Schedule D Case III on the current year basis under the 'savings income' rules. The most important examples of gross interest taxable under Schedule D Case III are:

- interest from National Savings Bank accounts; and
- interest from UK government stocks.

5   OTHER TAXED INCOME

5.1   Introduction

In addition to bank interest and building society interest certain other interest is received net of lower rate tax. The gross amount of income is taxable, and the taxpayer will receive a lower rate tax credit for the lower rate tax suffered at source or a repayment where tax is overpaid.

Taxed income received net of lower rate tax includes the following:

- interest on company loans and debentures;
- interest on UK government securities acquired before 6 April 1998 unless an election for gross payment has been made (except 3½% War Loan which is always paid gross); and
- interest on local authority stocks.

Such income is taxed under the same special 'savings income' rules applying to dividends and bank and building society interest.

One type of taxed income, patent royalties, is received net of basic rate tax and is not treated as 'savings income'.

5.2   Example - Taxation of savings income - higher rate taxpayer

Andrew, a single man, receives the following income for 1998/99.

	£
Salary	16,000
Building society interest	2,400 (net)
UK government stock interest (received net)	1,600 (net)
Patent royalties	770 (net)
UK dividends	8,000 (net)
Rental income	500

Calculate the income tax due.

5.3   Solution

	£	Non-Savings £	Savings £
Schedule E	16,000	16,000	–
BSI 2,400 × 100/80	3,000	–	3,000
UK government stock 1,600 × 100/80	2,000	–	2,000
Patent royalties 770 × 100/77	1,000	1,000	–
Dividends 8,000 × 100/80	10,000	–	10,000
Schedule A	500	500	–
STI	32,500	17,500	15,000
Less: PA	4,195	4,195	–
Taxable income	28,305	13,305	15,000

Income tax liability

		£
Non-savings:	4,300 @ 20%	860
	9,005 @ 23%	2,071
	13,305	
Savings:	13,795 @ 20%	2,759
	27,100	
	1,205 @ 40%	482
	28,305	
Income tax liability		6,172

		£
Less:	Tax credits:	
	BSI	600
	UK government stock	400
	Patent royalties	230
	Dividends	2,000
		3,230
		2,942

Note: This figure would be reduced by PAYE deducted and by any payments on account Andrew had paid on 31 January 1999 and 31 July 1999. Any balance remaining would be payable on 31 January 2000.

6 SCHEDULE D CASE VI

6.1 Introduction

Schedule D Case VI deals with income which the legislation seeks to tax but which is not assessable under any other Schedule or Case.

Examples of types of income which are assessed under Schedule D Case VI are:

- profits on the sale of patent rights;
- casual commission;
- sale of future earnings;
- post-cessation receipts;
- sales of certificates of deposit;
- enterprise allowance; and
- income from a discretionary trust.

6.2 Basis of assessment

In all instances it is the income and profits received in the actual fiscal year which are assessable. Note that Schedule D VI income is never treated as 'savings income'.

7 TRUST INCOME

7.1 Introduction

There are three types of trust from which an individual may receive income:

- an interest in possession trust, also known as a life tenant or life interest trust;
- a discretionary trust; and
- an accumulation and maintenance trust.

When an individual receives income from an interest in possession trust, it is net of basic rate tax (23%) or lower rate tax (20%) to the extent that it represents savings income. The savings income element is taxed on the individual just as for any other source of savings income.

Strictly the income, after paying trustee's expenses, belongs to the life tenant and is taxable on him whether the trustees physically pay it over. Such trusts are therefore said to be 'transparent'.

Income from the other two types of trust is paid net of tax at 34%. For example, £132 net from a discretionary trust is grossed up to £200 (£132 × 100/66) and carries a £68 tax credit. It is irrelevant whether the underlying income in the trust was 'savings' income. The gross amount of the income paid to the discretionary beneficiary is taxable, and he will receive a tax credit for the tax suffered, usually leading to a repayment where the tax is overpaid. In such trusts a beneficiary is not automatically entitled to trust income and only received what the trustees, at their discretion, choose to pay him. Income is assessable in the year it is received by the beneficiary.

8 PERSONAL EQUITY PLANS (PEPs)

8.1 Introduction

Individuals aged 18 or over who are resident and ordinarily resident in the UK may subscribe, in a year of assessment, up to a maximum of

- £6,000 in a general PEP which invests in European Community (EC) equities, investment trusts or unit trusts; and

- £3,000 in a single company PEP

and obtain specific tax exemptions. The subscriptions are not themselves allowable deductions for income tax purposes.

8.2   The investment

A PEP is operated as follows:

- the individual transfers cash or newly issued shares (eg, privatisation issues) to a plan manager;

- the plan manager purchases shares and holds them on behalf of the investor;

- the plan manager must invest the cash received in either quoted ordinary shares of EC companies, or investment trusts or unit trusts or hold the cash on interest earning deposits.

8.3   The relief

- Dividends from shares held in a plan are free of income tax. The plan manager makes a repayment claim and recovers the tax credit from the Revenue.

- Shares within a PEP are exempt from capital gains tax on disposal.

- Any interest earned whilst the investor's cash is held by a plan manager is free of tax providing it is reinvested in a PEP investment.

- When shares are transferred out of the plan their acquisition cost for capital gains tax purposes is the market value at the date of the transfer.

8.4   The phasing out

The new tax-free ISAs (individual savings accounts) are being introduced from 6 April 1999 to encourage the savings habit especially for those disinclined to provide for their old age. PEPs (and TESSAs) are therefore being phased out as they are seen - by the Labour government - as giving unnecessary incentives to wealthier individuals.

The phasing out rules are as follows:

- No new PEPs can be taken out after 5 April 1999.
- Existing PEPs will be allowed to continue to enjoy exemption from income tax and capital gains tax.
- A 10% tax credit will be repayable on dividends received in a PEP until 5 April 2004. (This is in line with the treatment of dividends in ISAs. Note that after 5 April 1999, tax credits on dividends will not generally be repayable.)

9   INDIVIDUAL SAVINGS ACCOUNTS (ISAs)

9.1   Introduction

Individuals aged 18 or over and both resident and ordinarily resident in the UK are eligible to subscribe to an individual savings account (ISA) to be offered by financial institutions such as banks and building societies from 6 April 1999.

Three kinds of investment are permitted:

- Cash (including National Savings)
- Life insurance; and
- Stocks and shares

The income and gains on investments held in an ISA are exempt from income tax and capital gains tax. In addition, for the first five years of the scheme, any UK dividends received in an ISA (or in respect of life insurance contracts held in an ISA) will attract a repayable 10% tax credit.

9.2   The rules

- There is a subscription limit of £5,000 in each tax year although the limit for 1999/00 will be set at £7,000 as a one-off;

- Within the £5,000 limit, no more than £1,000 can be held as cash (£3,000 for 1999/00) and there is a limit of £1,000 for investment in life insurance;

- The scheme is guaranteed to run for at least 10 years but otherwise there is no overall limit to the amount a saver can invest in his lifetime;

- There is no requirement to make a minimum investment and the capital and income of an ISA is available to be withdrawn at any time without losing the tax exemptions;

- Savers can either take out one ISA which can offer the full range of permitted investments or take out a separate ISA in respect of each of the three types of investment, ie, one for shares (max £3,000), one for cash (max £1,000, but £3,000 for 1999/00) and one for life insurance (max £1,000).

Investors who have been inclined to make regular use of the maximum PEP limits for stock market investments will be able to effectively continue this approach by using a 'full range' ISA which has a £5,000 limit (£7,000 for 1999/00) for investment in stocks and shares (provided the cash/life insurance options are ignored).

10   PENSIONS

10.1   Introduction

(a)   The point is often missed that payments into a pension scheme not only provide an individual with income during his retirement, but also represent a very tax efficient long term investment. Tax relief is available on contributions into a pension scheme (subject to certain restrictions). Both capital gains and income from the pension fund's investments are tax free, except that the tax credit on dividends received is not recoverable by the pension fund. On retirement a tax-free lump sum payment may be taken, though the pension itself is taxed as earned income.

(b)   The main ways of investing in a pension scheme are:

- an occupation pension scheme; or
- a personal pension scheme.

10.2   Occupational pension schemes

(a)   Occupational pension schemes are ones set up by employers for employees. Contributions must be made by the employer and, in addition, employees may contribute. If the scheme is Revenue approved, they enjoy considerable tax advantages.

(b)   For a Revenue approved occupational pension scheme the following apply:

- contributions made by an employee of up to a maximum of 15% of earnings are deductible from his Schedule E income. There is a restriction on the size of contribution that can be made, in that there is an earnings cap (£87,600 for 1998/99) which allows a maximum contribution of £13,140 (15% of £87,600) in 1998/99;

- employer's contributions are not treated as benefits in kind;

- employer's contributions are tax deductible for the employer;

- an employee may be paid a tax free lump sum on retirement (limited to 1½ of the lower of final salary or the earnings cap);

- the pension paid on retirement (limited to 2/3 of the lower of final salary or the earnings cap) is taxed as earned income.

- an employee benefiting from an occupational pension scheme may make further provision for his retirement by paying additional voluntary contributions (AVCs) either into his employer's scheme or into a separate scheme. They are tax deductible to the extent that they, plus any contributions made by him into his employer's scheme do not exceed 15% of earnings.

10.3   Personal pension schemes

Personal pension schemes are available to the self-employed and those in non-pensionable employment.

Non-pensionable employment includes employment where an occupational pension scheme is operating but where the employee has not joined the scheme.

Personal pension schemes are operated by individuals contracting with a pension provider and paying premiums into a fund. If an employer makes contributions into an employee's personal pension fund, the payments are not treated as benefits in kind providing that they are within the limit on contributions.

10.4   Tax relief available for personal pension schemes

The taxpayer may claim a deduction from earned income (net relevant earnings) for premiums paid. There is a limit on the amount of premium that can be relieved which is a percentage (age-related) of net relevant earnings.

The pension fund is free from capital gains tax and income tax, except that any tax credit on dividends received is not recoverable by the pension fund.

The pension received on retirement is taxed as earned income with facility for a tax-free lump sum (subject to limits) to be paid on retirement.

10.5   Allowable premiums

The maximum annual tax deductible premium is a percentage of net relevant earnings (limited by an earnings cap - £87,600 for 1998/99). The deductible percentages of net relevant earnings for 1998/99 are as follows:

Age at **start** of tax year	%
Up to 35	17½
36 to 45	20
46 to 50	25
51 to 55	30
56 to 60	35
61 and over	40

Where an employer makes contributions to the scheme these will operate to reduce the maximum relief otherwise allowable.

10.6   Method of giving relief

(a)   **Employees** – Relief is given at the basic rate by deduction at source when the contributions are paid.

Higher rate relief is usually given through the PAYE code or when the income for a tax year is self-assessed.

(b)   **Self-employed** – Contributions are paid gross. Relief given as an allowable deduction (against net relevant earnings) in the self-assessment calculation.

10.7   Net relevant earnings

(a)   Relevant earnings are

- emoluments from an office or employment assessable under Schedule E (including benefits in kind)

  Note: should an employee be a member of the employer's occupational pension scheme, then the income from that employment is *not* relevant earnings.

- profits of a trade, profession or vocation assessable under Schedule D (including profits from letting of furnished holiday accommodation).

(b)   Net relevant earnings – are relevant earnings less:

In the case of an employed person

- allowable expenses incurred wholly, exclusively and necessarily in the performance of the duties of the employment.

In the case of a self-employed person

- losses brought forward
- charges on income incurred wholly and exclusively for business purposes.

Note: In practice the Revenue permit business charges to be deducted from non-relevant income in priority, leaving the excess only to reduce relevant earnings.

10.8   Carry forward of unused relief

Unused relief arises when the premiums paid in a tax year are less than the maximum calculated as a percentage of net relevant earnings. It may be carried forward and used to relieve contributions paid in any of the next six years of assessment. Relief is given for the year in which the contribution is paid **provided** the maximum % relief for that year is fully absorbed first by the payments.

Unused relief for earlier years must be used before that for later years.

10.9   Carry-back of contributions

The individual may elect to have all or part of a contribution treated as if it were paid in the preceding year of assessment, or, if there were no NREs in that preceding year, in the year before that.   The election must be made not later than 31 January following the end of the year of assessment in which the contribution was actually paid.

The election to carry back contributions allows the taxpayer to take advantage of the situation where he has income taxed at a higher rate in the preceding year against which he can relieve his contribution.

10.10   Example: Personal pension premiums

Bernice, who was born on 6 June 1953, has run her own hairdressing business for many years. Results for 1998/99 are as follows:

	£
Schedule D Case I	25,000

Bernice's other income and payments for 1998/99 are as follows:

	£
Schedule D Case III	600
Mortgage interest (gross) paid under MIRAS	3,500
Trade charges (gross)	1,800

There is no unused pension contribution relief brought forward. Calculate the maximum personal pension premium that Bernice can set off in 1998/99.

10.11   Solution

Step 1   Calculate net relevant earnings.

1998/99 Net relevant earnings

	£	£
Schedule D Case I		25,000
Schedule D Case III	600	
Trade charges	(1,800)	
Unrelieved trade charges		(1,200)
Net relevant earnings		23,800

Note that trade charges are set against investment income before trading income.

Step 2   Calculate the appropriate percentage of net relevant earnings

Bernice is 44 at the start of the tax year.

Maximum pension premium is £23,800 × 20% = £4,760.

10.12   Example: Personal pension premium

Benjamin, born in 1970 started making payments into a personal pension plan in August 1995 on taking up his first employment since leaving university. He provides you with the following information:

	Net relevant earnings £	17½% of net relevant earnings £	Premiums paid £
1995/96	28,000	4,900	4,200
1996/97	30,000	5,250	5,125
1997/98	26,000	4,550	5,160
1998/99	32,000	5,600	5,760

How are the premiums paid relieved?

10.13   Solution

	£
1995/96	
17½% of net relevant earnings	4,900
Less premium paid	4,200
Unused relief	700
1996/97	
17½% of net relevant earnings	5,250
Less premium paid	5,125
Unused relief	125

	£
1997/98	
17½% of net relevant earnings	4,550
Unused relief (1995/96)(amount needed to balance)	610
	5,160
Less: Premium paid	5,160
	-
1998/99	
17½% of net relevant earnings	5,600
Unused relief (1995/96: balance remaining)	90
(1996/97) (amount needed to balance)	70
	5,760
Less: Premium paid	5,760

At 6.4.99 there is (125 – 70 =) £55 of 1996/97 unused relief remaining to carry forward.

Conclusion   Pensions are an extremely tax effective way to make long term investments.

Individuals can either pay into:

- an occupational pension scheme; or
- a personal pension scheme.

Occupational pension schemes are set up by employers for their employees. Tax relief is limited to 15% of earnings.

Personal pension schemes are entered into by self-employed individuals and people in non-pensionable employment. Tax relief is limited to an age related percentage of net relevant earnings subject to an earnings cap.

11   CHAPTER SUMMARY

This chapter has dealt with financial investments and sundry income. The following areas were covered:

- Tax-free income

- Dividends: note that dividends are grossed up by 20/80 and taxed at either the lower rate or higher rate of income tax, depending on the individual's level of income.

- Bank and building society interest: note that it is received net of 20% tax and taxed just as for dividends.

- Taxed income: this is taxed in the same way as dividends, bank and building society interest. The exception is patent royalties which are received net of basic rate tax and **not** subject to the 'savings' income tax regime.

- Schedule D Case III interest received gross: note the main examples of income not taxed at source.

- Schedule D Case VI income: note that the basis of assessment is the income received in the tax year.

- Trust income.

- Personal equity plans

- Individual savings accounts.

- Personal pensions.

12   SELF TEST QUESTIONS

12.1   What is the basis of assessment for bank and building society interest? (3.2)

12.2   What are the main examples of interest received gross? (4.1)

12.3   What exemption is available for National Savings Bank interest? (4.2)

12.4   Give examples of taxed income other than bank/building society interest. (5.1)

12.5   What is the maximum tax deductible contribution that an individual may make into an occupational pension scheme? (9.2)

12.6   What tax relief is available for premiums paid into a personal pension scheme? (9.4)

12.7   What constitutes net relevant earnings for personal pension scheme purposes? (9.7)

12.8   How is unused relief utilised? (9.8)

13   EXAMINATION TYPE QUESTION

13.1   Long Life

Long Life, a single man aged 35 on 6 April 1997, has been trading for many years as a barrel manufacturer. His adjusted trading results net of capital allowances for 1997/98 and 1998/99 were £14,400 and £23,000 respectively.

During 1998/99 he received building society interest of £1,984. His only other income assessable in 1998/99 was £3,300 interest which arose on his holding of 3½% War Loan. He also took out a £25,000 mortgage on 1 July 1998 for the purchase of his new residence. The net interest paid during 1998/99 under MIRAS was £1,725.

He also entered into two deeds of covenant payable annually from August 1998 as follows:

Save the Children (a charity)	£3,500 (gross)
His mother	£600 (gross)

He paid a personal pension contribution of £2,000 on 3 April 1998. He also paid personal pension plan contributions totalling £6,000 in 1998/99. There was no unused relief as at 6 April 1997.

Payments on account totalling £2,700 had been made on 31 January and 31 July 1999.

You are required to calculate Long Life's further tax payable for 1998/99 (taking advantage of any unused pension relief brought forward).

14   ANSWER TO EXAMINATION TYPE QUESTION

14.1   Long Life

Income tax computation 1998/99

			£
Earned income			
Schedule D Case I			23,000
Less: Personal pension plan contributions lower of:			
(i) amount paid	£6,000		
(ii) 20% × £23,000 (aged 36)	4,600		
Add: Relief b/f 1997/98 (W)	520		
	£5,120	(5,120)	
			17,880

Unearned income

Schedule D III	- Building Society interest £1,984 × 100/80	2,480
	- War loan	3,300
		23,660
Charges -	Charitable Deed of Covenant	(3,500)
		20,160
Less:	PA	(4,195)
Taxable income		15,965

Tax borne:

Non-savings:	4,300 × 20%	860
	5,885 × 23%	1,354
Savings:	5,780 × 20%	1,156
		3,370
Add:	Tax retained on charges	
	£3,500 × 23%	805
Tax liability		4,175
Less:	Tax suffered at source on BSI received	(496)
	Payments on account	(2,700)
Further tax payable (on 31 January 2000)		979

Note: mortgage interest within MIRAS is ignored in the income tax computation.

WORKING

Net relevant earnings for 1997/98	14,400
Relief @ 17½% (age 35 on 6.4.97)	2,520
Relief taken in 1997/98	(2,000)
Unused relief c/f for up to 6 years	520

5 DEDUCTIONS FROM INCOME AND FROM INCOME TAX LIABILITY

INTRODUCTION

There are certain allowable outgoings and personal reliefs that individuals are allowed to deduct from their income in order to arrive at their amount of taxable income.

It is important to be aware not only of the payments that can be deducted from income, but also how they are dealt with in the income tax computation.

Finance Act 1994 reduced the relief available on certain allowances and interest payments. These amounts are no longer deducted from taxable income; instead, a tax credit is given against the individual's tax liability.

1 INTRODUCTION

1.1 Context

It will be remembered from an earlier chapter that statutory total income comprises

	£
Net earned income	a
Unearned income	b
	c
Less: Charges on income	d
Statutory total income	£e

Having dealt with the constituents of earned income and unearned income, it is now necessary to consider exactly what is meant by the term charges on income.

1.2 Classification of charges

The following outgoings of an individual fall within the category of charges on income:

(a) annual interest
(b) annual payments.

The charges may be further classified according to method of payment

(a) paid under deduction of either 23% or 10% tax at source (known as retainable charges), for example

- deeds of covenant to charities (paid net of 23% tax)
- mortgage interest paid under the MIRAS scheme (paid net of 10% tax)

(b)   paid gross without deduction of tax at source (known as non-retainable charges), for example

- mortgage interest not coming under the MIRAS scheme
- maintenance payments under Court Orders.

1.3   Treatment in tax computations

(a)   Subject to points (b) and (c) below, charges paid under deduction of tax at source are grossed up for inclusion in the computation, and are deducted in arriving at a statutory total income.

Charges are **ALWAYS** dealt with on an actual year basis.

(b)   Mortgage interest on an only or main residence attracts relief at 10% and maintenance payments attract relief at 15% only. Where payments are made gross they are not allowed as a deduction from income; instead, a tax credit is given which reduces the individual's tax liability. (This is covered in more detail later in the chapter).

(c)   Mortgage interest paid under MIRAS has already received relief at 10%, and therefore no further entry in the computation is required. (Again, this is covered in more detail later).

2   ANNUAL INTEREST

2.1   Loans for qualifying purposes

Relief is given for interest **paid** on **fixed loans** incurred to finance expenditure for a **qualifying purpose**. Relief may be claimed for **any** payment of interest other than interest paid in excess of a reasonable commercial rate or for interest paid on bank **overdrafts** (or credit cards).

However, if the purpose of the debt is to finance expenditure wholly and exclusively in the course of a trade, profession or vocation, interest is deductible as a trading expense in arriving at the profit assessable under Schedule D Case I or II and is **not** dealt with as a charge on income in the personal tax computation.

The **qualifying purposes** to which the loan must be applied are as follows.

(a)   **Only or main residence**

The purchase of land or buildings in the UK and the Republic of Ireland (including static caravans and houseboats) provided the property is **used** at the time the interest is paid is the **only** or **main** residence of the borrower.

There is a limit on the total amount of loans which can qualify for relief. This limit is £30,000 and it applies to the **residence**, not the borrower, and is for purchase only. This means that individuals sharing the cost of purchase of a residence will not get £30,000 relief each, but instead the limit of £30,000 is divided between the number of borrowers.

(b)   **Partnerships.** The purchase of a share in a partnership, the contribution of capital or loans by a partner for the purchase of plant or machinery for use in the partnership. The partner borrowing the money may be any partner except a limited partner.

(c)   **Close companies.** The purchase of ordinary shares in, or loans to, a close (ie controlled by a limited number of persons) trading company.

(d)   **Employee-controlled companies.** Relief is available to full-time employees for loans taken out to acquire ordinary shares in an employee controlled UK resident, unquoted trading company.

(e)   **Employees.** The purchase of plant or machinery by an employed person for use in his employment. Relief is not given beyond the three fiscal years following that in which the debt was incurred.

(f)   **Commercial let property**

There is **no** upper limit on the amount of the loan (unlike the ceiling of £30,000 for loans on a main residence). Interest is also allowable on loans for improvements to the let property.

The loan interest on let property is **not** treated as a charge on income in calculating statutory total income but as an allowable business expense against rents assessable under Schedule A.

(g)   **Borrowers living in job-related accommodation**

(i)   Tax relief is also available where an individual is living in 'job related' accommodation and he is paying interest on a loan (up to £30,000) used to purchase a property which he intends will become his main residence.

(ii)   Accommodation is job related if it is provided for a person by reason of his employment where:

- it is necessary for the proper performance of the duties of his employment (eg, caretakers); or

- it is provided for the better performance of the employee's duties and it is customary for such employers to provide accommodation for their employees (eg policemen); or

- special security arrangements are in force and the employee resides in the accommodation as part of those arrangements because there is a threat to his security.

(iii)   Accommodation is also regarded as job related if a self-employed person is provided with accommodation by another person and required to trade on premises provided by that other person (eg, tenant of a brewery).

(h)   **Bridging loans**

Where, at a time when the borrower has a qualifying loan used to acquire his only or main residence, he raises a new qualifying loan to acquire a second property with the intention of using it as his new main residence and disposing of the only or main residence to which the first loan relates, relief is available temporarily for interest on both loans for 12 months (or such longer time as the Inspector may allow).

The Revenue apply the tax limit of £30,000 separately to both loans during this bridging period.

Relief is also available for mortgage interest for 12 months after moving out of the main residence, even when a loan has not been taken out to purchase a new home. This allows people moving into rented accommodation to continue benefitting from the relief while trying to sell their previous home.

(i)   **Purchase of annuity secured on property in the UK or the Republic of Ireland**

Interest will be allowed provided:

- the loan was made as part of a scheme under which not less than 90% of the proceeds of the loan are used by the borrower to purchase an annuity ending with his life or the life of the survivor of two or more persons and

- at the time of the loan the borrower was 65 or over and

- the loan is secured on the borrower's only or main residence and does not exceed £30,000

- the interest has been paid.

2.2   Mortgage Interest Relief At Source (MIRAS)

Most mortgage interest is paid net of 10% income tax under the MIRAS (mortgage interest relief at source) scheme.

(a)   **Outline of the scheme**

The essence of the scheme is that

- the borrower is entitled to deduct and retain income tax at 10% on making the payment, and

- the lender will recover from the Inland Revenue the amount of income tax deducted by the borrower.

The MIRAS scheme confers relief at 10% on non-taxpayers as well as on taxpayers, and there is no provision to recover this relief because the borrower is not a taxpayer.

(b)   **Income tax relief**

Mortgage interest attracts relief at 10% only. Where mortgage interest is paid under MIRAS it must be ignored in calculating the individual's income tax liability; relief is given when the payment is made.

2.3   Methods of giving relief for interest paid

There are two methods of giving relief for interest paid. The method of relief depends on the purpose of the loan.

The first method applies to interest on a loan

- used to purchase the borrower's only or main residence;

- used to purchase a property which is intended to be used as the borrower's only or main residence where the borrower lives in job-related accommodation;

- used by a person aged 65 or over to purchase a life annuity and secured on the borrower's only or main residence.

Where such interest is paid gross (ie, not under the MIRAS provisions) relief is given by deducting a tax credit of 10% of the gross amount from the individual's income tax liability. The tax credit is 23% in the case of the purchase of a life annuity.

Thus, if Gregory, who is single, and earns £33,525 a year pays mortgage interest of £2,500 (gross) in 1998/99 on a loan of £30,000 used to purchase his main residence, his tax position would be as follows:

(a)   If the loan is outside the MIRAS scheme

		£
Income		33,525
Less: Personal allowance		(4,195)
Taxable income		29,330

		£
Income tax liability		
£4,300 × 20%		860
£22,800 × 23%		5,244
£2,230 × 40%		892
Less: Tax credit on mortgage interest £2,500 × 10%		(250)
Income tax liability		6,746

(b)   If the loan is within the MIRAS scheme

		£
Income		33,525
Less: Personal allowance		(4,195)
Taxable income		29,330

		£
Income tax liability		
£4,300 × 20%		860
£22,800 × 23%		5,244
£2,230 × 40%		892
Income tax liability		6,996

The interest payment is ignored in the income tax computation. Relief is given when the interest is paid, which in 1998/99 will be £2,500 × 90% ie, £2,250.

The second method applies to interest on a loan

- used to purchase machinery or plant for business purposes;
- used to purchase an interest in a close company;
- used to purchase a share in a partnership;
- used to purchase shares in an employee-controlled company.

Where such interest is paid, relief is given by deducting the interest from the borrowers' income for the year.

Thus, if Gregory, from the previous illustration paid interest of £2,500 on a loan taken out to purchase a share in a partnership, his tax position would be as follows:

	£
Income	33,525
Less: Interest	(2,500)
	31,025
Less: Personal allowance	(4,195)
Taxable income	26,830

Income tax liability	
£4,300 × 20%	860
£22,530 × 23%	5,182
	6,042

Note that where the interest is deducted from income, relief is automatically available at lower, basic or higher rate as appropriate.

Conclusion   The methods of giving relief depend on the purpose of the loan

- Interest on loans to purchase the borrower's main residence

  - loan within MIRAS: relief given at the time of payment; ignored in income tax computation.

  - loan outside MIRAS: relief given by deducting a tax credit of 10% of the gross amount of mortgage interest from the income tax liability.

- Interest on loans for other eligible purposes; relief is given by deducting the amount of interest paid from the borrower's income.

3   DEEDS OF COVENANT

3.1   Introduction

A deed of covenant is a legally binding agreement under which one person agrees to make a series of payments without receiving consideration in return.

All deeds of covenant, in order to obtain tax relief, must satisfy **FOUR** conditions, namely

- payments under the covenant must be for a period **capable** of exceeding three years.
- the covenant must be irrevocable.
- the covenant must not have been made for valuable consideration.
- the covenant must be payable to a recognised charity.

All charitable covenants are fully allowable as charges on income, thereby benefiting from tax relief at both basic and higher rates.

Subscriptions to charities that offer free or reduced rates of admission are often paid by means of a covenant. Where such a benefit is offered, it does not infringe the general rule that a covenant must not have been made for a valuable consideration, so long as the charity's sole or main purpose is the preservation of property (as is the National Trust) or the conservation of wild life.

Because the covenantor deducts and retains basic rate relief at source at the time of payment, it is necessary to adjust for this in the individual's tax computation to prevent double relief being obtained. In order to calculate the final tax liability, the basic rate tax that has been retained by the taxpayer is added to tax borne. This is because the taxpayer must account to the Revenue for the tax retained.

Thus if Peter, who is single and earns £38,045 pays a charitable deed of covenant of £1,925 (net) each year, his tax position for 1998/99 would be as follows:

	£
Income	38,045
Less: Deed of covenant $(1,925 \times {}^{100}/_{77})$	(2,500)
Less: Personal allowance	(4,195)
	31,350
Income tax liability	
£4,300 × 20%	860
£22,800 × 23%	5,244
£4,250 × 40%	1,700
Income tax borne	7,804
Add: Tax retained on charges paid net (2,500 × 23%)	575
Income tax liability	8,379

The amount actually paid to the charity is £1,925 (ie, net of basic rate tax). In order to achieve relief at higher rate, for the taxpayer, the gross amount is included in the computation. As relief has already been given at basic rate at the time of payment, this must be added back at the bottom of the calculation. If this adjustment was not made, relief actually obtained would be as follows:

	£
£2,500 × 23% (at time of payment)	575
£2,500 × 40% (via tax computation)	1,000
	1,575

Note that although the taxpayer only pays £1,925 to the charity, the charity can reclaim the tax from the Revenue of £575 and thus receives £2,500 in total.

4   EXCESS CHARGES, S350 ASSESSMENTS

4.1   S350, ICTA 1988 assessments

If those charges on income which are paid under deduction of tax at source exceed an individual's total income from all sources, further special points arise.

(a)   **Charges paid net (other than mortgage interest under MIRAS)**

If a taxpayer has very little or no income (eg he is a trader and makes a loss), his charges on income may well exceed his income as follows:

1998/99	£
Schedule D Case I	Nil
Less: Charges on income:	
Deed of covenant to a charity	100
Statutory total income	Nil

Referring back to the example above it should be appreciated that the income tax computation becomes, in effect

	£
Income tax borne on nil taxable income	Nil
Add: Income tax relief deducted at source from	
deed of covenant £100 × 23%	23
Income tax payable	23

The tax is payable on £100 under *s350 ICTA 1988*.

(b)   **Mortgage interest paid net of income tax**

Where mortgage interest is paid net under the MIRAS scheme, income tax is deducted upon payment and retained but the tax does not have to be recovered by means of a *Sec 350* adjustment in circumstances similar to those above.

If a taxpayer has, for 1998/99, assessable earned income of £6,225; allowable gross interest on a £30,000 mortgage of £4,635 paid under MIRAS (tax saved at 10%: £463) and a personal allowance of £4,195, his income tax position is as follows:

Income tax computation 1998/99

	£
Earned income	6,225
Less: Personal allowance	4,195
Taxable income	2,030
Income tax borne and payable: (£2,030 × 20%) =	406

Thus, where the tax credit on mortgage interest paid under MIRAS exceeds an individual's total income tax borne, there is no requirement to make a repayment to the Revenue.

5   PAYROLL GIVING

An employee, included in the PAYE system, may make donations to charity by having the employer deduct the donations from wages or salary prior to calculation of PAYE deductions.

This is known as give-as-you-earn (GAYE). The maximum permitted donations are £1,200 pa. Donations made by deed of covenant do not qualify for this relief.

It is necessary for the employer to set up a Revenue approved scheme to deal with such deductions and to channel funds via an approved agent to the charities.

6   GIFT AID

For those who wish to give one-off gifts of money to charity the Gift Aid scheme is available.

Single charitable lifetime cash gifts of at least £250 (net of basic rate tax) per year of assessment will get tax relief at the donor's highest tax rate.

The payments must be made with basic rate tax deducted at source (ie, out of taxed income); the gross amount is relieved as a charge on income.

Donations by deed of covenant or under the payroll giving (GAYE) scheme are not affected.

There is no upper limit on the amount gifted.

The gift threshold is reduced to £100 and can apply to gifts which total at least £100 when made to charities under the Millennium Gift Aid extension. These charities must be supporting education or poverty projects in third world countries and gifts must be made by 31 December 2000.

7   VOCATIONAL TRAINING EXPENSES

Relief is given to UK resident individuals who pay for their own vocational training. Detailed provisions are as follows:

- Training must be towards a national vocational qualification, and may be up to degree level. Relief is not, however, conditional upon a qualification actually being obtained.

- Basic rate relief is given by deduction at source when course and examination fees are paid. Higher rate relief, if appropriate, is obtained in calculating the final tax liability.

- Basic rate relief will be given (by deduction at source) even if the trainee has no taxable income and/or where the training is unrelated to the trainee's present work.

Tax relief is not available for;

- Children under 16;
- Individuals aged 16 to 18 who are in full-time education at school;
- Training which is wholly or mainly for leisure purpose.

In addition, relief is given to individuals over the age of 30 who pay for their own retraining for new careers. Detailed provisions are as follows:

- Tax relief is given on fees paid for full-time vocational courses, lasting between four weeks and a year.

- Relief is available whether or not the training course leads to a National Vocational Qualification.

8   PERSONAL ALLOWANCES

8.1   Introduction

Various personal allowances (also known as personal reliefs) are available to taxpayers, depending on their status and circumstances. The method of giving relief depends on the type of allowance as follows:

- personal allowance and blind person's relief - deducted from statutory total income

- married couple's allowance, additional personal allowance and widow's bereavement allowance - a credit of 15% of the allowance is given against the income tax liability.

  Note that the tax credit may reduce the tax liability to nil but it can never lead to a repayment of tax.

8.2   Personal allowances (PA)

Each taxpayer (including children), resident in the UK is entitled to a personal allowance. The amount for 1998/99 is £4,195. Relief is available at lower, basic and higher rate of tax.

Surplus personal allowance cannot be transferred to any other taxpayer.

Rose, who is single, and earns £32,000, would have a tax position as follows for 1998/99

		£
Salary		32,000
Less: Personal allowance		4,195
		27,805
Income tax liability		
£4,300 × 20%		860
£22,800 × 23%		5,244
£705 × 40%		282
		6,386

Personal allowances are also available for some non-residents. Citizens of all states within the European Economic Area are entitled to UK personal allowances and to tax credits from UK company qualifying distributions, for example dividends paid by a UK company.

8.3   Married couple's allowance (MCA)

A man who is married and living with his wife for all, or any part of, a tax year is entitled to claim (on his tax return) the married couple's allowance in addition to his personal allowance.

The rate of married couple's allowance for 1998/99 is £1,900.

Relief is given by a deduction of 15% of the allowance from the income tax liability. (The rate will be 10% for 1999/2000).

The allowance is restricted in the year of marriage.

If a husband's tax liability is too small to use the whole married couple's allowance tax credit he can give notice to his Inspector that he wishes the surplus to be transferred to his wife.

Furthermore the wife may elect that the allowance be split equally between the couple, or the spouses together may elect that the allowance should be allocated wholly to the wife.

Thus Julie, who is married and has jointly elected with her husband to claim all the MCA, and earns £32,400 will have a tax position as follows:

		£
Salary		32,400
Less: Personal allowance		(4,195)
Taxable income		28,205

Income tax liability	
£4,300 × 20%	860
£22,800 × 23%	5,244
£1,105 × 40%	442
	6,546
Less: Tax credit in respect of MCA (£1,900 × 15%)	(285)
Total income tax liability	6,261

The tax credit calculation would be done in the same way, if instead of dealing with MCA, the widow's bereavement allowance or the additional personal allowance (see below) was available.

Tax credits should be deducted, before adding back tax retained on charges on income, if appropriate, in the following order:

- credit on APA
- credit on WBA
- credit on MCA

8.4   Allowances depending upon age

Taxpayers aged 65 and over at any time in the year of assessment are entitled to higher rates of personal allowance and married couple's allowance.

Personal allowance:
Those aged 65 – 74 get a higher rate (£5,410)
Those aged 75 and over get the highest rate (£5,600)
The allowance is given for the year of assessment in which the 65th or 75th birthday falls even if the taxpayer dies before the birthday.

Married couple's allowance
The amount depends upon the age of the older of the husband and wife by the end of the year.
The allowance is given to the husband.
For those aged 65 to 74 the allowance is £3,305, for those aged 75 or over, the allowance is £3,345.

For both the age related personal allowance and married couple's allowance an income restriction operates to reduce the level of the allowances. If the taxpayer's statutory total income is above £16,200 the age related allowance is reduced by half the difference between the statutory total income and £16,200 – but not so as to reduce the allowance to less than the basic personal allowance or married couple's allowance.

8.5   Example: Age allowance

Mr and Mrs Grey are living together throughout 1998/99. Mr Grey, aged 70, has statutory total income of £18,800. Mrs Grey, aged 69, has statutory total income of £12,600. Assume all the income is in the form of pensions.

Calculate their income tax liability.

8.6   **Solution**

Step 1   Calculate the allowances available to Mr and Mrs Grey.

		£	£	£
Mr Grey:	Total income		18,800	
	Limit		16,200	
	Excess		2,600	
	PA (Aged 65 – 74)		5,410	
	Less: ½ excess (£1,300) limited to		1,215	
	Reduced PA cannot be less than		4,195	4,195
	MCA (Aged 65 – 74)		3,305	
	Less: ½ excess	1,300		
	Less: Reduction in PA	1,215	85	
	Reduced MCA		3,220	3,220

Notes:

(1)   The restriction of age related MCA depends only on the husband's total income.

(2)   The reduction in any MCA due to husband's total income is less any reduction already made to his PA.

Mrs Grey: PA: Full PA allowance for 65 – 74.   5,410

Step 2   Calculate Mr and Mrs Grey's taxable income for 1998/99.

Computations 1998/99

	Mr Grey £	*Mrs Grey* £
Statutory total income	18,800	12,600
Less: Allowances		
PA (65 – 74)	(4,195)	(5,410)
Taxable income	14,605	7,190
Income tax liability		
£4,300 × 20%	860	860
£10,305/£2,890 × 23%	2,370	665
	3,230	1,525
Less: Tax credit in respect of MCA £3,220 × 15%	(483)	
Income tax liability	2,747	1,525

8.7   **Additional personal allowance (APA)**

The following classes of taxpayer may claim the additional personal allowance (APA), also known as the additional child allowance (ACA), provided they have **resident** with them a **qualifying child** or children.

- A widow or widower
- A man not entitled to married couple's allowance (eg a divorced man)
- An unmarried, separated or divorced woman
- A married man whose wife is totally incapacitated
- A married woman where husband is totally incapacitated.

A qualifying child is either

- the claimant's own child (including a stepchild or adopted child) who is born in or is under the age of 16 at the beginning of the year of assessment or who, being 16 or over, is either in full-time education or undergoing full-time training for a trade or profession, lasting for at least two years or

- any other child born in or under the age of 18 at the beginning of the year of assessment and maintained at the claimant's expense for at least part of the year.

The amount of the allowance is £1,900.

Relief is given by a deduction of 15% of the allowance from the income tax liability (10% for 1999/2000).

8.8   Widow's bereavement allowance (WBA)

This allowance is given to a widow for the year of assessment in which her husband died and for the next following year of assessment.

It is a condition that the husband was entitled for the year of his death to the married couple's allowance.

If the widow should remarry **in the year of bereavement** she will **not** be given the widow's bereavement allowance for the **next** following year.

There is no corresponding relief for widowers.

The amount of the allowance is £1,900.

Relief is given by a deduction of 15% of the allowance from the income tax liability (10% for 1999/2000).

8.9   Blind person's relief (BPR)

Any person who is registered with the local authority as a blind person may claim this relief.

The full relief is given even though the claimant may have been registered for part only of the fiscal year.

The amount of the allowance is £1,330.

Relief is given by deducting the allowance from statutory total income.

Conclusion Personal allowances are important reliefs available to all taxpayers; care must be taken in an income tax question to note whether the taxpayer is:

- married;
- aged 65 or over;
- is single and has a child resident with them; or
- is a recently widowed woman

as additional reliefs may be available.

9   CHAPTER SUMMARY

This chapter has dealt with deductions from income and deductions from income tax. The following areas were covered:

- the types of loan interest and their treatment: by far the most important type is mortgage interest;
- tax relief on charitable deeds of covenant;
- tax liabilities arising when charges paid net of basic rate tax exceed all other income;
- payroll giving;
- the gift aid scheme;
- relief for vocational training expenses;
- personal allowances.

10   SELF TEST QUESTIONS

10.1   What relief is available for interest paid where the purpose of the debt is to finance expenditure incurred wholly and exclusively in the course of a trade? (2.1)

10.2   What are the qualifying purposes to which a loan must be applied if relief is to be given for interest paid on the loan? (2.1)

10.3   What constitutes job-related accommodation? (2.2)

10.4   What conditions must a deed of covenant satisfy in order to obtain tax relief? (3.1)

10.5   What is the payroll giving scheme? (5)

10.6   What is the Gift Aid scheme? (6)

10.7   How does the Millennium Gift Aid scheme differ from the Gift Aid scheme? (6)

10.8   What relief is available for vocational training expenses? (7)

10.9   Who is entitled to claim a married couple's allowance? (8.3)

10.10   Who is entitled to claim an additional personal allowance? (8.7)

11   EXAMINATION TYPE QUESTION

11.1   Mr Brown

Mr Brown, who was born in 1935 is employed by the local bank.

63 (handwritten, above "1935")

For 1998/99 he received the following remuneration package:

	£
Salary	30,000
Benefits in kind	3,720

PAYE of £7,272 was deducted.

He received the following amounts from his investments in 1998/99.

	£
Building society interest	1,568
Interest on holding of £10,000 13% Treasury Stock 1999	1,040
National Savings Bank investment account	82

The National Savings Bank account was opened in 1995.

He has held the Treasury Stock since 1993 and has made no election to receive interest gross.

Mr Brown cashed in some National Savings Certificates, which he had purchased for £1,200 in 1992, from which he received £2,490.

In March 1998 Mr Brown invested £3,000 in a Tax Exempt Special Savings Account; he invested a further £1,800 in March 1999. The account was credited with £25 of interest by 5 April 1998 and a further £320 by 5 April 1999.

Mr Brown took out an endowment mortgage on 1 March 1998 of £40,000 to buy the house he lives in at a fixed rate of 7%. He pays the loan under the MIRAS system and actually paid £2,520 in 1998/99 (gross interest of £2,800 with tax relief at source of £280).

Mr Brown also pays £55 each year to the National Trust under a deed of covenant. This payment allows him and his family free access to all National Trust properties. Mr Brown lives with his wife, Ivy, who was born in 1933: she has no income of her own.

No payments on account were required on 31 January or 31 July 1999.

You are required to calculate Mr Brown's income tax liability for 1998/99.

12   ANSWER TO EXAMINATION TYPE QUESTION

12.1   Mr Brown

Outstanding income tax liability 1998/99	Savings	Non-savings	Total	
	£	£	£	
Earned income				
Schedule E - salary and benefits in kind		33,720	33,720	
Unearned income				
Schedule D Case III				
- Building society interest (× 100/80)	1,960		1,960	
- Government stock interest (× 100/80)	1,300		1,300	
- NSB investment account	82		82	
Less: Charge on income				
Deed of covenant to charity (£55 × 100/77)		(71)	(71)	
STI	3,342	33,649	36,991	
Less: Personal allowance	-	(4,195)	(4,195)	
Taxable income	3,342	29,454	32,796	

Income tax	£	£
4,300 × 20%		860
22,800 × 23%		5,244
5,696 × 40%		2,278
32,796		8,382
Less: Tax credit re MCA (1,900 × 15%)		(285)
Income tax borne		8,097
Add: Basic rate tax retained		
Deed of covenant £71 × 23%		16
Income tax liability		8,113
Less: PAYE	7,272	
BSI	392	
Government stock interest	260	
		7,924
Outstanding income tax liability		189

Notes:

(1)   TESSAs are exempt from tax providing no withdrawals are made greater than the interest credited less notional lower rate tax.

(2)   Encashments of National Savings Certificates are exempt.

(3)   Mr Brown is entitled to an age related married couple's allowance as his wife is 65; however, as his STI is £36,991 the allowance is restricted to the ordinary married couple's allowance of £1,900.

(4)   Mortgage interest paid under the MIRAS scheme is paid net of 10% tax. The payment is ignored in the tax computation.

(5)   As all the savings income clearly falls in the 40% band there is no need to show it separately in the computation of tax borne.

(6)   Where a taxpayer has no gross sources of income he is unlikely to have to make payments on account under self-assessment. Instead, all tax not collected at source or through PAYE, would be payable on 31 January following the tax year. Amounts under £1,000 are likely to be collected by restricting the PAYE tax code provided the Revenue receive the tax return by 30 September following the tax year.

6 HUSBANDS, WIVES AND CHILDREN

INTRODUCTION

All taxpayers are taxed separately on their own income, have their own personal allowance, and must make their own annual income tax return. However, there are still some very important tax implications that affect the married couple specifically and these are the subject of this chapter.

1 PERSONAL ALLOWANCES AND THEIR TRANSFER

1.1 Personal allowance

Whether or not it is unused, the personal allowance cannot be transferred between spouses.

1.2 Married couple's allowance

The following elections are available:

(a)   The wife may elect unilaterally that the married couple's allowance should be split equally between the couple;

(b)   The couple may jointly elect that the married couple's allowance should be allocated wholly to the wife.

Elections under (a) and (b) should be made before the beginning of the first tax year to which it is to apply. Once made, the election remains in force for future years until revoked.

These elections do not apply to the age related element in married couple's allowances. For example even if £3,305 is available only £1,900 or £950 may be allocated to the wife.

(c)   Where the husband has insufficient income tax liability to deduct all of the £285 (£1,900 × 15%) tax credit, the amount of the credit not deducted may be transferred to his wife.

In the same way, if the wife has insufficient income tax liability to deduct all of her tax credit, she may elect that the excess is set against her husband's income tax liability.

This election applies not only to the basic married couple's allowance, but also to the age related married couple's allowances.

The amount of tax credit that can be transferred is the amount surplus to income tax liability calculated **before** deducting credits for charges on income but **after** deducting credits for

- qualifying maintenance payments
- additional personal allowance
- widow's bereavement allowance

The election applies for one year only, and must be made within five years of 31 January following the relevant tax year.

1.3   Example: Transfer of excess married couple's allowance

The following information is relevant to Mr and Mrs Barefoot, both aged under 65, and living together throughout 1998/99. Mr Barefoot is a university undergraduate, his wife has a full-time job.

	Mr B £	Mrs B £
Salary		12,000
Vacation earnings	3,800	
Building society interest received	400	

Mr Barefoot gives notice that he wishes to transfer his surplus MCA to his wife. Show the position for 1998/99.

1.4   Solution

Transfer of married couple's allowance tax credit	£	£
MCA tax credit (1,900 × 15%)		285
Mr Barefoot's total income:		
Vacation earnings	3,800	
BSI £400 × 100/80	500	
	4,300	
Less: PA	4,195	
Taxable income	105	
Income tax liability £105 × 20%	21	
Less: MCA tax credit	(21)	(21)
Transferred to Mrs B		264

Tax position 1998/99	Mr B £	Mrs B £
Income	4,300	12,000
Less: PA	(4,195)	(4,195)
Taxable income	105	7,805
105/4,300 × 20%	21	860
3,505 × 23%		806
	21	1,666
Less: Tax credit re MCA	(21)	(264)
Income tax liability	Nil	1,402

2   YEAR OF MARRIAGE

2.1   Personal allowance

This is given for the year of marriage in the same way as for any other year.

2.2   Married couple's allowance

In the year of marriage the married couple's allowance is reduced by one-twelfth for each complete tax month (ending on the 5th) from 6 April to the date of marriage.

If the age-related married couple's allowance is due this is reduced first by any excess income restriction before applying the above rule.

2.3   Activity

Jack is considering marrying Jill on the following alternative dates:

(a)   5 May 1998
(b)   6 August 1998
(c)   5 April 1999

To how much married couple's allowance will he be entitled in 1998/99 in each case?

2.4   Activity solution

(a)   **5 May 1998** – the allowance of £1,900 will not be restricted since the marriage takes place before a complete tax month (ending on the 5th) after 6 April has expired.

(b)   **6 August 1998** – the fourth complete month since 6 April 1998 expired on 5 August 1998 – the allowance will be £1,900 less $\frac{4}{12}$ × £1,900 = £1,267.

(c)   **5 April 1999** – 11 **complete** months have expired – the allowance will be £1,900 less ($\frac{11}{12}$ × £1,900) = £158.

2.5   Additional personal allowance (APA)

In the year of marriage, a husband who is entitled to the additional personal allowance (for example, as a widower he had care of dependent children from a previous marriage) may choose to keep that allowance instead of (a reduced) married couple's allowance.

A woman can have the additional personal allowance for the year of marriage if she qualified by having a qualifying child living with her before the date of marriage. A wife cannot claim the additional personal allowance for any year throughout which she is living with her husband unless he is totally incapacitated.

3   YEAR OF SEPARATION OR DEATH

3.1   Death of wife

If his wife dies a husband is still entitled to the full married couple's allowance for that year of assessment.

3.2   **Death of husband**

Any election for the wife to receive half or all of the MCA is automatically void. The husband receives the full MCA in the year of his death as well as the full personal allowance.

The wife is entitled to her full personal allowance for the year of assessment in which her husband dies. In addition she can get:

(a)   any of the credit re the married couple's allowance which cannot be used against her husband's income (the husband's executors can give notice for the transfer of any surplus)

(b)   the additional personal allowance, if she has a qualifying child living with her after her husband's death

(c)   the widow's bereavement allowance for the year of husband's death and also for the following year (if she has not re-married by the start of that year)

3.3   **Separation**

(a)   The wife gets her full personal allowance for the year of separation, and in addition:

- any surplus married couple's allowance transferred to her by her husband; and

- the additional personal allowance, if she has a qualifying child living with her after the separation.

If she elects to be allocated any of the married couple's allowance, the sum of this allowance and the additional personal allowance must not exceed £1,900.

(b)   The husband will get his full personal allowance in the year of separation and in addition, he may claim the additional personal allowance if there is a qualifying child resident with him at some time after the date of separation.

The sum of the married couple's allowance and the additional personal allowance claimed in the year must not exceed £1,900.

(c)   These provisions may be illustrated as follows:

Michael and Jane separate permanently during 1998/99.

John, their only son is to spend six months of the year with each parent. Jane has elected to have half of the married couple's allowance allocated to her.

In 1997/98, the allowances available are as follows:

	Michael £	Jane £
Married couple's allowance	950	950
Additional personal allowance	950	950
	1,900	1,900

Note: if Michael and Jane had elected for all the married couple's allowance to be transferred to Jane, then she could not claim any additional personal allowance, but John may claim the full £1,900.

3.4   Example: Year of death of husband

John died on 6 October 1998 aged 48. The assessable income and allowable charge of John and his wife Sarah, aged 48, for 1998/99 were as follows

Income	John	Sarah
	£	£
Salaries from employment	17,000	18,395
Interest from National Savings Bank investment account (credited 31 December 1998)	–	850
Bank deposit interest		400
Building Society interest	480	600
Lump sum widow's payment from DSS		1,000

Outgoings

Building society interest paid under MIRAS before John's death on £18,000 mortgage (gross amount)	1,000

The National Savings Bank investment account was opened in 1997.

The mortgage on their house was paid off by Sarah using the proceeds of a mortgage protection insurance policy maturing on John's death.

COMPUTE the income tax liabilities of John and Sarah respectively for 1998/99.

3.5   Solution

(a)   **JOHN (deceased)**

Income Tax Computation 1998/99

	£
Earned income	
Schedule E – actual – salary	17,000
Unearned income	
Building society income	
$£480 \times \dfrac{100}{80}$	600
Statutory total income	17,600
Less: PA	4,195
Taxable income	13,405

	£
At lower rate (£4,300 + 600 = 4,900 × 20%)	980
At basic rate (£13,405 – 4,900 = 8,505 × 23%)	1,956
Less: Tax credit re MCA (1,900 × 15%)	(285)
Income tax liability	2,651

(b)   **SARAH (widow)**

Income Tax Computation 1998/99	£	£
Earned income		
Schedule E – actual – salary		18,395
Unearned income (all savings income)		
Bank deposit interest		
£400 × $\frac{100}{80}$	500	
Building society interest £600 × $\frac{100}{80}$	750	
NSB interest	850	2,100
Statutory total income		20,495
Less: PA		4,195
Taxable income		16,300
At lower and basic rate		
(£4,300 + 2,100 = 6,400 × 20%) + (£9,900 × 23%)		3,557
Less: Tax credit re WBA (1,900 × 15%)		(285)
Income tax liability		3,272

(*Note:* the lump sum widows payment is tax free.)

4   MAINTENANCE PAYMENTS

4.1   Court Orders and Agreements

Payments under Court Orders and under maintenance agreements are dealt with as follows

- the recipient is not taxed on any payments received

- where payments are made to **a former or separated spouse** or to such a person for the maintenance of a **child (under 21) of the family** the payer gets tax relief, up to a maximum limit equal to the amount of the married couple's allowance until the recipient re-marries

- the relief is given by way of a tax credit of 15% of the payment (or of the amount of the married couple's allowance, ie, £1,900 if less)

- all payments are made GROSS.

In the year of separation or divorce a husband will get the married couple's allowance for the whole year (there is no apportionment); he will also get relief up to the limit for maintenance payments made in the part of the year during which he is separated or divorced. On re-marriage the husband will be able to claim the married couple's allowance, as well as relief (up to the maximum) for maintenance payments to his ex-wife, either for her benefit or for the benefit of a child of the family.

5   JOINT INCOME

5.1   Introduction

Although a husband's and wife's incomes are calculated separately, special rules exist for dealing with income arising from jointly held assets.

5.2   The 50:50 rule

Income from assets held in their joint names by a married couple who live together will normally be split equally between them for tax purposes.

It is the amount of income assessable, either on an actual or current year basis, that is split.

5.3   Declaration of beneficial interests

A married couple whose actual entitlement to a jointly held asset and the income from it is unequal may make a joint irrevocable declaration of their actual beneficial interests in the asset and their income from it.

If a declaration is made each spouse will be assessed on their actual entitlements from those assets covered by the declaration.

6   MORTGAGE INTEREST

6.1   Introduction

A husband and wife are entitled to claim relief on the interest they each pay on a loan used to purchase their only or main residence. They share a joint ceiling for relief of £30,000. If the loan is in their joint names the £30,000 limit is normally divided equally between them so that each gets relief for payments of interest on up to £15,000. If the loan is in the name of only one of them, then that person will normally get tax relief on the interest paid, up to the £30,000 limit.

6.2   Election available

A husband and wife can jointly elect to share both the limit and the tax relief between them in any way they choose. For example, a wife can have all the tax relief even though the loan is in her husband's name. This is called an allocation of interest election.

To make an election a married couple must complete and sign the appropriate form. An election must be made by 31 January following the end of the tax year to which it applies. Once made, an election will apply for subsequent years until it is changed or withdrawn.

If the interest is paid under MIRAS the election is of no practical relevance.

7   CHARGES ON INCOME AND JOINT PAYMENTS

7.1   Introduction

Relief for charges on income is given to the spouse who qualifies for it. Where there is a limit to the amount of relief, each spouse separately is entitled to that limit (but see mortgage interest above).

7.2   Deeds of covenant

Each spouse gets relief on payments made under covenants separately entered into, and where spouses have jointly covenanted the amount actually paid by each person is the amount allowed. If this is not clear (eg paid from joint bank account), the 50:50 rule will apply.

7.3   **Joint bank accounts**

Where a married couple make payments out of a joint account to satisfy a joint liability attracting tax relief for which both qualify – the relief is divided equally.

Where joint funds are used to satisfy a debt attracting tax relief of one spouse only, that spouse will get the relief. (For example, a professional subscription relating to the wife's employment is paid from a joint bank account: the wife will get the whole amount allowed against her Schedule E assessment.)

8   **CHILDREN'S INCOME**

8.1   **General rules**

All income of a child is assessable on the child and is not aggregated with a parent's income. The child has full entitlement to a personal allowance.

Returns and claims may be made by a child, but normally these would be done by a parent or guardian.

Where the child has received taxed income covered by the personal allowance, a repayment of tax will arise.

8.2   **Aggregation with parent's income**

Where a child under the age of 18 and unmarried has investment income and this is derived from capital provided by either parent, then the income is treated as that of the parent who provided the capital. The capital could be provided by means of a formal trust or settlement or could simply be a gift of money (eg opening a NSB account in the child's name) or shares.

If the income does not exceed £100 in a year of assessment, then it is ignored for aggregation purposes.

9   **CHAPTER SUMMARY**

This chapter picks up the knowledge acquired in the earlier chapters and applies it to the family group. In most examination papers there is an income tax question based on some aspect of the husband/wife relationship. The whole of this chapter must be considered as essential required knowledge.

The following areas were covered:

- transfer of the married couple's allowance between spouses;
- the allowances available in the year of marriage, of separation or of death of a spouse;
- tax relief for maintenance payments;
- tax treatment of joint income;
- the treatment of charges; and
- childrens income.

10   **SELF TEST QUESTIONS**

10.1   What elections are available concerning the transfer of the married couple's allowance? (1.2)

10.2   How is the amount of tax credit for the married couple's allowance that can be transferred determined when a husband has insufficient income tax liability to use the full amount? (1.2)

10.3   How is the married couple's allowance in the year of marriage calculated? (2.2)

10.4   What allowances are available to a husband and wife in the year that they separate? (3.3)

10.5   What sort of maintenance payments qualify for tax relief? (4.1)

10.6   What is the tax position of the recipient of such payments? (4.1)

10.7   How is the income from assets held in the joint names of a married couple normally taxed? (5.2)

10.8   What declaration may a married couple make when the entitlement to the income of a jointly held asset is unequal? (5.3)

10.9   What election may a married couple make concerning tax relief on mortgage interest payments? (6.2)

10.10   How is the income of a child assessed? (8.1)

11   EXAMINATION TYPE QUESTION

11.1   John and Fiona

John Gathercole and Fiona Smeech (nee Scoles) have shared a house in Wisteria Avenue since the date of their marriage.

John and Fiona were married on 21 June 1998 and in 1998/99 they had the following income.

	John £	Fiona £
Salary (gross)	29,224	5,100
Tax under PAYE	(5,593)	(Nil)
Building society interest received	2,000	1,440
Bank interest received	320	-

John pays mortgage interest on the house under MIRAS on a loan of £40,000 from a building society and interest paid thereon amounted to £4,500 (gross).

Fiona paid interest of £2,900 on a loan of £25,000 from her uncle towards the purchase of her flat. On the date of their marriage, Fiona moved into John's house and put her flat up for sale. The flat was subsequently sold in May 1999.

John was a bachelor, but Fiona was divorced in 1992 and has a daughter, Verity aged 9, from her previous marriage who lives with her.

The divorce settlement took the form of a capital sum, and Fiona receives no maintenance.

John pays £275 net, under Deed of Covenant, to the Church of St James.

You are required to compute the income tax payable by or repayable to John and Fiona in respect of 1998/99.

12   ANSWER TO EXAMINATION TYPE QUESTION

12.1   John and Fiona

Income tax computation for John and Fiona 1998/99

	£	John £	£	Fiona £
Earned income				
Schedule E (actual)		29,224		5,100
Unearned income (all savings income)				
BSI (× 100/80)	2,500			1,800
Bank interest (× 100/80)	400	2,900		-
		32,124		6,900
Less Charges				
Deed of covenant (275 × 100/77)		(357)		-
Statutory total income		31,767		6,900
Less: PA		(4,195)		(4,195)
Taxable income - Fiona				2,705
Taxable income - John		27,572		

		John	Fiona
Tax borne			
Non-savings: 4,300 / 2,705 × 20%		860	541
$\dfrac{20,372}{24,672}$ × 23%		4,686	
Savings: $\dfrac{2,428}{27,100}$ × 20%		486	
$\underline{472}$ × 40%		189	
27,572		6,221	541

	John	Fiona
Less: Tax credit re mortgage interest		
2,900 × 10%		(290)
Tax credit re APA 1,900 × 15% (restricted)		(251)
Tax credit re MCA 1,900 × $^{10}\!/_{12}$ × 15%	(237)	
Add: Basic rate tax deducted on charge 357 × 23%	82	
Income tax liability	6,066	Nil

		John		Fiona
Less: Income tax paid				
(a) PAYE tax	5,593		Nil	
(b) Tax credits on:				
BSI	500		360	
BDI	80	6,173	-	360
Income tax repayable		(107)		(360)

*(**Tutorial note:** Fiona can reduce her income tax liability by the lesser of 15% of APA (1,900); or the amount that reduces her income tax liability to nil.)*

7 INCOME FROM EMPLOYMENT

INTRODUCTION

(a)   This chapter, concerning income from employment has two themes. The first is setting limits to the Schedule E charge and so it reviews the nature of assessable emoluments, when payments are treated as emoluments, and the vital distinction between employment and self-employment. Establishing the link between tax years and emoluments is also considered.

(b)   The second area covered by the chapter is the treatment of a variety of incentive schemes. What links them together is a lenient tax regime on certain payments (that would otherwise be charged more rigorously under Schedule E) when they are directly or indirectly tied to an employer's financial performance.

---

1   THE SCOPE OF SCHEDULE E

1.1   Assessable emoluments

(a)   Directors and employees are assessed on the amount of emoluments **received** in the year of assessment. The term emoluments includes not only cash wages or salary, but bonuses and commission and benefits-in-kind made available by the employer.

(b)   The following benefits are also taxed under Schedule E:

- statutory sick pay (SSP);
- statutory maternity pay (SMP);
- retirement pension and widow's pension; and
- jobseeker's allowance.

(c)   Exempt benefits include:

- child benefit;
- incapacity benefit (initial period only);
- maternity allowance; and
- widows' lump sum payment.

1.2   When payments are emoluments

(a)   There is a considerable body of case law on whether a payment is an 'emolument from an office or employment'. For example, payments may be received from persons other than an employer and still constitute emoluments from the office eg tips of waiters and porters; on the other hand payments may be received which have some connection with the holding of the office but are not derived from holding it.

(b)   Brief notes on some leading cases are given below.

- Tips received by an employee taxi-driver where held to be assessable as remuneration for services rendered. (Calvert v Wainwright 1947)

- The payment by a company for the defence of a director in a dangerous driving prosecution, a criminal offence, was held to be income of the director. (The expenditure would be allowable in the company's computation) (Rendell v Went 1964).

- Collections received by a professional county cricketer for meritorious performance as provided by the league rules, were held to be profits arising from his employment. (Moorhouse v Dooland 1954).

- An amount of £1,000, part of a bonus paid by the Football Association to the 'squad' from which the English side in the 1966 World Cup competition was chosen, and £750 paid by a manufacturer as prizes in a competition, were held not to be in the nature of rewards for services rendered and therefore, not assessable. (Moore v Griffiths 1972).

1.3   The time earnings are received

(a)   Because Schedule E assessments are on a receipts basis, the time that the emoluments are received is of critical importance. The statute stipulates that this time is when the **earliest** of the following events occurs:

- actual payment of, or on account of, emoluments; or
- becoming entitled to such a payment.

(b)   In the case of directors, who are in a position to manipulate the timing of payments, there are extra rules. They are deemed to receive emoluments on the earliest of the two general rules set out above and:

- when sums on account of emoluments are credited in the accounts;

- the end of a period of account, where emoluments are determined before the end of that period; and

- when the amount of emoluments for a period are determined, if that is after the end of that period.

(c)   These rules do not deal with the timing of when benefits-in-kind are assessable, which is dealt with under separate legislation (eg the provision of an asset as a benefit would normally be assessed initially when first made available). Similarly pensions are taxed on an accruals rather than receipts basis.

1.4   Employment or self-employment?

(a)   The distinction between employment and self-employment is fundamental - an employee is taxable under Schedule E whilst a self-employed person is assessed on the profits derived from his trade, profession or vocation under Schedule D Cases I or II.

(b)   In many instances, determining whether a person is either employed or self-employed is not difficult. However, in other cases the distinction is less clear. The following principles, laid down by case law decisions, are important matters taken into account in deciding whether a person is employed or self-employed.

(c)   The primary test of an employment as opposed to self-employment is the existence of a **contract of service** compared with a mere **contract for services** (Fall v Hitchen). However, even in the absence of a contract of service any of the following matters would corroborate the existence of a such a contract.

- obligations by the 'employer' to offer work and the 'employee' to undertake the work offered. An 'employee' would not normally be in a position to decline work when offered. (O'Kelly v Trusthouse Forte) Ability to work as much or as little at the individual's choice indicates self-employment. (Barnett v Brabyn)

- the manner and method of the work being controlled by the 'employer'. (Performing Rights Society Ltd v Mitchell and Booker)

- the 'employee' being committed to work a specified number of hours at certain fixed times (Global Plant Ltd v Secretary of State for Social Services)

- the 'employee' is obliged to work personally and exclusively for the 'employer' (Warner Holidays v Secretary of State for Social Services)

- the work performed by the 'employee' is an integral part of the business of the 'employer' and not merely an accessory to it (Cassidy v Ministry of Health)

- the economic reality of self-employment is missing - namely the financial risk arising from not being paid an agreed, regular, remuneration (Market Investigations v Ministry of Social Security)

2   LUMP SUM PAYMENTS ON TERMINATION OR VARIATION OF EMPLOYMENT

2.1   Principles

The tax treatment of payments made on cessation of employment largely depends on whether the employee has a right to them under a contract of employment, or not. If there is a legal right the payment is taxed in the same way as any other employment income. But, if the payment is an ex-gratia one it falls outside the scope of the normal Schedule E rules (because it is not in return for services as an employee) but is subject to a special tax regime.

2.2   Ex-gratia payments

Ex-gratia payments are subject to Schedule E tax, in principle, but the first £30,000 is exempt. Payments include not only cash but benefits in kind received (such as allowing the employee to keep his company car). Where an employee receives statutory redundancy pay the amount received counts as the first part of the £30,000 exempt band.

Where an ex-gratia payment is made to an employee approaching retirement age the Revenue can deem it to be made under an unapproved retirement benefit arrangement and thereby assessable in full under Schedule E (ie, without the £30,000 exemption). Retrospective approval can be given for the sum to be fully exempt provided there is no actual approved scheme and the amount is within the normal limits - eg, 3/80ths of final salary for each year of service.

2.3   Exempt payments

There are specific statutory provisions to exempt some payments made to former employees. These are:

- payments for injury, disability or death;
- statutory redundancy payments; and

- terminal grants to members of the Armed Forces.

Lump sum payments received from an approved pensions scheme are also exempt (although not paid by the former employer).

2.4 Example

Albert age 40 years received a lump-sum of £80,000 from his employers following his redundancy in December 1998. He has other earned income of £34,000 and income from furnished accommodation of £2,445 for 1998/99. There are no charges on income. Albert also received £5,000 statutory redundancy pay.

Calculate the income tax payable by Albert for 1998/99 assuming all tax reliefs are claimed for the lump sum.

2.5 Solution

Income tax computation - 1998/99

		£	£	£
Earned income (other than lump sum)				34,000
Lump sum			80,000	
Less: Exempt amount		30,000		
Less: Statutory redundancy pay		5,000		
			25,000	
				55,000
				89,000
Schedule A				2,445
STI				91,445
Less: Personal allowance				4,195
Taxable income				87,250

	£			£
On first	4,300	@ 20%		860
On next	22,800	@ 23%		5,244
On remaining	60,150	@ 40%		24,060
	87,250			30,164

3 INCENTIVE SCHEMES

3.1 Introduction

(a)   It has long been recognised by employers that there are commercial benefits in schemes to motivate employees that are linked to a company's profitability. These may take the form of profit-related pay (discussed above) or profit-sharing, allocation of company shares or the grant of options to buy company shares in the future.

(b)   Successive governments have encouraged this approach by giving tax privileges to such schemes, provided that they meet the relevant requirements. Schemes that do so are known as approved schemes and those that do not are referred to as unapproved schemes.

(c)   We look first at approved schemes and the conditions necessary for approval. At the end of this section there is an outline of the tax regime for unapproved schemes.

3.2   Approved profit-sharing schemes

(a)   Each scheme is administered by a trust (set up by the relevant company) using funds provided by the company to buy shares in the company (or its parent) for appropriation to the company's participating employees. An approved profit-sharing scheme provides for an annual amount of a company's authorised shares to be allocated to eligible employee participants, with no income tax liability arising on the benefit so obtained.

(b)   The employee must undertake not to dispose of, or assign, the shares allocated to him during the retention period, and must permit the trustees to hold the shares throughout that period. The retention period is from initial appropriation (to the employee) until the second anniversary of that date, the employee's death or reaching an age specified in the scheme (which must be between 60 and 75).

(c)   The maximum initial market value of shares which may be appropriated to any one participant in a year of assessment is the greater of:

  •   £3,000, or

  •   10% of the participant's remuneration for the relevant or preceding year of assessment;

subject to an overriding maximum of £8,000. Remuneration is that liable to PAYE ie, excluding benefits-in-kind and after deducting occupational pension contributions.

(d)   The shares must be quoted on a recognised stock exchange or be shares in a company not controlled by another.

(e)   An eligible employee is any person who is a full-time or part time employee or full-time director of the company concerned.

(f)   Any sums expended by a company participating in an approved scheme, by way of payment to the scheme trustees, are allowed as a deduction in computing assessable trading profits under Schedule D, as are the costs of establishing such a scheme.

(g)   When shares are appropriated to an individual by the trustees no charge under Schedule E arises, except where shares are appropriated to a participant in excess of the above mentioned limit.

(h)   A disposal of a participant's shares by the trustees before the third anniversary of the appropriation (the release date) gives rise to a Schedule E charge for the year of assessment in which the disposal takes place, on the locked-in value. The **locked-in value** is the initial market value of the shares or the disposal proceeds where they are lower.

3.3   Example

Goodenuff is a participant in his company's approved profit-sharing scheme. On 1 September 1995 the scheme trustees appropriated to him 5,000 25p ordinary shares (market value 40p). On 1 May 1998 the trustees sell 350 of the shares at 50p each on his behalf.

What charge under Schedule E, if any, will arise on Goodenuff as a result of the sale of shares in May 1998?

3.4 Solution

A Schedule E charge will arise as follows:

	£
1998/99	
Market value on appropriation 350 x 40p	140

Locked-in value = £140 and so the Schedule E charge is £140, being lower than the proceeds (350 × 50p × 100% = £175).

3.5 Savings-related share option schemes

(a) There is a favourable tax treatment for share option schemes:

- that are linked to a SAYE (Save As You Earn) contract with a maximum monthly contribution by any employee of £250 per month for 3, 5 or 7 years; and

- where the purchase price of the shares is met by the employee, out of the SAYE accumulated savings, and the shares so acquired become additional share capital of the company,

provided the price at which options are offered is not less than 80% of market value when purchased.

(b) If the options are exercised **more than three years** after the option was granted, no Schedule E charge arises on

- grant of the option
- exercise of the option.

(c) On subsequent disposal of the shares, the capital gains arising on the excess of net sale proceeds (or market value) at the date of disposal over the subscription price plus the cost of acquiring the options, will be taxable.

(d) The costs of setting up such a scheme are allowable as trading expenses.

3.6 Company share option plan

(a) This type of approved share option scheme differs from the SAYE schemes described above in that:

- the funds are provided by the employing company;
- the aggregate value of options granted is potentially much higher; and
- the company has much greater discretion in allocating options to employees.

(b) An approved scheme is one where an option to purchase shares is granted to an individual:

- by reason of employment or directorship; and
- in accordance with a scheme approved under the legislation.

(c)   Participation in the scheme need not be extended to all employees nor be on equal terms to all participants. Eligible employees must be either full-time directors (ie, working at least 25 hours per week) or full-time or part time employees. Close company directors with a material interest (>10%) are ineligible. Subject to the above, the company has complete discretion as to participants.

(d)   The price payable for the shares on exercise of the option must not be materially less than their market value at the time the option was granted.

(e)   The tax implications for the employee are:

- on grant of an option: no charge under Schedule E

- on exercise of an option: no charge under Schedule E, provided the right is

    - exercised not less than three nor more than ten years after grant, and
    - is not exercised within three years of the date another option under the plan was last exercised.

- on final disposal of scheme shares, CGT will be charged on any gain then arising. The gain would be net disposal proceeds (or market value) less the price paid on exercise and the cost of the option.

(f)   There is a £30,000 limit to the value of shares for which a participant may hold unexercised options at the time of any grant of options.

(g)   The costs of administering the scheme are allowable trading expenses for the company.

3.7   Employee share ownership trusts (ESOTs)

(a)   The purpose of an ESOT is similar to that of an approved profit sharing scheme described above. However, there is no limit on the value of shares that may be distributed, which provides a significant incentive to establish them.

(b)   A company making a payment to a qualifying share ownership trust will be able to deduct the expenditure in its corporation tax computation. The receipts will not be taxed in the share ownership trust provided the funds are spent on qualifying purposes. If subsequently the trustees do not distribute shares under the scheme, or spend funds other than for qualifying purposes, then a chargeable event occurs. The trustees will then be liable to tax under Schedule D Case VI.

(c)   Individuals who sell shares in the founding company to a qualifying share ownership trust can roll over the gain against the cost of chargeable assets acquired with the sale proceeds. This encourages the sale of shares to the ESOT.

(d)   A qualifying share ownership trust must:

- be established by deed;

- be established by a UK resident company, not controlled by any other company; and

- have at least three UK resident trustees, of which at least one must be a professional trustee. Most of the trustees must be employees of the founding company's group who do not hold a material interest (more than 5%) and must have been selected by the employees of the founding company's group (or a committee of them). Most must not be, or have been, directors of companies within the founding company's group.

(e)   The following requirements apply to beneficiaries.

*   Beneficiaries at any time *must* include individuals who have been employees or directors of the founding company's group for a least five years, working, in the case of directors, at least twenty hours per week.

*   Beneficiaries **may** include those who would have qualified under the first requirement if the employment period requirement was abolished.

*   Beneficiaries **may** include those who have left employment within the previous eighteen months.

*   Beneficiaries **must exclude** those who have a material interest (more than 5%) in the founding company, or had a material interest in the previous year.

(f)   The plan should be established to receive or borrow funds from the founding company, which are used to buy shares in that company. Borrowing from other sources is permitted. The shares must be transferred to the beneficiaries within seven years, or sold to an approved profit sharing scheme at open market value. Any cash not immediately expended must be kept as cash, or in a bank or building society account.

(g)   The shares purchased must be:

*   ordinary fully paid up shares of the founding company (which must not be controlled by another company);

*   not redeemable; and

*   not subject to any restrictions other than those attaching to all shares of the same class, or imposed by the articles of association.

(h)   If a UK resident company makes a payment to a qualifying employee share ownership trust, then, provided at least some of the company's employees are beneficiaries of the trust, and the trustees expend the sum on one or more qualifying purposes within nine months of the end of the company's accounting period, the company may deduct the sum in its corporation tax computation. The company must make a claim for the relief within two years of the end of the accounting period in which the sum was paid.

(i)   The qualifying purposes are:

*   the acquisition of shares in the founding company;
*   the repayment of loans;
*   the payment of interest on loans;
*   the payment to beneficiaries under the trust; and
*   the meeting of expenses.

Any expenditure incurred on establishing as ESOT will be allowable as a trading expense for the company despite it clearly being a capital cost.

(j)   The trustees' actions can give rise to a chargeable event which will result in a charge to income tax under Schedule D Case VI. Chargeable events include:

- the transfer of securities other than to a beneficiary of the plan or to the trustees of an approved profit sharing scheme for at least open market value;

- the transfer of securities to a beneficiary if the following conditions are not satisfied:

    -   all securities transferred at the same time are transferred on similar terms;
    -   securities have been offered to all the beneficiaries of the plan; and
    -   securities are transferred to all beneficiaries who accepted the offer;

- the retention of shares by the trustees for more than seven years from acquisition. Shares are disposed of on a FIFO basis; and

- the expenditure of a sum other than for a qualifying purpose.

3.8   Unapproved employee share schemes

The approved schemes described above enable limited benefits to be provided for directors and employees without attracting a tax charge.   However, all the above schemes impose severe limitations on use, and consequently, many employers and employees prefer to use unapproved schemes for the benefit of senior executives and to accept the resultant, mainly not significant, tax charge.

The main events giving rise to a tax charge on unapproved schemes are as follows.

(a)   Where a share option is exercisable more than 10 years after it was granted an immediate charge to income tax is made under Schedule E.

(b)   On exercise or earlier assignment of a share option the gain is then taxed as income under Schedule E.

(c)   Where an employee/director received any benefit arising from the shareholding which is not received by all holders of that class of shares - the benefit is charged as income under Schedule E.

(d)   If the shares are acquired at less than their market value an income tax charge is levied on that undervalue when the shares are sold.

(e)   If the shares are issued to the employee/director subject to restrictions, a Schedule E charge is raised whenever any of those restrictions are removed or varied such that the value of the shares increases.

(f)   Where the shares are in a subsidiary company, an income tax charge is raised on the seventh anniversary of their acquisition (or on earlier disposal) on any increase in their value at that time.

(g)   If shares are issued to an employee but are subject to forfeiture (eg, if the employee fails to meet performance targets) there is a charge when the risk of forfeiture is lifted based on the share value at that date. There is only a charge when the shares are first awarded if they can be at risk of forfeiture for a period of more than five years.

(h)   If the shares are sold for a price in excess of their market value, the excess is assessed to tax as income rather than as a chargeable gain.

(i)   Where the shares are acquired without immediate payment for their full price, the under value is treated as a beneficial loan subject to an income tax charge at the official rate of interest. (This charge does not apply to shares in close companies.)

4   SELF TEST QUESTIONS

4.1   What are the rules governing the time emoluments are deemed to be received by an employee? (1.3)

4.2   What factors do the Courts take into account in distinguishing between employment and self-employment? (1.4)

4.3   What impact does the receipt of statutory redundancy pay have on the taxation of an ex-gratia payment received on termination of employment? (2.2)

4.4   What conditions apply to shares of a company that has set up an approved profit sharing scheme? (3.2)

4.5   What discretion does a company have in deciding on the participants in a company share option plan? (3.6)

4.6   Who must and who may be included as beneficiaries in an employee share ownership trust (ESOT)? (3.7)

1 What are the rules governing the taxation of benefits received by an employee (1.2)?

8 BENEFITS IN KIND

INTRODUCTION

This chapter looks at the principles of the taxation of benefits and expense deductions. A distinction is drawn between the way benefit charges are imposed on employees earning less than £8,500 pa on the one hand and those earning more, and directors, on the other.

1 PRINCIPLES OF TAXATION OF BENEFITS

1.1 Introduction

(a) The scope of the Schedule E charge, set out above, was defined in terms of the emoluments from an office or employment. In addition to salary, the term emoluments also covered perquisites and profits, which are better known as benefits-in-kind.

(b) The general rule for valuing benefits in kind provided to employees was established by case law (Tennant v Smith, 1892). Employees are taxed on the cash equivalent of the benefit, which is the cash value the employee would receive if he disposed of the benefit to a third party. Occasionally a benefit can be taxed without the need to consider the value to a third party. In Heaton v Bell (1969) an employee was assessed on an amount of income he would have received from his employer had he given up a benefit provided (the loan of a car).

1.2 Exceptions to the general principle

There are three types of exception to the general rule derived from case law outlined above:

(a) some benefits, that are assessable on all employees, are subject to specific statutory rules;

(b) benefits received by a group that broadly comprises employees earning £8,500 pa or more and directors are taxed, in general, under a different general principle imposed by statute; the cost of providing the benefit; and

(c) some specific benefits that are taxable only in the hands of employees earning £8,500 pa or more and directors are subject to specific statutory valuation rules.

2 BENEFITS ASSESSABLE ON ALL EMPLOYEES

2.1 Introduction

The general rule (the cash value of the benefit on disposal to a third party) is used as a fall back measure where the benefit provided does not fall into one of the categories below that have specific rules.

2.2 Vouchers and credit tokens

(a) Vouchers are broadly documents with which an individual can obtain goods and services. Cash vouchers are subject to PAYE when handed over to an employee and thus no further benefit arises on them since tax has already been paid. Non-cash vouchers are assessable on the employee at the cost of providing them. By concession luncheon vouchers are not taxed unless they are worth more than 15 pence per working day.

(b)   Use of credit tokens (such as a company credit card) are assessable on the value of goods and services bought with them.

(c)   No assessable benefit arises where the employee can show that the use of either vouchers or credit tokens was wholly, exclusively and necessarily in the performance of the duties of his employment.

2.3   Living accommodation

(a)   Where an employee is provided with living accommodation as a result of his employment, he is assessable on the higher of:

- the accommodation's annual value; and
- the rent actually paid for it by the provider of the accommodation.

(b)   Annual value is the rent the premises would command in the open market assuming that the tenant pays occupier's taxes and the owner pays for insurance, maintenance and repairs. You will not be expected to calculate such a value in your examination. Where necessary it will be provided for you. Normally annual value is assumed to be rateable value, in spite of the abolition of domestic rates.

(c)   To the extent that the accommodation is used wholly, exclusively and necessarily for business purposes the employee's benefit amount is reduced. Similarly, it is reduced by any contribution the employee makes for the accommodation.

(d)   There is no assessable benefit at all if the accommodation is job-related. To qualify as such it must be provided:

- where it is necessary for the proper performance of the employee's duties (eg a caretaker); or

- for the better performance of the employee's duties and, for that type of employment, it is customary for employers to provide living accommodation (eg hotel-worker); or

- where there is a special threat to the employee's security and he resides in the accommodation as part of special security arrangements.

(e)   A director can only claim one of the first two exemptions if:

- he has no material interest in the company; and

- he is a full-time working director or the company is a non-profit making organisation.

A material interest is broadly, more than 5% in the company's ordinary share capital.

(f)   There is an additional benefit assessed on expensive living accommodation. It applies where the cost of providing the accommodation exceeds £75,000 and there is a charge under the normal accommodation rules described above. So, however expensive the accommodation, it does not apply where it qualifies as job-related. It does, however, apply when there is no normal charge only because the employee pays rent equal to the rateable value of the property.

(g) The benefit is calculated as the additional value of the accommodation to the employee which is:

(cost of provision - £75,000) × the appropriate percentage

Cost of provision is the purchase price of the property plus expenditure on improvements incurred before the start of the tax year. The appropriate percentage is the official rate of interest used for beneficial loans in force at the start of the tax year.

To prevent avoidance, where the accommodation has been owned by the provider throughout a period of six years preceding the employee's taking up residence in it, the calculation of the benefit uses the property's market value when first used by the employee rather than the original cost. This applies even if the value has declined.

Deductions from the assessable benefit are available both for bona fide business use of the accommodation and for rent paid by the employee that exceeds the benefit assessable under the normal charge.

(h) It should be emphasised that the benefit for use of expensive accommodation is an extra assessable benefit, **not** a replacement for the 'normal' charge.

2.4 Activity

Barber, a sales manager, occupies a flat owned by his employer. Its annual value is £4,000 and Barber pays his employer £500 pa for use of the flat. The flat was purchased in 1992 for £120,000. The Inspector has agreed that 25% of the use of the flat may be attributed to business use.

Calculate the total benefit assessable on Barber, assuming an official rate of interest of 10%.

2.5 Activity solution

	£	£
Normal accommodation benefit	4,000	
Less: 25% business use	1,000	
		3,000
Less: Contribution for personal use		500
		2,500
Additional accommodation benefit		
(120,000 - 75,000) × 10%)	4,500	
Less: 25% business use	1,125	
		3,375
Total assessable benefit		5,875

3 BENEFITS ASSESSABLE ON EMPLOYEES EARNING £8,500 OR MORE AND DIRECTORS

3.1 Principles of assessment

(a) Instead of being taxed under the general principle for valuing benefits (effectively the second hand sale value of the benefit) these employees and directors are taxed under a separate set of statutory rules.

(b)   Whoever actually meets the cost, the measure of the benefit provided is the cost of providing it. Where a part of an expense benefits the employer rather than employee (such as entertaining company guests in a house used by the employee) the cost of provision may be apportioned between the amount spent exclusively for the employer's benefit and the remainder. The taxable benefit on the employee is the latter.

(c)   Where employers provide in-house benefits (such as free tickets for employees of a coach travel company) the measure of the benefit is the additional or marginal cost incurred by the employer as a result - not a proportion of the total cost (Pepper v Hart, 1993).

(d)   A benefit is deemed to have been provided to an employee not only when it is provided to him directly but also when it is provided to a member of his family or household. For the sake of brevity, throughout this section benefits are described as being made available to an employee but it should be borne in mind that on each occasion the charge to tax is also incurred when the benefit is provided to a member of the employee's family or household.

(e)   To be taxed under these principles a benefit must be provided to the employee by reason of his employment.

3.2   The threshold income level

In broad terms, the calculation to ascertain whether a person reaches the threshold income level of £8,500 assumes (in the calculation of benefits) that he does so. A calculation of the following kind is required in cases of doubt.

	£
Salary	x
Benefits assessable on all employees *	x
Benefits assessable only on £8,500 (or more) earners	x
Total emoluments (for test purposes)	x

* except the additional charge for living accommodation

If the total amounts to £8,500 or more the individual becomes subject to the benefits regime for the 'higher-paid'. Note that there is no deduction for business expenses in calculating this total.

3.3   Expenses connected with living accommodation

(a)   Under the general benefits in kind rule, expenses connected with living accommodation, such as lighting and heating, are taxable on an employee where the cost is met by his employer.

(b)   Such costs can total a considerable sum and so there is a limit on the amount taxable as a benefit where **the employee's accommodation is job-related**.

(c)   The limit applies to the following types of expense.

• heating, lighting and cleaning
• repairing, maintaining or decorating the premises
• furniture and other goods normal for domestic occupation.

(d)   The taxable limit is 10% of net emoluments (salary plus benefits other than the ancillary benefits in question less any expenditure deductible against employment income).

3.4   Use of assets

(a)   Many benefits in kind constitute payment of expenses on behalf of an employee. Sometimes, however, assets are provided for an employee's use while legal ownership remains with the employer. The most common example is the company car, which has special rules of its own considered later on in this chapter, but there is a general rule that applies to other assets.

(b)   Except for cars, car fuel, vans, mobile phones and accommodation, the general rule is that an employee is taxed on a benefit amounting to 20% of an asset's market value at the time it is first provided. So, if the employee is provided with a television costing £500, he is subject to a benefit in kind charge under Schedule E of £100 (£500 × 20%). The benefit is assessed for **each** tax year in which it is provided (not just the one in which it was first made available).

(c)   Where the employer rents the asset made available to the employee instead of buying it, the employee is taxed on the rental paid by the employer rather than 20% of market value if the rental is the higher figure. So if the annual rental for the television mentioned above is £120, that would be assessed on the employee.

(d)   Payments made by the employee for the use of the asset reduce (or eliminate) the taxable benefit.

3.5   Gifts of assets

(a)   If an employer purchases a new asset and gives it to an employee immediately, the employee is taxed on the cost.

(b)   Where an asset is given to an employee that is second-hand, different rules may apply. In these circumstances the employee is taxed on the **higher** of the asset's market value when **given to him** and:

 •   the asset's market value at the time it was **first made available** to the employee

      less

 •   the benefit assessed on the employee during the time he had the use of it but did not own it.

(c)   The purpose of the special rule for gifts of used assets is to prevent employee's gaining from gifts of assets that depreciate in value rapidly once they are used.

(d)   Where the employee buys the asset, the payment is deducted in calculating the benefit.

3.6   Activity

Brian's employer, X Ltd, purchased a dishwasher for his use on 1 June 1997, costing £600. On 6 April 1998 it gave the dishwasher to Brian (its market value then being £150).

Calculate the benefit assessable on Brian on the basis of:

(a)   the circumstances as set out above; and

(b)   if Brian paid X Ltd £100 for the dishwasher.

3.7 **Activity solution**

(a)   Gift of dishwasher

	£
Market value when first made available to Brian	600
Less: Benefit already assessed	
1997/98 £600 × 20% × 10/12	100
Taxable benefit in 1998/99	500

The benefit is £500 since this is greater than the dishwasher's market value when given to Brian (£150).

(b)   Sale of dishwasher to Brian for £100

	£
Benefit as calculated in (a) above	500
Less: Price paid	100
Taxable benefit in 1998/99	400

Note: where the benefit of use is provided for only part of a tax year the benefit is reduced proportionately.

3.8   **Cars**

(a)   The 'company car' has been one of the benefits most widely provided for employees. The amount of the benefit depends on the cost, age and amount of business use the car is put to.

(b)   In line with the approach to taxing benefits, there is no assessment where a car is not intended to be available for private use and, as a matter of fact, there is none. Remember that travel between home and work counts as private use, **not** business use.

(c)   No individual using a 'pool car' is assessed on a car benefit. To qualify as a 'pool car' **all** of the following conditions must be met during the tax year in question.

- The car must be used by more than one employee (and not usually by one employee to the exclusion of the others).

- It must not normally be kept overnight at or near the residence of any of the employees making use of it.

- Any private use by an employee must be merely incidental to his business use of it.

(d)   It should be noted that if any employee breaks these conditions he exposes all other users of the car to a benefit charge, not just himself.

(e)   Unless the employee is exempted because he makes no private use of an employer's car, or it is a pool car, he is subject to a benefit in kind charge.

The car benefit charge is a percentage of the car's price, which will be either:

- its list price published by the manufacturer, importer or distributor (as appropriate); or

- if there is no list price, its 'notional price' (which is equivalent to its market value when new).

(f)   The list price of a car is further defined as the inclusive price (ie, including taxes) appropriate for the car on the assumption that it is sold in the UK as an individual sale in the retail market. Consequently employees of large companies cannot benefit from bulk discounts their employer might negotiate. It is the list price **on the day before the car's first registration** that is used.

(g)   Where the car is fitted with accessories the list price of these (or market value where there is no list price) is added to the list price of the car subject to a maximum price of £80,000.

(h)   An employee may reduce the price on which his car benefit charge is calculated by making a capital contribution. There was no provision for capital contributions under the old car benefit system. The price is reduced by the lower of:

- the capital contribution towards the cost of the basic car and its accessories; and

- £5,000.

(i)   The standard car benefit will be 35% of the price of the car subject to a maximum price of £80,000.

(j)   The standard 35% applies to low business mileage (or none at all). There are then reductions as follows:

- a 1/3 reduction for business mileage of 2,500 to 17,999 miles in the tax year: or

- a 2/3 reduction for business mileage of 18,000 miles or more.

(k)   When more than one car is made available to an employee, any car, other than the car with the most business use, is assessed as 35% of the list price with no reductions unless the business use is 18,000 miles or more, in which case the reduction is 1/3.

(l)   Further reductions may then be made in the following order.

- Where the car is four years old or more at the end of the tax year, a reduction is made of 1/3 of the benefit after taking account of the appropriate business mileage reduction.

- Where the car is unavailable for part of the tax year because it was first provided or ceased to be provided part way through a tax year the benefit (after taking account of business mileage and the car's age) is reduced proportionately.

    The car may also be unavailable for a period during the tax year but was available both before and after (for instance if it was under repair after a crash). The benefit charge that would otherwise apply is proportionately reduced provided that it was unavailable for a continuous period of 30 days.

- Lastly, a reduction is made where the employee makes a financial contribution as a condition of the car being available for his private use. (This should not be confused with a capital contribution made towards the purchase cost of the car, which is deducted from the price on which the percentage car benefit is based.)

(m)   The charge for cars available for private use takes into account the running expenses of the vehicle, so there is no additional taxable benefit when the employer pays for insurance, road fund licence, maintenance etc.   If a chauffeur is provided with the car however it constitutes an additional benefit.   A separate benefit-in-kind charge is made for car fuel (see below).

(n)   A special system applies to 'classic cars' (which were favourably treated under the old system).   A classic car is one that is at least 15 years old at the end of the tax year, has a market value of £15,000 or more and has a higher market value than list price.

(o)   The percentage benefit charge for classic cars will be based on market value (on the last day of the tax year or when the car ceased to be available to the employee if that occurred during the tax year).   As with ordinary cars, there is a reduction (up to a £5,000 maximum) for capital contributions towards the cost of the car made by the employee.

3.9   Car fuel

(a)   Scale charges apply to car fuel provided for private motoring in a car provided by reason of a person's employment.   They are based on engine size only, without reference either to the age of the car or its original market value (unless it has no cylinder capacity) or the amount of business mileage.

(b)   The scale charges for **petrol** cars for 1998/99 are:

Engine size	£
1,400 cc or less	1,010
1,401cc - 2,000cc	1,280
2,001 cc or more	1,890

For **diesel** cars the equivalents are:

Engine size	£
2,000cc or less	1,280
2,001 cc or more	1,890

(c)   Proportionate reductions in the fuel scale charge apply where the car is unavailable for part of the tax year.   These are calculated on the same basis as reductions in the car charge.

(d)   No reduction is made in the fuel scale charge for payments made by the employee unless he pays for **all** fuel used for private motoring.   In which case the charge would be cancelled. Since the fuel scale charge applies only to vehicles for which there is a car benefit charge, it does not apply to 'pool cars'.

3.10 Activity

Charles took up employment with Weavers Ltd on 1 July 1998. His remuneration package included a 5 year old 2,500cc petrol-driven car, list price £24,000. He took delivery of the car on 1 August 1998 and during the remainder of the tax year drove 15,000 miles on business and 18,000 miles for private purposes. As a condition of the car being made available to him for private motoring, Charles paid £100 per month for the car and £50 per month for petrol.

Weaver's Ltd incurred the following expenses in connection with Charles' car

	£
Servicing	450
Insurance	780
Fuel (of which £1,150 was for business purposes)	2,500
Maintenance	240

Calculate Charles' assessable benefits for 1998/99 in connection with his private use of the car

3.11 Activity solution

	£	£
Benefit - £24,000 × 35%	8,400	
Less: High business mileage reduction (W1) ($\frac{2}{3}$)	5,600	
	2,800	
Less: Reduction for age of car £2,800 × $\frac{1}{3}$	933	
	1,867	
Less: Reduction for non-availability (W2)	622	
	1,245	
Less: Payment for use (W3)	800	
		445
Fuel - standard scale charge	1,890	
Less: Reduction for non-availability (W4)	630	
		1,260
Assessable benefit		1,705

WORKINGS

(W1)   High business mileage reduction - car

High business mileage threshold reduced due to non-availability to $18,000 \times 8/12 = 12,000$ miles. Thus Charles qualifies for the $\frac{2}{3}$ reduction.

(W2)   Reduction for non-availability - car

Car first made available on 1 August 1998. Thus not available for 4 months of 1998/99. Reduction is thus £622 ($£1,867 \times 4/12$).

(W3)   Payment for use

Payment made for 8 months @ £100/month = £800.

(W4)   Reduction for non-availability - car fuel

Same proportionate reduction applies as for car benefit charge. Reduction is thus £1,890 × 4/12 = £630.

Notes:

(1)   The amount of Charles' private mileage has no impact on the calculations.

(2)   Charles does not qualify for a reduction in the fuel scale charge because he does not pay for all fuel used for private motoring.

3.12   Cars and cash alternatives

Where employees are offered either a company car or a cash alternative, the employee will pay tax on the option that they have taken ie, either on the cash or the car benefit figure based on list price. Without this rule the Heaton v Bell principle would apply to reduce the value, of the car benefit to the (usually lower) amount of salary 'sacrificed'. The same applies for NICs; if the cash is taken, the employee and employer will pay Class 1 NICs on the cash alternative, if the company car is taken, the employer will pay Class 1A NIC on the benefit figure based on list price.

3.13   Activity

Sally and Ray are both employed by Buddle Ltd. As part of their remuneration package, they are offered the choice between a company car and a cash alternative of £400 per month.

Sally chooses a Volvo 850 with a list price of £19,500. She travels 2,000 business miles in 1998/99. Ray chooses the cash alternative.

Calculate the assessable benefit for Ray and Sally for 1998/99.

3.14   Activity solution

Sally's assessable benefit:

£19,500 × 35%   £6,825

Ray's assessable benefit

£400 × 12   £4,800

3.15   Vans and heavier commercial vehicles

(a)   Where employers' vans are made available to employees for their private use, a benefit in kind scale charge applies.

(b)   A distinction has to be drawn between cars, vans and heavier commercial vehicles. Vans are defined as vehicles primarily designed for carrying goods or burden (and cars are defined in opposite terms). Between vans and heavier commercial vehicles the distinction is one of weight. Vehicles up to 3.5 metric tonnes are vans. Any weight above this level counts as a heavier commercial vehicle.

(c)   Unless a heavier commercial vehicle is provided wholly or mainly for an employee's private use (which would be unusual) there is no taxable benefit. Vans, however, are subject to a taxable benefit, the size of which depends on the age of the van and whether it is made available for private use to just one employee or is shared. As with cars, there is an exemption from the charge for pooled vans and the same definition of pooled applies to both cars and vans.

(d)   Where a van is made available for private use to only one employee the scale charge is £500 if it is less than four years old at the end of the tax year. Older vans attract a £350 scale charge. Proportionate reductions in the scale charge are made where a van is unavailable (using the same definition as for cars). Again following the car benefit principle, a reduction is made for payments made by the employee for private use of the van.

(e)   Where employees share the private use of the van, or vans, a different calculation applies. The £500 scale charge (or £350 for vans at least four years old) is totalled for all the shared vans and the resulting figure is divided equally over all the employees who made any private use of any of the vans during the tax year regardless of the amount of private use.

(f)   A shared van is one that is available to more than one employee of the same employer (either at the same time or consecutively) unless one employee has the sole use of it for a period of more than 30 days.

(g)   If, for any of the vans involved, it was available exclusively to any one employee for a period of 30 days or more, the proportion of the scale charge applying to that van is apportioned to that one employee and is correspondingly deducted from the aggregate scale charges of the shared vans.

(h)   No employee sharing the private use of vans can incur a scale charge higher than £500.

(i)   An employee can elect for his scale charge to be calculated on an alternative basis when he shares the private use of a van or vans. This basis looks to the number of days on which the employee has a shared van available for private use; the scale charge is £5 per day. The election will benefit employees who make relatively little private use of a shared van.

3.16   Mobile telephones

(a)   Mobile telephones made available to an employee attract a separate scale charge of £200 pa unless the employee:

- makes no private use of it; or

- is required to reimburse the full cost of private use to the provider and actually does so.

(b)   Reductions in the scale benefit are made for periods in the tax year during which the telephone is unavailable (before it is first made available, after it ceases to be so, or for a continuous period of 30 days or more).

(c)   It should be noted that (as for car fuel) there is no reduction for partial reimbursement of cost to the provider; the scale charge is an all or nothing one.

(d)   The scale charge for a mobile telephone applies even where it is fitted in a car that attracts a car benefit charge; it is **not** subsumed within the car benefit.

3.17   Beneficial loans

(a)   Beneficial loans are those made to an employee below the **official rate of interest** (broadly an approximation to the prevailing commercial mortgage rate).

(b)   Employees are liable to a benefit in kind charge on the difference between the interest that would be payable on the loan (had interest been charged at the official rate) and the interest actually paid in respect of the tax year, whether paid during it or afterwards.

An exemption for small loans applies where all the employee's cheap or interest free loans, excluding loans which qualify for tax relief, total no more than £5,000.

(c)   There are two methods of calculating the benefit, the averaging method and the accurate method. The former uses the average of the loan outstanding at the beginning and end of the tax year. If the loan was taken out or redeemed during the tax year that date is used instead of the beginning or end of the tax year. The latter method calculates the benefit day by day on the balance actually outstanding. Either the taxpayer or the Revenue can decide that the accurate method should be used.

(d)   If an interest-free or cheap loan is one that would ordinarily attract tax relief, tax relief is available on the appropriate amount of the loan at the official rate of interest.

(e)   If all or part of a loan to an employee (whether or not made on low-interest or interest-free terms) is written off, the amount written off is treated as a benefit in kind and charged to income tax.

(f)   Where an employee dies with a loan outstanding, no benefit in kind accrues after the date of death and there is no charge to tax if the employer writes it off.

3.18   Activity

Daniel was granted a loan of £35,000 by his employer on 31 March 1998 to help finance the purchase of a yacht. Interest is payable on the loan at 3% pa. On 1 June 1998 Daniel repaid £5,000 and on 1 December 1998 he repaid a further £15,000. The remaining £15,000 was still outstanding on 5 April 1999. Daniel earns £30,000 pa.

Calculate the assessable benefit for 1998/99 under

(a)   the averaging method; and
(b)   the accurate method

assuming that the official rate of interest was 10% pa until 5 August 1998 and 8% pa thereafter.

3.19   Activity solution

(a)   Averaging method

	£	£
6.4.98 - 5.8.98 (official interest rate 10%)		
$\dfrac{35,000 + 15,000}{2} \times 10\% \times 4/12$		833
6.8.98 - 5.4.99 (official interest rate 8%)		
$\dfrac{35,000 + 15,000}{2} \times 8\% \times 8/12$		1,333
		2,166
Less: interest paid		
6.4.98 - 31.5.98 £35,000 × 3% × $^2/_{12}$	175	
1.6.98 - 30.11.98 £30,000 × 3% × $^6/_{12}$	450	
1.12.98 - 5.4.99 £15,000 × 3% × $^4/_{12}$	150	
		(775)
		1,391

(b)   Accurate method

                                  £

6.4.98 - 31.5.98 (56 days)

$$£35,000 \times \frac{56}{365} \times 10\%$$ 537

1.6.98 - 5.8.98 (66 days)

$$£30,000 \times \frac{66}{365} \times 10\%$$ 542

6.8.98 - 30.11.98 (117 days)

$$£30,000 \times \frac{117}{365} \times 8\%$$ 769

1.12.98 - 5.4.99 (126 days)

$$£15,000 \times \frac{126}{365} \times 8\%$$ 414

                                      2,262

Less: Interest paid   (775)

                                        1,487

3.20   Loans with mortgage interest relief

The rules for taxing cheap and interest-free loans provided by employers where mortgage interest relief applies are as follows:

- First, the value of the loan for tax purposes is calculated; which is the difference between the interest (if any) paid by the employee and the interest which he would have paid at the official rate of interest.

  This amount is added to his other income and taxed at his marginal rate of tax.

- Second, the employee will be entitled to tax relief at 10% on the loan, up to £30,000, as if he had paid interest at the official rate.

3.21   Activity

Grace has a £50,000 home loan at 2% provided by her employer. She is a higher rate tax payer.

Calculate the net tax payable on the loan assuming that the official rate of interest is 8%.

3.22 **Activity solution**

Tax liability

	£	£
Interest saved £50,000 @ (8% – 2%) 6%	3,000	
Tax due £3,000 @ higher rate 40%		1,200

Tax relief

	£	£
Interest actually paid £50,000 @ 2%	1,000	
Interest treated as paid	3,000	
Total	4,000	
Mortgage interest relief on £4,000 × $^{30}/_{50}$ @ 10%		240
Net tax payable		960

3.23 **Exemption for commercial loans**

There is an exemption for loans made to employees on commercial terms by employers who lend to the general public. The exemption will apply where

- the loans are made by an employer whose business includes the lending of money;

- loans are made to employees on the same terms and conditions as are available to members of the public; and

- a substantial number of loans on these terms are made to public customers.

3.24 **Scholarships**

(a) In principle, if a scholarship is provided to a member of an individual's family or household, the cost of it is taxable as a benefit in kind.

(b) There is an exemption, however, for the 'arm's length' grant of scholarships. No taxable benefit arises where:

- the scholarship is awarded from a separate trust scheme;

- the person receiving it is in full-time education at a school, college or university; and

- not more than 25% of payments made in the tax year from the scheme are made by reason of a person's employment.

(c) In the hands of the recipient scholarship income is exempt.

3.25 **Payment of director's tax liability**

(a) Where tax should have been deducted from a director's emoluments under the PAYE system, but was not, and the tax is paid over to the Revenue by someone other than the director, the director is treated as receiving a benefit in kind.

(b)   The measure of the benefit is the amount of tax accounted for, less any reimbursement by the director (if any).

(c)   Note that this benefit in kind rule applies only to directors (not employees earning more than £8,500). In addition, a director without a material interest in the company and who either is a full-time working director or the company is charitable or non-profit making, is exempted.

4   EXEMPT BENEFITS

The following are the more important exempt benefits-in-kind

(a)   the **employer's contribution** to an approved pension scheme. Although many schemes also require contributions by the employee (also tax deductible against his Schedule E salary), the ultimate benefit-in-kind will be a non-contributory scheme

(b)   the use of subsidised on-site **restaurant or canteen** facilities, provided such facilities are available for all employees

(c)   luncheon vouchers up to a value of 15p per working day

(d)   entertainment provided for an employee, by reason of his employment, by a **genuine third party** eg, a ticket or seat at a sporting or cultural event provided for a business contact or client to generate goodwill. NB: Revenue has long accepted that, in practice, no tax liability will arise on the typical working lunch or dinner

(e)   gifts received, by reason of his employment, from genuine third parties, provided the cost from any one source does not exceed £150 in a year of assessment

Long service awards in kind (eg gold watches) are exempt up to a cost of £20 for each year of service of 20 years or more

(f)   the provision of a benefit of a car parking space provided at or near the place of work, including the reimbursement of the cost of such a parking place

(g)   provision of travel, accommodation and subsistence during public transport disruption caused by industrial action

(h)   provision of transport between home and place of work for severely disabled employees

(i)   medical insurance for treatment and medical services where the need for treatment arises while abroad in performance of duties

(j)   Christmas parties, annual dinner dances etc for staff generally. Modest cost (up to £75 pa per head) will not be assessed

(k)   security assets and services

Where a security asset or security service is provided by reason of employment, or where reimbursement is made for the cost of such measures.

Relief is not, therefore, available where the director or employee himself bears the cost.

The asset or service must meet a special threat to the employee's personal physical safely (as opposed to his property). Security assets include such things as intruder alarms, bullet-resistant glass and floodlighting. Security services include such things as bodyguards and specially trained chauffeurs

(l)   work-place nurseries for child (under 18) care

Nurseries run by the employer (who must be responsible for finance and management) at the workplace or at other non-domestic premises will not be an assessable benefit-in-kind.

Included are facilities run jointly with other employers or local authorities and similar facilities for older children after school or during school holidays.

Note: the provision of cash allowances or vouchers to meet child care expenses remain assessable.

(m)   Recreational or sporting facilities.

No benefit arises on the provision of such facilities by a person's employer (directly or indirectly). But the following are **excluded** from exemption:

- use of cars, ships, aircraft and hovercraft;
- facilities that include or are associated with overnight accommodation; and
- facilities provided on domestic premises.

(n)   Removal expenses and benefits.

No assessable benefit arises on payment or reimbursement of removal expenses and benefits provided that:

- the expenses are incurred in connection with a change in the employee's principal private residence resulting from:

    - taking up a new employment; or
    - an alteration in the duties of an employment; or
    - a change in the location at which the employee's duties are carried out;

- the costs met or reimbursed are qualifying expenses. These are widely drawn so as to include costs of disposing of the first house, travel and subsistance when looking for a new house, removal expenses and interest on a bridging loan whilst the employee owns both the old and new homes;

- the expenditure is incurred by the end of the tax year following the one in which the employment change occurred; and

- only the first £8,000 of the total expenditure met or reimbursed is exempt.

(o)   Counselling services for employees

No assessable benefit arises on counselling services provided to an employee made redundant provided that:

- the recipient has been a full-time employee throughout the previous two years;

- the services are provided in the UK;

- their purpose is to enable the employee to find another employment or become self-employed; and

- the services consist wholly or mainly of advice and guidance, developing skills or using office facilities.

The exemption also extends to travel expenses necessarily incurred in receiving the counselling services.

(p) Expenses incurred by employees whilst away overnight on company business

Where employers pay personal expenses, such as telephone calls home, laundry and so on, for employees who stay away from home on business, these expenses are not a taxable benefit for employees, provided that they fall below the de-minimis limit of £5 per night in the UK and £10 per night overseas.

This exemption applies regardless of how the employer meets the expenses. For instance, the employer may:

(i) pay hotel bills directly; or
(ii) provide a nightly allowance; or
(iii) reimburse the employee with the actual expenses incurred.

If an amount above the limit is paid, the whole amount is taxable.

(q) Insurance

No assessable benefit arises where employee liability insurance is paid by an employer.

(r) Reimbursement for business mileage incurred in an employee's own car where the Fixed Profit Car Scheme (FPCS) limits are not exceeded:

Size of car engine	On the first 4,000 miles in the tax year	On mileage in excess of 4,000 miles in the tax year
Up to 1,000cc	28p	17p
1,001cc - 1,500cc	35p	20p
1,501cc - 2,000cc	45p	25p
over 2,000cc	63p	36p

If the employer reimburses less than the FPCS value, the employee can claim tax relief for the amount of the deficit.

5 DEDUCTIBILITY OF EXPENSES FROM EMPLOYMENT INCOME

5.1 Introduction

Relief for expenditure against employment income, taxed under Schedule E, is of two types. Firstly, certain types of expenditure are specifically permitted by statute. The most important of these are:

(a) contributions to approved pension schemes, personal pensions. or retirement annuity plans (within certain limits);

(b) fees and subscriptions to professional bodies and learned societies, provided that the recipient is approved for the purpose by the Revenue and its activities are relevant to the individual's employment; and

(c) payments to charity made under a payroll deduction scheme operated by an employer (up to a maximum of £1,200 pa).

Secondly, unspecified expenditure on travel and other expenditure is deductible to the extent that it complies with very stringent rules. These are discussed below.

5.2 Travel expenditure

(a) Travelling expenses may be deducted (s198(1A) (a) ICTA 1988) where they are incurred:

- necessarily; and
- in the performance of the duties of the employment.

(b) In deciding whether travelling expenses are necessarily incurred the Courts look to whether it is the requirements of the job that make the expenditure necessary, or the circumstances of the individual. If it is the former, the 'necessarily' test is passed but otherwise it is not.

(c) The Courts have looked at the phrase, 'in the performance of the duties of the employment' in many cases. With regard to travelling expenses the following principles have emerged.

- The costs of travelling from home to work are not deductible (Cook v Knott, 1887), except in the rare case when it can be shown that the duties are started before leaving home (Owen v Pook, 1969).

- Costs of travelling from one employment to another are not deductible (Mitchell and Edon v Ross, 1962).

- If an employee has more than one place where the duties have to be performed, travelling expenses between them are allowable (Jardine v Gillespie, 1906).

(d) Travel expenses are also allowed (s198(1A(b) (ICTA 1988) for journeys an employee makes to or from a place he has to attend in the performance of his duties, other than normal commuting journeys. For example, where James lives in Swindon and normally works at his employer's office in London (his permanent workplace) he will be allowed tax relief for the travel and subsistence expenses of travelling from his home to a temporary work location in Manchester.

(e) Travel and subsistence costs are allowed for 'site-based' employees provided that attendance at the site is not expected to last more than 24 months.

5.3 Other expenses

(a) The rule covering deductibility of non-travelling expenses is even more strict. In addition to the two tests required for travelling expenditure, such expenses must also be incurred wholly and exclusively in the performance of the duties. So severe are these tests that one judge thought that the words of the rule 'are found to come to nearly nothing at all'.

(b) The test that expenditure must be incurred '**in the performance** of the duties' means that there is no deduction for expenditure incurred beforehand to gain the requisite knowledge or experience to do the work. So, for example, the cost of attending evening classes by a schoolteacher has been disallowed (Humbles v Brooks, 1962).

(c) For expenditure to be 'necessarily' incurred it must be inherent in the job, not something imposed by the employee's circumstances. Thus an employee with poor eyesight was unable to deduct the cost of spectacles. In other words, to be necessary expenditure, each and every person undertaking the duties would have to incur it.

(d)   For expenditure to be incurred 'wholly and exclusively' it must be with the sole objective of performing the duties of the employment. It does not matter that some personal benefit is acquired from the expenditure as long as it is incidental. Two examples show this distinction. If an employee is required to wear clothes of a high standard, and so purchases them, the expenditure is **not** deductible. The employee's clothes satisfy both professional and personal needs. On the other hand expenditure on a home telephone can be partly deductible. Business calls are made 'wholly and exclusively' and so are deductible. But, on the same reasoning as applied to the clothes no part of the line rental for a home phone may be deducted.

6   SELF TEST QUESTIONS

6.1   What general principle is applied (unless overridden by a specific statutory rule) to the valuation of benefits provided to employees earning £8,500 or more and directors? (1.2)

6.2   In what circumstances does the additional benefit on living accommodation apply? (2.3)

6.3   What tests must travelling expenditure comply with to be deductible against Schedule E income? (5.2)

7   EXAMINATION TYPE QUESTION

7.1   Mr F Darcy

Mr F Darcy, managing director of the Pemberley Trading Co Ltd, is paid an annual salary of £36,000 and also bonuses based on the company's performance. Pemberley's accounting year ends on 31 December each year and the bonuses are normally determined and paid on 31 May thereafter. In recent years bonuses have been

Year to 31 December 1996	£4,000
Year to 31 December 1997	£8,000
Year to 31 December 1998	£4,000

Mr Darcy pays 7% of his basic salary to an approved occupational pension scheme. He uses a company car (3,500cc) purchased in 1996 for £20,000, for 25,000 miles during 1998/99, of which 25% is for non-business use. Running expenses including car fuel paid by the company were £2,600 in the year.

On 2 April 1997 the company set up a scholarship fund for its employees and their relatives. Mr Darcy's son, who is 23 years old and has no income of his own, was awarded a scholarship of £2,940 per year for three years from 1 October 1998 to continue to study for a doctorate at the University of London while continuing to live with his father. It is paid each year on 1 December.

Under the terms of the company's approved profit-sharing scheme Mr Darcy was allotted 1,000 ordinary £1 shares of the company, the market value of which is £4.25 per share, on 21 January 1999.

Mr Darcy pays charitable deeds of covenant totalling £4,235 (net).

Mr Darcy's wife died in 1990. He is a UK resident.

You are required to compute Mr Darcy's income tax payable for 1998/99. Briefly give reasons for your treatment of items included or excluded in arriving at his taxable income.

8   ANSWER TO EXAMINATION TYPE QUESTION

8.1   Mr F Darcy

Computation of income tax payable for 1998/99

	£	£
Earned income		
Schedule E:		
Salary		36,000
Bonus *(note 1)*		8,000
		44,000
Benefits		
Car 20,000 × 35%	7,000	
Less: 7,000 × ⅔ *(note 2)*	(4,667)	
Car fuel *(note 2)*	1,890	
Scholarship paid for son	2,940	
Excess shares under profit sharing scheme *(note 3)*	102	
		7,265
		51,265
Less: Pension contributions 7% × £36,000		2,520
		48,745
Less: Charitable deed £4,235 × 100/77		5,500
Statutory total income		43,245
Less: PA		4,195
Taxable income		39,050

£	£
4,300 @ 20%	860
22,800 @ 23%	5,244
11,950 @ 40%	4,780
Less: Tax credit re APA (1,900 × 15%)	
(son in full time education)	(285)
Income tax borne	10,599
Add: Tax withheld on £5,500 charitable covenant	1,265
Income tax payable	11,864

Explanation of treatment

(1)   Under the receipts basis for directors under Schedule E the bonus is treated as received, and therefore taxed, when it is determined. Thus the bonus determined in May 1998 is taxable in 1998/99.

(2)   The car benefit is reduced by ⅔ as Mr Darcy drives more than 18,000 business miles per year. There is no reduction in the car fuel benefit.

(3)   The limit of value which may be apportioned under an approved profit sharing scheme is 10% of salary for PAYE purposes (ie, excluding benefits in kind, but after deduction of pension contributions). The higher of the current year or preceding year's remuneration may be used

1998/99   £36,000 + 8,000 − 2,520 = £41,480
1997/98   £36,000 + 4,000 − 2,520 = £37,480

	£
Value of shares allotted 1,000 × 425p	4,250
Limit 10% × £41,480 (less than the £8,000 overriding limit)	4,148
	102

9 SCOPE OF BUSINESS INCOME TAX

INTRODUCTION & LEARNING OBJECTIVES

(a)   The following chapters are concerned with the detail of the income tax regime as it applies to unincorporated businesses (ie, sole traders). Before that can be considered, however, the limits of the system must be defined.

(b)   Definition: Case I: the annual profits arising or accruing in respect of any trade carried on in the UK or elsewhere;

Case II: the annual profits arising or accruing in respect of any profession or vocation not contained in any other Schedule.

When you have studied this chapter you should be able to do the following:

- Identify whether an activity will be regarded as trading or non-trading by using the 'badges of trade'
- Adjust an accounting profit for the deductions and additions required to calculate Schedule D Case I profit
- Calculate the assessments in the opening years of a business including the overlap relief to carry forward
- Understand the adjustments on a change of accounting date
- Calculate the assessment for a business ceasing.

1   BADGES OF TRADE

1.1   Introduction

(a)   It is Schedule D Case I that most concerns us and it can be seen from the definition above that the key element is the concept of a trade.

   Definition   'Trade includes every trade, manufacture, adventure or concern in the nature of trade'.

(b)   Although the above is the statutory definition of a trade, in practice it is not a very helpful one. What constitutes a trade has been reviewed by the Courts in many decided cases. The criteria that emerge from these were set out by a Royal Commission and are known as the 'badges of trade'. They are:

- the subject matter of the realisation;
- the length of the period of ownership;
- the frequency or number of similar transactions by the same person;
- supplementary work on or in connection with the property realised;
- the circumstances that were responsible for the realisation; and
- motive.

(c)   Each of these principles is dealt with individually below. It is vital to appreciate that no one 'badge' is decisive. In any set of circumstances one 'badge' may indicate trading and another the opposite. It is the overall impression, using all relevant factors, that is important.

1.2   Identifying and investigating areas of concern

It is important to decide whether an activity amounts to a trade. Depending on the circumstances, the profit or gain on a transaction may, if not caught under Schedule DI, be assessable under another income tax Schedule or Case, or be assessable as a capital gain, or quite simply exempt tax altogether.

Also the whole issue of whether an individual can claim that he is trading under Schedule D or is assessable under Schedule E on his earnings raises significant issues concerning the information that the individual presents to the Revenue. The Revenue will consider closely the evidence to see whether it supports a Schedule D or Schedule E assessment.

In addition another area of concern is the allowability of expenditure. In computing the taxable trading income, the taxpayer will present information of expenses paid that he considers allowable and the Revenue will have to satisfy themselves that these are amounts validly expended in accordance with the legislation for the purpose of the trade. The main areas of concern are covered in paragraph 2 below.

1.3   Subject matter

The type of goods involved in a transaction is relevant in deciding whether the transaction concerns an investment (in which case it is capital in nature and not subject to Schedule D Case I) or goods for the private use of the individual (or his family) or stock in trade. Normally, to be considered as an investment, the goods must either be income producing (such as land or shares) or liable to be held for aesthetic reasons (such as works of art). So, for example, when an individual acquired 1,000,000 rolls of toilet paper and resold them at a profit he was held not to have acquired and resold an investment and consequently was judged to have made a trading profit (Rutledge v CIR, 1929).

1.4   Length of period of ownership

As a general rule the longer the period between acquisition and disposal of assets the greater the likelihood that the resale will not be treated as a trading transaction. Care must be taken in applying this principle and in particular the nature of the assets has to be taken into account. For instance, it would be necessary to hold land for far longer than quoted shares to obtain the benefit of this rule, since normally the market in land operates much more slowly than that in shares.

1.5   Frequency of similar transactions

A single transaction may be enough for a person to be regarded as trading, as was seen in the toilet rolls case above, but the more often similar transactions are entered into the more likely they will be regarded as trading activities. Again the nature of the assets involved is important. In Salt v Chamberlain (1979) the taxpayer was held to be trading on the evidence of over 200 Stock Exchange sales and purchases over a period of three years. But in Pickford v Quirke (1927) the director of a spinning company was engaged in buying the shares of a mill-owning company and then causing it to sell its assets (asset stripping). One transaction of this kind might have been regarded as capital in nature but when he had done the same thing four times over he was held to be trading.

1.6   Supplementary work on assets before resale

If work is done on an asset before it is sold this may indicate a trade. In Cape Brandy Syndicate v CIR (1921) the purchase of brandy in bulk and subsequent blending and re-casking before resale was held to be a trade.

1.7   Circumstances in which the assets were acquired

An individual who deliberately purchases goods is more likely to be regarded as trading than one who acquires them accidentally, for example by inheritance or by gift.

1.8   Motive

The more obvious an individual's intention to profit from a transaction the more likely it is that it will be viewed as trading. When the comedian, Norman Wisdom, purchased a large quantity of silver bullion as a hedge against devaluation of sterling, the profit resulting from its resale was regarded as a trading profit. The Court of Appeal held that the motive for the transaction was to make a profit in sterling terms and that, since it could not be characterised as an investment, it was a trading profit.

It is important to appreciate, however, that the absence of a profit motive does not **of itself** preclude the transaction from being treated as trade.

2   COMPUTING TAXABLE TRADING INCOME

2.1   Introduction

(a)   Schedule D Case I profit is rarely the same figure as the profit shown in a trader's profit and loss account, although accounting profit before tax is the starting point for the series of adjustments that are normally necessary. The adjustments that need to be made to move from accounting profit to taxable profit are of four types, as follows:

- expenditure that has been charged in the profit and loss account but which tax law prevents from being an allowable deduction;

- income taxable under Schedule D Case I that has not been included in the accounts;

- expenditure that is deductible for tax purposes but not charged in the profit and loss account; and

- profits taken into the profit and loss account that are not subject to Schedule D Case I.

The first two types of adjustment increase the Schedule D Case I profit and the second two reduce it.

(b)   Before considering the adjustments in detail two important points need to be emphasised. Firstly, it is only an individual's Schedule D Case I profit that is being calculated. The fact that an item of income (such as interest received) is excluded does not mean that it is not taxable; only that it is not taxable under Schedule D Case I. Secondly, the starting point for all adjustments is the principles of normal commercial accountancy. These apply unless overridden by tax law (derived either from statute or decided cases).

2.2   Deductible and non-deductible expenditure

Non-deductible expenditure (also known as disallowable expenditure) is by far the most common form of adjustment to accounts. The necessary adjustments reflect a series of principles which are examined below.

(a)   **Expenditure not incurred 'wholly and exclusively' for trading purposes**

Such expenditure may be disallowed because it is too remote from the purposes of the trade (the remoteness test) or because it has more than one purpose and one of them is not trading (the duality principle).

Expenditure is regarded as being too remote from the trade when it is incurred in some other capacity than that of a trader. The leading case in this area remains Strong & Co of Romsey Ltd v Woodifield (1906) in which the company paid damages to an individual injured by a collapsing chimney at an inn which it owned. The House of Lords held that the payment was not allowable for tax purposes because the taxpayer paid it in its capacity of property owner rather than as part of its trade of innkeeping.

The duality principle is also best illustrated by decided cases. In Caillebotte v Quinn (1975) a self-employed person was unable to eat lunch at home and claimed the extra cost as a tax deduction. It was held that the expenditure was not allowable. The duality of purpose lay in the fact that the taxpayer needed to eat to live, not just to work! Similarly, in Mallalieu v Drummond (1983), a female barrister was refused a tax deduction for her expenditure on the black clothing necessary for court appearances. It was held that the expenditure had been for her personal needs as well as professional ones.

Although there is this general principle that prohibits the deduction for tax purposes of expenditure that has a dual purpose, in practice some types of expenditure, notably on cars, is apportioned between the amounts that relate to business and private use, with the business element treated as being allowable.

(b)   **Subscriptions and donations**

The treatment of subscriptions and donations follows both the 'wholly and exclusively' rule set out above and various pieces of legislation.

Subscriptions and donations to political parties are generally not deductible.

Trade or professional association subscriptions are normally deductible since they will be made wholly and exclusively for the purposes of the trade.

A charitable donation must meet three tests to be allowable. Firstly, it must be 'wholly and exclusively' for trading purposes (for example promoting the business' name). Secondly, it must be local and reasonable in size in relation to the donor's business. Thirdly, it must be made to an educational, religious, cultural, recreational or benevolent organisation.

Non-charitable gifts are not allowable except as set out below.

(c)   **Capital expenditure**

Expenditure on capital assets is not allowed in computing Schedule D Case I profits, so any amount charged in the form of depreciation, loss on sale of fixed assets or lease amortisation must be added back to profit for tax purposes. Similarly the profit on sale of a fixed asset should be deducted from the accounting profits.

Adjustments are also necessary, when expenditure is on the borderline between what might be regarded as revenue and capital expenditure. Most commonly this occurs in distinguishing between repairs expenditure (treated as revenue expenditure and so allowable) and renewals expenditure (treated as capital expenditure and so disallowed). The distinction between repairs and renewals expenditure for tax purposes is based on a few important cases.

The cost of initial repairs to an asset are not deductible where they are necessary to make it serviceable for the trade (Law Shipping Co Ltd v CIR, 1923). But the cost of initial repairs is deductible if the assets can be put into use before the repairs are carried out, if they are to make good normal wear and tear and the purchase price was not reduced to take account of the necessary repair work (Odeon Associated Theatres v Jones, 1971).

Other than initial repairs the principal source of dispute is the treatment of restoration costs. Here the principle to be applied is whether the restoration renews a subsidiary part of an asset (in which case it is an allowable repair to the larger asset) or whether it is the renewal of a separate asset (in which case it is treated as non-allowable capital expenditure. So, for example, the replacement of a factory chimney was held to be a repair to the factory (Samuel Jones & Co (Devondale) Ltd v CIR, 1951) but the replacement of an old stand with a new one at a football club was held to be expenditure on a new asset and thus disallowable capital expenditure (Brown v Burnley Football and Athletic Club Ltd, 1980).

Expenditure on certain categories of capital assets such as plant and machinery or industrial buildings attract tax allowances known as capital allowances (see following chapter). Capital allowances are deductible as if they were a trading expense.

(d)   **Entertaining and gifts**

Expenditure on gifts and entertainment needs to be looked at in terms of the recipient.

Small gifts, normally but not exclusively, to customers (with a cost of not more than £10 per recipient) are allowable provided that firstly, the gift is not of food, drink, tobacco or vouchers exchangeable for goods and secondly, the gift carries a conspicuous advertisement for the donor. The cost of gifts which do not meet these restrictive conditions are disallowed unless they are to charities (examined above) or to employees. Gifts to employees will normally be allowable in the hands of an employer but will usually result in an income tax charge to an employee under the benefits in kind rules (looked at in an earlier chapter).

Despite the fact that they might not be regarded as being made wholly and exclusively for the purposes of the trade, gifts to UK educational establishments of articles either manufactured by the donor or used in his trade are allowable, provided that they either would qualify as plant or machinery in the hands of the educational establishment or did qualify in the hands of the donor. In most cases no adjustment to the accounts will be necessary because no income will have been credited (for a manufactured article) and any cost charged in the profit and loss account will be allowed. However, the donor is obliged to make a specific claim by 31 January following the year of assessment in whose basis period the gift was made.

Entertainment expenditure is disallowed. The only exception is for expenditure relating to an employer's staff, provided it is not merely incidental to the entertainment of others.

(e)   **Legal and professional charges**

Legal and professional charges are allowable provided that they are incurred in connection with the trade and are not related to capital items. So, for example, the following commonly met types of professional charge are allowed:

- legal fees to collect trade debts
- charges incurred in defending title to fixed assets

Using the same principle, the following are not deductible:

- Fees incurred when acquiring new fixed assets
- (For companies) fees arising as a result of issuing new share capital

The principle of allowing or disallowing professional fees by relating them to the type of expenditure with which they are connected is broken in the case of fees incurred in obtaining loan finance. Fees and other incidental costs of obtaining loan finance are specifically allowable.

(f)   **Appropriations**

Appropriations are the withdrawal of funds from a business's profits rather than expenses incurred in earning them. The obvious examples are charges described as a proprietor's salary, or interest on capital invested in the business. Similarly any private element of expenditure relating to a proprietor's car, telephone and so on is also disallowed under this heading.

Other items commonly found in a profit and loss account also count as appropriations rather than expenses. These are notional expenses (in the sense that they do not represent money spent by the business) such as general provisions against doubtful trade debts and stocks. In contrast, writing off a trade debt or stock and specific provisions against them are allowable (on the grounds that they represent a best estimate of an actual cost to the business). Consequently, when making adjustments to the figure of accounting profits in respect of write offs of, or provisions against, trade debts and stocks, all that needs to be done is to add back any increase or deduct any decrease in the **general** provision that has occurred during the course of the year. Bad debts that are not trade debts are not allowable (which includes debts to employees).

(g)   **Charges on income**

Charges on income are deducted for tax purposes from all income. Consequently, in computing Schedule D Case I income, they must be added back to the figure of accounting profit. Common examples are royalties and interest on long term business loans. Remember that the amount deductible for charges against total income is the amount paid in the period (rather than the amount accrued in the accounts which is added back in the Schedule D Case I computation).

(h)   **Interest payable**

Interest on short term borrowings such as business account overdrafts, credit cards or hire purchase contracts is allowable on an accruals basis and thus no adjustment is needed to the accounts. It was noted above that long term interest is allowed as a charge, not as a Schedule D Case I expense.

Interest on overdue tax is never allowable and likewise repayment supplement is not taxable.

(i)   **Pre-trading expenditure**

Pre-trading expenditure is specifically deductible by statute (since it might otherwise fall foul of the wholly and exclusively rule). Provided that the expense is of a kind that would have been deductible had the trade been carried on at the time, pre-trading expenditure incurred in the seven years before the trade begins is allowable. The expenditure is treated as though it had been incurred on the first day of trade.

(j)   **Other items**

The items dealt with above are the more important ones that you are likely to meet in the course of adjusting expenditure charged in a trader's accounts. Set out below is a list of some other items you may meet and a brief description of how to treat them. Although most are items that appear to fall foul of the 'wholly and exclusively' rule or 'revenue not capital' rule, they are nevertheless allowable due to a specific statutory or case law rule.

Type of expenditure	Treatment in computation	Notes
Compensation for loss of office	Allow	Only if for benefit of trade
Cost of contributing to expenses of agent handling payroll deductions for charity	Allow	
Contributions to approved local enterprise agency	Allow	
Contributions to business links - which provides a single point of access for all key local business support agencies	Allow	
Cost of registering patents and trademarks	Allow	
Cost of seconding employees to charities	Allow	
Counselling services provided in the UK for redundant employees	Allow	
Damages paid	Allow	Only if paid in connection with trade matter
Defalcations	Allow	Only if by employee, not a director or proprietor
Educational courses	Allow	Only if for trade purposes
Fines	Disallow	Unless parking fines incurred on business by employee (not director or proprietor)
Payment that constitutes a criminal offence	Disallow	
Payments made in response to threats, menaces, blackmail and other forms of extortion	Disallow	
Pension contributions to an approved pension scheme	Allow	Provided paid (not accrued) by the year end
Removal expenses	Allow	Provided not an expansionary move or expenses relating to personal move of proprietor

Salaries accrued at year end	Allow	Provided paid not more than nine months after year end
Travelling expenses to trader's place of business	Disallow	Unless trader has no fixed place of business
Waste disposal site preparation or restoration costs	Allow	

2.3   Income taxable under Schedule D Case I but not included in accounts

This adjustment is normally needed only when a trader removes goods from the business for his own use. So, for example, if a car dealer removes a vehicle from stock to become his own vehicle he may not have recorded it as a sale. Nevertheless in computing Schedule D Case I profits he must include the market value of the vehicle as income (and likewise is entitled to a deduction for its purchase cost).

2.4   Deductible expenditure not charged in the profit and loss account

(a)   There are two common types of expenditure that fall into this category. The first concerns a premium paid for a short lease. A trader is entitled to deduct a proportion of the amount assessable on his landlord in his trading accounts. This will not be reflected in his accounts, however, since the cost of the lease will be reflected in an annual amortisation charge. The adjustments for the lease are thus to add back the amortisation charged in the accounts (disallowable as capital) and deduct the proportion of the Schedule A charge (which does not feature in the accounts at all).

The Schedule A charge assessable on the landlord is

	£
Premium	X
less: $2\%(n-1) \times$ premium	(X)
	X

where n =   duration of lease in years

The allowable deduction is the Schedule A charge spread evenly over the period of the lease.

(b)   The second example is rentals on finance leases that have been capitalised in the trader's accounts in accordance with SSAP 21. The trader's accounts will show a depreciation charge for the capitalised asset and an interest charge that is the part of the lease rental that represents a finance charge. Both these need to be added back and the lease payments, which did not appear in the profit and loss account, are deducted.

2.5   Profits recognised in the accounts but not charged under Schedule D Case I

These tend to fall into three categories as follows:

(a)   capital receipts (which may be subject to capital gains tax for individuals or corporation tax for companies);

(b)   income taxed other than under Schedule D Case I (such as rents charged under Schedule A, interest received under Schedule D Case III or income taxed at source); and

(c)   income that is exempt from tax (notably repayment supplement).

Such receipts must be deducted from the figure for accounting profit. Amounts that are subject to income tax must then be included elsewhere in an individual's personal income tax computation.

2.6   Activity

You are presented with the accounts of Mr Cornelius for the year to 31 December 1998, as set out below. Mr Cornelius runs a small printing business and wishes to know the amount of his Schedule D Case I profit.

	£	£
Gross profit on trading account		25,620
Profit on sale of premises		1,073
Building society interest received		677
		27,370
Advertising	642	
Staff wages	12,124	
Rates	1,057	
Repairs and renewals	2,598	
Car expenses	555	
Bad debts	75	
Telephone	351	
Heating and lighting	372	
Miscellaneous expenses	347	
Depreciation - printing presses	1,428	
- office equipment	218	
- Mr Cornelius' car	735	
		20,502
Net profit before tax		6,868

Notes:

(1)   Staff wages includes an amount of £182 for a staff Christmas lunch.

(2)   Mr Cornelius' car is used 75% for business purposes and 25% for private purposes.

(3)   Repairs and renewals comprises the following expenditure:

	£
Refurbishing second hand press before use in the business	522
Redecorating administration offices	429
Building extension to enlarge paper store	1,647
	2,598

(4)   Miscellaneous expenses included:

	£
Subscription to Printers' Association	45
Contribution to local Enterprise Agency	50
Gifts to customers - calendars costing £7.50 each	75
- 2 food hampers	95

(5)   The profit on the sale of premises relates to the sale of a small freehold industrial unit in which Mr Cornelius used to store paper before building his extension.

(6)   The charge for bad debts was made up as follows:

	£
Write off of specific trade debts	42
Increase in general provision for bad debts	50
	92
Less: recovery of bad debt previously written off	17
Charge to profit and loss account	75

Calculate Mr Cornelius' Schedule D Case I income

2.7   Activity solution

Mr Cornelius - Schedule D Case I income - Year ended 31 December 1998

		£
Net profit before tax		6,868
Add: Disallowable expenditure		
repairs and renewals (522 + 1,647)	2,169	
car expenses (555 × 25%)	139	
bad debts	50	
gifts to customers (food hampers)	95	
depreciation (1,428 + 218 + 735)	2,381	
		4,834
		11,702
Less: Income not chargeable under Schedule D Case I		
profit on sale of premises	1,073	
interest received	677	
		1,750
Schedule D Case I income		9,952

Notes:

(1)   The expenditure on the Christmas lunch is allowable in the hands of the employer. Provided it is not excessive it will not produce a benefit in kind in the hands of employees.

(2)   Refurbishment of the second hand press is disallowed on the grounds that the expenditure was necessary before it was brought into use in the business. The extension of the stockroom created a new asset and was not the repair of part of an existing one.

(3)   Car expenses represent a common instance of apportioning an expense between business and private use. In practice such apportionment of car expenses is permitted by the Revenue, although there is a general rule against apportionment (the duality principle) which prevents apportionment in many cases.

(4)   Gifts to customers are disallowed unless they amount to £10 or less per customer during the year and display a conspicuous advert for the business. Gifts of food (or drink or tobacco) are disallowed irrespective of their cost.

3   **BASIS PERIODS AND TAX YEARS**

3.1   **Introduction**

(a)   Income tax is charged for tax years (also known as fiscal years or years of assessment) that run from 6 April to the following 5 April. Since traders normally do not make up their profit and loss accounts to coincide with the tax year there needs to be a system for attributing profits earned in a period of account to a particular tax year. Both Schedule D Case I and Schedule D Case II use the same method and so for simplicity they are both referred to here as Schedule D Case I.

(b)   The profit-earning (or loss-making) period that is attributed to a particular tax year is known as the 'basis period' for that tax year.

3.2   **Extensions to trade**

A taxpayer is taxed on the results of a particular trade and if he carries on more than one trade they are assessed separately. The concept of a trade is important throughout tax law but is particularly so when dealing with losses (see later chapter) and extensions to a trade.

The question of whether new activities constitute an extension of an existing trade or the start of a new one is one of fact. Its importance lies in the fact that the profits or losses of an extension of an existing trade are amalgamated with those of current activities but where there is a new trade the commencement rules of assessment apply. Sometimes the amalgamation of two trades is treated as the cessation of both and the commencement of a third. For example, this was treated as occurring when two individuals set up in partnership; one of them had formerly had a trade of contracting for the processing of films and the other a trade of film processing. Although the trades appear similar it was decided that the merged business carried on by the partnership was not an extension of either of the former trades (George Humphries & Co v Cook, 1934).

3.3   **Apportionment on a daily basis**

In paper 7, apportionment of Schedule D Case I profits, losses and capital allowances for income tax businesses is performed on a daily rather than monthly basis.

The ACCA will provide you with a calendar as given below to help you calculate any daily apportionments required. Note that you are expected to ignore the fact that there are 29 days in February in a leap year.

Month	No of days	Month	No of days
January	31	July	31
February	28	August	31
March	31	September	30
April	30	October	31
May	31	November	30
June	30	December	31

4   **ASSESSMENT ON THE CURRENT YEAR BASIS - ONGOING YEAR RULES**

4.1   **The basic principles**

The basic rule is that the profits for a year of assessments are the adjusted profits shown by the accounts ending in that year.

4.2   Example

Jerry prepares accounts to 30 September annually. He commenced trading on 6 April 1997. His profits for the 2 years to 30 September 2000 were:

	£
Year to 30 September 1999	20,000
Year to 30 September 2000	22,000

These form the basis for the assessable amounts for 1999/2000 and 2000/01:

	£
1999/2000 (Year to 30.9.99)	20,000
2000/01 (Year to 30.9.2000)	22,000

5   CURRENT YEAR BASIS - OPENING YEAR RULES

5.1   Introduction

There are special provisions to deal with the opening and closing years.

The basis of assessment in the opening years is normally as follows:

Year 1	Actual profits from commencement to 5 April

Year 2   Either:

(a)   Where there is an accounting date in the year, the 12 months ending on that accounting date; or

(b)   Where there is an accounting date in the year that is not preceded by 12 months of profits, the first 12 months from the commencement date; or

(c)   Where there is no accounting date in the year, the fiscal basis applies.

Year 3   12 months ending with the accounting date in the year.

The following examples illustrate the three possible situations that can arise in Year 2. Remember that any apportionments have to be made on a daily basis.

5.2   Example 1

Arthur commenced trading on 1 July 1997. He prepared accounts to 30 June each year. His adjusted trading profits for the first two years were as follows:

	£
Year ended 30.6.98	24,000
Year ended 30.6.99	28,000

The Schedule DI assessable amounts are as follows

		£
1997/98		
(1.7.97 - 5.4.98)		
24,000 × 279/365		18,345
1998/99 (see note)		
(year to 30.6.98)		24,000
1999/2000		
(year to 30.6.99)		28,000

Note. Because there is an accounting date which is preceded by 12 months of profits in the year, the assessment is the 12 months ending on that accounting date (rule (a)).

5.3   Example 2

Edwina commenced trading on 1 July 1997. She prepared accounts to 31 March 1999 and annually thereafter. Her adjusted trading profits for the first two periods were as follows:

	£
21 months ended 31.3.99	42,000
Year ended 31.3.2000	27,000

The Schedule DI assessable amounts are as follows:

		£
1997/98		
(1.7.97 - 5.4.98)		
42,000 × 279/639		18,338
1998/99 (see note)		
(year to 31.3.99)		
42,000 × 365/639		23,991
1999/2000		
(year to 31.3.2000)		27,000

Note. There is an accounting date in the second year of assessment which is preceded by 12 months of profits, so the assessment is the 12 months ending on that accounting date (rule (a) again). Note that it doesn't matter whether the 12 months preceding the accounting date form the whole or part of an accounting period.

5.4   Example 3

Pattie commenced trading on 1 September 1997. She prepared accounts to 30 June 1998 and annually thereafter. Her adjusted trading profits for the first two periods were as follows:

	£
10 months ended 30 June 1998	30,000
Year ended 30 June 1999	48,000

The Schedule DI assessable amounts are as follows:

	£
1997/98	
(1.9.97 - 5.4.98)	
30,000 × 217/303	21,485
1998/99 (see note)	
(1.9.97 - 31.8.98)	
30,000 + (62/365 × 48,000)	38,153
1999/2000	
(year to 30.6.99)	48,000

Note. Because the accounting date ending in the second year of assessments is not preceded by 12 months of profits, the assessment is the first 12 months of profits from the date of commencement (rule (b)).

5.5   Example 4

Cordelia commenced trading on 1 July 1997. She prepared accounts to 30 April 1999 and annually thereafter. Her adjusted trading profits for the first two periods were as follows:

	£
22 months ended 30.4.99	55,000
Year ended 30.4.2000	32,000

The Schedule DI assessable amounts are as follows:

	£
1997/98	
(1.7.97 - 5.4.98)	
55,000 × 279/669	22,937
1998/99 (see note)	
(6.4.98 - 5.4.99)	
55,000 × 365/669	30,007
1999/2000	
(year to 30.4.99)	
55,000 × 365/669	30,007

Note. Because there is no accounting date in the second year of assessment, the assessment is the profits for the period 6.4.98 to 5.4.99 - the fiscal basis (rule (c)).

5.6   Overlap profits

In each of the above four opening year examples it can be seen that some of the profits have been included in the assessable amounts for more than one year. The portion of profits which were assessed in more than one year are known as the 'overlap profits'.

The overlap profits are carried forward and are ultimately deducted from the assessable amount for the period in which the business ceases (see below) to equalise the profit earned with the profits taxed over the life of the business. Relief may not therefore be obtained for many years if the business continues for a long while.

Example 5

The assessable amounts for the first two years in example 1 were:

		£
1997/98		
(1.7.97 - 5.4.98)		
24,000 × 279/365		18,345
1998/99		
(year to 30.6.98)		24,000

The overlap profits which were assessed twice are those of the period 1.7.97 - 5.4.98 ie, 24,000 × 279/365 = £18,345.

Example 6

The assessable amounts for the first two years of trading in example 2 were:

		£
1997/98		
(1.7.97 - 5.4.98)		
42,000 × 279/639		18,338
1998/99		
(year to 31.3.99)		
42,000 × 365/639		23,991

In this case there are only 5 days of overlap profits (1.4.98 - 5.4.98) ie, 5/639 × 42,000 = £329. (Check: £18,338 + £23,991 − £42,000 = £329.)

Example 7

The assessable amounts for the first three years in example 4 were:

		£
1997/98		
(1.7.97 - 5.4.98)		
55,000 × 279/669		22,937
1998/99		
(6.4.98 - 5.4.99)		
55,000 × 365/669		30,007
1999/2000		
(year to 30.4.99)		
55,000 × 365/669		30,007

The overlap profits are those of the period 1.5.98 - 5.4.99 ie, 55,000 × 340/669 = £27,952. (Check: £22,937 + £30,007 + £30,007 − £55,000 = £27,951 ie, overlap profits within error for rounding.)

6   CHANGE OF ACCOUNTING DATE

6.1   Introduction

Provided certain conditions are met, a self-employed person is allowed to change his or her accounting date. There may be tax advantages in doing so, or the change may be made for commercial reasons. For example, it may be easier to take stock at certain times of the year.

6.2   Conditions to be met

A change in accounting date will only be valid if the following conditions are met:

(a)   The change of accounting date must be notified to the Inland Revenue on or before 31 January following the tax year in which the change is to be made.

(b)   The first accounts to the new accounting date must not exceed 18 months in length.

If the period between the old accounting date and the proposed new accounting date is longer than 18 months, then two sets of accounts will have to be prepared.

(c)   There must not have been another change of accounting date during the previous five tax years.

This condition may be ignored if the Inland Revenue accept that the present change is made for genuine commercial reasons. Not surprisingly, obtaining a tax advantage is not accepted as a genuine commercial reason.

6.3   Failure to meet the conditions

If the conditions are not met, the old accounting date will continue to apply. If accounts are made up to the new accounting date, then the figures will have to be apportioned accordingly.

6.4   Calculation of assessable profits

If the conditions are met, then the basis period for the tax year in which the change of accounting date is made will either be less than or more than 12 months in length.

6.5   Basis period of less than 12 months

Where the period between the end of the previous basis period and the new accounting date is less than 12 months, the basis period will be the 12 month period ending with the new accounting date.

Because this will result in some profits being assessed more than once, overlap profits will arise. These will be carried forward and offset in exactly the same way as overlap profits arising upon the commencement of trading.

6.6   Example: Basis period of less than 12 months

Andrea, a sole trader, has always made up her accounts to 31 March. She decides to change her accounting date to 30 June by making up accounts for the three month period to 30 June 1998. Andrea's tax adjusted profits are as follows:

	£
Year ended 31 March 1998	60,000
Three months to 30 June 1998	20,000
Year ended 30 June 1999	85,000

The Schedule D1 assessable amounts will be as follows:

		£
1997/98	Year to 31.3.98	60,000
1998/99	12 month period to new accounting date of 30.6.98	
	Year to 31.3.98 60,000 × $^{274}/_{365}$	45,041
	Period to 30.6.98	20,000
		65,041
1999/2000	Year to 30.6.99	85,000

The profits of £45,041 taxed in 1998/99 are overlap profits, since they were also taxed in 1997/98. They will be carried forward and would normally be offset when Andrea ceases trading.

If Andrea had instead made up accounts for the 15 month period to 30 June 1999, then the total assessable profits for 1998/99 and 1999/2000 would have been the same. Suppose the tax adjusted profit for the 15 month period ended 30 June 1999 is £105,000:

		£
1997/98	Year to 31.3.98	60,000
1998/99	12 month period to new accounting date of 30.6.98	
	Year to 31.3.98 60,000 × $^{274}/_{365}$	45,041
	Period to 30.6.99 105,000 × $^{91}/_{456}$	20,954
		65,995
1999/2000	Year to 30.6.99 105,000 × $^{365}/_{456}$	84,046

The basis period for 1998/99 is to the new accounting date of 30 June, since there are no accounts made up to a date in 1998/99. Overlap profits are still £45,041.

6.7   Basis period of more than 12 months

Where the period between the end of the previous basis period and the new accounting date is more than 12 months, then that period becomes the basis period.

Because the basis period is more than 12 months, it will be possible to offset a corresponding proportion of any overlap profits that arose upon the commencement of trading.

6.8   Example: Basis period of more than 12 months

Peter, a sole trader, commenced trading on 1 July 1995, and has always made up his accounts to 30 June. He has now decided to change his accounting date to 30 September by making up accounts for the 15 month period to 30 September 1998. Peter's tax adjusted profits are as follows:

		£
Year ended 30 June 1996		18,000
Year ended 30 June 1997		24,000
Period ended 30 September 1998		30,000
Year ended 30 September 1999		36,000

The Schedule D1 assessable amounts will be as follows:

			£
1995/96	1.7.95 to 5.4.96		
	$£18,000 \times {}^{279}\!/_{365}$		13,759

The profits of £13,759 are overlap profits and the overlap period is 279 days.

1996/97	Year to 30.6.96	18,000
1997/98	Year to 30.6.97	24,000

1998/99	15 month period to 30.9.98	30,000
	Less: Overlap profits $13,759 \times {}^{92}\!/_{279}$	4,537
		25,463

1999/2000	Year to 30.9.99	36,000

In 1998/99 profits for 15 months are assessed. Because the normal basis of assessment is that only 12 months profits are assessed, Peter is allowed to offset 3 months (92 days) worth of his overlap profits that arose when he commenced trading. These overlap profits are for a period of 279 days, so the offset is based on a fraction of ${}^{92}\!/_{279}$.

7   CURRENT YEAR BASIS - CLOSING YEAR RULES

7.1   Introduction

The basis of assessment in the closing years is as follows:

Closing year   Actual profit from the end of the basis period of the previous year of assessment until cessation.

Deduct any unrelieved overlap profits

7.2   Example 8

Michael commenced trading on 1 May 1997. After trading profitably for some years, he ceased trading on 31 March 2005. His adjusted trading profits for the final three periods are as follows:

	£
Year ended 30.4.2003	40,000
Year ended 30.4.2004	42,000
Period ended 31.3.2005	38,000

Assume his overlap profits (for the period 1.5.97 - 5.4.98) were £27,000

The Schedule DI assessable amounts are as follows:

		£
2003/04		
(year to 30.4.2003)		40,000
2004/2005		
(23 months from 1.5.2003 to 31.3.2005)		
(42,000 + 38,000)		80,000
Less overlap profits		27,000
Final assessable amount		53,000

8   CURRENT YEAR BASIS - TREATMENT OF CAPITAL ALLOWANCES

Capital allowances are treated as a trading expense of the accounting period.

This can be illustrated as follows:

	£
Adjusted profits for year ended 31.3.99	X
Less: capital allowances (basis period y/e/ 31.3.99)	(X)
DI profit for year ended 31.3.99	X

This amount will be assessed in 1998/99.

9   AVERAGING RELIEF FOR FARMERS

9.1   Introduction

(a)   Compare two businesses that each earn profits over two years of £40,000. One earns £20,000 each year and the other £40,000 in the first year and £nil in the second. The second business pays more tax than the first because there is a liability to higher rate tax in year one whereas the first business doesn't pay tax above the basic rate in either year.

(b)   Farmers are particularly vulnerable to volatile changes in the profitability of their businesses from year to year due to good or bad weather. Consequently, they are entitled to a special relief that protects them from the effects of higher rate tax in the sort of circumstances described above.

9.2   Principles of averaging relief

(a)   The relief is available to farmers and market gardeners, either trading alone or in partnership. It comes fully into play when one of two consecutive year's profits is 70% or less of the other's, although there is a more restrictive form of the relief that becomes available when one of the two year's profits drops to 75% or less of the other's. The profits figure on which the comparison is made is the tax-adjusted figure but before taking into account loss relief of any kind. It is not available in the first or last tax year of trade.

(b)   Once a profit figure has been subject to averaging it is used for all tax purposes.

(c)   Where averaging has occurred the later year's result (after averaging) can be compared with the next year's result and, if it meets the criteria, re-averaged. However, the earlier year cannot be reaveraged with the year that preceded it, so the practical consequence is that when dealing with several years the earliest year of the series is taken first (subject to the time limit mentioned below).

(d)   The farmer or market gardener must specifically claim the relief by 31 January following the end of the later tax year affected.

9.3   Mechanics of the relief

(a)   Where one of two consecutive years profits is 70% or less of the other the profits of both are adjusted to the average of the two. If one of the years is loss making it is treated as zero and so both years are treated as making half the profits of the other year.

(b)   The adjustment for the restrictive form of the relief, which operates when the lower of the profits of two consecutive years is more than 70% but not more than 75% of the higher is a little more cumbersome. An amount, computed from the expression set out below, is added to the lower profits and deducted from the higher.

The expression is:

$3(H-L) - 3H/4$, where

H is the higher profits; and
L is the lower profits.

9.4   Activity

Smith is a market gardener who commenced trading on 1 May 1995 and prepared his first accounts to 31 October 1995, tax-adjusted profits as follows:

Year to 31 October 1996	£16,500
Year to 31 October 1997	£25,500
Year to 31 October 1998	£29,150
Year to 31 October 1999	£22,000

Calculate the final assessments for all years affected by the above results, assuming that any possible averaging claim is made within the appropriate time limit.

9.5   Activity solution

The profit for 1996/97 (£16,500) is less than 70% of that for 1997/98 (£25,500) and so the full averaging procedure applies, as follows.

		£
1996/97		16,500
1997/98		25,500
		42,000
£42,000/2 =		21,000

Thus £21,000 is the final assessable amount for 1996/97 but the averaged profit for 1997/98 may be averaged again with 1998/99.

The averaged profit of £21,000 for 1997/98 is greater than 70% but less than 75% of the 1998/99 profit figure (£29,150). Thus partial averaging applies.

The adjustment to be made is calculated as:

3(29,150 - 21,000) -(3/4 × 29,150)   = £2,588.

The final assessable amount for 1997/98 is thus £23,588 (21,000 + 2,588) and that for 1998/99 is £26,562 (29,150 - 2,588).

Since the adjusted profit for 1999/2000 (£22,000) is more than 75% of the averaged 1998/99 assessment, no further averaging is currently possible (although averaging of 1999/2000 and 2000/2001 may be possible when the adjusted profit for the year ending 31 October 2000 is known).

10   CHAPTER SUMMARY

(a)   Schedule D Case I tax is chargeable only on the profits of trade, but since 'trade' is defined by statute in a circular fashion it has been left to the Courts to define the limits of what is considered to be trading activity.   The Courts look at the overall outcome from the following tests:

Test	*Comment*
(i) What type of goods are the subject matter of the transaction?	If of a type normally traded rather than held as an investment, it implies trading.
(ii) How long were the goods owned?	The shorter the period of ownership the more likely that trading is taking place.
(iii) How many transactions of a similar kind have there been?	The more transactions there have been, the more likely it will be treated as trading.
(iv) Has there been any supplementary work done to the goods?	Supplementary work increases the likelihood that the activity will be treated as trading.
(v) In what circumstances were the goods sold?	A person who has deliberately acquired goods is more likely to be treated as trading than one who acquires them by gift or inheritance.
(vi) What was the motive behind the transaction?	The more obvious an individual's intention to profit from a transaction the more likely that it will be treated as trading.

Remember that it is the **overall** impression from these tests that determines whether or not an activity is treated as trading, not the result of one test in isolation.

(b)   A series of adjustments are normally needed to a trader's accounting profit to calculate his profit taxable under Schedule D Case I. The adjustments are of four types:

(i)   expenditure charged in the profit and loss account that is disallowed in computing Schedule D Case I tax. Such adjustments may arise because the expenditure is not allowed for tax purposes at all (such as on entertaining) or relief is given in some other way (such as interest on long term loans allowable as a charge on income).

(ii)   income taxable under Schedule D Case I that is not recognised in the accounts. This normally concerns stock removed by a proprietor for his own use (treated as a sale at market value for tax);

(iii)   deductible expenditure under Schedule D Case I that is not charged in the profit and loss account. Such adjustments are relatively rare and occur most often when a trader deducts a proportion of the amount assessable on his landlord for the lease of his business premises; and

(iv)   profits recorded in the profit and loss account that are not subject to Schedule D Case I, such as capital receipts, income taxed in another way and exempt income.

(c)   Because businesses do not normally make up accounts for years coinciding with the tax year, a system is needed to link a period of account with a tax year.

Businesses are taxed on the current year basis with special rules in opening year's.

(d)   Averaging relief for farmers allows farmers (and market gardeners) to average the tax profits (before loss relief) of two adjacent years if one of them is 70% or less of the other. A more restricted form of relief applies where the smaller profit is between 70% and 75% of the higher.

11   SELF-TEST QUESTIONS

11.1   How is a trade defined for tax purposes? (1.1)

11.2   What are the six badges of trade? (1.1)

11.3   What are the four types of adjustment needed to calculate Schedule D Case I from accounting profit? (2.1)

11.4   What are the two tests used to decide whether or not expenditure is incurred wholly and exclusively for trading purposes? (2.2)

11.5   What types of item tend to be recognised as profit in accounts but are not charged to tax under Schedule D Case I? (2.5)

11.6   How is a business assessed in the closing years? (7.1)

11.7   What is the expression used to calculate the adjustment to a farmer's (or market gardener's) profits when the profits of one tax year are between 70% and 75% of those of an adjacent year. (9.3)

12   EXAMINATION TYPE QUESTION

12.1   Holly

The following is the profit and loss account of Holly who has carried on business for many years in the UK as a wholesale supplier of consumer goods for the home market.

Profit and loss account - Year ended 30 November 1998

	£	£		£
Wages		33,500	Gross profit	85,353
NI contributions (staff)		5,000	Sale proceeds of	
Rent		2,343	typewriter	240
Business rates		496	Interest on Government	
Insurance (premises & stock)		243	securities (gross)	1,540
Light and heat		1,101		
Motor car expenses		1,380		
Advertising		840		
Holly - speeding fine		150		
Depreciation				
Equipment	866			
Motor car	1,200	2,066		
Bad and doubtful debts		623		
Trade expenses		11,549		
Income tax (Schedule D)		12,800		
Professional charges		2,284		
Net profit		12,758		
		87,133		87,133

(a)   25% of the car mileage relates to private use.

(b)   Bad or doubtful debts

	£		£
Bad debts written off		General provision on	
as irrecoverable	438	debtors at 1.12.97	535
General provision		P & L account	623
2% on debtors at 30.11.98	720		
	1,158		1,158

(c)   Trade expenses

	£
Stationery	2,250
Printing	3,350
Subscriptions	
Political party	200
Trade association	500
Entertaining customers	2,249
Redecoration of offices	3,000
	11,549

(d)   Professional charges

	£
Accountancy	1,712
Debt collecting	332
Legal charges re renewal of lease for 21 years	240
	2,284

(e)   Holly has taken goods from the business for his own use during the year, but no entry has been made in the books of account. The goods cost £1,350. Holly's normal mark-up on such goods is 40% on cost.

(f)   Holly resides over the business premises and $\frac{1}{3}$ of rent and light and heat relates to private use. Holly paid a lease premium of £4,000 on 7 February 1998 for renewal of his lease for 21 years, determinable by either party after each period of 7 years. No entry was made in the profit and loss account for this item.

You are required to compute the adjusted Schedule D Case I trading profit for the year ended 30 November 1998.

13   ANSWER TO EXAMINATION TYPE QUESTION

13.1   Holly

Adjustment of trading profits - y/e 30.11.98

	− £	+ £
Net profit per accounts		12,758
Rent $\frac{1}{3} \times 2,343$		781
Light and heat $\frac{1}{3} \times 1,101$		367
Motor car expenses $\frac{1}{4} \times 1,380$		345
Holly - speeding fine		150
Depreciation		2,066
Increase in provision for doubtful debts		185
Subscriptions - Political party		200
Entertaining customers		2,249
Income tax		12,800
Goods for own use $1,350 \times \dfrac{140}{100}$		1,890
Legal fees $\frac{1}{3} \times 240$ (private use element)		80
		33,871

Less:	Proceeds of typewriter	240	
	Interest on Government securities	1,540	
	Proportion of lease premium paid		
	Assessed to Schedule A on landlord -		
	Premium	4,000	
	less: 2% $(7 - 1) \times 4,000$	(480)	
		3,520	

Annual cost to Holly

$$\frac{3,520}{7} = 503 \times \frac{2}{3} \times \frac{297}{365}$$

	−	+
	273	2,053
Adjusted Schedule D Case I profit		31,818

Note: it is assumed that the trade association has entered into the usual arrangement with the Revenue to pay tax on its excess income.

10 CAPITAL ALLOWANCES ON PLANT AND MACHINERY

INTRODUCTION & LEARNING OBJECTIVES

(a)   This chapter is concerned with capital allowances available to traders and others on the purchase of plant and machinery. There are, however, a number of preliminary points that need to be considered. Is the person who has incurred the expenditure eligible for capital allowance? Does the asset acquired count as plant or machinery? If it does qualify, what allowances are available and for which accounting periods are they given?

(b)   Once the rules for deciding these questions are appreciated the arithmetical calculations are fairly straight forward. Provided that the computations are laid out clearly and with an appropriate structure, the resulting figures should readily fall into place.

When you have studied this chapter you should be able to do the following:

● Identify whether capital expenditure falls within the definition of plant and machinery evolved by the Courts

● Determine whether an item is included in any of the types of expenditure deemed to be plant by specific pieces of legislation

● Allocate expenditure to the general pool, the car pool or specific items as appropriate

● Identify whether expenditure qualifies for first year allowance, and calculate the allowance.

● Calculate writing down allowances on the basis of the unrelieved expenditure available and restrict the allowances where particular rules make this relevant

● Deal with disposals of plant and machinery and calculate the balancing charge or balancing allowance that may arise

● Apply the rules for determining the circumstances in which balancing allowances occur

● Restrict the allowances given where the asset in question is an expensive car or an asset used partly for private purposes by the trader

● Calculate capital allowances applying to assets acquired by hire purchase

● Calculate capital allowances on long life assets

1 ELIGIBILITY

1.1 Qualifying assets

Capital allowances are given at statutory rates on qualifying expenditure on certain fixed assets. The allowances are not only given on original cost, but also on all subsequent qualifying expenditure of a capital nature which has been disallowed in the adjusted profits computation (eg, improvements). Contributions towards cost received from public, government, or local authority sources must be deducted from the cost to obtain the expenditure eligible for capital allowances.

The allowances are available for expenditure on:

(a)   plant and machinery;
(b)   industrial buildings and structures;
(c)   qualifying hotels;
(d)   agricultural buildings and works; and
(e)   patents and know-how.

Plant and machinery is considered in this chapter and the other categories in the following chapter.

1.2   Who may claim capital allowances

Capital allowances are available to persons who:

(a)   buy and use capital assets (as indicated above) in a trade or profession assessable under Schedule D Case I or II, or in an employment the income from which is assessable under Schedule E;

(b)   receive royalty income from patents or rent from industrial or agricultural property; or

(c)   receive rent from unfurnished lettings of property (other than (b) above) and incur expenditure on plant used for property maintenance.

1.3   Mechanism for giving relief

(a)   Capital allowances are given as a trading expense in calculating the Schedule D Case I profit. It is therefore the net figure that is used when using the current year basis period rules described in an earlier chapter.

(b)   Capital allowances are given for each period of account instead of for a tax year. Where there is a short or long period of account, the writing down allowance (25% pa for plant) is contracted or expanded on a pro rata basis. First year allowances are not contracted or expanded for short or long periods of account. However, if the period of account exceeds eighteen months it must be divided, for capital allowance purposes into a 12 month period of account and a second period of account to deal with the remaining months.

1.4   Activity

Grace commenced trading on 1 August 1998. Results, adjusted for income tax purposes but before capital allowances, have been as follows:

	£
Year ended 31 July 1999	25,500
Year ended 31 July 2000	30,000

On 9 July 1999 she bought machinery for £6,000.

Calculate the amounts assessable under Schedule D Case I for 1998/99 and 1999/2000.

1.5   Activity solution

Capital allowances for 12 months ended 31 July 1999 are £1,500 (£6,000 × 25%)

Schedule D Case I amounts assessable.

	£
1998/99	
1.8.98 - 5.4.99 248/365 × (25,500 − 1,500)	16,307
1999/2000	
y/e 31.7.99 (25,500 − 1,500)	24,000

Note: If the first period of account was instead for the 14 month period to 30 September 1999, the capital allowances would be £1,751 (£6,000 × 25% × 426/365).

2   MEANING OF PLANT AND MACHINERY

2.1   Introduction

There is no statutory definition of plant except that it includes vehicles and ships.   The most informative definition was given in the case of Yarmouth v France (1887).   Plant was said to include

> Whatever apparatus is used by a businessman for carrying on his business - not his stock-in-trade which he buys or makes for sale - but all goods and chattels, fixed or moveable, live or dead, which he keeps for permanent employment in his business.

This is obviously a very far-reaching definition.   It includes not only the obvious items of plant and machinery, but also such items as moveable partitions, office furniture and carpets, heating installations, motor vehicles, computers, lifts and any expenditure incurred to enable the proper functioning of the item such as reinforced floors or air conditioning systems for computers.

2.2   The Courts' interpretation of 'plant'

(a)   The original definition of plant in **Yarmouth v France** provides a good starting point but has been refined by the Courts.   In particular, the test that has been applied is a **functional** one.   It asks, is the item simply part of the setting or premises **in which** the trade is carried on or is it something **with which** the trade is carried on?   If it is part of the setting or premises it is not plant, and thus no capital allowances are available, but if it fulfils a function it is plant.

(b)   The dividing line between an asset that is functional and one that is merely part of the setting in which the trade is carried on is not always clear.   Examples below show how the Courts have reacted to claims for capital allowances in these circumstances.

  (i)   In Dixon v Fitch's Garage Ltd, a canopy covering petrol filling pumps was held to be part of the setting and not plant and machinery.   (It did not assist in serving petrol to customers.)

  (ii)   In Hampton v Fortes Autogrill Ltd, false ceilings in a restaurant were held not to be plant.   (All it did was to hide unsightly pipes.)

  (iii)   In Cooke v Beach Station Caravans Ltd, swimming pools at a caravan park were held to be plant and machinery - the caravan park as a whole was the setting.

  (iv)   In Jarrold v John Good & Sons Ltd, moveable partitioning in an office was held to be plant and machinery.

2.3   Assets deemed to be plant

There are various types of expenditure that would not be thought of as plant using the approach set out above but are treated as plant by specific legislation.   These are:

(a)   thermal insulation in an industrial building;

(b)   cost of complying with fire regulations;

(c)   expenditure to comply with regulations on safety at sports grounds;

(d)   expenditure on a security asset which is one used to counter a threat to an individual's security that arises due to the trade involved. Some items are excluded from being treated as security assets notably cars and dwellings;

(e)   cost of alterations to buildings needed for the installation of plant;

(f)   expenditure on acquiring computer software outright or under licence (to the extent that it is capital rather than revenue expenditure).

On disposal the first four categories above are treated as being sold for nothing which means that no balancing charge can arise. Balancing charges are considered later in the chapter.

2.4   Clarification on the meaning of plant

There is no general statutory definition of plant for tax purposes. The Finance Act 1994 introduced provisions with the intention of making the issue clearer by providing that land, buildings and structures cannot be plant. In particular the provisions give detailed lists of items associated with buildings which are part of the building and not plant. However, it is not intended that expenditure on buildings and structures which specific decisions of the courts have shown to be plant should cease to qualify.

3   CALCULATING THE ALLOWANCES

3.1   Pooling expenditure

(a)   Generally, the cost of all plant and machinery purchased by a trader becomes part of a *pool of expenditure* on which capital allowances may be claimed. When an addition is made, the pool increases; on disposal the pool is reduced by the sale proceeds.

(b)   Exceptionally, certain items are not included in the pool. They are:
   • motor cars;
   • assets with private usage by the proprietor; and
   • expenditure incurred on **short-life** plant where an election to de-pool is made.

These exceptional treatments are dealt with below.

3.2   First year allowances (FYA)

(a)   Expenditure on plant and machinery by small and medium sized businesses in the period 2 July 1997 to 1 July 1999 qualifies for FYAs.

(b)   A business is small or medium sized if it satisfies two of the following three criteria:

   • turnover does not exceed £11.2 million;
   • assets do not exceed £5.6 million;
   • there are not more than 250 staff;

or if it was small or medium sized the previous year.

(c)   FYAs are given at the rate of 50% on expenditure between 2 July 1997 and 1 July 1998 and at the rate of 40% for expenditure between 2 July 1998 and 1 July 1999. Thus if expenditure of £8,000 is incurred on the purchase of new plant on 11 October 1998, FYAs of £8,000 @ 40% = £3,200 are available.

(d)   Expenditure on which FYAs are given is **not** added to the pool of expenditure in the year in which it is incurred. Instead the expenditure, net of the FYA is added to the pool of expenditure at the start of the following year. This ensures that FYAs and WDAs are not both given in the same year on the same expenditure.

(e)   A trader may claim (in his income tax return) the whole or only part of the allowance to which he is entitled. If only part of the available FYAs are claimed, then the expenditure is treated as if part qualified for FYAs, and the remainder did not. Thus if, in (c) above, the trader claimed FYAs of £2,400 then $\frac{2,400}{3,200} \times £8,000 = £6,000$ is treated as expenditure qualifying for FYAs, and the balance of £8,000 – £6,000 = £2,000 is treated as expenditure not qualifying for FYAs.

(f)   No FYA may be claimed in the final period of trade.

(g)   Where a new trade is being established capital expenditure incurred before it starts is treated as being made on the first day of trade. However, it is the actual date of expenditure which determines whether FYA is available.

3.3   Writing down allowances (WDA)

(a)   An annual WDA of 25% is given on a reducing balance basis by reference to the unrelieved expenditure in the pool brought forward at the beginning of the year (ie, cost of all pool assets less allowances already given against the pool, including expenditure incurred in the previous year on which FYAs were given, less those FYAs) adjusted for additions and disposals during the year. The WDA is given on the allowable cost in the year of purchase.

(b)   Looking at a proforma helps to understand how the WDA is calculated. Suppose that Brian has been trading for several years preparing accounts to 31 December each year, and has a balance of unrelieved expenditure brought forward at 1 January 1998.

	Pool £
Unrelieved expenditure b/f, say	50,000
Less: Disposal proceeds	14,000
	36,000
WDA @ 25%	9,000
Unrelieved expenditure c/f to 1 January 1999	27,000

(c)   The important point to note is when in the sequence the WDA is available on assets disposed of during the year. Their disposal proceeds are deducted first from the pool balance. Note that if the disposal proceeds for any asset are greater than its original cost, the amount deducted from the pool is limited to **original cost**.

(d)   Next the WDA is calculated on the balance remaining after excluding disposals.

(e)   No WDA may be claimed in the final period of trade.

(f)   If the profits basis period for a tax year is less than 12 months long the WDA is scaled down proportionately. This rule affects the first tax year of a new business (where it is based on less than 12 months of profits) and companies' accounting periods that are shorter than 12 months.

(g)   Where a new trade is being established capital expenditure incurred before it starts is treated as being made on the first day of trade.

(h)   An individual may claim (in his income tax return) the whole or only part of the allowance to which he is entitled. If a partial claim is made in one year, WDAs in subsequent years will be calculated on a higher figure than if the allowances had previously been claimed in full, but as a consequence relief for the expenditure incurred will be delayed.

3.4   Expenditure on plant and machinery: notification

No claim for FYA or WDA in respect of expenditure on plant or machinery may be made unless the expenditure is notified to the Inspector within two years of the end of the chargeable period to which the claim relates.

3.5   Length of ownership in the basis period

The WDA is never restricted by reference to the length of ownership of an asset in the basis period.

3.6   Activity

Bertram commenced trading on 1 January 1998, preparing accounts to 31 December annually. He purchased the following items of machinery:

1 November 1998	cost £2,000
1 April 1999	cost £8,700 (plus cost of installation £300)
1 March 2000	cost £4,000
1 December 2002	cost £5,875

Compute the capital allowances for the years ended 31 December 1998 to 31 December 2003.

3.7   Activity solution

	Expenditure qualifying for FYA £	Pool £	Allowances £
Year ended 31 December 1998			
Additions - Cost 1 November 1998	2,000		
FYA - 40%	800		800
Written down value (WDV) c/f		1,200	
Year ended 31 December 1999			
WDA - 25%		300	300
		900	
Additions - Cost 1 April 1999			
(8,700 + 300)	9,000		
FYA 40%	3,600		3,600
		5,400	3,600
Total allowances			3,900
WDV c/f		6,300	
Year ended 31 December 2000			
Addition - Cost 1 March 2000		4,000	
		10,300	
WDA - 25%		2,575	2,575
WDV c/f		7,725	
Year ended 31 December 2001			
WDA - 25%		1,931	1,931
WDV c/f		5,794	

Year ended 31 December 2002

Addition - Cost 1 December 2002	5,875	
	11,669	
WDA - 25%	2,917	2,917
WDV c/f	8,752	

Year ended 31 December 2003

WDV - 25%	2,188	2,188
WDV c/f	6,564	

Year ended 31 December 2004

WDV - 25%	1,641	1,641
WDV c/f at 31.12.2004	4,923	

3.8   Sale of plant

(a)   Where plant is sold during the basis period the disposal value is deducted from the balance of unrelieved expenditure in the pool. The WDA for the year is then calculated on the resultant figure (ie, pool brought forward less sale proceeds of current year disposals). The normal rule is that the sale proceeds must be deducted from the pool after bringing in acquisitions not qualifying for FYA in the same basis period but **before** calculating the WDA.

(b)   The disposal value deducted from the pool must never exceed the original cost of purchasing the asset. An excess of proceeds over original cost may be charged to capital gains tax, but not income tax. Thus on a disposal always deduct from the pool the lower of the disposal value and the original cost.

3.9   Activity

Sandy commenced trading on 1 October 1995, preparing accounts to 30 ~~June~~ September annually. In the year to 30 September 1999 the following transactions took place.

30 December 1998	Plant sold (originally purchased for £4,000) for £800
20 August 1999	Plant purchased for £2,000

Compute the capital allowances for the year ended 30 September 1999 assuming that the pool balance on 1 October 1998 was £4,900.

3.10   Activity solution

	Pool £	Allowances £
Year ended 30 September 1999		
Pool balance b/f at 1.10.98	4,900	
Additions not qualifying for FYA - 20 August 1999	2,000	
	6,900	
Less: Sale proceeds - 30 December 1998	800	
	6,100	
Less: WDA - 25%	1,525	1,525
Pool WDV c/f at 30.9.99	4,575	

3.11   Balancing charges

(a)   If, on disposal of an asset in the pool, disposal proceeds exceed the pool balance brought forward, the excess allowances previously given will be recovered and charged to tax by means of a balancing charge.

(b)   If expenditure qualifying for FYA has been incurred during the period, the trader may choose to claim less than the full FYA so as to avoid a balancing charge since the expenditure on which FYA is not claimed is included in the pool of expenditure.

(c)   A balancing charge is treated as an addition to the Schedule D Case I profits and the capital allowances are deducted from the total.

3.12   Activity

Nelson commenced trading on 1 July 1995, preparing accounts to 30 June annually. In the year ended 30 June 1999 he had the following transactions

1 July 1998	Sold plant (originally purchased for £6,000) for £6,200
1 January 1999	Purchased new plant for £2,500

The balance in the pool of plant at 1 July 1998 was £4,000.

Compute the capital allowances available for the year ended 30 June 1999, if any.

3.13   Activity solution

(a)   **Full FYA claimed**

	Expenditure qualifying for FYA £	Pool £	Allowances £
Year ended 30 June 1999			
Pool balance b/f at 1.7.98		4,000	
Less: Sale proceeds 1 July 1998:			
limited to cost		6,000	
Balancing charge		2,000	(2,000)
Expenditure qualifying for FYA	2,500		
FYA @ 40%	1,000		
			1,000
WDV c/f		1,500	

(b)   **20% of FYAs claimed**

	Expenditure qualifying for FYA £	Pool £	Allowances £
Year ended 30 June 1999			
Pool balance b/f at 1.7.98		4,000	
Additions not qualifying for FYA:			
1 January 1999 80% of £2,500		2,000	
		6,000	
Less: Sale proceeds 1 July 1998:			
limited to cost		6,000	
		-	
Additions qualifying for FYA:			
1 January 1999 40% × £2,500	500		
FYA @ 40%	200		200
WDV c/f		300	

3.14   Balancing allowances

(a)   The basic idea underlying capital allowances is that over the life of a business a trader will obtain relief for the total cost less subsequent sale proceeds of his plant. Where the trade is permanently discontinued and there is still a balance of unrelieved expenditure in the pool (ie, a balance after deducting final sale proceeds), the trader is entitled to claim relief for that unrelieved balance by means of a balancing allowance (it is effectively a last year allowance).

(b)   To summarise

   •   The only time a balancing allowance will arise in the general pool is in the period of account at the end of which the trade is permanently discontinued.

   •   A balancing allowance is computed by reference to the excess of the pool balance at the end of the final period of account over the sale proceeds received on ultimate disposal of the plant.

   •   No FYA or WDA are available for the period of account, the cost of any additions being merely added in. This is logical, since relief for unrelieved expenditure will be given by means of a balancing allowance instead.

3.15   Example

Joad prepares accounts to 5 April annually. He ceased to trade on 5 April 1999, on which date he sold the whole of his plant for £10,000. The balance in the pool at the beginning of the final period of account (ie, on 6 April 1998) was £14,000 and he had purchased plant in June 1998 for £5,000.

Compute the balancing allowance for the year ended 5 April 1999.

3.16   Solution

	£
Pool balance b/f	14,000
Addition during year	5,000
	19,000
Less: Sale proceeds	10,000
Balancing allowance for the year ended 5 April 1999	9,000

3.17   Assets acquired by hire purchase and leased assets

(a)   The essence of a **hire purchase** contract is that on making the final payment the payer becomes the asset's legal owner. Although the payer only hires the asset beforehand this is effectively ignored for capital allowances purposes and he is treated as though he had bought the asset in the first place. Consequently:

- the hire purchase interest is treated as a trading expense of the period of account in which it accrues (and is deductible in computing Schedule D Case I profits);

- the full cash price of the asset is brought into the pool in the period of first use; and

- capital allowances are made on the full cash price irrespective of the actual instalments paid in the period of account.

(b)   Legal title to **leased assets** remains with the lessor. The lessee (the user of the asset) is hiring it and this is reflected in the tax treatment. Lease payments are treated as deductible, on an accruals basis, in computing Schedule D Case I profits and no capital allowances are available to the lessee.

4   CARS AND ASSETS WITH PRIVATE USE BY TRADER

4.1   Cars costing £12,000 or less

(a)   The cost of acquisition of a car is put into a separate **car pool**, unless the cost of the car exceeds £12,000, or the car is used for private as well as business purposes by the owner.

(b)   The expenditure does not qualify for FYA, even if acquired in the period 2 July 1997 to 1 July 1999.

(c)   If there is a balance brought forward on the car pool the cost of acquisition is added before dealing with disposals or computing the WDA. This rule ensures that balancing charges are avoided or minimised where acquisitions and disposals occur in the same period of account.

(d)   The 'car pool' is deemed to be a separate trade for the purposes of capital allowances so that if all the cars in the pool are disposed of the 'trade' ceases and a balancing allowance or balancing charge must be computed.

4.2   Cars costing more than £12,000

(a)   The cost of a car where it exceeds £12,000 (£8,000 before 11 March 1992) must not be brought into either the general or car pool. The capital allowances on each such car must be separately computed.

(b)   FYAs are not available on expenditure on cars.

(c)   The WDA is restricted to a maximum, in one year period of account, of £3,000 (£2,000 for cars bought before 11 March 1992). Once the car has been written down to below £12,000 the WDA will be computed in the normal way (ie, 25% of written down value) but the car remains in its separate column of the computation. It must not be brought into the general or car pool.

(d)   Each pool (car) is deemed to be a separate trade so that when the car is sold a balancing allowances or charge must be computed on the difference between the written down value and the sale proceeds.

4.3   Private use of an asset by the owner

Where an asset is used by the proprietor/owner partly for business and partly for private purposes (eg, a motor car), only a proportion of the available FYAs and WDAs is given. This proportion is computed by reference to the percentage of business use to total use. Where an asset is used partly privately, the following rules must be followed in computing the allowances available and the allowances given

(a)   The cost must not be brought into the general or car pool, but must be the subject of a separate computation (in the same way as a car costing over £12,000).

(b)   The written down value of the asset is based on its full cost but only the business proportion of any allowance (FYA or WDA) is actually given.

(c)   On disposal of the asset, a balancing adjustment is computed by comparing sale proceeds with the written down value (if a profit, there is a balancing charge and vice versa). Having computed the balancing adjustments, the amount assessed or allowed is then reduced to the business proportion.

(d)   Where the asset concerned is an 'expensive' car WDAs are first restricted to the £3,000 limit (for written down values still over £12,000) and then the business proportion of £3,000 is actually given as an allowance.

(e)   Private use by an employee of an asset owned by the business has no effect on the business's entitlement to capital allowances (although there will normally be a benefit-in-kind charge on the employee).

4.4   Activity

Mr Fish prepared annual accounts to 30 September. As at 1 October 1997 the following written down values were brought forward for capital allowance purposes

	£
General pool (of plant)	12,500
Car (costing £7,000 in May 1997) with 30% private use by Fish	5,250

Subsequently the following additions and disposals of plant and machinery were made

Additions   3.6.98 Car, cost £14,000 (no private use)
12.6.98 Car, cost £7,500 (no private use)
12.9.98 Car, cost £9,000 (no private use),
purchased on HP for 8 quarterly payments of £1,300
commencing on 12.9.98.

Disposals   1.1.98 Milling machine sold for £4,300 (original cost £11,000)
1.1.99 Car purchased May 1997 sold for £2,750

Mr Fish claims maximum allowances.

Compute the capital allowances available for the years ended 30 September 1998 and 30 September 1999.

4.5   Activity solution

	General pool £	Car pool £	Expensive Car £	Car with 30% private use £	Allowances £
Year ended 30 September 1998					
WDV b/f at 1.10.97	12,500			5,250	
Acquisitions (6.98, 9.98)		16,500	14,000		
	12,500				
Disposal of plant (1.98)	4,300				
	8,200				
WDA - 25%	2,050	4,125	3,000		9,175
			(max)		
- 25%				1,313 (70%)	919
WDV c/f at 30.9.98	6,150	12,375	11,000	3,937	10,094
Year ended 30 September 1999					
Disposal of car (1.99)				2,750	
Balancing allowance				1,187 (70%)	831
WDA - 25%	1,537	3,094	2,750		7,381
WDV c/f at 30.9.99	4,613	9,281	8,250		8,212

5   **SUMMARY OF COMPUTATIONAL TECHNIQUE**

(a)   Bring forward unrelieved expenditure from the previous year for

    (i)   the general pool
    (ii)   the car pool
    (iii)   cars costing over £12,000 (£8,000 before 11.3.92) (separate column for each)
    (iv)   assets used partly privately (separate column for each).

(b)   Add, in the appropriate column, costs of items acquired not qualifying for FYAs.

(c)   Deduct, in the appropriate column, the sale proceeds (or cost if lower) of any assets disposed of during the period, calculating the balancing charge where one arises (or balancing allowance in the case of (iii) and (iv) only.

(d)   Compute the WDAs available (restricting to £3,000 (£2,000) pa each in the case of expensive cars), and then reduce for any private use by the owner.

(e)   Compute the FYAs available on expenditure qualifying for FYA, and then reduce for any private use by the owner.

6   **ELECTION FOR DE-POOLING OF SHORT-LIFE ASSETS**

6.1   **The election**

(a)   The election is designed to enable traders to accelerate capital allowances on certain short-life machinery or plant, where it is the intention to sell or scrap within five years of acquisition.

(b)   An election must be made by 31 January following the year of assessment containing the end of the period of account in which the expenditure was incurred and is irrevocable.

(c)   Any plant and machinery can constitute a short-life asset, except, principally:

    •   motor cars;
    •   assets with private use; and
    •   ships.

6.2   **Computations**

(a)   The treatment of short-life assets corresponds in most respects to that applied to motor cars costing over £12,000 and assets with private use. Thus:

    •   each short life asset is the subject of a separate computation; and
    •   FYAs and WDAs are given under the normal rules; and
    •   on disposal within five years a separate balancing allowance is given or balancing charge arises.

(b)   However, unlike the treatment of expensive cars and assets with private use, if no disposal has taken place by the fourth anniversary of the end of the period of account in which the acquisition took place, the unrelieved balance is transferred back to the general pool in the first period of account following that anniversary. This ensures that no tax advantage arises from making the election where it ought not, in retrospect, to have been made.

6.3   Activity

Tango prepared annual accounts to 30 June. At 1 July 1997 he had a general pool of qualifying expenditure of £8,000. On 1 August 1997 he purchased two microcomputers with peripheral hardware for £6,000 each. Tango's policy is to replace computers every two to three years. One computer was sold for £200 on 20 September 2000 but the other was still in use at 30 June 2002. Short life asset elections were made in respect of both computers.

Calculate the capital allowances available to Tango for all the years ended 30 June 1998 to 30 June 2003.

6.4   Activity solution

	General pool £	Short life assets No 1 £	No 2 £	Allowances £
Year ended 30 June 1998				
WDV b/f at 1.7.97	8,000			
WDA - 25%	2,000			2,000
	6,000			
Additions - microcomputers:		6,000	6,000	
FYA - 50%		3,000	3,000	6,000
		3,000	3,000	8,000
Year ended 30 June 1999				
WDA - 25%	1,500	750	750	3,000
	4,500	2,250	2,250	
Year ended 30 June 2000				
WDA - 25%	1,125	563	563	2,251
	3,375	1,687	1,687	
Year ended 30 June 2001				
Disposal proceeds (20.9.2000)		200		
Balancing allowance		1,487		1,487
WDA - 25%	844		422	1,266
	2,531		1,265	2,753
Year ended 30 June 2002				
WDA - 25%	633		316	949
	1,898		949	
Year ended 30 June 2003				
Transfer of short life asset to qualifying pool	949		949	
	2,847			
WDA - 25%	712			712
WDV c/f at 30.6.2003	2,135			

Notes:

(a)   The disposal of one microcomputer within the short life period has resulted in full allowances being given during the period of use in the business (1 August 1997 - 20 September 2000).

(b)   Since the other microcomputer is used beyond its anticipated short life, the unrelieved balance is transferred over to the general pool immediately after the fourth anniversary of the end of the period of account in which it was acquired.

7   CAPITAL ALLOWANCES ON LONG LIFE ASSETS

7.1   Introduction

Finance Act 1997 has introduced provisions to bring the tax treatment of long life assets more closely into line with normal accountancy practice. The rules appear below and apply to assets acquired on or after 26 November 1996.

7.2   The rules

(a)   Writing down allowances of 6% per annum on the reducing balance basis will be given on machinery and plant which has an expected working life when new of 25 years or more. Allowances are calculated by pooling all such expenditure.

(b)   If the expenditure is incurred in the period 2 July 1997 to 1 July 1998, first year allowances of 12% will be available. (Note that the 40% FYA rate for expenditure between 2 July 1998 and 1 July 1999 on general plant is **not** available on long life assets.)

(c)   These rules will not apply where expenditure on long life assets does not exceed a *de minimis* limit of £100,000 per year.

The limit applies to companies, individuals and to partnerships.

(d)   If a long life asset is sold for less than its tax written down value in order to accelerate allowances, it will be treated as sold for its tax written down value.

8   FIXTURES IN BUILDINGS WHICH QUALIFY AS MACHINERY AND PLANT

8.1   Introduction

Capital allowances are available for fixtures in buildings. Finance Act 1997 has corrected certain defects in the rules. The current rules apply to expenditure on or after 24 July 1996.

8.2   Current position

(a)   Provisions have been introduced which

- prevent allowances from being given on fixtures both as machinery and plant and under some other category eg, enterprise zones or scientific research

- limit allowances given on fixtures as machinery and plant in total to the original cost of the fixture, and

- if a fixture is sold for less than its tax written down value in order to accelerate allowances, treat it as sold at the tax written down value.

(b)   The purchaser and vendor of a building may make a joint election determining how much of the sale price relates to the fixtures.

9   CHAPTER SUMMARY

(a)   Capital allowances are available only for capital expenditure on certain types of fixed asset. The most important of these is plant and machinery. Allowances are given as a trading expense in computing the Schedule D Case I profits for traders and from Schedule E income of employees (where applicable).

         For Schedule D Case I businesses they are given for periods of account by reference to transactions in that period of account.

(b)   Most plant and machinery expenditure is pooled. The principal exceptions are cars costing over £12,000, assets partly used privately by the proprietor and assets for which a 'short-life' election has been made. Cars costing £12,000 or less are pooled but in a separate pool of their own.

(c)   First year allowances at the rate of 50% are available to small and medium sized businesses in respect of expenditure incurred in the period 2 July 1997 to 1 July 1998. This has been extended a further year to give FYAs at 40% on expenditure between 2 July 1998 and 1 July 1999.

(d)   Writing down allowances at the rate of 25% are calculated on the pool balance brought forward plus purchases not qualifying for first year allowances less disposal proceeds (or original cost if lower).

(e)   For a non-12 month period of account WDA is reduced or increased proportionately. The time during a period of account after an asset is purchased is never relevant in calculating the amount of allowance due.

(f)   Balancing charges arise whenever disposal proceeds (or original cost, if lower) exceed the balance on the pool. In contrast balancing allowances occur only when there is an unrelieved pool balance when trade ceases (or is deemed to have ceased on the disposal of any asset whose capital allowances are calculated individually).

(g)   An election can be made to de-pool plant and machinery (other than, principally, cars and assets with private use). An asset not disposed of by the fourth anniversary of the end of the period of account in which it was acquired is then transferred to the general pool at its written down value (and thus the benefit of the election is lost).

(h)   Long life assets, ie, those with an expected working life of at least 25 years qualify for writing down allowances of only 6% pa (unless the £100,000 demininis limit is not exceeded). Expenditure between 2 July 1997 and 1 July 1998 qualifies for 12% FYA, if incurred by a small or medium sized business.

10   SELF-TEST QUESTIONS

10.1   Who may claim capital allowances? (1.2)

10.2   How is relief for capital allowances given to unincorporated traders? (1.3)

10.3   What distinction does the functional test make in determining whether an asset qualifies as plant or not? (2.2)

10.4   What assets are specifically deemed to be plant by legislation? (2.3)

10.5   What expenditure qualifies for first year allowances? (3.2)

10.6   On what amount are writing down allowances calculated? Is the taxpayer required to use his entitlement? (3.2)

10.7   When plant is sold what are the alternative amounts that may be deducted from unrelieved expenditure? (3.7)

10.8   In what circumstances do balancing allowances arise? (3.14)

10.9   How are allowances calculated on assets used partly for private purposes by the trader? (4.3)

10.10   How does the calculation of capital allowances on short-life assets differ from that of 'normal' assets? (6.2)

10.11   In what circumstances are writing down allowances reduced to 6%? (7.2)

11   EXAMINATION TYPE QUESTION

11.1   Baldy

Baldy has been trading for many years in Barnet, preparing accounts to 31 December annually.

His general pool of unrelieved expenditure on plant and machinery brought forward on 1 January 1997 was £7,000.

In the two years ended 31 December 1998 the following transactions took place.

Year ended 31 December 1997

10 May 1997	Sold two lorries (purchased for £8,450 each) for £2,500 each. Purchased two replacement lorries for £5,250 each.
1 Nov 1997	Purchased plant costing £9,000
1 Dec 1997	Purchased two cars costing £6,600 each. It is agreed with the Inland Revenue that one of the cars is used 30% for private purposes by Baldy.

Year ended 31 December 1998

1 Nov 1998	Purchased plant costing £1,000 40%
18 Nov 1998	Purchased two cars costing £5,200 each (used wholly for business purposes)
1 Dec 1998	Sold both cars purchased in December 1997 for £2,000 each.

You are required to compute the capital allowances available to Baldy for the years ended 31 December 1997 and 31 December 1998.

12   **ANSWER TO EXAMINATION TYPE QUESTION**

12.1   **Baldy**

Baldy - capital allowances on plant and machinery

	General pool	Car pool	Car(30%) private use	Total allowances
	£	£	£	£	£
Year ended 31 December 1997				
Balance b/f at 1.1.97	7,000			
Additions not qualifying for FYA				
10.05.97 Lorries	10,500			
1.12.97 Motor cars		6,600	6,600	
Sale proceeds - lorries	(5,000)			
	12,500			
WDA (25%)	3,125	1,650	1,650 (× 70%)	5,930
	9,375	4,950	4,950	
Additions qualifying for FYA				
1.11.97 Plant	9,000			
FYA (50%)	4,500			4,500
	4,500			
WDV c/f at 31.12.97	13,875	4,950	4,950	10,430
Year ended 31 December 1998				
Additions not qualifying for FYA				
18.11.98 Motor cars		10,400		
		15,350		
Sale proceeds 1.12.98		(2,000)	(2,000)	
		13,350	2,950	
Balancing allowance			(× 70%)	2,065
WDA (25%)	3,469	3,338		6,807
	10,406			
Additions qualifying for FYA				
1.11.98 Plant	1,000			
FYA (40%)	400			400
	600			
				9,272
WDV c/f at 31.12.98	11,006	10,012		

11 CAPITAL ALLOWANCES ON INDUSTRIAL BUILDINGS AND MISCELLANEOUS ASSETS

INTRODUCTION & LEARNING OBJECTIVES

Allowances on plant and machinery were dealt with in the previous chapter. This chapter considers the other principal categories of asset for which capital allowances are available.

When you have studied this chapter you should be able to do the following:

- Decide whether a building will qualify under the statutory definition of an industrial building or qualifying hotel

- Calculate the proportion of expenditure incurred that is eligible for industrial buildings allowances

- Decide whether the initial allowance is available on a particular item of expenditure and if so decide the rate of allowance

- Decide whether a writing down allowance may be made in respect of a particular period of account and calculate it when appropriate

- Determine whether a sale of an industrial building gives rise to a balancing adjustment

- Calculate the balancing charge or allowance arising on sale and deal with the different calculations required when the building has been used throughout its period of use for industrial purposes, and when non-industrial use has occurred.

- Judge whether allowances are available to a purchaser of a used industrial building and, where appropriate, calculate them

- Determine whether particular expenditure qualifies for capital allowances as expenditure on agricultural buildings and works

- Be able to compute the capital allowances due to both the seller and purchaser of an agricultural building when it is sold

- Calculate allowances due to and charges arising on owners of patent rights and know-how

- The implication of the capital goods scheme on industrial buildings allowances.

1 INDUSTRIAL BUILDINGS

1.1 Definition of an industrial building

Specifically, the Capital Allowances Act 1990 states that buildings used for a variety of specific purposes qualify as industrial buildings. The more important of these are:

(a) a trade carried on in a mill, factory or similar premises,

(b) a trade which consists in the manufacture of goods or materials or the subjection of goods or materials to any process,

(c)   a trade which consists in the storage of

- goods or materials used for manufacturing purposes, or which are to be subjected to any process, or

- finished goods or materials which have been manufactured or subjected to any process.

In addition, the following structures are also industrial buildings:

(a)   any building or structure provided by the person carrying on one of the above trades for the welfare of the employees and in use for that purpose, eg, a canteen or workplace nursery

(b)   a drawing office used for the preparation of plans for manufacturing or processing operations etc (CIR v Lambhill Ironworks Ltd)

(c)   a sports pavilion used in any trade

(d)   a building or structure in use for the purpose of a (private) toll road undertaking. The allowance is given for the cost of construction by a person with the right to charge a toll on the road

(e)   a highway undertaking (ie, an undertaking relating to the design, building, financing and operation of any roads). The allowance is given to a person with the right to receive money by reference to use of the roads

(f)   a warehouse used to store imported goods at their point of arrival in the UK

1.2   Excluded buildings

Specifically excluded from classification as industrial buildings are

(a)   dwelling houses
(b)   retail or wholesale premises
(c)   showrooms
(d)   hotels (except qualifying hotels)
(e)   offices (except offices directly involved in production).

1.3   Qualifying hotels

Provided that an hotel meets the conditions for qualification, it is treated as an industrial building qualifying for allowances.

A qualifying hotel is one that satisfies **all** the following five conditions.

(a)   The building must be a hotel (not defined).

(b)   The accommodation must be in a permanent building or buildings.

(c)   The hotel must be open for at least 4 months (120 days) in the season (1 April to 31 October each year).

(d)   When open in the season the hotel must have at least 10 bedrooms which are available for short-term letting to the public (ie, not more than 30 days per letting).

(e)   When open in the season, the services provided for guests must normally include breakfast, evening meal, room cleaning and the making of beds.

1.4   Enterprise zones

(a)   Enterprise zones have been designated for the purpose of encouraging and accelerating economic redevelopment within certain existing urban areas (eg, Inverclyde, Motherwell, Sunderland, East Durham).

(b)   Advantageous capital allowances on the cost of construction of industrial and commercial buildings in these zones form part of the package of incentives.

(c)   The buildings that qualify for IBAs (industrial building allowances) are:

- industrial buildings

- qualifying hotels

- any other commercial buildings used for trading or professional purposes. (This covers hotels that do not count as 'qualifying hotels', retail premises, and offices generally.)

- offices - whether or not they are used for trading or professional purposes.

Dwelling houses are **not** covered

(d)   The expenditure must be incurred within 10 years of the date on which the area is designated an enterprise zone if it is to rank for the enhanced allowances.

2   QUALIFYING COST OF CONSTRUCTION

2.1   Principles

(a)   Expenditure must be incurred in construction; thus the cost of the land and the incidental expenses associated with its acquisition do not rank for IBAs. However, costs of work on the land that is preliminary to construction do qualify, as follows:

- the preparation of the site in order to lay foundations; and
- cutting, tunnelling and levelling the land in connection with the construction.

(b)   Professional fees, notably those of architects, incurred as part of a construction project for an industrial building also qualify for IBAs.

(c)   Where part of a single building is not used for a qualifying purpose and the expenditure on that non-industrial part does not exceed 25% of the total qualifying cost of the whole building, then the IBAs will be given on the cost of the whole building. Conversely, if the non-industrial part costs more than 25%, IBAs will be given on the industrial part, only. For hotels, any part occupied by the proprietor or his family is treated as a 'non-industrial' part and is disqualified if it exceeds the 25% limit.

(d)   Capital expenditure on alterations to an existing industrial building also qualifies for IBAs unless the alteration is incidental to the installation of plant and machinery, in which case it ranks for plant and machinery allowances as part of the cost of the plant.

(e)   The total cost of constructing a qualifying building is eligible for IBAs (subject to the rule on non-qualifying parts of a building) if built by or for the trader. If it was acquired after construction (but before use) the eligible expenditure depends on the type of vendor. When purchased from a builder it is the purchase price (including the builder's profit margin), otherwise it is the **lower** of the purchase price and the construction expenditure incurred.

2.2   Example

Jumbo erected a factory block for use in his manufacturing business. The total price of £370,000 was apportioned as follows

	£
Freehold land (including cost of conveyancing)	60,000
Cutting and tunnelling of site	2,000
Construction of building comprising	
Factory	267,000
Employee's canteen	12,000
General offices	29,000
	370,000

2.3   Solution

The expenditure qualifying for IBAs would be as follows

	£
Total cost	370,000
Less: Land and associated legal costs	60,000
Cost of construction of whole structure	310,000

The cost of the non-qualifying part of the structure (ie, the offices) of £29,000 does not exceed 25% of the cost of the whole structure of £310,000. Therefore IBAs are available on the cost of the whole structure.

3   CALCULATING INDUSTRIAL BUILDINGS ALLOWANCES FOR A NEW BUILDING

3.1   Initial allowance

(a)   The initial allowance for general industrial buildings and hotels (but not enterprise zone buildings) was phased out in the mid 1980s. However, it was temporarily reintroduced for expenditure incurred under a contract entered into between 1 November 1992 and 31 October 1993. The rate is 20% of the eligible expenditure on the building and it was given for the basis period in which the expenditure was incurred.

(b)   The building had to be put into use as an industrial building by 31 December 1994 (at the latest) if it was to qualify for the initial allowance. If the initial allowance had already been given, but the building was not brought into industrial use by 31 December 1994, it was withdrawn.

(c)   If the expenditure is incurred before trading starts then:

*   for the purpose of deciding the basis period in which the transaction falls, the expenditure is treated as having been made on the first day of trade; but

*   for deciding whether the initial allowance is due the actual date of the expenditure decides the point.

(d)   The initial allowance for qualifying buildings located in enterprise zones is 100%. This allowance has been, and continues to be, available for such expenditure incurred outside the 12-month reintroduction of the general initial allowance. Although the special tax regime for enterprise zones lasts only ten years from the date of designation, where expenditure on industrial buildings is incurred within the 10-year time limit but the buildings are sold, unused, after the 10-year period has expired the enterprise zone IBAs remain available.

3.2   Writing down allowance

(a)   Unlike WDAs on plant and machinery, those for industrial buildings are given on a **straight line basis** on the cost of the qualifying capital expenditure. The WDA is proportionately reduced where the period of account is of less than 12 months duration and proportionately increased where the period of account exceeds 12 months.

(b)   A WDA is given provided the building is in use as an industrial building at the end of the period of account. **Temporary** disuse of an industrial building does **not** affect the allowances given but use for non-industrial purposes does. Non-industrial use is dealt with below. Unlike plant, it is possible to get both IA (where available) and WDA given for the same period of account if the building was brought into use by the end of the period of account in which the expenditure was incurred.

(c)   The rate of WDAs is 4% for industrial buildings and hotels outside enterprise zones. Normally there is no WDA for enterprise zone buildings as the full cost is relieved through the 100% IA. Where a reduced IA is taken, however, the annual WDA is 25% of qualifying expenditure, with any balance taken in the final year.

(d)   The WDA is given to the person who possesses the relevant interest at the end of the period of account.

(e)   The relevant interest in the building (eg, freehold, leasehold) is that which the person who incurred the capital expenditure was entitled to at the time the expenditure was incurred (ie, the WDA will normally go to the person who incurred the cost of construction).

3.3   Writing down period

(a)   New industrial buildings are deemed to have a tax life of 25 years from the date the building was first used. The tax life is important insofar as no balancing adjustment will arise on the sale of the building after the 25-year period has elapsed. Similarly, no allowances will be available to a purchaser of a building where its tax life has already expired.

(b)   Where use commenced before 6 November 1962 the tax life was deemed to be 50 years and the WDA was accordingly 2% of qualifying expenditure. Even where the tax WDV of such a building has been written down to nil (because of an initial allowance) a balancing charge could still arise if it is sold within its 50 year tax life.

3.4   Sales of buildings without non-industrial use

(a)   On disposal of an industrial building a balancing adjustment is computed by comparing disposal proceeds with its WDV (known as the 'residue before sale').

(b)   Where the disposal proceeds are **less** than the residue before sale a balancing allowance is given.

(c)   A balancing charge arises when the disposal proceeds are **more** than the residue before sale. The balancing charge can never exceed the allowances previously given on the building (this restriction applies where the building is sold for more than original cost). The surplus over original cost may be charged to capital gains tax.

3.5   Example

Expenditure as in the earlier example (see 2.2). The factory block was completed and paid for on 1 June 1998 and taken into use on 1 August 1998. Jumbo commenced trading on 1 April 1997 and prepared accounts to 31 March annually.

On 1 August 2002 the factory was sold for £500,000 (including £100,000 for the land) to Mumbo.

Compute the IBAs available to Jumbo for each of the years concerned.

3.6   Solution

	£	£
Year ended 31 March 1999		
Qualifying expenditure incurred 1.6.98		310,000
WDA (4%) on cost (in use 31.3.99)	12,400	
Years ended 31 March 2001 to 2002		
WDA - £12,400 pa for three years	37,200	
		49,600
WDV before sale		260,400
Year ended 31 March 2003		
Qualifying sale proceeds - 1.8.2002 - £400,000.		
Restricted to allowable cost		310,000
(no WDA: building not in use by Jumbo on 31.3.2003)		
Balancing charge (recovers all IBAs given)		49,600

3.7   Building sold after non-industrial use - for more than cost

(a)   Where an industrial building is being used for non-industrial purposes at the end of a period of account **no WDA is given**. However, the cost of the building is written down by a **notional WDA** (calculated in the normal way - but not given to the taxpayer).

(b)   If, after non-industrial use, the building is sold for more than it originally cost, any balancing charge that arises is limited to the total allowances **actually given**.

3.8   Example

Facts as in the example above, except that Jumbo used the building as retail premises between 1 March 2001 and 30 April 2002.

Calculate the balancing charge arising on disposal.

3.9   Solution

	£	*Allowances given* £
Year ended 31 March 1999		
Qualifying expenditure (1.6.98)	310,000	
WDA (4%)	12,400	12,400
	297,600	
Year ended 31 March 2000	12,400	12,400
	285,200	
Year ended 31 March 2001 - 31 March 2002 - notional WDAs		
(2 x £12,400)	24,800	-
	260,400	
Year ended 31 March 2003		
Sale proceeds - limited to cost	310,000	
Balancing charge	49,600	
Balancing charge limited to allowances given		24,800

3.10   Building sold after non-industrial use - for less than cost

Where an industrial building is sold for less than original cost, having been, for part of its tax life, not used for a qualifying industrial purpose, the balancing charge is calculated as the excess of allowances actually given over the adjusted net cost.

Adjusted net cost is 'cost minus sales proceeds' multiplied by the fraction

$$\frac{\text{Period(s) of qualifying industrial use since date of first use}}{\text{Total period of use since date of first use}}$$

3.11   Example

Mille who commenced trading on 1 December 1995 and makes up accounts to 30 November, had an industrial building constructed in the year ended 30 November 1997 at a cost of £1,000,000 (excluding land) and put it into use on 1 October 1997. During the period 1 April 1999 to 30 September 2002 the building was used for non-industrial purposes. It was subsequently used again for industrial purposes until 31 December 2008 when it was sold for £900,000.

3.12   Solution

As the building was sold for less than original cost the computation will be:

	£	£
Cost		1,000,000
WDA y/e 30.11.97 and y/e 30.11.98 - 4% × 2	80,000	
Notional WDAs y/e 30.11.99 to y/e 30.11.2001 - 4% × 3	120,000	
WDA y/e 30.11.2002 to 30.11.2008 - 4% x 7	280,000	480,000
WDV before sale (Residue before sale)		520,000

The balancing adjustment for y/e 30.11.2009 is

Net cost = £1,000,000 - £900,000 = £100,000

Adjusted net cost is then:

£

$$\text{Net cost} \times \frac{\text{Periods of qualifying use}}{\text{Period from first use to disposal}}$$

$$£100,000 \times \frac{(1.10.97 - 31.3.99) + (1.10.02 - 31.12.08)}{(1.10.97 - 31.12.08)}$$

$$£100,000 \times \frac{1 \text{ year, } 182 \text{ days} + 6 \text{ years, } 92 \text{ days}}{11 \text{ years and } 92 \text{ days}} \qquad 68,882$$

IBAs actually given £(480,000 - 120,000)   360,000

Balancing charge y/e 30.11.2009   291,118

4   ALLOWANCES FOR USED INDUSTRIAL BUILDINGS

4.1   Principles

Provided the building is to be used in a qualifying trade, a subsequent purchaser of the building (the tax life of which has not expired) is entitled to an annual WDA (having acquired the relevant interest). This annual allowance is computed as follows

$$\frac{\text{Residue of expenditure after sale}}{\text{Remaining tax life of building from date of first use}} = \text{Annual WDA}$$

The residue of expenditure after sale is the written down value of the building prior to a sale, plus any balancing charge assessed on the vendor (or minus any balancing allowance) but if this results in a figure greater than the price the purchaser paid for the building it is restricted to purchase price.

Remaining life of the building means the unexpired part of the 25 year tax life.

4.2   Example

Jones who commenced trading on 1 January 1996 makes up accounts to 31 December, sells an industrial building for £750,000 on 1 December 2003. The building was constructed for his use at a cost of £300,000 and brought into use on 1 June 1998. The residue before sale is £240,000.

Calculate the annual WDA for the purchaser.

4.3   Solution

£

Residue before sale   240,000
Add: Balancing charge (300,000 - 240,000)   60,000

Residue after sale   300,000

$$\text{Annual WDA} = \frac{300,000}{25 - 5 \text{ years } 183 \text{ days}} = £15,386$$

Note: the purchaser obtains IBAs only on the original construction price of the building (£300,000) rather than the £750,000 he paid for it.

5   AGRICULTURAL BUILDINGS AND WORKS

5.1   Introduction

This is a capital allowance on expenditure on the construction (including alterations and improvements) of qualifying works and buildings. The allowance is available to owners or tenants of agricultural land and is given to the person who incurred the expenditure.

5.2   Qualifying expenditure

(a)   The Capital Allowances Act 1990 refers to buildings and other works in the UK. These include:

> farmhouse (see below)
> farm buildings
> fences
> drainage works
> water and electrical installations
> farm cottages used by employees (need not be on the land being farmed)
> shelter belts of trees
> glasshouses on market garden land.

The cost of the land is not included.

(b)   Not more than one third of the capital expenditure on a farmhouse qualifies for relief. The proportion may be further reduced where the accommodation and amenities are not in keeping with the size and nature of the agricultural undertaking.

(c)   Improvement and other grants from local authorities or government departments must be deducted from the qualifying expenditure.

5.3   Allowances

(a)   Allowances for agricultural buildings (ABAs) closely follow the system for industrial buildings allowances.   There are initial allowances (temporarily) and writing down allowances. However, there is sometimes a departure from the industrial buildings system when agricultural buildings are sold and this is dealt with below.

(b)   An initial allowance of 20% was available on capital expenditure incurred by the owner of agricultural land on the construction of (or extension and improvement to) the types of work set out above. As for industrial buildings, the expenditure must have been incurred under a contract made between 1 November 1992 and 31 October 1993. Similarly the building must have been brought into use for agricultural purposes by 31 December 1994 and, if it is not, any initial allowance already made is withdrawn.

(c)   Annual writing down allowances of 4% are made where the building is in use for agricultural purposes at the end of the period of account. Following the industrial buildings system, the WDA is made for the period of account in which the expenditure was incurred if the building has been brought into agricultural use by the end of the period of account. Thus, potentially, ABAs of 24% were available (temporarily) for periods that included the 12 months 1 November 1992 to 31 October 1993.

5.4   Methods of giving relief

(a)   Allowances are given to traders as a trading expense of the period of account (ie, deducted in arriving at the Schedule D Case I profits).

(b)   For investors in agricultural property agricultural buildings allowances are instead treated as a property letting expense, and so deducted from rental income.

5.5   Disposal of agricultural buildings

(a)   The WDA for the period of account in which the disposal takes place is apportioned between the vendor and purchaser - the new owner is then entitled to the WDA for the balance of the 25 year writing down period. The apportionment is made as follows

Vendor: from start of (vendor's) period of account to date of sale
Purchaser: from date of sale to end of (purchaser's) period of account

Where the buyer and seller make up accounts to different dates this apportionment results in a total WDA being claimed in the year of sale that is more (or less) than normal. A compensating adjustment is made on the buyer in the last year for which WDA is available. The purchase price of the building is **irrelevant**.

(b)   Alternatively, the two parties concerned may elect to regard the transaction as a balancing event. In this case there is no WDA in the period of account of transfer, and the former owner is subject to a balancing adjustment. The balancing adjustment is computed as for industrial buildings. The new owner will be entitled to a WDA based upon the residue of expenditure, which must be written-off over the rest of the 25 year writing down period. The 25 year period starts on the first day of the period of account in which the original expenditure was incurred.

(c)   The transaction is treated as a balancing event only if a joint election is made by vendor and purchaser by 31 January following the year of assessment in which the period of account of sale ended.

(d)   A balancing event election is also available where a building is demolished or otherwise destroyed during its 25 year tax life. In which case the 'vendor' makes the election and a balancing allowance is made of the residue of expenditure at that point.

5.6   Example

Sugden, who commenced trading as a farmer on 1 January 1996 and who prepares accounts to 31 December annually, erected a new dairy building, for use in his farming business, at a cost of £10,000 on 1 April 1997. Sugden sold the building for £9,500 on 1 January 1999 to NY Estates a partnership which prepares accounts to 30 June. A joint election is made to treat the disposal as a balancing event.

Calculate the agricultural buildings allowances for both parties.

5.7   Solution

	Allowances £	WDV £
Year to 31 December 1997		
Cost of dairy		10,000
WDA 4%	400	
Year to 31 December 1998		
WDA 4%	400	
		800
	800	
WDV before sale		9,200
Year to 31 December 1999		
Balancing charge	(300)	(300)
Sale proceeds		9,500
ABAs are equal to net cost of	500	

NY Estates

Annual WDA : $\dfrac{\text{WDV before sale } + \text{ balancing charge}}{\text{remainder of writing - down period}}$

ie, $\dfrac{£(9,200+300)}{1.1.99-31.12.21} = \dfrac{£9,500}{23\,\text{years}}$

ie,   £413 pa for 23 years starting in the year to 30 June 1999.

6   PATENT RIGHTS

6.1   Introduction

Patent rights means the right to do, or authorise the doing of, anything which would, but for that right, be an infringement of a patent. Allowances are available on the capital expenditure incurred on the purchase of existing patent rights. Patent Office fees for registration etc of patents are, on the other hand, allowable expenses in calculating adjusted trading profits.

6.2   Allowances available and balancing adjustments

(a)   For any period of account a writing down allowance of 25% is given in respect of

- the tax written down value of patent rights brought forward in the pool of patent right expenditure, plus

- the cost of patent rights incurred in the relevant period of account, less

- the sale proceeds (or, if lower, the original qualifying cost) of patent rights sold in the period of account.

(b)   Where the period of account is other than 12 months long, the WDA is restricted or expanded on a time basis by reference to the length of the period of account.

(c)   On disposal of patent rights in whole or in part, if disposal proceeds exceed the balance of cost in the pool (including current basis period expenditure) a balancing charge arises. A balancing allowance is made for the period of account in which the trade ceases or the last patent is sold, where the sale proceeds are less than the patents' written down value.

(d)   If disposal proceeds exceed the original qualifying cost of the patent rights, the capital profit is assessed as income under Schedule D Case VI in six equal annual instalments, commencing with the actual fiscal year (not period of account) in which the disposal took place. However, the taxpayer may elect, by 31 January following the end of that fiscal year, for the whole excess to be assessed in the tax year of disposal.

6.3   Activity

Brainstawm, who prepares accounts to 30 September annually, had the following transactions in patent rights

1 May 1998   Acquired the rights to a new machine design for £12,500

1 October 1999   Acquired the rights to a new manufacturing process for £10,000

1 January 2002   Sold the patent rights to the manufacturing process for net sale proceeds of £14,800

1 December 2002   Acquired the rights to a new computer language for £8,000.

Calculate the allowances attributable to Brainstawm's patent rights from the year ended 30 September 1998.

6.4   Activity solution

		Pool of patent rights £	Allowances (charges) £
Year ended 30 September 1998			
1.5.98	Cost of rights	12,500	
	Less: WDA - 25%	3,125	3,125
		9,375	
Year ended 30 September 1999			
	WDA - 25%	2,344	2,344
		7,031	
Year ended 30 September 2000			
1.10.99	Cost of rights	10,000	
		17,031	
	Less: WDA - 25%	4,258	4,258
		12,773	
Year ended 30 September 2001			
	WDA - 25%	3,193	3,193
		9,580	
Year ended 30 September 2002			
1.1.2002	Net sale proceeds, restricted to original cost	10,000	
	Balancing charge	420	(420)
Year ended 30 September 2003			
1.12.2002	Cost of rights	8,000	
	Less: WDA - 25%	2,000	2,000
	WDV c/f	6,000	

7   KNOW-HOW

7.1   Introduction

(a)   An alternative to the normal course of undertaking a programme of research is to buy the results of someone else's research in the form of know-how. This is more widely defined as industrial information or techniques likely to assist in

- the manufacture or processing of goods or materials
- the working of (or searching for) mineral deposits
- agricultural, forestry or fishing operations.

(b)   Know-how purchased as a separate entity qualifies for relief under this heading. However, if it was an asset acquired as part of a purchase of a business, it is part of a transaction dealt with under capital gains rules unless both parties elect, within two years of the transfer, for it to be dealt with under income tax rules.

7.2   Allowances available and balancing adjustments

(a)   Qualifying expenditure on acquiring know-how attracts tax relief in the same way as expenditure on patents described above.

(b)   However, the full amount of disposal proceeds is deducted from the know-how pool even if it exceeds the relevant original amount of qualifying expenditure. Thus, any capital gain may be assessed as a balancing charge.

8   SCIENTIFIC RESEARCH

8.1   Introduction

Expenditure on scientific research can take two forms: revenue and capital. Revenue expenditure (eg, salaries of research personnel, rent of premises for research purposes, etc) is allowed in the normal way in computing profits. Capital expenditure that does not rank for other reliefs (as plant and/or industrial buildings) qualifies for a capital allowance under this heading.

8.2   Allowances available and recovery of allowances

(a)   Capital expenditure on scientific research related to the trade qualifies for a 100% allowance in the period of account in which the expenditure is incurred.

(b)   No allowance is given for expenditure on the acquisition of land or rights over land. The one exception to this is expenditure on a building (or on plant and machinery which forms part of such a building) that has already been constructed, if the amount of such expenditure can be ascertained by apportionment on a just and reasonable basis.

(c)   Expenditure on a dwelling is not allowable: however, where a building is partly used as a dwelling and partly for research then, provided the proportion of cost relevant to the dwelling does not exceed 25%, the whole cost will be allowed.

(d)   When an asset which qualified for a scientific research allowance ceases to belong to the claimant (the relevant event) an adjustment is necessary. The nature of the adjustment depends upon whether or not the 100% allowance has already been made by the time the asset ceases to belong to the person concerned, ie

(e)   Where the 100% allowance is made for the period of account in which the relevant event occurs (or was made in an earlier period of account) the trader is deemed to have received trading income at the time of the relevant event equal to the lower of

- (Disposal value + allowances made) – expenditure incurred, or
- the amount of the allowance.

(f)   Where the relevant event occurs before the period of account for which the allowance is due to be made - the allowance is not made and the trader is allowed, as a trading expense in the tax period of account in which the relevant event occurs, any excess of expenditure incurred over disposal value.

9   CHAPTER SUMMARY

(a)   Industrial buildings include:

- mills, factories or similar premises used for a trade;
- buildings in which a trade of manufacturing or processing goods is carried on;
- canteens used in the trades mentioned above; and
- sports pavilions used in any trade.

(b)   Some buildings are specifically disqualified from industrial buildings' status. These are:

- dwelling houses;
- retail or wholesale premises;
- hotels (except qualifying hotels); and
- offices.

(c)   Qualifying hotels are treated as industrial buildings for IBA purposes.

(d)   Enterprise zones: any commercial building (but **not** dwelling houses) qualifies as an industrial building. Accelerated allowances (100% in year of expenditure) are available during their 10-year designation period.

(e)   Qualifying cost is normally the cost of construction. Where part of the cost is incurred on non-qualifying construction (such as administrative offices) it will nevertheless qualify if it does not exceed 25% of the total cost of construction (ie, including the doubtful costs).

(f)   Where an industrial building is purchased unused from the person that built it the qualifying cost to the purchaser is the lower of the purchase cost and the cost of construction. If it is bought unused from a builder the price paid is the qualifying amount and the cost of construction by the builder is irrelevant.

(g)   Initial allowances are available on qualifying costs of construction between 1 November 1992 and 31 October 1993 at a rate of 20%.

(h)   Writing down allowances at 4% of cost (on a straight line basis) may be claimed provided that the building is in use as an industrial building at the end of the period of account. It is not available if the building is being used for non-industrial purposes at the end of a period of account, but temporary disuse is ignored.

(i)   Buildings have a tax life of 25 years from the date of first use. Its significance lies in the fact that a balancing adjustment arises on sale within this period but not after it has expired.

(j)   When industrial buildings are sold any balancing adjustment is computed by comparing disposal proceeds with the tax written down value (known as the residue before sale) at the time of sale. A balancing allowance or charge arises depending on whether the building is sold for more or less than its written down value. A balancing charge must not exceed the allowances previously given on the building.

(k)   If the building is sold for more than cost after non-industrial use any balancing charge is limited to the total allowances actually given. If the sale is for less than cost the balancing charge is the excess of allowances actually given over the adjusted net cost.

(l)   Writing down allowances to a second or subsequent user of an industrial building are given over its remaining tax life in equal annual amounts.

(m)   Capital allowances on agricultural buildings closely follow the industrial buildings allowances system. Initial and writing down allowances are given in the same way. On a sale of an agricultural building a balancing charge or allowance may be calculated if the buyer and seller elect for this treatment. Otherwise the writing down allowance of the year of sale is apportioned between them.

(n)   Patent rights and know-how are pooled in a similar way to plant and machinery with WDAs of 25% pa.

10   SELF TEST QUESTIONS

10.1   What buildings are specifically disqualified from being industrial buildings? (1.2)

10.2   What conditions must an hotel meet to be treated as a qualifying hotel? (1.3)

10.3   Do dwelling houses attract industrial buildings allowances in enterprise zones? (1.4)

10.4   What is the limit on the expenditure incurred on a non-industrial part of a building if the whole of it is to qualify for IBAs? (2.1)

10.5   What are the rates of initial allowance and writing down allowance for general industrial buildings and those located in enterprise zones? (3.1, 3.2)

10.6   How long is the tax life of an industrial building and what is its significance? (3.3)

10.7   In what way is a balancing charge restricted where a building is sold for more than original cost after non-industrial use? (3.7)

10.8   What buildings and works qualify for agricultural buildings allowances? (5.2)

10.9   What are the two alternative methods of calculating allowances due to the seller and purchaser of an agricultural building for the period of account in which it is sold? (5.5)

10.10   When the disposal proceeds of patent rights exceed the original qualifying cost, how is the excess taxed? (6.2)

10.11   What condition must be fulfilled for a building used for employee welfare to qualify as an industrial building? (1.1)

10.12   What costs are eligible for industrial buildings allowances? (2.1)

10.13   What is the relevant interest for the purposes of the writing down allowance? (3.2)

10.14   Where a building is sold for less than cost after non-industrial use, what is the fraction applied to net cost to calculate adjusted net cost? (3.10)

10.15   How are writing down allowances calculated for the second or subsequent user of an industrial building? (4.1)

11   EXAMINATION TYPE QUESTIONS

11.1   Arthur and Lancelot

Arthur acquired and paid for new business premises on 1 September 1998 at a cost of £271,250, made up as follows

	£	£
Cost of land		30,000
Legal costs of conveyancing title, etc		750
Cost of clearing site and preparing foundations		2,250
Cost of structure		
Factory	200,000	
Integral design and drawing office	3,750	
Administration area	5,250	
Staff and works canteen	15,750	
		224,750
Heating and air conditioning plant		13,500
		271,250

From 1 September 1998 until 1 August 2003 Arthur used the premises for his trade as manufacturer of reproduction medieval weapons. From then on until the complex was sold to Lancelot for £500,000 (including land £60,000; plant £3,000) on 31 August 2009, it was used for non-industrial purposes. From 1 September 2009 Lancelot used the premises as a factory.

Both Arthur and Lancelot make up accounts to 31 March annually, and they are not associated for tax purposes.

You are required to show the capital allowances computations of Arthur and Lancelot for the years 31 March 1999 to 31 March 2010 based on the above information.

11.2   Charlie Ceasing

Charlie Ceasing who commenced to trade on 6 August 1995 making up his accounts to 5 August in each year, ceases to trade on 5 August 2001.

The tax written down value of the pool after computing the capital allowances for the year ended 5 August 1997 was £410. Capital expenditure in the later periods of account was as follows

Year ended 5 August 1998

		£
1 November 1997	Purchased motor car solely for business use	16,100
30 April 1998	Purchased office equipment	450
1 May 1998	Sold office equipment	100
2 June 1998	Purchased delivery van	2,550 (second hand)
10 June 1998	Sold plant and machinery	250

Year ended 5 August 1999

		£
5 March 1999	Purchased office equipment (deposit paid £200 - balance £1,000 paid over 24 months from 5 April 1999)	1,200 (on HP)
1 July 1999	Purchased new delivery van (van purchased in 1998 taken in part exchange at value of £700)	5,800 (full price)
10 July 1999	Sold office equipment	100

Following the cessation of trading, the remaining plant and equipment was sold for £2,250, the delivery van for £2,163 and the trader kept the motor car for his own use. The market value of the motor car at 5 August 2001 was £5,675.

You are required to set out the capital allowances computations for the trader for the years ended 5 August 1998 to 5 August 2001.

(Ignore VAT)

12   ANSWERS TO EXAMINATION TYPE QUESTIONS

12.1   Arthur and Lancelot

Capital allowances

(a)   **Allowable expenditure**

			£
Industrial building:	Site clearance, etc		2,250
	Structure		224,750
			227,000
	(Admin area within limit)		227,000
Plant and machinery:	Heating and air conditioning plant		£13,500

(b)   **Allowances claimed by Arthur**

	Industrial Buildings		Plant and machinery (Pool)	Total allowances
Year to 31 March 1999	£	£	£	£
Allowable expenditure		227,000	13,500	
WDA 4%	9,080			9,080
FYA 40%			5,400	5,400
WDV			8,100	
				14,480
Y/e 31.3.00 WDA 4%/25%	9,080		2,025	11,105
			6,075	
Y/e 31.3.01 WDA 4%/25%	9,080		1,519	10,599
			4,556	
Y/e 31.3.02 WDA 4%/25%	9,080		1,139	10,219
			3,417	
Y/e 31.3.03 WDA 4%/25%	9,080		854	9,934
		45,400	2,563	
		181,600		

	Industrial Buildings £	£	Plant and machinery (Pool) £	Total allowances £
Y/e 31.3.04 Notional WDA 4%/25%	9,080		641	641
			1,922	
Y/e 31.3.05 Notional WDA 4%/25%	9,080		480	480
			1,442	
Y/e 31.3.06 Notional WDA 4%/25%	9,080		360	360
			1,082	
Y/e 31.3.07 Notional WDA 4%/25%	9,080		270	270
			812	
Y/e 31.3.08 Notional WDA 4%/25%	9,080		203	203
			609	
Y/e 31.3.09 Notional WDA 4%/25%	9,080		152	152
		54,480	457	
Residue before sale		127,120		
Y/e 31.3.10		£437,000	3,000	
Balancing charges				
Plant			(2,543)	(2,543)
Buildings - since proceeds of sale exceed cost, balancing charge is limited to allowances **actually given**		£(45,400)		(45,400)
				(47,943)

(c)   **Allowances claimable by Lancelot**

Year to 31 March 2010	£	£	Allowances £
Industrial buildings			
Cost = residue of expenditure after sale ie, £(127,120 + 45,400)	172,520		
WDA: Based on residue of expenditure, spread over balance of tax life (1.9.09 - 31.8.23) (172,520 ÷ 14 years)	12,323		12,323
Plant and machinery			
Cost (second-hand)		3,000	
WDA at 25%		750	750
WDV c/f	160,197	2,250	
			13,073

12.2   Charlie Ceasing

		General pool	Expensive car	Capital allowances
	£	£	£	£
Year ended 5 August 1998				
Tax WDV b/f at 6.8.97		410	-	-
Additions: Car			16,100	
Less: Disposals:				
Office equipment	100			
Plant and machinery	250	(350)		
		———		
		60		
WDA @ 25% (restricted for car)		(15)	(3,000)	3,015
Additions qualifying for FYA				
Office equipment	450			
Delivery van	2,550			
	———			
	3,000			
FYA @ 50%	(1,500)			
	———	1,500		1,500
Total capital allowances for y/e 5 August 1998				4,515
		———		———
Year ended 5 August 1999				
Tax WDV b/f at 6.8.98		1,545	13,100	
Less: Disposals:				
Delivery van	700			
Office equipment	100	(800)		
	———			
		745		
WDA @ 25% (restricted for car)		(186)	(3,000)	3,186
		———		
		559		
Additions qualifying for FYA				
Office equipment	1,200			
Delivery van	5,800			
	———			
	7,000			
FYA @ 40%	(2,800)			2,800
	———	4,200		
Total capital allowances for y/e 5.8.99				5,986
				———
Year ended 5 August 2000				
Tax WDV b/f at 6.8.99		4,759	10,100	
WDA @ 25%		(1,190)	(2,525)	3,715
		———	———	
Total capital allowances for y/e 5.8.00				3,715
				———
Year ended 5 August 2001				
Tax WDV b/f at 6.8.00		3,569	7,575	
Less: Disposal proceeds/mv		(4,413)	(5,675)	
Balancing charge		(844)		(844)
		———		
Balancing allowance			1,900	1,900
			———	———

12 TRADING LOSSES

INTRODUCTION & LEARNING OBJECTIVES

(a)   When dealing with the income tax regime for traders in this text it has so far been assumed that their trades are profitable and thus it has been with the calculation of the tax due on those profits with which we have been concerned. However, there is also provision in the Taxes Acts for dealing with losses incurred by traders and this is the subject of this chapter.

(b)   A tax loss arises in a trade when an accounting result is adjusted for tax purposes in the usual way but the adjusted figure is negative. One of the most important points to appreciate in dealing with trading losses is that where the result for a period of account is a loss the assessable profit for that period is nil.

(c)   Although you are not required to learn the sections of legislation for your examination, it is usual for loss reliefs to be referred to by their section number and, since there are relatively few of them, it takes no great feat of memory.

When you have studied this chapter you should be able to do the following:

- Calculate the amount of loss that may be carried forward under S385 ICTA 1988 against future trading profits and deal with its set off

- Ascertain the charges on income that may be carried forward with a S385 loss

- Calculate the amount of loss for the purposes of relief against total income under S380 ICTA 1988

- Set the S380 relief off correctly against the taxpayer's statutory total income

- Judge when a claim may be made to set off trading losses against net chargeable gains for the year

- Calculate the relief due under S381 ICTA 1988 and set it off correctly against the total income of the three preceding tax years.

- Calculate the relief for losses in closing years under S388 ICTA 1988.

---

1   RELIEFS FOR BUSINESSES UNDER THE CURRENT YEAR BASIS

1.1   Introduction

The reliefs available for a trading loss, as explained in the following sections, are as follows:

(a)   S385 ICTA 1988 carry forward against future trading profits;
(b)   S380 ICTA 1988 relief against STI;
(c)   S381 ICTA 1988 opening year loss relief against STI;
(d)   S388 ICTA 1988 terminal loss relief against previous trading profits.

2 LOSS RELIEF BY CARRY FORWARD: S385 ICTA 1988

2.1 Principles of the relief

(a) This is the most straightforward of the loss reliefs. A trading loss may be carried forward and set against the **first** taxable profits arising in the **same** trade. If the subsequent profits are not high enough to use all the loss then so much of the loss is used so as to reduce the profits to nil, with the remainder being carried forward again until further profits arise, and so on.

(b) The loss itself may be carried forward indefinitely (until such time as there are profits against which to set it off) but a claim must be made to establish the amount of the loss to be carried forward within five years of 31 January following the end of the tax year in which the loss arose. Once the claim has been established the loss will be used automatically against the future trading profits without the need for a further claim.

(c) When dealing with set off of losses it is useful to adopt a columnar layout, presenting each year in a separate column. Keep a separate working to show when, and how much, of the loss has been used up.

2.2 Activity

Edward, who has been trading since 1 January 1995, has had the following recent tax adjusted results:

Year to 31 December 1997	Loss	£5,000
Year to 31 December 1998	Profit	£3,000
Year to 31 December 1999	Profit	£10,000

Assuming that Edward wishes to claim loss relief only under S385 ICTA 1988, calculate his assessable amounts for 1997/98 to 1999/00 inclusive.

2.3 Activity solution

	1997/98 £	1998/99 £	1999/00 £
Schedule D Case I (CYB)	nil	3,000	10,000
Less: S385 relief	nil	3,000	2,000
Net Schedule D Case I amounts	nil	nil	8,000

Working - loss memorandum

	£
Trading loss	5,000
Less: S385 relief in 1998/99	3,000
	2,000
Less: S385 relief in 1999/00	2,000
Loss carried forward to 2000/01	nil

Note: The loss is set off against the first profits to arise, to the maximum extent possible. Thus £3,000 of the loss is set off in 1998/99 and the remainder carried forward to 1999/00, where it is set off against more substantial profits.

3   RELIEF AGAINST TOTAL INCOME: S380 ICTA 1988

3.1   Introduction

In a prolonged difficult period for a business relief under S385 may take a long time to materialise. Consequently there is another potential option made available to taxpayers; they may relieve trading losses against the statutory total income of the tax year of the loss and/or the previous one. This claim is made under S380 ICTA 1988.

3.2   Calculating the loss

(a)   The loss is calculated on an accounting period basis (ie, in the same way as profits).

A loss for the year ended 31 December 1998 is relieved against STI of 1998/99 and/or 1997/98.

(b)   Capital allowances are treated as an expense in arriving at the tax adjusted profit or loss so they are relieved as an integral part of the loss.

3.3   Example

Graham has been in business since 1 January 1995, making up accounts to 31 December annually. His recent tax adjusted results are as follows:

Year to 31 December 1997	Profit	£10,000
Year to 31 December 1998	Loss	£6,000
Year to 31 December 1999	Profit	£12,000

What loss relief is available under s.380?

3.4   Solution

The loss is £6,000 for the tax year 1998/99 (in which Graham's loss-making period of account ended). This is available under s.380 against STI of 1998/99 and/or 1997/98.

3.5   Obtaining relief for the loss

(a)   As shown above, the loss may be set off against the taxpayer's statutory total income of the year of the loss. If that relief is chosen the taxpayer cannot decide to set only part of his loss against total income; it must be set off to the maximum possible extent. Remember that statutory total income comprises income from all sources less charges on income. However, personal allowances are deducted after any loss relief and so a claim under S380 may involve wasting them.

(b)   The loss could instead be carried back against the STI of the previous year whether or not the trade was being carried on in that previous year. A claim under S380 may be made for either the tax year of the loss or the previous year or both. The two years are treated separately and thus a claim is required for each year. A written claim must be made within one year of 31 January following the end of the tax year of loss.

(c)   A taxpayer may have losses for two consecutive tax years and wish to relieve both under S380. In these circumstances statutory total income of a year is relieved by the loss of that year in priority to the loss carried back from the following year.

3.6   Activity

Adrian makes up accounts annually to 31 December. His recent results have been:

Year ended 31 December 1997	Profit	£34,000
Year ended 31 December 1998	Loss	£48,000
Year ended 31 December 1999	Profit	£60,000

For 1997/98 Adrian has other income of £5,000 and charges on income of £2,800. In 1998/99 the figures are £6,000 and £2,500 respectively.

Show how relief for the loss would be given under S380 ICTA 1988, assuming that Adrian makes all claims to the extent that they are beneficial. What loss, if any, is available for carry forward against trading profits after all S380 claims have been made?

3.7   Activity solution

The loss is incurred in 1998/99. Thus S380 claims may apply for 1998/99 and 1997/98.

	1998/99
	£
Schedule D Case I (y/e 31 December 1998)	nil
Non-trading income	6,000
	6,000
Less: Charges on income	2,500
STI	3,500
Less: S380 relief - ignore as STI covered by PA	-
	3,500
Less: PA	3,500 (max)
Taxable income	nil

	1997/98
	£
Schedule D Case I (y/e 31 December 1997)	34,000
Non-trading income	5,000
	39,000
Less: Charges on income	2,800
STI	36,200
Less: S380 relief (W)	36,200
Taxable income	nil

Losses of £11,800 (W) remain unrelieved after a claim for 1997/98 has been made under S380 and they are thus available for carry forward under S385.

Working - loss memorandum

	£
1998/99 - loss of y/e 31.12.98	48,000
Less: Used in 1997/98	36,200
Available for carry forward against future trading profits	11,800

Note: by making a claim for only 1997/98 under S380 Adrian obtained relief for his loss as rapidly as possible, without needlessly wasting his personal allowance for 1998/99. In this way he has maximised the amount of loss to carry forward to use against future trading profit. The best course of action would depend on the personal circumstances of each case but as a general principle there is clearly no point in claiming S380 where the personal allowance already covers all or most of the STI (as here in 1998/99).

3.8   S380 relief in opening years

(a)   In the first year of trade, the assessable profit (or loss) period starts on the day trade commences and finishes on 5 April following. Unless the trader prepares his accounts to 5 April, this will require the profit (or losses) of a period straddling 5 April to be apportioned. (Remember, daily apportionment is required.)

(b)   A loss may only be relieved once. If, in the opening years, a loss has been relieved, it is treated as nil when calculating the next assessment.

3.9   Activity

Geraldine starts trading on 1 August 1998. Her results, as adjusted for tax purposes, are:

		£
10 months to 31 May 1999	Loss	(20,000)
Year ended 31 May 2000	Profit	48,000

Calculate Geraldine's Schedule D Case I assessable amounts for 1998/99 and 1999/00 on the assumption that she claims relief under S380 against STI of £30,000 of 1998/99.

3.10   Activity solution

Schedule D Case I assessments

	£
1998/99 (actual basis)	
1.8.98 - 5.4.99 248/304 × (20,000) = (£16,316)	Nil
1999/00 (accounts in second fiscal year less than 12 months after commencement; therefore first 12 months)	
1.8.98 - 31.7.99	
Loss	(20,000)
Less: Relieved under s.380	16,316
	(3,684)
Profits 61/365 × 48,000	8,022
	4,338

(*Tutorial note:* When calculating the amount assessable under Schedule D Case I for 1999/00, the loss already relieved under S380 must be deducted.)

3.11   Relief of trading losses against capital gains

(a)   A limited relief is available to permit traders to set off trading losses against chargeable gains, the purpose of which is to put unincorporated businesses on a closer footing to companies.

(b)   The relief works by acting as an extension to S380 relief described above (under rules given in S72 FA 1991). It only becomes available, however, if the statutory total income of the year in question has been reduced to zero by the trading loss under a normal S380 claim and yet the loss is not fully relieved. There is no need to make a S380 claim for the previous year (or any other claim for loss relief) but relief against capital gains is only granted to the extent that the loss remains after being used to relieve income.

(c)   The remaining unrelieved trading loss may be set off as a deemed capital loss against the taxpayer's net chargeable gains for the year; that is after setting off current year capital losses and any capital losses brought forward against current year capital gains. It takes precedence over both taper relief and the CGT annual exemption.

3.12   Example

Charles, who makes up accounts annually to 31 December, made a trading profit of £3,000 and loss of £14,000 in his periods of account ended 31 December 1998 and 1999 respectively. He has income taxed at source of £4,500 in 1998/99 and also realised capital gains of £16,000 and capital losses of £5,000 in that tax year. There was no capital gains taper relief.

Calculate the amounts that remain in charge to tax for 1998/99, assuming that Charles claims relief against both income and gains under S380 for that year and no other year.

3.13   Solution

	1998/99 £
Schedule D Case I (y/e 31.12.98)	3,000
Income taxed at source	4,500
	7,500
Less: s 380 relief against income	7,500
Taxable income	nil
Capital gains	16,000
Less: Capital losses	5,000
Net gains	11,000
Less: S380 relief against chargeable gains (14,000 - 7,500)	6,500
Gains remaining in charge before annual exemption	4,500

4   TRADE CHARGES: S387 ICTA 1988

4.1   Introduction

(a)   Charges on income, whether trade charges (such as patent royalties) or non-trade charges (such as charitable covenants) are both deducted from the aggregate of a taxpayer's income rather than from any particular type of income.

(b)   Where aggregate income is low, the charges to be deducted may exceed the available income. For non-trade charges this is simply bad luck for the taxpayer; no relief is obtained for them. But excess **trade** charges are treated as though they were a trading loss and may be carried forward to be relieved against future trading profits in exactly the same way as a trading loss carried forward under S385.

(c)   If the taxpayer had both trade and non-trade charges, the non-trade charges are deducted in priority against any aggregate income to avoid wasting them.

4.2   Activity

Edward has the following income and expenditure

	1998/99 £	1999/00 £
Schedule D Case I	1,000	21,000
Investment income	3,000	3,000
Charitable covenant paid (gross)	5,000	5,000
Patent royalty paid (gross)	6,000	6,000

What is Edward's statutory total income for each year?

4.3   Activity solution

		1998/99 £	1999/00 £
Schedule D Case I		1,000	21,000
Less: 'Loss' (trade charge brought forward)			6,000
		1,000	15,000
Investment income		3,000	3,000
		4,000	18,000
Less:	Non-trade charges	4,000 *	5,000
		-	13,000
	Trade charges		6,000
Statutory total income		nil	7,000

* there is sufficient income to deduct only £4,000 of non-trade charges. Relief for the remaining £1,000 is lost. The trade charges not deducted in 1998/99 are carried forward in the same way as a s 385 loss (and so are deducted in 1999/00).

5   RELIEF OF TRADING LOSSES IN THE EARLY YEARS OF TRADE

5.1   Introduction

(a)   Particular consideration is given to taxpayers who have recently established businesses since they are more likely to incur losses. There are special loss relief rules that apply to the first four tax years of a trade.

(b)   The special relief, under S381 ICTA 1988, is available only in these early years of trade. It is important to appreciate, however, that this is only one alternative; the reliefs under S385 and S380 described earlier in this chapter can be used if the taxpayer prefers. Which claim or combination of claims is most appropriate depends on the taxpayer's personal circumstances.

5.2   Relief under S381 ICTA 1988

(a)   A trading loss suffered may be set off under S381 against the taxpayer's statutory total income of the three tax years preceding the tax year of the loss. So if a loss is suffered in, say, 1998/99 it may be set off against the total income of 1995/96, 1996/97 and 1997/98. There is no need for the trade to have been carried on in earlier years. Potentially, for example, the relief can be set against income under Schedule E if a taxpayer gave up employment to start a business.

(b)   Unlike S380 relief, where separate claims are required for relief in the current year and the previous year, relief under S381 operates automatically for all three years, beginning with the earliest and ending with the latest.

(c)   The loss available for S381 relief must be computed in the same way as described for S380 relief ie, in the same was as profits.

(d)   Remember that capital allowances are automatically deducted in arriving at the Schedule D Case I profit or loss figure.

(e)   The additional relief against chargeable gains is **not** available under S381.

5.3   Example

Caroline started in business as a sheep shearer on 1 July 1997. Her results, as adjusted for tax purposes, for the first two years are as follows:

		£
Year ended 30 June 1998	Loss	(12,000)
Year ended 30 June 1999	Profit	2,500

Before becoming a sheep shearer, Caroline had been employed as a dress maker. Her remuneration from this employment, which ceased on 30 September 1996, for recent years was:

	£
1996/97	5,868
1995/96	11,050
1994/95	9,520

Caroline is single and has other income of £4,500 (gross) pa.

Calculate taxable income for all years:

(a)   after claiming relief under S381 ICTA 1988; and
(b)   after claiming relief under S380 ICTA 1988, instead of claiming under S381 ICTA 1988.

Assume tax rates and allowances for 1998/99 apply throughout.

5.4   Solution

(a)   **Taxable income computations**

	1994/95	1995/96	1996/97	1997/98
Schedule E	9,520	11,050	5,868	-
Other income	4,500	4,500	4,500	4,500
	14,020	15,550	10,368	4,500
Less: S381 (W2)	(9,173)	(2,827)	-	-
	4,847	12,723	10,368	4,500
Less: PA	(4,195)	(4,195)	(4,195)	(4,195)
Taxable income	652	8,528	6,173	305

	1998/99	*1999/00*
Schedule D Case II	-	2,500
Other income	4,500	4,500
	4,500	7,000
Less: PA	(4,195)	(4,195)
Taxable income	305	2,805

(*Tutorial note:* The loss of 1997/98 is set against STI of 1994/95, then if any loss remained, it would be set against STI of 1995/96 then 1996/97.

WORKINGS

(1) **New business: assessments**

	£
1997/98 1.7.97 - 5.4.98	Nil
1998/99 (y/e 30.6.98)	Nil
1999/00 (CYB: y/e 30.6.99)	2,500

(2) **Loss**

1997/98 (1.7.97 - 5.4.98)	
(279/365 × 12,000)	9,173
1998/99 (y/e 30.6.99)	
(12,000 – 9,173)	2,827

(b)

	1994/95	*1995/96*	*1996/97*	*1997/98*
Schedule E	9,520	11,050	5,868	-
Other income	4,500	4,500	4,500	4,500
	14,020	15,550	10,368	4,500
S380			(9,173)	(2,827)
Less: PA	(4,195)	(4,195)	(1,195)	(1,673)
Taxable income	9,825	11,355	Nil	Nil

	1998/99	*1999/00*
Schedule D Case II	-	2,500
Other income	4,500	4,500
	4,500	7,000
Less: PA	(4,195)	(4,195)
Taxable income	305	2,805

Tutorial notes:

(1)   The personal allowance is assumed throughout to be £4,195.

(2)   Under S380:

      (a)   the loss for 1997/98 (£9,173) is set against STI of 1997/98 and/or 1996/97;
      (b)   the loss for 1998/99 (£2,827) is set against STI of 1998/99 and/or 1997/98.

In the example, relief is taken in the earliest year possible.

There is no requirement that the trade be carried on in the earlier year that a S380 claim is made.

(3)   It is more tax efficient to use S381 as this avoids wasting personal allowances in this situation. In part (b) it would be better to use the loss of 1998/99 under S385 in 1999/00 (limited to £2,500) as this avoids wasting the personal allowance.

6   LOSSES IN CLOSING YEARS : S388 ICTA 1988

6.1   Introduction

(a)   Without special provision, the only effective relief for trading losses incurred in the final year of trade would be a current year (or previous year) claim under S380. No claim is possible under S385 (because there will be no trade to generate future profits).

(b)   To alleviate this lack of opportunity to relieve final year trading losses there is a special relief provided under S388 ICTA 1988. Broadly, it permits the trading loss and trade charges of the final 12 months of trade that remain unrelieved to be set against the available profits (as defined) for the year of cessation and then carried back and set against the available profit for the three tax years preceding.

(c)   There are two elements in dealing with S388 relief:

      •   calculating the amount of the 'terminal loss'; and
      •   calculating the amount of 'available profit' against which the terminal loss may be set off.

6.2   Calculating the terminal loss

(a)   The terminal loss is made up by totalling the following elements:

      (i)   trading loss incurred in the final tax year (ie from 6 April to date of cessation);

      (ii)   unrelieved business charges of the final tax year;

      (iii)   trading loss incurred from 12 months before cessation to the start of the final tax year;

      (iv)   a proportion of the business charges of the penultimate tax year.

(b)   In calculating these amounts bear the following in mind.

      (i)   Any overlap relief created when the trade commenced is deductible in the final year of assessment thereby increasing any trading loss (or, perhaps, turning a trading profit into a loss) appearing in (i) above.

(ii)   If the calculation of trading losses in either (i) or (iii) above in fact shows a profit, treat it as £nil.

(ii)   The proportion of business charges of the penultimate tax year is calculated at the **lower** of:

• any amount unrelieved; and

• $\dfrac{\text{number of days in (iii) above}}{365} \times$ total charges for the year

(iii)   If any of the losses that might appear in the terminal loss calculation have been relieved by some other means (eg s 380), they must be excluded.

6.3   Available profit

Definition   The available profit for each year of assessment is the adjusted Schedule D Case I profit less the excess of trading charges over non-trading income (ie, those amounts which would have been carried forward for relief had cessation not intervened). The assessments are also reduced by any loss relief given in those years under S380.

6.4   Activity

Yves ceased trading on 30 June 2001. His final period of trade was the 9 months to 30 June 2001 and beforehand he made up accounts annually to 30 September. His tax-adjusted trading results and charges on income are as follows

Period of account	Trading result	£
9 months to 30.6.01	Loss	7,200
Year to 30.9.00	Profit	100
Year to 30.9.99	Profit	7,300
Year to 30.9.98	Profit	7,500

Tax Year	Trade charges £
2001/02	420
2000/01	560
1999/00	560
1998/99	560

There was overlap relief of £1,800 brought forward.

Calculate the terminal loss claim available to Yves and show how relief may be obtained for it. Yves had no other sources of income.

6.5   Activity solution

	1998/99 £	1999/00 £	2000/01 £	2001/02 £
Income available (W1)	6,940	6,740	nil	nil
Less: terminal loss relief (W2)	(ii) 3,083	(i) 6,740	nil	nil
	3,857	nil	nil	nil

WORKINGS

(W1)   Income available for terminal loss relief

	1998/99 £	1999/00 £	2000/01 £	2001/02 £
Schedule D Case I (CYB)	7,500	7,300	100	-
Less: charges not set against non-trading income	560	560	560	-
Available income	6,940	6,740	nil	nil

(W2)   Calculation of terminal loss

	£	£
Loss in 2001/02 (86/273 × £7,200)		2,268
Overlap relief		1,800
Unrelieved trading charges of 2001/02		420
Loss in 2000/01: 1.7.00 – 5.4.01		
(92/365 × £100) + (187/273 × £-7,200)		4,907
Trade charges of 2000/01.		
Lower of:		
Unrelieved charges (£560 – £100 (W1))	460	
279/365 × total charges (£560)	428	
		428
Terminal loss		9,823

The remaining loss of £25 (£7,200 – 2,268 – 4,907) could be relieved under s.380 had Yves any other sources of income.

7   SELF TEST QUESTIONS

7.1   By what time must a claim be made to establish the amount of loss that may be carried forward under S385 ICTA 1988? (2.1)

7.2   Is it possible to deal with capital allowances separately from a trading loss? (1.1)

7.3   If a taxpayer has claimed loss relief against total income of the same tax year is there any restriction on his claiming relief against total income of the previous year? (3.1)

7.4   How are losses calculated in the first year of trade for the purposes of S380 ICTA 1988? (3.8)

7.5   What is the time limit for a claim under S380 ICTA 1988? (3.5)

7.6   Which years can be relieved by a s.388 ICTA 1988 claim. (6.1)

7.7   In what circumstances may a trading loss be relieved against chargeable gains? (3.11)

7.8   How are trade charges given relief under S387 ICTA 1988? (4.1)

7.9   For which tax years may a S381 ICTA 1988 claim be made? (5.1)

7.10 Does the taxpayer need to make separate claims for each of the three tax years that may be relieved under a S381 ICTA 1988 claim? (5.2)

8 EXAMINATION TYPE QUESTION

8.1 Ebb

Ebb, a married man, commenced trading as a part-time pleasure boat operator on 1 April 1995. Recent results have been as follows.

	Schedule DI profit/(loss)
	£
Year ended 31 March 1999	7,055
Year ended 31 March 2000	(8,375)

Mr and Mrs Ebb's other income comprises

	Years ended 5 April	
	1999	*2000*
	£	£
Ebb:		
Part-time salary from Deephaven Docks Ltd	2,200	2,225
Building society interest received	2,816	1,600
Mrs Ebb:		
Part-time salary from Deephaven Docks Ltd	3,455	3,555
Interest from bank deposit account	512	576

You are required to calculate the taxable income of Mr and Mrs Ebb for the years 1998/99 and 1999/2000 assuming loss relief is taken at the earliest opportunity.

Assume FA 1998 rates and allowances apply for future years.

9 ANSWER TO EXAMINATION TYPE QUESTION

9.1 Ebb

(a) **Taxable income computations - Mr Ebb**

	1998/99		*1999/2000*
	£	£	£
Earned income			
Schedule E - salary		2,200	2,225
Schedule DI profits		7,055	-
		9,255	2,225
Unearned income			
Building society interest (× 100/80)		3,520	2,000
Statutory total income		12,775	4,225
Loss arising in 1999/2000	(8,375)		
Loss relief under S380 TA 88	8,375	(8,375)	-
Revised STI		4,400	4,225
Less: PA		(4,195)	(4,195)
Taxable income		205	30

(b) **Taxable income computations - Mrs Ebb**

	1998/99 £	1999/2000 £
Earned income		
Salary	3,455	3,555
Unearned income		
Bank interest £512/576 × 100/80	640	720
	4,095	4,275
Less: PA	(4,095) max	(4,195)
Taxable income	-	80

13 TAXATION OF PARTNERSHIPS

INTRODUCTION & LEARNING OBJECTIVES

A partnership is a body of persons carrying on business together with a view to profit (Partnership Act 1890).

Although a partnership is a single trading entity, for tax purposes each individual partner is effectively treated as trading in their own right. This chapter deals with allocating the income between partners.

When you have studied this chapter you should be able to do the following:

- Allocate trading profits between partners
- Deal with partnerships commencing and ceasing, and partners joining or leaving partnerships
- Allocate trading losses between partners and set out the loss reliefs available to each partner
- Calculate chargeable gains on disposals of partnership assets outside the partnership, and on changes in the profit sharing ratio

---

1 THE ALLOCATION OF PROFITS AND LOSSES

1.1 The computation of partnership profits and losses

(a) The principles of computation of a partnership's tax adjusted profit or loss are the same as those for a sole trader.

(b) Partners' salaries and interest on capital are not deductible, since these are an allocation of profit.

1.2 The allocation of the profit or loss

(a) The tax adjusted profit or loss is allocated between the partners according to their profit sharing arrangements for that period of account.

(b) Partners may be entitled to salaries (a fixed allocation of profit) and interest on capital. The balance will be allocated in the profit sharing ratio.

(c) A partnership may have non-trading income such as a Schedule A profit or bank interest.

Such income will be allocated between the partners according to the profit sharing ratio.

(d) A partnership may pay annual charges, such as an annuity to a retired partner.

These are also allocated between the partners according to the profit sharing ratio.

1.3   A change in the profit sharing ratio

If a partnership changes its basis of profit sharing during a period of account, then the profit or loss will need to be time apportioned accordingly prior to allocation.

1.4   Example

David and Peter are in partnership Their tax adjusted profit for the year ended 30 September 1998 was £16,500.

Up to 30 June 1998 profits were shared between David and Peter 3:2, after paying salaries of £3,000 and £2,000.

From 1 July 1998 profits were shared 2:1 after paying salaries of £6,000 and £4,000.

Show the allocation of profits for 1998/99.

1.5   Solution

The 1997/98 partnership profits will be allocated as follows:

	Total £	*David* £	*Peter* £
1.10.97 to 30.6.98			
(profits £16,500 × $^{273}/_{365}$ = £12,341)			
Salaries ($^{273}/_{365}$)	3,740	2,244	1,496
Balance (3:2)	8,601	5,161	3,440
	12,341	7,405	4,936
1.7.98 to 30.9.98			
(profits £16,500 × $^{92}/_{365}$ = £4,159)			
Salaries ($^{92}/_{365}$)	2,520	1,512	1,008
Balance (2:1)	1,639	1,093	546
	4,159	2,605	1,554
Total allocation	16,500	10,010	6,490

1.6   Partnership capital allowances

(a)   Capital allowances are deducted as an expense in calculating the tax adjusted profit or loss.

The profit allocated between the partners is therefore after capital allowances.

(b)   Individual partners cannot claim capital allowances on their own behalf.

If assets are owned privately (such as motor cars), then the business proportion of such assets must be included in the partnership's capital allowances computation. The total capital allowances are then deducted as an expense.

2   COMMENCEMENT AND CESSATION

2.1   Introduction

(a)   The normal commencement and cessation rules apply upon the commencement and the cessation of a partnership.

(b)   The rules are applied after the allocation of the profit or loss between the partners.

(c)   Each partner is therefore effectively taxed as a sole trader in respect of their share of profit or loss.

        A partner will be treated as commencing when he or she joins the partnership (which will be upon the commencement of the partnership for the original partners), and will be treated as ceasing when he or she leaves the partnership (or the partnership ceases).

(d)   Each partner may therefore have his or her own overlap relief.

2.2   A change in the membership

(a)   The membership of a partnership may change as the result of the admission, death or retirement of a partner.

(b)   Provided that there is at least one partner common to the business before and after the change, the partnership will automatically continue.

(c)   However, the commencement and cessation rules will apply to the individual partner who is joining or leaving the partnership.

2.3   Example

Able and Bertie have been in partnership since 1 July 1996 making up their accounts to 30 June each year. On 1 July 1998 Carol joins the partnership.

The partnership's tax adjusted profits are as follows:

	£
Year ended 30 June 1997	10,000
Year ended 30 June 1998	13,500
Year ended 30 June 1999	18,000

Profits are shared equally.

Show the amounts assessed on the individual partners for 1996/97 to 1999/00.

2.4   Solution

Profits will be allocated between the partners as follows:

	Total £	Able £	Bertie £	Carol £
y/e 30.6.96	10,000	5,000	5,000	–
y/e 30.6.97	13,500	6,750	6,750	–
y/e 30.6.98	18,000	6,000	6,000	6,000

Able and Bertie will both be assessed as follows, based upon a commencement on 1 July 1996:

		£
1996/97	1 July 1996 to 5 April 1997 £5,000 × $^{279}\!/_{365}$	3,822
1997/98	Year ended 30 June 1997	5,000
1998/99	Year ended 30 June 1998	6,750
1999/00	Year ended 30 June 1999	6,000

They will both be entitled to overlap relief of £3,822.

Carol will be treated as commencing on 1 July 1998, and will be assessed on her share of the partnership profits as follows:

		£
1998/99	1 July 1998 to 5 April 1999 £6,000 × $^{279}\!/_{365}$	4,586
1999/00	Year ended 30 June 1999	6,000

She will be entitled to overlap relief of £4,586.

2.5   Sole traders

If a sole trader takes someone into partnership, the commencement rules will apply to the new partner, whereas the sole trader will be treated as continuing.

Similarly, when a business goes from partnership to sole trader, the sole trader will be treated as continuing, while the other partner(s) will have a cessation.

3   PARTNERSHIP LOSSES

3.1   Notional losses

(a)   Loss relief is only available if the partnership as a whole makes a loss.

(b)   The basis of allocating profits between partners may result in one partner showing a loss, and yet the partnership as a whole has made a profit.

(c)   The loss is only notional, and is reallocated to the other partners according to the amount of profits each partner was originally allocated.

3.2   Example

Maud, Nigel and Olive are in partnership. Their adjusted profit for the year ended 30 April 1998 is £1,200. They share profits equally after salaries of Maud £4,200, Nigel £3,000 and Olive £1,800.

Show the allocation of profits between the partners for 1998/99

3.3   Solution

	Total £	Maud £	Nigel £	Olive £
Salaries	9,000	4,200	3,000	1,800
Share of balance (1/3 each)	(7,800)	(2,600)	(2,600)	(2,600)
	1,200	1,600	400	(800)
Olive's loss is reallocated to Maud and Nigel 1,600:400		(640)	(160)	800
	1,200	960	240	–

3.4 The allocation of trading losses

Losses are allocated between partners in exactly the same way as profits.

3.5 Loss relief claims available

(a) The loss relief claims available to partners are the same as those for sole traders.

(b) A partner joining a partnership may be entitled to claim under S381 ICTA 1988 where a loss is incurred in the first four years of his membership of the partnership.

This relief would not be available to the existing partners.

(c) A partner leaving the partnership may be entitled to claim for a terminal loss under S388 ICTA 1988.

Again, this relief will not be available to the partners remaining in the partnership.

3.6 Example

Peter, Paul and Mary are in partnership making up their accounts to 5 April. During 1998/99 Paul left the partnership and Maggie joined in his place.

For the year ended 5 April 1999 the partnership made an adjusted loss of £20,000.

State the loss relief claims that will be available to the partners.

3.7 Solution

Paul will be entitled to terminal loss relief under S388 ICTA 1988 since he has actually ceased trading.

Maggie will be entitled to claim opening years relief under S381 ICTA 1988 since she has actually commenced trading.

Peter and Mary will not be entitled to either of the above reliefs.

All the partners will be entitled to relief under S380 ICTA 1988.

All the partners except Paul will be entitled to relief under S385 ICTA 1988.

4 PARTNERSHIP CAPITAL GAINS

4.1 Introduction

Each partner is assessed separately on his or her share of the partnership's capital gains.

You may prefer to come back to this section after studying the chapters on capital gains.

4.2 A disposal by the partnership

(a) Capital gains are normally allocated according to the profit sharing ratio unless a different basis has been agreed.

(b) Strictly, the proceeds and cost of the asset should be allocated between the partners so that each partner has his or her own separate capital gains computation.

It is usually acceptable, however, to calculate the gain and then allocate this one figure between the partners.

4.3   Example

Jim, James and June are in partnership. During 1998 they disposed of a freehold building and made a chargeable gain of £60,000. (Ignore taper relief).

The partners share profits 40:35:25.

Allocate the gain between the partners.

4.4   Solution

The gain will be allocated:

		£
Jim	(40%)	24,000
James	(35%)	21,000
June	(25%)	15,000

4.5   Reliefs

(a)   Each partner will be entitled to their own annual exemption of £6,800 to use against their gains on partnership and other assets.

(b)   Each partner will qualify for retirement relief individually. A partner under 50 will not qualify as a result of all the other partners being over 50.

(c)   Rollover relief will be available to each partner as they choose. Thus some partners may claim to rollover their share of a gain against their share of a replacement asset whilst others may not.

(d)   The same principle will apply to any other reliefs that are available, such as holdover relief in respect of the gift of business assets.

4.6   A change in the profit sharing ratio

(a)   Partners in relation to the acquisition and disposal of partnership assets pursuant to bona fide commercial arrangements, are generally not classed as connected persons.

(b)   This means that where there is a disposal between partners, the market value of the asset will not be used as the disposal price. The disposal price will instead be the value of that asset as shown in the partnership balance sheet.

(c)   A change in the partners profit sharing ratio does not by itself give rise to a charge to CGT, even though this will result in some partners having a reduced share (a disposal) of the partnership assets.

(d)   However, a revaluation of assets on the partnership balance sheet followed by a change in the partners profit sharing ratio will result in a charge to CGT.

The disposal price for partners who reduce their share of partnership assets will be the value in the balance sheet.

4.7   Example

Adam and Barry are in partnership. In December 1997 they decided to include the value of the partnership goodwill in their balance sheet at a value of £100,000.

The partners have always allocated profits and losses equally, but decided to change this in December 1998 to Adam 70% and Barry 30%.

Calculate the chargeable gains that will be assessed on the partners. (Ignore taper relief).

4.8   Solution

The inclusion of goodwill in the balance sheet in December 1997 does not give rise to a chargeable gain.

The subsequent change in profit sharing in December 1998 will result in a chargeable gain based on the value of goodwill reflected in the balance sheet of £100,000.

Barry' share of goodwill is reduced from 50% to 30% and so he will be treated as making a disposal of 20%, as follows:

		£
Share of goodwill before change in profit sharing	100,000 × 50% =	50,000
Share of goodwill after change in profit sharing	100,000 × 30% =	30,000
Deemed proceeds		20,000

Since the goodwill has no cost, he will be treated as making a chargeable gain of £20,000 for 1998/99.

Adam's share of the goodwill is increased from 50% to 70% and he therefore does not have a capital gain He will now have a base cost for goodwill equivalent to Barry's deemed proceeds of £20,000.

4.9   A change in the membership

(a)   The CGT rules relating to a change in the members of a partnership are exactly the same as for a change in the partners profit sharing ratio.

(b)   The admission or retirement of a partner will only result in a charge to CGT if the partnership has previously revalued assets on the balance sheet.

(c)   Where partnership assets have not been revalued, an incoming partner will simply take over a share of the cost of the partnership assets and will be entitled to indexation from their original date of purchase.

4.10   Example

Cathy and Des are in partnership, and allocate profits equally.

In June 1997 they admitted Eve as a partner. Profits were still allocated equally.

At the date that Eve was admitted to the partnership, goodwill was valued at £120,000, but this was not revalued in the partnership balance sheet neither did it have a CGT base cost.

The partners decided to cease trading in May 1999 and sold the goodwill for £150,000.

Show the chargeable gains that will be assessed on the partners. (Ignore taper relief).

4.11   Solution

On Eve's admission to the partnership there was no charge to CGT since goodwill was not revalued in the partnership balance sheet.

The cessation in May 1999 is a straightforward disposal of a partnership asset resulting in a chargeable gain of £150,000 This will be shared equally between the partners (£50,000 each), and will be assessed in 1999/00.

5   SELF TEST QUESTIONS

5.1   How are profits allocated between partners? (1.2)

5.2   How are annual charges allocated between partners? (1.2)

5.3   How are capital allowances given for assets owned privately by partners? (1.6)

5.4   When will the commencement rules apply to a partner? (2.1)

5.5   When will a partnership automatically continue when there is a change in the membership? (2.2)

5.6   How is a notional loss reallocated? (3.1)

5.7   What loss relief claims are available to partners? (3.5)

5.8   How are a partnership's capital gains assessed? (4.1)

5.9   When will a partner qualify for retirement relief? (4.5)

5.10   When will the change in the profit sharing ratio result in a charge to CGT? (4.6)

6   EXAMINATION TYPE QUESTION

6.1   Alf and Bob

Alf aged 56 and Bob aged 57 have been in partnership together since 1 December 1994.

The partners sold their business on 30 November 1998 for its market value of £520,000.
The partnership assets at 30 November 1998, and the chargeable gains (after indexation) arising on the disposal), were as follows:

	Market Value £	Chargeable Gain £
Freehold property	322,000	133,000
Goodwill	100,000	100,000
Plant and machinery	58,000	–
Net current assets	40,000	–
	520,000	233,000

The Schedule D Case I amounts for the final four years before dividing between the partners are as follows:

	Profit/(Loss) £
1995/96	15,000
1996/97	14,000
1997/98	11,200
1998/99	(33,500)

Profits and losses have always been shared 40% to Alf and 60% to Bob.

Alf is single and had no other income or outgoings.

Bob is single and also has no other income or outgoings apart from bank interest of £1,250 (gross) received on 1 December 1998.

Assume the 1998/99 rates and allowances apply to all years. Ignore taper relief.

You are required to:

(a)   Calculate the chargeable gains that will be assessed on Alf and Bob for 1998/99.

(b)   (i)   Advise the partners of the possible ways of relieving the partnership loss for 1998/99.

(ii)   Advise the partners as to which loss relief claims would be the most beneficial.

(iii)   After taking into account the advice in (ii), calculate the partners' taxable income for 1995/96 to 1998/99, and their net chargeable gains for 1998/99.

7   ANSWER TO EXAMINATION TYPE QUESTION

7.1   Alf and Bob

(a)   The capital gains of £233,000 arising on the disposal of the business will be split between the partners in their profit sharing ratios as follows:

		£
Alf	– 40%	93,200
Bob	– 60%	139,800

Both partners are over 50 and will therefore qualify for retirement relief, with the relevant qualifying period being 4 years.

Alf's chargeable gains of £93,200 are fully covered by retirement relief (£250,000 × 40% = £100,000).

Bob's chargeable gains for 1998/99 are as follows:

	£	£
Share of capital gains		139,800
Retirement relief		
250,000 × 40%	100,000	
(139,800 – 100,000) × 50%	19,900	
		119,900
Chargeable gains		19,900

(b)   There are two possible ways that the partnership loss can be relieved.

(i)   A claim can be made under S380 ICTA 1988 against total income for 1998/99 and/or 1997/98.

Subject to this claim being made, it would then be possible to extend the claim under S72 FA 1991 against chargeable gains of the same year.

(ii)   Terminal loss relief can be claimed under S388 ICTA 1988.

The final Schedule D Case I assessments will be split between the partners as follows:

	Alf 40% £	Bob 60% £
1995/96	6,000	9,000
1996/97	5,600	8,400
1997/98	4,480	6,720
1998/99	(13,400)	(20,100)

The most beneficial loss relief claim available to Alf would appear to be a terminal loss claim under S388 ICTA 1988.

Bob could also make a terminal loss claim, but this would waste his personal allowances for several years. He would be advised to make a claim under S380 ICTA 1988 against his statutory total income of £1,250 for 1998/99, and then claim under S72 FA 1991 against his chargeable gains of £19,900 for 1998/99.

Alf - taxable income:

	1995/96 £	1996/97 £	1997/98 £	1998/99 £
Schedule D Case I	6,000	5,600	4,480	–
Terminal loss	(3,320)	(5,600)	(4,480)	–
	2,680	–	–	–
PA	(2,680)	–	–	–
Taxable income	–	–	–	–

Bob - taxable income:

	1995/96 £	1996/97 £	1997/98 £	1998/99 £
Schedule D Case I	9,000	8,400	6,720	–
Bank interest	–	–	–	1,250
	9,000	8,400	6,720	1,250
Loss claim S380 ICTA 1988				(1,250)
PA	(4,195)	(4,195)	(4,195)	–
Taxable income	4,805	4,205	2,525	–
Chargeable gains				19,900
Loss claim S72 FA 1991 (20,100-1,250)				18,850
				1,050
Annual exemption				1,050
Net chargeable gains				–

14 OVERVIEW OF CAPITAL GAINS TAX

INTRODUCTION & LEARNING OBJECTIVES

When capital assets are sold at a profit, the profit is taxed; if the disposer is an individual, the profit will be charged to capital gains tax, if a company, to corporation tax. These chapters are concerned with explaining how the profit (the gain) is calculated, and the reliefs that are available.

When you have studied this chapter you should have learned the following:

- The scope of capital gains tax.
- In what circumstances a person is a chargeable person.
- The principal categories of exempt persons.
- Which assets are chargeable, and which exempt.
- The scope of the term 'disposal'.
- The position of companies with respect to capital gains.
- The operation of Taper Relief.
- The interaction of Taper Relief and loss relief.
- How loss relief is given and its interaction with the annual exemption.
- How assets are valued.
- The scope and significance of the term 'connected persons'.
- Rates of capital gains tax and when tax may be paid in instalments.

---

1 SCOPE OF CAPITAL GAINS TAX

1.1 Introduction

(a) Although it needs some elaboration, the scope of capital gains tax can be stated briefly. Capital gains tax is charged on gains arising on chargeable disposals of chargeable assets by chargeable persons. Such gains are not taxed individually, however. They are aggregated for a year of assessment (identical to the income tax year, 6 April to the following 5 April).

(b) The taxpayer's capital transactions for the tax year are entered in a computation, as follows.

Proforma CGT computation - Mr Brown - 1998/99

	£
Total 1998/99 chargeable gains, say	20,000
Less: Total 1998/99 allowable losses, say	4,000
	16,000
Less: Allowable losses brought forward at 6 April 1998, say	5,000
	11,000
Less: Annual exempt amount for 1998/99	6,800
Taxable gains for 1998/99	4,200

(c)   Loss relief for capital gains tax and the annual exempt amount are considered later in this chapter.

(d)   Taper relief is given against gains net of losses and depends on the period for which the asset giving rise to the gain has been held. This is also considered later in this chapter.

1.2   Chargeable and exempt persons

(a)   Only a chargeable person can be subject to capital gains tax and he is liable on all disposals of assets whether in the UK or abroad. A chargeable person is one who is either resident in the UK for the tax year in question (or part of it) **or** ordinarily resident. Residence is based on the same principles as for income tax, and thus a person is resident if:

- he is present in the UK for 183 days or more (normally ignoring days of departure or arrival); or

- he visits the UK habitually and the visits average more than three months per year.

Ordinarily residence can be regarded as habitual residence, so a person may be ordinarily resident in a tax year that he is not resident (because he is out of the UK for more than half that year).

These rules may be regarded as commonsense. They ensure that individuals who are actually UK resident in a tax year, or are normally so, pay UK tax. Equally their effect is to prevent the charge applying to foreign residents.

A Frenchman selling his factory in Paris would find it odd to receive a demand for capital gains tax from the Inland Revenue!

By concession, the Revenue allow a taxpayer to be neither resident nor ordinarily resident if he goes abroad for full-time employment and his overall period of absence includes a complete tax year. Limited visits to the UK within this period are allowed under the concession without losing non-R and non-OR status. However, this concession was misused for CGT avoidance so the following rule applies for taxpayers leaving the UK after 16 March 1998.

If a taxpayer leaves the UK and sheds R and OR status he still remains chargeable to CGT if he has been resident for at least four of the previous seven tax years and resumes R or OR status within the five tax years following his departure. Gains made during his absence will be chargeable on him in the year of return.

(b)   A chargeable person, as defined above, is not restricted to individuals. In addition the following may be chargeable persons if they meet the residence tests.

- companies
- partnerships
- personal representatives
- trustees.

(c)   Since the scope of 'persons' subject to capital gains tax is so all-embracing, the law makes specific provision for a variety of persons it wishes to exempt from the tax. The principal ones are:

- approved pension funds
- charities (to the extent that they use the gains for charitable purposes)

- authorised unit trusts and approved investment trusts
- local authorities
- registered friendly societies.

1.3   Chargeable and exempt assets

(a)   All forms of property are chargeable assets unless exempted. Note that it is irrelevant where in the world the asset is situated. The list of exempt assets is therefore long, but the main ones are set out below.

- foreign currency for personal expenditure.

- motor vehicles including veteran and vintage cars (except those unsuitable for private use)

- decorations for valour (unless acquired by purchase)

- some chattels (dealt with later in the text)

- gilt edged securities and qualifying corporate bonds

- debts (other than debts on a security)

- personal equity plan investments

- pension and annuity rights

- National Savings certificates.

- Prizes and betting winnings.

(b)   Exempt assets are outside the scope of capital gains tax. Consequently, whilst gains are not taxable, losses are not allowable either.

1.4   Chargeable disposal

(a)   The general term 'disposal' is not defined in the capital gains tax legislation, so its natural meaning, as amplified by case law decisions, has to be used. An asset may be regarded as disposed of when its ownership changes. Consequently the following are 'disposals';

- sales of assets
- gifts of assets

(b)   However, legislation and case law takes the meaning of 'disposal' further than might be thought from its everyday use. In particular, the following are also regarded as 'disposals' for capital gains tax purposes:

- sale of part of an asset (such as a half share in a painting)

- receipt of a capital sum derived from an asset

- loss or total destruction of assets (irrespective of whether or not the owner is compensated by a capital sum for the loss).

Remember that capital gains tax can only be charged if there is a chargeable disposal of a chargeable asset by a chargeable person. All three elements must be present and even then there may be a relief from tax.

1.5   Companies

Companies were included in the list of chargeable persons set out earlier in the chapter. Their position, however, is rather different from that of individuals. Although companies' gains and losses are computed broadly in the same way as individuals', they are not subject to capital gains tax itself but rather suffer corporation tax on their chargeable gains. The tax year is not the basis period for companies; their gains form part of their profits chargeable to corporation tax for the accounting period in which they arise.

1.6   Annual exempt amount

(a)   Every individual receives an exempt amount for each tax year. For 1998/99 it is £6,800 (1997/98 = £6,500). If his gains for the year do not exceed that amount, he is not chargeable to tax. Otherwise, he is chargeable on gains over and above the exempt amount.

(b)   Companies receive no exempt amount and are thus taxable on chargeable gains in full.

2   TAPER RELIEF

2.1   Introduction

(a)   Since March 1982 taxpayers have been entitled to a form of relief for inflation, referred to as indexation allowance, based on the movement of the retail prices index (RPI) from the month of acquisition to the month of disposal. This is explained in detail in the next chapter. The Labour government coming to power in 1997, however, decided to reform the system of CGT for individuals (but not for companies) with effect from 6 April 1998. Individuals making disposals of assets in 1998/99 and later years will only be entitled to an indexation allowance up to April 1998. For example, where an asset is acquired on 1 March 1993 and sold on 15 July 1998, relief for inflation is restricted by giving the indexation allowance only from March 1993 to April 1998.

(b)   Indexation allowance for individuals for periods after 5 April 1998 is being replaced by a taper relief dependent on the period of ownership after that date.

(c)   One of the objects of the reform is to encourage longer term investment in businesses so the taper relief for 'business' assets is more generous than for non-business assets.

(d)   Taper relief is given as a percentage reduction of a gain that would otherwise be chargeable. In other words it reduces the gain remaining after it has been reduced by indexation allowance. Similarly it reduces the gain remaining after deducting any available loss relief. We will return to these two points later.

(e)   Taper relief is given by reference to the number of complete years that an asset has been held since 5 April 1998. For example, an asset purchased in July 1998 and sold in May 2004 will have 5 years worth of taper using the scale below.

(f)   There is a bonus year given where an asset was acquired before 17 March 1998 (when the new regime was announced). For example, if the above asset sold in May 2004 had been acquired in July 1997 there would be 7 years worth of taper relief - 6 years for post 5 April 1998 ownership plus a bonus year for holding the asset by 17 March 1998.

(g)   The Taper Relief Table:

No. of complete years after 5 April 1998 (including the bonus year if available)	Taper relief percentages	
	Business	*Non-business*
1	7.5%	0%
2	15%	0%
3	22.5%	5%
4	30%	10%
5	37.5%	15%
6	45%	20%
7	52.5%	25%
8	60%	30%
9	67.5%	35%
10 or more	75%	40%

2.2   Activity

James disposes of an asset in July 1998 making an indexed gain of £80,000. The asset had been acquired in March 1986 and qualified as a business asset. The indexation allowance used to compute the gain had been based on the RPI movement from March 1986 to April 1998.

Calculate the gain remaining chargeable assuming his annual exemption is unused and comment on the difference had the asset been a non-business asset.

2.3   Activity solution

Indexed gain before taper relief	£80,000
Less: Taper relief - 7.5% as 'bonus' year applies	6,000
Gain after taper relief	£74,000
Less: Annual exemption	(6,800)
Gain remaining chargeable	£67,200

If the asset had been a non-business asset no taper relief would be available. In fact, taper relief for such assets will not apply for disposals made before 6 April 2000 (2 years post 5 April 1998 plus a bonus year) at the earliest.

2.4   Business and non-business assets

A business asset is defined as:

- an asset used for the purposes of a trade carried on by an individual either as a sole trader or in partnership; or

- an asset used for the purposes of a trade carried on by an individual's 'qualifying company'; or

- an asset held for the purposes of an office or employment to which the individual owner is required to devote substantially the whole of his time; or

- shares in a 'qualifying company'.

A 'qualifying company' is a trading company (or the holding company of a trading group):

- where the individual holds at least 5% of the voting rights and is a full time working director or employee; or

- where the individual holds at least 25% of the voting rights.

An asset not qualifying as a business asset is consequently a non-business asset.

3   LOSSES

3.1   Introduction

(a)   Losses and gains are calculated in the same way, as set out in the next chapter.

(b)   Where allowable losses arise they are set off against chargeable gains arising in the same tax year (or accounting period for companies).

(c)   Set off against gains is made to the maximum possible extent. There is no possibility of restricting the set off to avoid wasting all or part of the annual exemption. For example, if in 1998/99, Bill has chargeable gains of £14,000 and allowable losses of £9,000, his net chargeable gains are £5,000. This is covered entirely by his annual exemption of £6,800. Bill does **not** have the option of deducting only £7,200 of losses so that his net gains are £6,800 (which would be covered exactly by the annual exemption).

(d)   Losses are set against gains before deducting taper relief and the amount of taper relief is calculated on the gain net of any loss relief. Fortunately, the taxpayer is entitled to set any loss against gains which attract no taper relief or lower rates of taper relief.

(e)   Where a taxpayer cannot set off allowable losses against gains in the tax year they arise (because the gains are insufficient), he is entitled to carry the loss forward.

(f)   Losses brought forward are deducted only if the taxpayer has net chargeable gains for the tax year (or accounting period for companies). Current year losses are deducted in priority. For individuals, losses brought forward reduce net chargeable gains only to the level of the annual exemption for the year. Any additional losses brought forward are carried forward again to the next year. Since companies have no annual exemption this point does not apply to them.

(g)   Taper relief is given against net gains remaining after deducting current losses and losses brought forward. If this has resulted in net gains equal to the amount of the annual exemption there is no point in then calculating the taper relief (if any).

3.2 Activity

Tom, Dick and Harry made chargeable gains and allowable losses for the years 1998/99 and 1999/00 as set out below.

	Tom	Dick	Harry
1998/99			
Chargeable gains	12,000	4,000	5,000
Allowable losses	8,000	7,000	6,000
1999/00			
Chargeable gains	10,000	9,800	7,000
Allowable losses	2,000	1,000	2,000

An none of the assets giving rise to the chargeable gains were business assets taper relief can be ignored.

Assuming that the annual exemption for 1999/00 remains at its 1998/99 level, calculate the taxable gains for Tom, Dick and Harry for both 1998/99 and 1999/00 and the amount of any losses carried forward at the end of 1999/00.

3.3 Activity solution

Tom

1998/99	£
Chargeable gains	12,000
Allowable losses	8,000
Net chargeable gains	4,000

Net chargeable gains are covered by the annual exemption. No losses to carry forward to 1999/00.

1999/00	£
Chargeable gains	10,000
Allowable losses	2,000
Net chargeable gains	8,000
Less: Annual exemption	6,800
Taxable gains	1,200

Tom is taxed on gains of £1,200 in 1999/00.

Dick

1998/99	£
Chargeable gains	4,000
Allowable losses	4,000
Net chargeable gains	Nil

Dick is unable to use his 1998/99 annual exemption since his gains are all covered by current year losses. He has losses of £3,000 (7,000 – 4,000) to carry forward to 1999/00.

1999/00	£
Chargeable gains	9,800
Allowable losses	1,000
Net chargeable gains	8,800
Less: Losses brought forward (1998/99)	2,000
	6,800
Less: Annual exemption	6,800
Taxable gains	Nil

Dick used £2,000 of his losses brought forward, to reduce his net chargeable gains to the level of the annual exemption. He still has losses of £1,000 (3,000 – 2,000) to carry forward to 2000/2001.

Harry

1998/99	£
Chargeable gains	5,000
Allowable losses	5,000
Net chargeable gains	Nil

Like Dick, Harry wastes his 1998/99 annual exemption as all his 1998/99 gains are covered by current year losses. He has losses of £1,000 (6,000 – 5,000) to carry forward to 1999/00.

1999/00	£
Chargeable gains	7,000
Allowable losses	2,000
Net chargeable gains	5,000
Less: Annual exemption	6,800
Taxable gains	Nil

Harry's net chargeable gains for 1999/00 are all covered by his annual exemption. His losses brought forward from 1998/99 (£1,000) are thus carried forward to 2000/2001 untouched.

3.4 Activity

Henry makes the following (pre-taper) gains and loss in 1998/99:

Gain on disposal of shares in a qualifying company	£28,000
Gain on disposal of quoted shares (not a business asset)	£20,000
Loss on an asset used in Harry's business	£9,000

He has unrelieved capital losses of £3,000 brought forward from 1997/98. Taper relief of 7.5% was available on the qualifying company shares.

Compute the chargeable gains net of the annual exemption.

3.5   Activity solution

Where a loss is to be deducted start with the gain attracting the lowest rate of taper. It is clear that the loss brought forward can be applied in full without reducing the net gains (before taper relief) below £6,800.

		£
Gain on the quoted company shares		20,000
Less: Loss (current and brought forward)		12,000
		8,000
Gain on the business asset	28,000	
Less: taper relief @ 7.5%	2,100	
		25,900
Gains before annual exemption		33,900
Less: Annual exemption for 1998/99		6,800
Gains chargeable in 1998/99		27,100

3.6   Losses in the year of death

In general the rule for capital gains tax is that allowable losses may not be carried back to earlier periods for relief. This applies to companies and, with one exception, to individuals.   The exception is for losses incurred in the tax year in which an individual dies. Note that this does **not** apply to losses brought forward to that year.

Losses an individual suffers in the year of death may be carried back to the three tax years preceding the tax year of death. However, the carry back is possible only after the losses have been relieved to the maximum extent against gains of the same tax year (even if this entails wasting part or all of the annual exemption).

When losses are carried back they are relieved against the net gains of the earlier year (that is, the earlier years' own losses are relieved first). Losses carried back are relieved against the most recent year first and only to the extent that net gains before taper relief are reduced to the level of the annual exemption for that year. Any remaining losses are then carried back to the next earliest year, and so on.

If the loss is carried back to a year where taper relief has been given, it may be necessary to recalculate the taper relief. This applies if the carried back loss reduces the net chargeable gain attracting taper relief.

3.7   Activity

Jenny has made chargeable gains and suffered allowable losses as follows. She died on 31 March 1999.

	1995/96	1996/97	1997/98	1998/99
	£	£	£	£
Chargeable gains	20,000	4,000	8,800	7,000
Allowable losses	4,200	–	2,000	19,000

(a)   What are Jenny's taxable gains for 1995/96 to 1998/99 inclusive?
(b)   What difference would it make, if any, had Jenny died on 8 April 1999?

Note: the annual exemption was £6,000 for 1995/96, £6,300 for 1996/97 and £6,500 for 1997/98.

3.8   Activity solution

(a)   The year of death is dealt with first.

1998/99 £

Chargeable gains	7,000
Less: Allowable losses of the year	7,000
Taxable gains	Nil

Losses carried back to 1997/98 £12,000 (19,000 – 7,000).

1997/98 £

Chargeable gains	8,800
Less: Allowable losses for the year	2,000
	6,800
Less: Annual exemption	6,500
	300
Less: Losses carried back from 1998/99	300
Taxable gains	Nil

Losses carried back to 1996/97 £11,700 (12,000 – 300).

1996/97 £

Chargeable gains	4,000
Less: Annual exemption	6,000
Taxable gains	Nil

No carried back losses used as chargeable gains covered by the annual exemption. Losses carried back to 1995/96.

1995/96 £

Chargeable gains	20,000
Less: Allowable losses	4,200
	15,800
Less: Annual exemption	6,000
	9,800
Less: Losses carried back	9,800
Taxable gains	Nil

Losses of £1,900 (11,700 – 9,800) remain unrelieved as they cannot be carried back further. As capital gains tax will already have been paid for 1995/96 and 1997/98, it will now be repaid.

(b)   If Jenny had died on 8 April 1999 rather than 31 March 1999 the losses incurred in 1998/99 could not have been carried back as they would not be losses of the tax year in which the death occurred.

4   VALUATION OF ASSETS

4.1   Introduction

In most circumstances the value of an asset is what a purchaser is prepared to pay for it. However, if transferor and transferee strike a bargain that is not 'at arm's length' the asset's market value is substituted. This happens by default where they are 'connected persons' (the scope of which is considered later in this chapter). A bargain made 'at arm's length' is effectively one made at market value. An asset's market value is that which it might reasonably be expected to fetch on a sale in the open market.

4.2   Negligible value

If the value of an asset becomes negligible for whatever reason, the owner may claim to the Inspector that this has occurred. Provided that the Inspector agrees the owner is then treated as having disposed of, and immediately reacquired, the asset at its negligible value. This treatment crystallises a loss. (How gains and losses are computed is dealt with later in the text).

The deemed disposal is treated as occurring at the date of the claim although the taxpayer can treat it as having occurred up to two years before the start of the tax year in which the claim was made (accounting period for companies). The back dating of the loss applies only if the asset was actually of negligible value at both the date of the claim and the earlier date.

4.3   Shares and securities

Quoted shares and securities have a special valuation rule of their own. Their value is taken from prices quoted in the Stock Exchange Daily Official List and is the lower of:

(a)   the lower quoted price plus a quarter of the difference between the lower and higher quoted prices; and

(b)   the average of the highest and lowest recorded bargains.

4.4   Activity

Shares in XYZ plc are quoted in the Stock Exchange Daily Official List at 230p – 270p. On the same day the highest and lowest recorded bargains were 224p and 276p.

If a disposal of XYZ plc shares were made on that day other than on an arm's length bargain, what would be their value for capital gains tax?

4.5   Activity solution

Value of XYZ plc shares is the lower of:

(a)	Lower price	230p
	Add: (270p – 230p) × 1/4	10p
		240p
(b)	Average of lowest and highest recorded bargains	
	(224p + 276p) × 1/2	250p

Their value is thus 240p.

5   CONNECTED PERSONS

5.1   Introduction

Earlier in the chapter it was noted that capital gains calculations for bargains not made at arm's length use an asset's market value rather than the actual price paid for it. Connected persons are assumed not to have made an arm's length bargain and thus market value is always used for their transactions.

Two points are considered in this section: firstly, what relationships are regarded as 'connected', and, secondly, what impact that has for the treatment of capital losses.

5.2   Scope of 'connected persons'

An individual is 'connected' with the following individuals (and vice-versa).

(a)   **Family**

•   the individual's spouse;

•   any relative of the individual or his or her spouse ('relative' is defined below);

•   the spouse of any relative of the individual or his or her spouse.

A relative is a brother, sister, ancestor or lineal descendent.

These relationships are most easily seen in diagrammatic form as shown below.

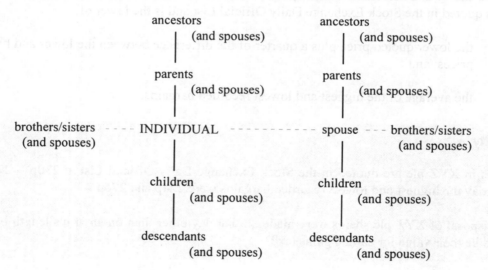

(b)   **Business associates**

•   partners
•   spouses of partners
•   relatives of partners

(except in relation to bona fide transactions in partnership assets).

(c)   **Companies**

•   over which the individual has control

•   over which he and persons connected with him have control together

A company (say X) is connected with another company (say Y) if:

- the same person (say A) has control of both X and Y; or
- A has control of X and other persons connected with him have control of Y; or
- A has control of X and A plus persons connected with him have control of Y; or
- A group of two or more persons control both X and Y.

5.3 Connected persons and loss relief

The purpose of defining 'connected persons' and treating transactions between them as having been made at market value is to ensure that they do not avoid tax or obtain loss relief with artificial transactions.

Except for disposals between spouses, which are subject to separate rules set out later in the text, where a transaction between connected persons results in a loss it is not available for general relief of chargeable gains as set out above. Its use is restricted to relief of gains on disposals to the **same** connected person.

6 ADMINISTRATION AND PAYMENT OF TAX

6.1 Introduction

Like income tax, capital gains tax is charged for tax years, so chargeable gains and allowable losses arising on transactions between 6 April 1998 and 5 April 1999 are subject to tax for the tax year 1998/99.

Companies pay corporation tax on their chargeable gains. Their chargeable gains and allowable losses are thus aggregated for an accounting period and form part of their profits chargeable to corporation tax.

For 'self-assessment' purposes, CGT is automatically due on 31 January following the tax year - eg, by 31 January 2000 for 1998/99.

Interest is payable on tax paid late. The system works in the same way as for income tax (see chapter on payment of tax). Repayment supplements are also calculated in the same way as for income tax.

6.2 Rates of tax

In broad terms, the rate at which an individual pays capital gains tax is dependent on the rate at which he pays income tax.

To ascertain the rate at which capital gains tax is paid, the gain is treated as though it were income, taxable at the individual's marginal rate of income tax. Note, however, that unused personal allowances cannot be used to reduce capital gains.

6.3 Example

Lucy has chargeable gains of £8,000 for 1998/99 (after deducting the annual exemption). What capital gains tax does she pay if her 1998/99 income after deducting personal allowances is:

(a)   £Nil (unused PA is £600)
(b)   £12,000
(c)   £22,000
(d)   £30,000.

6.4   Solution

(a)   Income of £Nil.

Lucy has no income chargeable to income tax but cannot use her surplus PA against the gains. Her capital gains tax payable is thus:

	£
First £4,300 @ 20%	860
Next £3,700 @ 23%	851
	1,711

(b)   Income of £12,000

If treated as income, the whole of Lucy's gains would fall in the basic rate band. Her CGT payable is thus:

£8,000 @ 23%	£1,840

(c)   Income of £22,000

Part of her gains, if treated as the top part of her income, will cause her to pay higher rate income tax. Her capital gains tax payable is thus:

	£
First £5,100 (remainder of basic rate band) @ 23%	1,173
Remaining £2,900 @ 40%	1,160
	2,333

(d)   Income of £30,000

In this case Lucy's basic rate band is wholly used up. Thus her CGT payable is:

£8,000 @ 40%	£3,200

6.5   Returns of information

A taxpayer is obliged to give written notice of his chargeable gains to the Inspector within 6 months of the end of the tax year. The normal way to do this is via a tax return but, if the Revenue does not issue a return, that does not excuse the taxpayer from failing to give notice.

Failure to give the required notice of liability renders the taxpayer liable to a penalty of up to the amount of tax unpaid on 31 January following the year of assessment.

There are a few exceptions to the requirement to provide information. The most commonly used concerns gains of small amounts. Where in a tax year an individual realises chargeable gains (before deduction of allowable losses) of not more than the annual exemption and the disposal proceeds are not more than twice the annual exemption, a simple statement to this effect constitutes the required notice. It is then up to the Inspector to decide whether to request further details. Secondly, no notice is required on the disposal of certain exempt assets, notably:

(a)   cars;
(b)   foreign currency for personal expenditure; and
(c)   prizes and betting winnings.

6.6   Payment of tax by instalments

It was noted earlier in the chapter that capital gains tax is due on 31 January following the tax year.

In two sets of circumstances, however, the tax may be paid in instalments.

(a)   If the seller is paid the consideration for the sale in instalments over a period of more than 18 months, the seller has the option to pay the associated CGT in instalments too.   The instalments may then be spread over the shorter of:

- eight years; and
- the period over which payment of the disposal proceeds is spread.

(b)   In some circumstances, capital gains tax due on gifts may be paid by instalments.   The donor cannot be entitled to hold over relief for business assets (explained later in the text) and the gift must fall into one of the following categories.

- land, or an interest in land; or

- shares or securities in a company that gave the donor control of it immediately before the sale; or

- shares or securities in a company that did **not** give control, but which are not quoted on a recognised stock exchange or the Unlisted Securities Market.

Where tax is paid in instalments because the consideration is paid by instalments, no interest on overdue tax is paid.   But for disposals by gift all instalments other than the first (which is due on the normal due date) carry interest calculated in the usual way.

7   CHAPTER SUMMARY

(a)   Capital gains tax is charged when a chargeable disposal of a chargeable asset is made by a chargeable person.

(b)   Companies pay corporation tax on their chargeable gains.   Whereas an individual is chargeable for a tax year, companies' gains are chargeable for accounting periods.   Their gains form part of profits chargeable to corporation tax.   Individuals receive an annual exemption (£6,800 for 1998/99) but companies do not.

(c)   Allowable losses are set off first against chargeable gains of the same tax year (accounting period for companies).   Taper relief (if any) is deducted next in the case of individuals (but not companies); this can involve wasting all or part of the annual exemption.   Where losses cannot be set off entirely in the year in which they arise they may be carried forward indefinitely and used to reduce future net chargeable gains as soon as they arise.   Losses incurred by an individual in the tax year in which he or she dies may be carried back to the three previous tax years, taking later years before earlier ones.   The annual exemption is not displaced when losses are carried back.

(d)   The value of an asset is normally the price at which it is sold.   Where it is gifted, sold at an undervalue or exchanged, its value is deemed to be market value.   Quoted shares and securities have their own method of valuation.

(e)   Connected persons are deemed not to have made a bargain 'at arm's length' and market value is used to calculate gains and losses for their transactions.   Broadly, relatives, business partners and companies that an individual controls are 'connected' with him.   Losses that arise on a disposal to a connected person may be relieved only against gains made to the **same** connected person.

(f)   Under self assessment CGT is payable on 31 January following the tax year.

(g)   A taxpayer is obliged to give notice of his liability of CGT to the Inspector within 6 months of the end of the tax year. CGT is not normally payable in instalments but this may be available where consideration is received in instalments or on certain assets where holdover relief for gifts of business assets does not apply.

8   SELF TEST QUESTIONS

8.1   On what gains is CGT charged? (1.1)

8.2   When is a person a chargeable person? (1.2)

8.3   Other than individuals, who may be a chargeable person for CGT purposes? (1.2)

8.4   What forms of property are chargeable assets? (1.3)

8.5   Other than sales and gifts, in which circumstances may there be a disposal for CGT purposes? (1.4)

8.6   How are companies' chargeable gains taxed? (1.5)

8.7   How do loss relief and taper relief interact? (3.1)

8.8   In what circumstances may losses be carried forward to a later period? (3.1)

8.9   How are quoted shares and securities valued other than on a bargain at arm's length? (4.3)

8.10   Against what gains may losses incurred in a disposal to a connected person be relieved? (5.3)

8.11   At what rate does an individual pay capital gains tax? (6.2)

15 THE CALCULATION OF GAINS AND LOSSES

INTRODUCTION & LEARNING OBJECTIVES

This chapter deals with the capital gains tax calculation. It covers disposal proceeds, acquisition costs and the indexation allowance. It is essential to fully master this chapter, which covers the basic calculation, before moving on to the various reliefs available.

When you have studied this chapter you should have learned the following:

- The form of a capital gains tax calculation.
- The rule for determining when a disposal occurs.
- How disposal proceeds are measured.
- Which types of expenditure are deductible in a capital gains tax calculation and which disallowed.
- How to identify and treat incidental costs of disposal and acquisition.
- The tests that improvement expenditure must meet to be allowable.
- How the indexation allowance is calculated and used in a capital gains tax calculation.
- The special rules for assets held since 31 March 1982.
- How to calculate allowable expenditure when the disposal is a part disposal of the asset.
- The treatment of improvement expenditure on a part disposal.
- The circumstances in which a disposal is deemed to take place on a 'no gain/no loss' basis.

1 INTRODUCTION

1.1 Overview of the calculation

In principle, although not in detail, capital gains tax is straightforward. The essence of a capital gain is the increase in value of an asset during the time it has been owned by the taxpayer and is therefore a comparison between the price he paid for it and the price he is now selling it for.

An illustrative computation, showing the main elements of the calculation, is set out below. The chargeable gain or allowable loss arising from the calculation then forms part of the individual's personal capital gains tax computation which was outlined in the previous chapter. In the case of the company it forms part of the company's profit chargeable to corporation tax for the accounting period in question.

1.2   Illustrative capital gains tax calculation

	£
Disposal proceeds	80,000
Less: Incidental disposal costs (see note below)	500
	79,500
Less: Allowable expenditure	30,000
Unindexed gain	49,500
Less: Indexation allowance	26,000
Chargeable gain	23,500

To the extent that this gain remains chargeable after any exemptions or deferrals or loss relief, it can be reduced further by taper relief provided the vendor is an individual and not a company. As the amount of taper relief for any particular gain therefore potentially depends on a number of other factors we generally omit it in the following calculations. The principles of taper relief have been shown in the previous chapter.

Note: incidental disposal costs form part of the allowable expenditure but they are shown separately in the calculation for reasons connected with the calculation of the indexation allowance.

The remainder of this chapter is devoted to outlining the basic rules for calculating each of the elements of the computation. Special cases and reliefs from tax are dealt with in later chapters.

1.3   Date of disposal

Unlike income tax and corporation tax, there is no question of apportioning a gain between different tax periods; the whole gain falls into the tax year (for individuals) or accounting period (for companies) in which the disposal takes place. Thus it is vital to be able to determine the date on which the disposal occurs.

The normal rule for capital gains tax is that the date of disposal is the date the contract is made (rather than the date of transfer of the asset which may be different).

2   DISPOSAL PROCEEDS

2.1   The general rule

The general rule, in the sense that it applies to the vast majority of disposals, is that the disposal proceeds taken into account in the computation is the amount of consideration received for the asset. This rule is applied provided that the disposal occurs through a bargain made at arm's length. So, if Mr Jones sells some shares to Mr Smith for £20,000, it is £20,000 that Mr Jones takes into his capital gains computation.

It should be noted that it is the gross disposal proceeds that are taken into the computation, before taking into account any costs associated with the disposal. Allowance may be made for these (see later in this chapter) but not by way of adjustment to the disposal proceeds themselves.

2.2   Other situations

Where actual consideration is not used the market value of the asset is usually substituted. The market value is the price which the asset might reasonably be expected to fetch on a sale on the open market, without any reduction being made for the effect of placing the whole of the asset on the market at one time.

Market value is substituted for actual proceeds either because, in fact, the bargain was not made at arm's length or because the law assumes that it was not made at arm's length. In particular, it is assumed that transactions between connected persons and gifts are bargains not made at arm's length and so market value is used for disposal proceeds in the capital gains tax computation.

3   ALLOWABLE EXPENDITURE

3.1   Introduction

As can be seen from the proforma capital gains tax computation earlier in this chapter allowable expenditure is deducted from the disposal consideration to calculate the unindexed gain.

The four types of expenditure which rank as allowable deductions are:

(a)   the purchase cost of the asset;

(b)   expenditure on enhancing the value of the asset (improvement expenditure);

(c)   expenditure incurred to establish, preserve or defend the taxpayer's title to the asset; and

(d)   incidental costs arising both on the acquisition of the asset and its disposal.

In all cases the expenditure has to be incurred 'wholly and exclusively' for the required purpose.

No deduction is permitted (even if the expenditure would fall within one of the categories set out above) if it is any of the following:

(a)   money paid out of public funds;

(b)   payments under insurance policies against damage, injury, loss or depreciation of the asset;

(c)   payments of interest; or

(d)   payments which are deductible in computing income tax.

The taxpayer is also prevented from deducting any amount representing the notional amount of his own labour.

3.2   Incidental costs

Broadly the same types of expenditure are deductible as incidental costs of acquisition or disposal. For the most part these are fairly obvious and consist of the following:

(a)   fees and commissions for professional services (surveyors, valuers, auctioneers, accountants, legal advisors, stockbrokers, or other agents);

(b)   advertising costs to find a buyer or seller;

(c)   the costs of a legal conveyance or transfer (including stamp duty); and

(d)   reasonable costs incurred in making valuations necessary for computing the gain particularly where market value is required.

Although incidental in nature, one must make a distinction between the incidental costs of acquisition and those of disposal because they are treated differently for the purposes of the indexation allowance (see later in this chapter).

3.3   Acquisition cost

In the great majority of cases acquisition cost is simply the price paid when the asset was originally purchased. Where, however, the owner acquired the asset by a transaction which required the previous owner to use the asset's market value in calculating his own gain, that same market value is used by the current owner as his cost of acquisition.

3.4   Improvement expenditure

To be deductible improvement expenditure must meet two tests:

(a)   it must be spent with the purpose of enhancing the value of the asset; and

(b)   it must be reflected in the state or nature of the asset at the time of disposal.

3.5   Preservation of title

This category of allowable expenditure, is fairly rare. Such expenditure is deductible if it is incurred in either establishing, or preserving, or defending the owner's title to or right over the asset in question. So, for example, legal costs in successfully resisting a claim to ownership of a piece of land is allowed under this heading.

The main reason for its comparative rarity is that such payments would often be deductible in computing income tax and are therefore disallowed in computing capital gains tax (see earlier in this chapter).

4   INDEXATION ALLOWANCE

4.1   Introduction

The indexation allowance is a rough and ready measure that attempts to ensure that capital gains are subject to tax only to the extent that they represent an increase in real terms of an asset's value. Notional or inflationary gains are excluded.

For capital gains tax inflation is measured via the Retail Prices Index (RPI).

A fraction is used to calculate the indexation factor, as follows:

$$\frac{\text{RPI in month of disposal}* - \text{RPI in month of expenditure}**}{\text{RPI in month of expenditure}**}$$

*   because the indexation allowance system has been superseded by taper relief for individuals by the FA98, the RPI for April 1998 is used where the individual held the asset by then and disposed of it after that month. This restriction does not apply where the vendor is a company.

**   as the relief was introduced by the FA82 the month of expenditure is taken as March 1982 or the month in which the expenditure was actually incurred, whichever is the later.

The fraction is rounded to three decimal places before use in a capital gains tax computation.

You will find the retail price indices in the rates and allowances at the front of this text.

4.2   Example

Mammoth Ltd sold a chargeable asset in January 1999 which it had bought in February 1987.

What is the indexation factor used in the calculation of its chargeable gain?

4.3   Solution

RPI in month of expenditure (February 1987) = 100.4
RPI in month of disposal (January 1999) = 164.8

Indexation factor is thus

$$\frac{164.8-100.4}{100.4} = 0.641 \text{ (rounded to three decimal places).}$$

4.4   Calculation of the indexation allowance

The indexation factor, as calculated above, is applied to each element of allowable expenditure other than incidental costs of disposal (which do not qualify for indexation allowance even if incurred before the month of disposal).

In the interests of accuracy the indexation allowance is calculated separately for each element of allowable expenditure that was incurred at a different time.

4.5   Example

Pye bought an investment property for £25,000 on 1 April 1983. On 15 July 1986 he spent £7,000 on a loft extension. He sold the property on 31 August 1998.

(a)   What indexation allowance is Pye entitled to on disposal of the property?

(b)   Would the indexation allowance have been different if the owner of the property had instead been Eye Ltd, all other dates and amounts being the same.

4.6   Solution

(a)   Indexation factor for acquisition expenditure:

$$\frac{161.2 \ (\text{RPI for April 1998}) - 84.28 \ (\text{RPI for April 1983})}{84.28 \ (\text{RPI for April 1983})}$$

= 0.913 (rounded to three decimal places)

The indexation allowance for the acquisition expenditure is:

£25,000 × 0.913 = £22,825

Indexation factor for improvement expenditure:

$$\frac{161.2 \ (\text{RPI for April 1998}) - 97.52 \ (\text{RPI for July 1986})}{97.52 \ (\text{RPI for July 1986})}$$

= 0.653 (rounded to three decimal places)

The indexation allowance for the improvement expenditure is:

£7,000 × 0.653 = £4,571

Pye's total indexation allowance is thus £27,396 (£22,825 + £4,571).

(b) If Eye Ltd had sold the property on 31 August 1998 the indexation allowance would have been calculated differently (using August 1998 rather than April 1998 as the month to which the indexation allowance is calculated disposal). In this case the indexation factors would have been as follows.

On acquisition expenditure:

$$\frac{162.2 - 84.28}{84.28} = 0.925$$

On improvement expenditure:

$$\frac{162.2 - 97.52}{97.52} = 0.663$$

The company's indexation allowance would then have been:

	£
On acquisition expenditure: £25,000 × 0.925 =	23,125
On improvement expenditure = £7,000 × 0.663 =	4,641
	27,766

A company in the same circumstances receives a further £370 (£27,766 - £27,396) of indexation allowance but will not be entitled to taper relief whatever type of asset or length of ownership applies.

4.7 Fall in the RPI

If there is a fall in the RPI between the date the allowable expenditure was incurred and the date of disposal (or April 1998, if appropriate) there is no indexation allowance given. Note that there is no 'negative indexation allowance' to be added to an unindexed gain.

4.8 Example

Linden Ltd acquires some land on 1 July 1998 for £40,000 and resold it on 30 August 1998 for £45,000.

What indexation allowance is it entitled to, if any?

4.9 Solution

RPI in month of disposal (August 1998) = 162.2
RPI in month of purchase (July 1998) = 162.6

Since the RPI was higher in the month of purchase than the month of sale, Linden Ltd has no indexation allowance.

4.10 Indexation allowance and capital losses

Indexation is only available to extinguish a capital gain, it is not available to create or increase a capital loss.

For disposals prior to 30 November 1993, indexation could create or increase a loss.

4.11   Activity

Cedric purchased an asset for £10,000 and later sold it in December 1998 for £12,000, the indexation allowance computed up to April 1998 is £4,000

What is the capital gains tax position?

4.12   Activity solution

		£
Proceeds		12,000
Less: cost		(10,000)
Unindexed gain		2,000
Indexation allowance (restricted)		(2,000)
		Nil

4.13   Indexation allowance on no gain/no loss disposals

In such cases it is assumed that the disposal proceeds of the vendor (and thus the base cost to the purchaser) are such that the vendor makes neither a gain nor a loss.

The most common instance of no gain/no loss disposals are those between spouses (see later in this chapter).

The indexation allowance is calculated in the normal way and added to the vendor's allowable expenditure to calculate the deemed disposal proceeds.

If an asset is acquired through a 'no gain/no loss' transfer on or after 30 November 1993, and is subsequently sold for less than the deemed disposal proceeds of the no gain/no loss transfer, the indexation allowance on the no gain/no loss transfer is restricted so that it neither creates nor increases a loss.

5   ASSETS HELD AT 31 MARCH 1982

5.1   Introduction

When capital gains tax was first introduced in 1965 the level of inflation was relatively low. Since that time, however, it has periodically reached high levels and consequently the value of most assets has increased greatly in nominal, if not real, terms. For many years it was thought that ignoring inflation prior to 31 March 1982 was a major source of injustice in the capital gains tax regime and this situation was rectified in the Finance Act 1988 by 'rebasing' to March 1982.

Towards the end of the 1990s inflation has fallen to modest levels and shows no sign of increasing. The FA98 therefore froze the inflation relief entitlement for individuals at its April 1998 value and switched the emphasis to relieving gains by reference to length of ownership. As the government was unsure whether this would be appropriate for companies, corporate taxpayers continue with the indexation allowance system for the present.

The FA98 taper relief system with the freezing of the indexation allowance does not alter the way the following rebasing rules work.

5.2   Rebasing

The FA88 rules, which involve a system known as 'rebasing', apply to assets held on 31 March

1982 and disposed of on or after 6 April 1988 (for individuals or companies). The system works by assuming that the person sold the asset on 31 March 1982 and immediately re-acquired it for its market value on that date. For assets held on 31 March 1982 the deemed acquisition cost (market value on that date) normally replaces original cost in the CGT computation. This ensures that the 'base date' for capital gains tax is effectively 31 March 1982.

5.3   Interaction with old rules

Before rebasing was introduced in 1988 capital gains tax calculations were normally based on the purchase price of an asset. Occasionally, where the value of an asset went down between the date of purchase and March 1982, substituting its 31 March 1982 value for the original cost on a post 1988 disposal would cause the taxpayer to be taxable on a higher gain. So, to ensure fairness, there is a requirement to calculate the gain using original cost too.

The results of the two calculations are compared and the one used depends on the outcome, as follows:

(a)   if either result produces a result of £nil or one of them a gain and the other a loss - neither result is used, the transaction is assumed to be for no gain/no loss;

(b)   if both calculations result in gains - the smaller gain;

(c)   if both calculations result in losses - the smaller loss.

Suppose an asset were sold such that a loss of £1,500 was the result of the 'cost calculation' and a loss of £1,200 the result of the 'March 1982 value' calculation, the loss of £1,200 (the smaller of the two) would be used.

5.4   Indexation allowance under 'rebasing'

Although the results of the two calculations have to be compared, the same indexation allowance is used in each of them. The indexation allowance is always based on the higher of original cost or 31 March 1982 value.

5.5   Election for March 1982 value for all disposals

If the taxpayer wishes, the complexities of making these comparisons each time an asset owned on 31 March 1982 is sold can be avoided. He can make an election to have all gains and losses computed on the basis of their March 1982 values.

The election is relevant to all assets held on 31 March 1982. Once made, it is irrevocable. The time limit for making the election is two years after the end of the tax year (or accounting period for companies) in which the first disposal was made to which it could apply (that is an asset held on 31 March 1982). The election applies not only to disposals occurring after the election was made but those before it too.

Where such an election is made the indexation allowance is automatically based on the asset's value at 31 March 1982.

5.6   Example

In 1974 White purchased a second home for £14,000 which he planned to use in his retirement. In 1978 the Department of Transport announced plans for a bypass which would pass near to the property and, in consequence, the house was worth only £10,000 on 31 March 1982. In 1984 a different route was chosen for the by-pass and when, on 31 March 1999, White sold the property he obtained a price of £50,000. (Ignore taper relief).

(a)   Calculate the chargeable gain arising.

(b)   What would the chargeable gain have been had a different route for the by-pass been chosen in 1981, and the 31 March 1982 value been £20,000?

5.7   Solution

(a)

	Cost	31.3.82 value
	£	£
Disposal proceeds	50,000	50,000
Less: Purchase price/ March 1982 value	14,000	10,000
Unindexed gain	36,000	40,000
Less: Indexation allowance (to April 1998)		
$\frac{161.2 - 79.44}{79.44}$ (= 1.029) × £14,000	14,406	14,406
Chargeable gain	21,594	25,594

The result used is thus a gain of £21,594.

(b)

	Cost	31.3.82 value
	£	£
Disposal proceeds	50,000	50,000
Less: Purchase price/March 1982 value	14,000	20,000
Unindexed gain	36,000	30,000
Less: Indexation allowance (to April 1998)		
$\frac{161.2 - 79.44}{79.44}$ (= 1.029) × £20,000	20,580	20,580
Chargeable gain	15,420	9,420

In this case the result used is a gain of £9,420. Again the smaller gain is taken, but this time it is based on the March 1982 value. The indexation allowance is higher because it is always based on the higher of the two alternatives (in this case £20,000).

5.8   Example

Meo bought a painting for £9,000 in January 1976 and sold it for £65,000 on 30 June 1998. In March 1982 it was professionally valued at £50,000.

Calculate the chargeable gain arising.

5.9   Solution

	Cost	31.3.82 value
	£	£
Disposal proceeds	65,000	65,000
Less: Purchase price/March 1982 value	9,000	50,000
Unindexed gain	56,000	15,000
Less: Indexation allowance (to April 1998)		
$\frac{161.2 - 79.44}{79.44}$ (= 1.029) × £50,000	51,450	51,450
Chargeable gain	4,550	Nil

The indexation allowance in the 31 March 1982 calculation can only extinguish a gain, it cannot create a loss.

In this case the result from the cost calculation is a gain, and that from the 31 March 1982 calculation is nil. Thus the result used is nil; neither a gain nor a loss.

6   PART DISPOSALS

6.1   Introduction

It is not simply the complete disposal of assets that triggers a charge to capital gains tax; part disposals do too (except in some cases when they are very small - see below).

The problem with part disposals is identifying the part of the allowable expenditure to deduct from the sale proceeds. This is done by calculating the fraction set out below and multiplying it by the whole cost. The fraction is:

$$\frac{A}{A+B}, \text{ which equals}$$

$$\frac{\text{Disposal consideration for the part disposed of}(A)}{\text{Disposal consideration for the part disposed of}(A) + \text{Market value of the remainder* } (B)}$$

* at the time of disposal.

6.2   Example

Carruthers purchased a commercial building for £250,000. He later sold part of it for £100,000 and at that time the part he retained was worth £200,000.

Calculate the allowable expenditure available to Carruthers on the part disposal.

6.3   Solution

The part disposal fraction is:

$$\frac{\text{Disposal consideration }(£100,000)}{\text{Disposal consideration }(£100,000) + \text{Market value of remainder }(£200,000)}$$

$$= \frac{100,000}{300,000} = \frac{1}{3}$$

Thus the allowable expenditure is:

$$\text{Original cost }(£250,000) \times \frac{1}{3} = £83,333.$$

6.4   Improvement expenditure

Care is needed when dealing with improvement expenditure on a part disposal. There are three possibilities:

(a)   the improvement expenditure applies equally to the whole asset (in which case it too is apportioned using the part disposal fraction); or

(b)   the improvement expenditure applies wholly to the part disposed of (in which case all of it is deducted in the part disposal computation); or

(c)   the improvement expenditure applies wholly to the part retained (in which case none of it is deducted in the part disposal computation).

6.5   Example

Higgins purchased a commercial building and annexe for £175,000 on 1 September 1988. On 31 December 1989 he incurred costs of £20,000 on installing air conditioning in the main building (but not the annexe). He sold the main building (without the annexe) for £250,000 on 10 October 1998. At that time the annexe was worth £50,000.

Calculate the chargeable gain arising.

6.6   Solution

	£	£
Disposal proceeds		250,000
Less: Allowable expenditure (W)		165,833
Unindexed gain		84,167

Less: Indexation allowance (to April 1998)

(a)   on original cost

$$\frac{161.2-108.4}{108.4} \ (=0.487) \times £145,833 \text{(W)} \qquad 71,021$$

(b)   on improvement expenditure

$$\frac{161.2-118.8}{118.8} \ (=0.357) \times £20,000 \qquad 7,140$$

		78,161
Chargeable gain		6,015

If this were a 'business' asset, taper relief of 7.5% would be available.

Working - allowable expenditure

Higgin's expenditure comprises a part of his original purchase plus the whole of the improvement expenditure

	£
Part of the original cost:	
$£175,000 \times \dfrac{250,000}{250,000+50,000}$	145,833
Improvement expenditure	20,000
	165,833

6.7   Small part disposals of land

When a person disposes of a small part of a holding of land he is able to elect to defer any capital gains tax until a later disposal that goes beyond the definition of 'small'. This is done by subtracting the small disposal proceeds from the allowable expenditure deductible on the future occasion.

What counts as 'small' depends on the circumstances. If the disposal is made to an authority that has compulsory purchase powers 'small' means that the consideration received is less than 5% of the market value of the land (including the part sold).

Alternatively, if the sale is to someone else, a disposal is small if:

(a)   the disposal proceeds are not more than 20% of the value of the land holding before disposal; and

(b)   the proceeds (plus any other proceeds from land sales in the tax year) are not more than £20,000.

7   NO GAIN/NO LOSS DISPOSALS

7.1   Introduction

Certain transactions, notably between spouses (provided they are not separated) are effectively ignored for capital gains tax purposes. The rationale is that married couples are essentially single economic entities and thus capital gains tax is imposed only when there is a disposal to a third party.

The way capital gains tax is sidestepped in these circumstances is to treat disposals between spouses as occurring at a price that provides the disposer with neither a gain nor a loss. When the transfer is made the transferor is deemed to dispose of the asset at its purchase cost plus indexation allowance from the date of acquisition to the date of transfer. The transferee is deemed to have paid the same amount to acquire the asset (and so this amount is used in any later disposal to a third party).

7.2   Activity

Jack acquired a chargeable asset for £25,000 on 1 September 1992 and transferred it to his wife, Jill, on 31 January 1995. Jill sold the asset to a third party on 1 August 1998 for £39,000.

Compute the chargeable gain or allowable loss on Jill's disposal in August 1998.

7.3   Activity solution

	£
Disposal proceeds	39,000
Less: Deemed acquisition cost (W)	26,175
Unindexed gain	12,825
Less: Indexation allowance (April 1998 - Jan 1995)	
$\dfrac{161.2-146.0}{146.0}$ (= 0.104) × £26,175	2,722
Chargeable gain	10,103

Working - deemed acquisition cost

	£
Purchase price in September 1992	25,000
Add: Indexation allowance (Jan 1995 - Sept 1992)	
$\dfrac{146.0-139.4}{139.4}$ (= 0.047) × £25,000	1,175
	26,175

7.4   Assets transferred after 31 March 1982

It was noted above that the rationale for no gain/no loss transfers is to treat the transferor and transferee as one economic entity and so effectively ignore transfers between them. The transferee 'stands in the shoes' of the transferor.

A particular problem arises where the transferor acquired an asset on or before 31 March 1982 and it is acquired by the transferee after that date. Since the rebasing rule requires the disposer to have owned the asset on 31 March 1982 the transferee would not obtain any benefit from them were it not for a special set of rules. These simply deem the transferee to have owned the asset on 31 March 1982. If the March 1982 value is the one used (rather than the transferor's original cost) indexation allowance for the transferee applies from that date too.

7.5   Activity

Stuart purchased a chargeable asset on 1 November 1980 for £18,000 and transferred it to his wife, Hannah, on 1 June 1983. On 31 May 1998 Hannah sold the asset for £50,000 and its value on 31 March 1982 was £21,000.

Calculate the chargeable gain or allowable loss arising on Hannah's disposal in May 1998.

7.6   Activity solution

	Cost	31.3.82 value
	£	£
Disposal proceeds	50,000	50,000
Less: Cost/March 1982 value	18,000	21,000
Unindexed gain	32,000	29,000
Less: Indexation allowance (to April 1998)		
$\dfrac{161.2 - 79.44}{79.44}$ $(= 1.029) \times £21,000$	21,609	21,609
Chargeable gain	10,391	7,391

The lower gain, £7,391 is taken.

7.7   Assets transferred on or after 30 November 1993

Where one spouse makes a disposal to the other, the asset is transferred at cost plus indexation allowance. This indexation allowance will not be available to create or increase a loss for assets acquired in no gain/no loss transfers on or after 30 November 1993 on the final disposal. In this case, the base cost of the asset will be its original cost plus restricted indexation allowance (if any).

7.8   Activity

Charlotte purchased a chargeable asset on 1 March 1989 for £20,000, and transferred it to her husband, Nicholas, on 1 May 1994. On 31 March 1999 Nicholas sold it for £22,000.

Calculate the chargeable gain or allowable loss on Nicholas' disposal in March 1999.

7.9   Activity solution

	£
Disposal proceeds	22,000
Less: Deemed acquisition cost £25,780 (W) restricted to	22,000
Allowable loss	Nil

	£
Working - deemed acquisition cost	
Purchase price in March 1989	20,000
Add: Indexation allowance (Mar 1989 - May 1994)	
$\dfrac{144.7-112.3}{112.3}$ (=0.289) × £20,000	5,780
	25,780

7.10   Assets transferred after 5 April 1998

Where an asset is transferred between spouses after 5 April 1998 the transferee spouse will be entitled to taper relief on a subsequent sale to a third party by reference to their combined periods of ownership since 5 April 1998, with entitlement to a bonus year if the transferor spouse had owned the asset on 17 March 1998. The business asset rates of taper relief apply provided the asset is a business asset in the hands of the transferee spouse regardless of its status in the transferor spouse's hands.

8   CHAPTER SUMMARY

The general form of a capital gains tax calculation is essentially straightforward. It involves deducting a person's allowable expenditure from his disposal consideration to obtain an unindexed gain and from this the indexation allowance is deducted to find the chargeable gain.

It is helpful to view the calculation as a series of separate elements, taken in the following order.

(a)   Decide the date of disposal (the date the contract for sale is made). The tax year or accounting period is then known.

(b)   Ascertain the disposal consideration to be taken into account (normally it is the sale price but the asset's market value is used when the disposal is a gift, a sale at an undervalue or a transaction between connected persons).

(c)   Calculate the allowable expenditure, remembering in particular that to qualify, improvement expenditure must be reflected in the state or nature of the asset at the time of disposal.

(d)   Calculate the indexation allowance separately for allowable expenditure incurred at different times. Remember that incidental costs of disposal do not attract indexation allowance.

For assets owned on 31 March 1982 and disposed of after 5 April 1988 (for individuals or companies) the rebasing rules apply. A comparison is made to decide which result is used (or, if appropriate no gain/no loss) unless the taxpayer has elected for all disposals to be calculated using March 1982 values.

Individuals are not entitled to indexation allowance beyond April 1998. Taper relief does not form part of the capital gain calculations. Instead it is a deduction to make after applying loss reliefs and certain other reliefs (see later chapters).

Capital gains tax applies to part disposals as well as disposals of entire assets. The form of the calculation is the normal one but care must be taken to ascertain the proportion of allowable expenditure to deduct. Small part disposals of land do not trigger a capital gains charge; it is deferred until a larger disposal of the land.

9   **SELF-TEST QUESTIONS**

9.1   On what date does a disposal occur for capital gains tax? (1.3)

9.2   What are the two alternatives that may be used as disposal consideration? (2.2)

9.3   What are the four categories of allowable expenditure? (3.1)

9.4   Why must incidental costs of acquisition and disposal be treated separately? (3.2)

9.5   What tests must improvement expenditure meet to be deductible? (3.4)

9.6   What formula is used to calculate the indexation factor? (4.1)

9.7   When is indexation allowance restricted or denied on a disposal? (4.4)

9.8   What is the 'base date' for capital gains tax? (5.2)

9.9   An election may be made to have all disposals of assets held on 31 March 1982 computed on the basis of their value on that date. What is the time limit for the election? (5.5)

9.10   What fraction is used to apportion part of the cost of an asset when a part disposal is made? (6.1)

16 PRINCIPAL PRIVATE RESIDENCES

INTRODUCTION

Relief is available on the disposal of certain assets, and on certain types of disposal, so that the full gain is not taxed at the time of the disposal.

The type of relief falls into two broad categories:

- Exemption; and
- Deferral.

If a gain is exempt it means that it is not chargeable now, nor in any time in the future; the gain is eliminated. This type of relief is available on the disposal of a principal private residence (see below) and also on the disposal of a business, or shares in a business, when the vendor is at least 50 years old and certain conditions are met (retirement relief).

If a gain (or part of a gain) is deferred, it will not be taxed at the time of disposal, but may be taxed on some future event. One instance where this relief is available is where there is a disposal followed by reinvestment in a new asset; the gain is either rolled over to reduce the base cost of the new asset or is simply put into suspense. When the new asset is eventually sold the gain is generally crystallised. This type of relief is available in several situations, examples are:

- reinvestment in business assets (gains rolled over)
- reinvestment in certain unquoted shares (gains put into suspense)

When studying the various capital gains tax reliefs in the ensuing chapters, it is important to establish whether the particular relief exempts the gain, or simply defers it.

These are the most important reliefs available:

- Principal private residence: this **exempts** the gain on an **individual's** house if it has been occupied as his principal private residence.

- Retirement relief: this **exempts** the gains on the disposal of an **individual's** business, or shares in a trading company.

- Rollover relief (replacement of business assets relief): this **defers** the gain when an **individual** or **company** disposes of a business asset, and reinvests in another one.

- Gift relief: this **defers** the gains on the gift, by an **individual**, of business assets and certain other assets.

- Rollover relief on reinvestment: this **defers** the gain on the disposal of any asset by an **individual** when he reinvests by subscribing for qualifying shares.

When an individual disposes of a business, the following reliefs may be relevant:

- retirement relief
- gift relief
- reinvestment relief
- rollover relief

When an individual disposes of shares in a business, the following reliefs may be relevant:

- retirement relief
- gift relief
- reinvestment relief.

Taper relief is only given against gains that are chargeable. If a gain is wholly exempt there is no taper relief. If a gain is only partly exempt, taper relief can apply to the amount that remains chargeable. Similarly if a gain is rolled over (ie, deferred), taper relief cannot apply as the gain has not become chargeable.

This chapter deals with one of the more important capital gains tax reliefs - the relief for principal private residences. With this relief the gain (or part of the gain) on the disposal of a principal private residence is exempt. This relief is examined fairly frequently; the questions tend to be quite straightforward, often covering periods of occupation and periods of absence.

---

1   INTRODUCTION

1.1   Overview

Any gain on the disposal of a private residence, which has been an individual's principal residence throughout his period of ownership, is exempt from capital gains tax. The sale of most private homes benefit from this exemption and thus relatively little capital gains tax is paid on the transfer of private residential property. Equally, any losses sustained by the taxpayer on the disposal of such property are not allowable for CGT. This chapter is concerned with the scope of the CGT exemption and the conditions and restrictions which deny it or reduce it in particular cases.

1.2   Scope of the exemption

Normally the taxpayer's principal private residence and up to half a hectare of adjoining ground may benefit from the exemption. If, however, the size and character of the house warrant it, a larger area may be permitted. The test is whether a larger area is needed 'for the reasonable enjoyment of it.'

2   DWELLING HOUSE

2.1   Introduction

In order to obtain the relief, the property disposed of must be a dwelling house.

2.2   Meaning of 'dwelling house'

The meaning of 'dwelling house' is not defined in the legislation and so it has been left to the courts to determine the limits of the expression. A number of principles have emerged from decided cases.

(a)   Caravans connected to mains services such as electricity and water do qualify as dwellings for the purposes of the relief (Makins v Elson, 1976).

(b)   In Batey v Wakefield (1981) the taxpayer sold a bungalow and a small amount of land that was within the grounds of his house and which had been occupied by a part-time caretaker. The Court of Appeal upheld a decision of the General Commissioners that the bungalow provided services for the benefit of the main house, was occupied by the taxpayer through his employee, and so qualified as part of the taxpayer's residence. A test resulting from this case is that buildings must together form an entity which can be regarded as a dwelling house, albeit divided into different buildings performing different functions. From a tax planning perspective, the physically nearer a dependent building is to the main house, the better will be the taxpayer's opportunity to show that the dependent building forms part of his principal private residence. More recent cases (Markey v Sanders, 1987 and Lewis v Rook, 1992) have reaffirmed this principle.

(c)   The case of Green v CIR (1982) showed that the Revenue may split a property between that used as the taxpayer's private residence and the part which is not, despite the property being all one building. The taxpayer sold a mansion house which comprised a central block with two wings connected to it by corridors. During reconstruction and redecoration work the taxpayer and his family occupied parts of the central block but not the wings. Thus, where the taxpayer owns a large property which is divided into several self contained units, only those parts which the taxpayer actually occupied qualify for exemption.

(d)   In Varty v Lynes (1976) the taxpayer first sold his house and part of his garden and then, about a year later, sold the remainder of the garden at a substantial profit. The court held that the principal private residence exemption applied only to the first disposal, because when the remainder of the land was sold, it no longer formed part of the individual's principal private residence. Although not the subject of a decided case, it is likely that if the order of sales in the Varty case were reversed, the land sold independently of the buildings would still not qualify for relief. In any event, the Revenue takes this point only when the land sold separately has development value.

3   RESTRICTIONS ON EXEMPTION

3.1   Periods of non occupation

In general, if the owner does not occupy his property for a period, any gain arising ceases to be exempt from capital gains tax. The exempt gain is then calculated by a fraction as follows:

$$\frac{\text{Total gain} \times \text{period of occupation}}{\text{Total period of ownership}}$$

The period before 31 March 1982 is ignored in calculating both periods of occupation and periods of ownership.

There are a number of sets of circumstances, in which despite being absent, an individual is nevertheless treated as being resident. These are:

(a)   the 36 months directly preceding the disposal of his property;

(b)   any period or periods which together do not last more than 3 years;

(c)   an unlimited period throughout which the individual was employed abroad;

(d)   any period or periods that together do not last more than 4 years, throughout which the individual was prevented from residing in his property because:

•   his place of work was too far from his property; or

- his employer required him to reside elsewhere

(e)   any period during which the individual resides in job related accommodation.

Relief for the final 36 months is extremely useful, especially for relatively short term ownership of property. Unlike the rules for most of the other periods of deemed occupation, there is no need for the owner to occupy or reoccupy the property at the end of it. He may even let his property or elect for another property to be treated as his principal residence without losing the benefit of the exemption. It should be noted, however, that the exemption is lost for any part of the property used for business purposes during this period.

For any of the permitted periods of absence in (b), (c) and (d) above to apply, it is vital that at some time both before and after the absence the property must have been the individual's only or main residence. This is a question of fact and so a period of deemed occupation under one heading does not count as a period of residence, either before or after, for another heading. There is one exception to this, provided by extra statutory concession, which removes the need for actual residence after a period of absence so long as an individual is unable to resume residence in his previous home because the terms of his employment require him to work elsewhere. Where an individual is absent for longer than the periods permitted by (b) or (d) the Revenue regard only any gain accruing in the additional absence as taxable (not the whole of it).

Note that actual occupation before 31 March 1982, although ignored for exemption purposes, will qualify as actual owner occupation preceding a period of absence.

It is important to appreciate that the periods of deemed occupation are cumulative and so, in exceptional circumstances, a taxpayer could find himself benefiting from all of them at different times.

Permitted absence whilst staying in job related accommodation can apply to both the employed and the self employed.

3.2   Example

In September 1978 Mr Flint purchased a house in Southampton for £15,000, which he lived in until he moved to a rented flat on 1 July 1982. He remained in the flat until 1 October 1984 when he accepted a year's secondment to his firm's New York office. On coming back on 1 October 1985 he moved into a relative's house, where he stayed until he returned to his own home on 31 January 1986. On 1 July 1986 he changed jobs and rented a flat near his new employer's offices in Newcastle. Here he remained until he sold his Southampton house on 1 February 1999 for £95,000. In March 1982 it was estimated to be worth £25,000.

Calculate the gain arising on the disposal, if any.

3.3   Solution

Calculation of chargeable gain

	£
Disposal proceeds	95,000
Less: 31 March 1982 value *	25,000
Unindexed gain	70,000
Less: Indexation allowance (to April 1998)	
$\dfrac{161.2 - 79.44}{79.44}$ (=1.029) × £25,000	25,725
Indexed gain	44,275
Less: Principal private residence (PPR) exemption (W)	19,069
Chargeable gain	25,206

* March 1982 value clearly produces lower gain than cost.

Working - chargeable and exempt periods of ownership

		Chargeable months	Exempt months
Sept 1978 - March 1982	(irrelevant)	-	-
April 1982 - June 1982	(resident)	-	3
July 1982 - Sept 1984	(absent - any reason)	-	27
Oct 1984 - Sept 1985	(absent - employed abroad)	-	12
Oct 1985 - Jan 1986	(absent - any reason)	-	4
Feb 1986 - June 1986	(resident)	-	5
July 1986 - Jan 1996	(absent - see tutorial note)	115	-
Feb 1996 - Jan 1999	(final 36 months)	-	36
		115	87

Total period of ownership (115 + 87) = 202 months.

Exempt element of gain is thus 87/202 × £44,275 = £19,069.

Note: after Mr Flint left his residence to work in Newcastle he never returned. Consequently he broke the condition for exemption that work away from home is granted only when there is actual residence both before and after the absence. In contrast the exemption for the final 36 months of ownership has no such restriction and was thus still available.

4   BUSINESS USE AND LETTING

4.1   Business use

Where a house, or part of it, is used wholly and exclusively for business purposes, it clearly cannot be used as residential accommodation at the same time.

Consequently, to the extent it is used for business purposes and for the period of use, it loses its CGT exemption and becomes taxable. It should be noted particularly that the taxpayer cannot benefit from any of the rules of deemed occupation (including that of the final 36 months of ownership) for any part of his property used for business purposes.

The exact proportion of the gain that becomes taxable in this way is subject to negotiation between the taxpayer and the Inspector. Common methods of apportionment, however, are the percentage of the floor area used for business purposes or to use the same percentage used in the taxpayer's income tax computation to apportion running costs to the area used for business purposes.

It should be noted that effective relief from capital gains tax may still be obtainable for the part of the property used for business purposes. Provided that the other conditions for the relief are met, the taxpayer can claim rollover relief on the gain attributable to the business use (see later in text). Similarly, if the gain is attributable to a business asset, the higher rate of taper relief will apply to any part of the gain remaining chargeable - for 1998/99 disposals of property held on 17 March 1998, for example, this would be 7.5%.

4.2   Letting

Where an individual lets out his house for residential use (but not commercial use) the principal private residence exemption is extended to cover gains accruing while the property is let. Before considering the details of this relief, two points need to be made. Firstly, where the individual takes in a lodger who shares the family's accommodation and takes meals with them the letting exemption is unnecessary. In these circumstances the whole of the property is treated as remaining the individual's principal private residence throughout the period of letting. Secondly, it relieves gains which would otherwise be chargeable to tax and therefore does not apply during periods of deemed occupation, which are already exempted.

The gain which is exempt as a result of letting relief is subject to an overriding monetary limit, currently £40,000 and cannot in any case exceed the amount of the main residence exemption. Note that the relaxation comes in the form of exempting a gain which would otherwise be chargeable to tax; it cannot convert a gain into an allowable loss.

The letting exemption applies whether the owner is absent from his property and lets the whole of it or lets part of it and still occupies the remainder. To benefit from the relief, however, the letting must form a part of the individual's own residence.

The letting exemption is restricted to the lowest of:

(a)   £40,000;
(b)   the amount of the gain exempted by the normal principal private residence rules;
(c)   the part of the gain attributable to the letting period.

Where a taxpayer lets only a part of his property the gain attributable to the letting is calculated by first apportioning the overall gain between the period in which the property was let and the period in which it was not and subsequently reducing the gain relating to the letting period according to the proportion of the property which was let.

5   OWNERSHIP OF MORE THAN ONE RESIDENCE

5.1   Nomination of main residence

Where an individual has more than one residence he is entitled to nominate which of them is to be treated as his principal residence for capital gains purposes by notifying the Inspector of Taxes in writing. The election must be made within two years of acquiring an additional residence otherwise it is open to the Inspector as a question of fact to decide which residence is the main residence.

5.2   Married couples

Provided that they are not treated as being separated or divorced, a married couple is entitled to only one residence between them for the purposes of the private residence exemption.

Where more than one residence is owned any election specifying which one is to be treated as the principal residence has to be made by both the husband and wife, irrespective of who owns the legal title to the properties.

Special rules apply on marriage breakdown. Where one spouse ceases to occupy the property in these circumstances, he or she is treated as still residing there for the purposes of capital gains tax. This treatment is subject to the following conditions:

(a)   the departing spouse must have owned or had an interest in the matrimonial home;

(b)   the other spouse must have continued to live in the house;

(c)   one spouse must have disposed of his interest in the property to the other; and

(d)   the departing spouse must not have made an election to treat some other property as his or her principal private residence.

6   SELF TEST QUESTIONS

6.1   What is the normal maximum permitted area of ground that may be sold with a main residence and qualify for PPR exemption? (1.2)

6.2   What test is applied in deciding whether a dependent building forms part of the main residence? (2.2)

6.3   Is the owner required to occupy his property during the final 36 months of ownership to qualify for the PPR exemption? (3.1)

6.4   What is the earliest date that can be relevant in calculating the 'period of ownership'? (3.1)

6.5   If the property is used for business purposes during the final 36 months of ownership is PPR exemption affected? (4.1)

6.6   What is the maximum letting exemption? (4.2)

6.7   What happens if the taxpayer does not elect within two years of acquiring a second residence as to which is his main residence? (5.1)

6.8   What principal private residence relief is a married couple entitled to? (5.2)

7   EXAMINATION TYPE QUESTIONS

7.1   Lucas

Lucas sold his only residence for £135,475 on 31 March 1999. He bought it on 1 April 1979 for £14,000. He used the whole property exclusively for himself and his wife for the first ten years, and then for the last ten years let the basement, comprising one-third of the house. No structural alterations were made and the basement was not a self-contained flat. The market value of the house on 31 March 1982 was £35,000.

Lucas elects for market value at 31 March 1982 basis to be used for all assets owned on that date.

Compute the amount of the chargeable gain, assuming any necessary elections are made.

7.2   Butler

On 6 April 1967 Butler purchased a freehold house for £6,215. The house was empty until 6 October 1968, when Butler commenced occupation. On 6 October 1970 he moved to France, and was employed there as a saleman until 6 October 1973, when he returned to work in England in an employment which required him to live away from home in rented accommodation.

On 6 October 1978 he resumed occupation until 6 October 1988 when again his employment required that he live some distance from his home. On 6 October 1995, having been told he was going to work permanently in the distant location, Butler returned to his house for a month's holiday during which he redecorated the house and put it on the market. It was sold on 6 July 1998 for £86,175 (net). Market value at 31 March 1982 was agreed to be £35,000.

Compute any chargeable gain arising.

8   ANSWERS TO EXAMINATION TYPE QUESTIONS

8.1   Lucas

	£	£
Net sale proceeds		135,475
Less: MV 31.3.82 by election		35,000
Unindexed gain		100,475

Less: Indexation allowance (March 1982 - April 1998)

$$\frac{161.2 - 79.44}{79.44} (1.029) \times 35,000 \qquad (36,015)$$

		64,460

Less: (i) Whole residence exempt for 10 years since 31.3.82: 7 years exclusive use and last 3 years in any event:

	£64,460 × $\frac{10}{17}$	37,918	
(ii)	Two-thirds only remaining 7 years exempt while let £64,460 × $\frac{7}{17}$ × $\frac{2}{3}$	17,695	55,613

Gain (otherwise) chargeable on letting		8,847

Less: Letting exemption, the lowest of:
  (i)   PPR exemption of £55,613
  (ii) Gain attributable to letting period, £8,847   8,847
  (iii) the monetary limit, £40,000

Chargeable gain		**Nil**

8.2   Butler

	Cost £	MV 31.3.82 £
Net sale proceeds	86,175	86,175
Less: Cost/MV 31.3.82	6,215	35,000
Unindexed gains	79,960	51,175

Less: Indexation allowance (March 1982 - April 1998)

$$\frac{161.2 - 79.44}{79.44} (=1.029) \times £35,000$$

	(36,015)	(36,015)
Lower gain chargeable	43,945	15,160

Less: Exemption
  (i)   Periods before 1.4.82 ignored
  (ii) 1.4.82 - 5.10.88   -   occupied
  (iii) 6.10.88 - 5.10.92 -   deemed occupation (4 years allowed due to location of workplace)
  (iv) 6.10.92 - 5.10.95 -   deemed occupation (3 years absence allowed for any reason)
  (v)   6.10.95 - 5.11.95 -   occupied
  (vi) 6.11.95 - 6.7.98   -   part of last 3 years

		15,160
Chargeable gain		**Nil**

17 SHARES AND SECURITIES

INTRODUCTION & LEARNING OBJECTIVES

Shares and securities are chargeable assets and any gain made on their disposal is taxable, and any loss, allowable. It is important to thoroughly understand this chapter and to master the matching rules and rules for bonus and rights issues, as these are examined frequently.

When you have studied this chapter you should have learned the following:

- The reason for needing matching rules to deal with the sale of shares and securities.

- The order in which matching takes place for post 5 April 1998 disposals.

- How to re-construct the pre-6 April 1998 share pool and deal with purchases and sales affecting it.

- What 'operative events' are and how they affect the calculation of the indexation allowance.

- What shares constitute the 1982 holding to reflect bonus and rights.

- How to alter the share pool and 1982 holding to reflect bonus and rights issues.

- How to recalculate the 31 March 1982 value to reflect bonus and rights issues.

- The rules for dealing with changes in share capital (reorganisations and takeovers)

- The terms of the exemption given to gilts and qualifying corporate bonds.

1 INTRODUCTION

1.1 Overview

Shares and securities present a particular problem for capital gains tax computations because any two shares in a company (of a particular class) are indistinguishable. Where shares have been acquired on more than one occasion this creates difficulties in identifying just which have been disposed of on a sale. For instance Jones buys ordinary shares in Smith plc as follows.

	Shares	Cost
		£
16 December 1985	1,000	2,500
17 June 1988	1,500	4,500

If, in January 1998 Jones sells 600 shares, which has he sold; some from the earlier purchase, some from the later purchase or a mixture of the two?

The answer matters because, in order to calculate Jones' chargeable gain or allowable loss his allowable expenditure and indexation allowance must be known. It also matters for calculating taper relief.

This chapter is devoted to setting out the capital gains tax rules as they apply to shares and securities. The essential principles of capital gains tax remain but they are overlain by a system needed to keep track of just which shares or securities are being sold.

2   THE MATCHING RULES

2.1   Introduction

The matching rules are needed to solve the problem of being unable otherwise to identify acquisitions with disposals, as illustrated above. They apply when a person has made more than one purchase of shares or securities of the same class in the same company. But no matching rules are needed where, for example, someone buys both preference shares and ordinary shares in a company as they are distinguishable.

Shares and securities are subject to the same rules and so, for the rest of the chapter, the term 'shares' covers both.

For individual shareholders (but not company shareholders) the matching rules have changed for disposals made after 5 April 1998. Essentially, the old matching rules were based on share pooling so, in the example above, Jones has a pool of 2,500 Smith plc shares costing £7,000. As shown below the indexation allowance could be accommodated by keeping an indexed cost column. Disposals were then made at average pool cost. The pooling technique, however, is not compatible with taper relief so, for individual shareholders, shares acquired after 5 April 1998 have to be separately identified and not added to any existing pools.

Thus we have 'old' matching rules which applied for disposals up to 5 April 1998 for individuals and continue to apply for corporate shareholders. There are also 'new' matching rules which apply for individuals on disposals after 5 April 1998.

2.2   The new matching order

Shares sold by an individual on or after 6 April 1998 are matched against acquisitions in the following order:

(a)   shares acquired on the same day as the sale;
(b)   shares acquired within the following 30 days;
(c)   shares acquired on or after 6 April 1998 (on a LIFO basis);
(d)   shares in the pool;
(e)   shares in the 1982 holding.

2.3   Example

On 18 February 1999 Frank sells 5,000 shares in Fosdyke Ltd (a qualifying company for taper relief purposes) for £26,000.

His acquisitions have been as follows:

15 March 1999	500 shares for £3,000
10 August 1998	1,000 shares for £3,600
16 April 1998	2,000 shares for £4,000

In addition his 'pool' of shares in Fosdyke Ltd as at 5 April 1998 consisted of 7,000 shares with a cost indexed to April 1998 of £700. All these shares had been acquired by 17 March 1998.

Calculate the gain arising and indicate how taper relief applies assuming that there are losses available for 1998/99 of £7,800 on other disposals and no other gains.

2.4   Solution

5,000 shares sold are matched with:

(a)	Shares purchased within the following 30 days	
	15 March 1999	500
(b)	Shares acquired since 6 April 1998 (LIFO)	
	10 August 1998	1,000
	16 April 1998	2,000
		3,500
(c)	Balance from share pool at 5 April 1998	1,500
		5,000

Gains are computed holding by holding

15.3.99	Sale proceeds 500/5,000 × £26,000	2,600
	Less: Cost	3,000
	Loss	400
10.8.98	Sale proceeds 1,000/5,000 × £26,000	5,200
	Less: Cost	3,600
	Gain	1,600
16.4.98	Sale proceeds 2,000/5,000 × £26,000	10,400
	Less: Cost	4,000
	Gain	6,400
5.4.98	Sale proceeds 1,500/5,000 × £26,000	7,800
	Less: Pool cost (indexed) 1,500/7,000 × £700	150
	Gain	7,650

Summary

Gains not qualifying for taper relief

10.8.98	1,600
16.4.98	6,400
	8,000
Less losses (400 + 7,800)	8,200
Excess losses	200

Gain qualifying for taper relief	7,650
Less: Loss remaining	200
	7,450
Less: Taper relief (1 bonus year) @ 7.5%	559
	6,891
Less: Annual exemption	6,800
Gains finally chargeable	91

2.5   The old matching order

Where shares are sold by a company or, prior to 6 April 1998, by an individual they are matched against acquisitions in the following order:

(a)   shares acquired on the same day (as the sale);

(b)   shares acquired during the nine days before the sale (taking earlier acquisitions first if there are more than one);

(c)   shares in the pool;

(d)   shares in the 1982 holding.

Even where individual shareholders are concerned, it is still necessary to know the old matching order to construct the pool which exists at 5 April 1998.

2.6   Indexation allowance

No indexation allowance is given for disposals matched against either same day acquisitions or acquisitions made during the previous nine days. This rule applies to the latter, even when the disposal falls in the month following the acquisition.

For individual shareholders, indexation allowance is only given up to April 1998 (as applies on assets held by individuals generally).

3   THE POOL

3.1   Introduction

It is easier to deal with shares as one asset (that increases and decreases in size as shares are bought and sold) so shares held for more than nine days are aggregated in a pool. Unfortunately this long standing and relatively easy technique of pooling was abolished for shares acquired by an individual after 5 April 1998.

It is likely that for individuals, the examiner will give details of the shares held in the pool at 5 April 1998, together with their cost and indexed cost. The examiner has also indicated that detailed calculations will not be required for companies, but the rules are set out below for completeness. In particular, it is crucial to understand how to deal with the indexed rise when making a disposal from the pool.

3.2   Composition of the pool

The pool (sometimes known as the FA 1985 pool because the rules were introduced in the Finance Act 1985) contains the following:

(a)   shares held on 6 April 1985 (1 April 1985 for companies) that were acquired after 5 April 1982 (31 March 1982 for companies); and

(b)   shares acquired on or after 6 April 1985 (1 April 1985 for companies) and, only in the case of individuals, before 6 April 1998.

The pool only ever contains shares of the same class of the same company, so any person may have several 'pools', each one concerned with a different class of share or shares in different companies.

3.3   Setting up the pool

The pool records, at any time, the number of shares held, their unindexed cost, and their indexed cost (that is original cost plus indexation to date).

Where a person held shares on 6 April 1985 (or 1 April 1985 for companies) that were acquired after 5 April 1982 (or 31 March 1982 for companies) the pool calculations begin by introducing the cost of them.

An indexation allowance is then calculated for each acquisition from the date of purchase to April 1985. The total of original cost and the indexation allowance forms the indexed cost.

3.4   Example

Daisy purchased 1,200 shares in Handley plc for £3,000 on 28 September 1983 and a further 2,000 shares for £5,750 on 2 January 1985.

Calculate the pool's indexed cost at 6 April 1985.

3.5   Solution

	Shares	Unindexed cost £	Indexed cost £
28 September 1983 purchase	1,200	3,000	3,000
2 January 1985 purchase	2,000	5,750	5,750
	3,200	8,750	8,750

Indexation allowance:

on September 1983 purchase

$$\frac{94.78 - 86.06}{86.06} \ (= 0.101) \times £3,000$$

303

on January 1985 purchase

$$\frac{94.78 - 91.20}{91.20} \ (= 0.039) \times £5,750$$

224

Indexed cost on 6 April 1985

9,277

3.6   Dealing with purchases between 6 April 1985 and 5 April 1998

Broadly, shares are added to the pool when a purchase is made and removed from it on a sale. The allowable cost is added to the totals in the unindexed pool and indexed pool and an indexation allowance (known as an 'indexed rise') is added to the pool of indexed cost immediately before each 'operative event' and so covers inflation on the total investment from one operative event to the next. For the most part operative events are purchases or sales but, strictly, they can be any event that changes the total indexed cost and so includes other events too (such as rights issues which are dealt with later in the chapter).

Note that the indexed rise is calculated in just the same way as any other indexation allowance, except for three features:

(a)   the fraction is not rounded to three decimal places; and

(b)   it is multiplied by the indexed cost total immediately after the previous operative event (even if this was a sale); and

(c)   there is no wait until the asset is sold to calculate the allowance (its added bit by bit as the indexed cost total alters).

Where the operative event is the first after April 1985 the indexed rise is calculated from April 1985 to the operative event.

3.7   Example

Continuing the previous example, suppose that Daisy bought a further 500 shares for £1,300 on 6 July 1985 and another 1,300 shares for £3,300 on 10 October 1988.

What is the value of the indexed cost pool on 10 October 1988?

3.8   Solution

	Shares	Unindexed cost £	Indexed cost £
b/f at 6 April 1985	3,200	8,750	9,277
6 July 1985 - purchase			
indexed rise £9,277 × $\dfrac{95.23 - 94.78}{94.78}$			44
			9,321
additional shares	500	1,300	1,300
	3,700	10,050	10,621
10 October 1988 - purchase			
indexed rise £10,621 × $\dfrac{109.5 - 95.23}{95.23}$			1,592
			12,213
additional shares	1,300	3,300	3,300
Total holding at 10 October 1988, and unindexed cost	5,000	13,350	
Indexed cost at 10 October 1988			15,513

3.9   Making disposals from the pool

When shares are sold that are matched against the pool, the number of shares sold is deducted from the share column, a proportionate part of the unindexed cost is deducted from the unindexed cost column, and a proportionate part of the indexed cost is deducted from the indexed cost column. As this is a part disposal the proportionate cost should be calculated using the A/(A + B) formula (as seen in a previous chapter). However, we are not usually given the value of the remaining shares (B in the formula), in which case average cost is used.

The gain or loss on disposal is calculated as follows:

	£
Proceeds	X
Less: Unindexed cost	(X)
Less: Indexation allowance	
(Indexed cost - unindexed cost)	(X)
	X

3.10   Example

Following on from the previous example, let us suppose that Daisy sold 3,000 shares in Handley plc for £14,000 on 1 February 1998.

Calculate the chargeable gain arising on the disposal.

	Shares	Unindexed cost £	Indexed cost £
b/f at 10 October 1988	5,000	13,350	15,513
1 February 1998 - sale			
indexed rise £15,513 × $\dfrac{160.3 - 109.5}{109.5}$			7,197
			22,710
sale of shares	3,000		
reduction of unindexed and indexed cost			
$\dfrac{3,000}{5,000}$ × £13,350/22,710		8,010	13,626
Bal c/f	2,000	5,340	9,084

	£
Sale proceeds	14,000
Less: Unindexed cost (above)	8,010
Unindexed gain	5,990
Less: Indexation allowance (13,626 – 8,010)	5,616
Chargeable gain	374

3.11   Pooling after 5 April 1998

Where the shareholder is a company the normal pooling treatment and the old matching rules continue to apply.

For individual shareholders, however, the pool is brought up to date for indexation at April 1998 and any purchases made after 5 April 1998 are kept outside the pool as separate assets.

In the example above the 2,000 pool shares will be carried forward with an indexed cost of £9,135 (9,084 + 9,084 × (161.2 − 160.3)/160.3).

4   THE 1982 HOLDING

4.1   Introduction

As indicated earlier in the chapter shares acquired (in the same company and of the same class) before 6 April 1982 (for individuals) or 1 April 1982 (for companies) are not put into the pool. The reason for the rule is straightforward. When they were originally acquired there was no indexation allowance and it is thus arithmetically simpler to deal with indexation separately for each disposal.

No new shares (other than rights or bonus issues) are ever added to the 1982 holding; its shares have been 'frozen' and it remains in existence only until those shares are disposed of.

The 1982 holding normally contains shares purchased between 6 April 1965 (when capital gains tax was introduced) and 1982 (as set out above). When a partial disposal of the holding occurs the proportion of the cost that is deductible is calculated by using the A/(A + B) formula if the values are given, but otherwise by taking an average of the cost of the shares in the holding. Then, as for other assets held at 31 March 1982, a comparison is made between the gain arising using purchase cost and that arising from using the March 1982 market value.

4.2   Example

Parrott bought 650 shares in Zenith plc on 1 March 1978 for £2,000 and a further 1,000 shares on 1 February 1982 for £3,200. On 1 December 1998 he sold 1,200 shares for £9,000. The price of Zenith plc shares on 31 March 1982 was £3.50. The shares are not business assets for the purpose of taper relief.

Calculate the chargeable gain arising on the disposal.

4.3   Solution

Chargeable gain

	Cost	31.3.82 value £
Disposal proceeds	9,000	9,000
Less: Cost (W)	3,782	
March 1982 value (£3.50 × 1,200)		4,200
Unindexed gain	5,218	4,800
Less: Indexation allowance (to April 1998)		
$\dfrac{161.2 - 79.44}{79.44}$ (= 1.029) × £4,200	4,322	4,322
Chargeable gain	896	478

Both results produce chargeable gains and so the smaller one, £478, is taken.

Working - 1982 holding

	Shares	Cost £
1 March 1978 - purchase	650	2,000
1 February 1982 - purchase	1,000	3,200
	1,650	5,200
1 December 1998 - sale	1,200	*3,782
Remaining shares c/f	450	1,418

* Cost of shares sold: $\dfrac{1,200}{1,650} \times £5,200 = £3,782$

5   CHANGES IN SHARE CAPITAL

5.1   Introduction

So far we have looked at how capital gains are calculated when a person acquires shares, sometimes in several transactions spread over a lengthy period, and then sells some or all of them. Although matching rules are needed to keep track of which shares have been sold (and from that the attributable cost and indexation allowance) the shares sold were at least the ones originally purchased.

On occasion, however, entirely new shares enter the picture, such as on bonus or rights issues. It helps to understand the rules for dealing with these issues if one remembers that the shareholder acquires them as a direct result of the holding he already owns.

5.2   Bonus issues

Bonus issues (sometimes known also as scrip or capitalisation issues) are fairly straightforward to deal with. Additional shares are issued, but at no extra cost to the shareholder.

The only complication produced by bonus issues is how to treat the extra shares for the purpose of the matching rules when a disposal is made. Quite simply, every purchase of shares made before the bonus issue takes place has the appropriate number of bonus shares added to it. Thus the number of shares in the pool (and the 1982 holding where applicable) is increased proportionately.

5.3   Example

Rayner acquired shares in Pollock plc as follows:

FA85 holding as at 6 April 1998	2,500 shares
5 May 1998 purchased	4,000 shares
7 August 1998 purchased	1,000 shares
9 November 1998 1 for 5 bonus issue	
3 February 1999 purchased	1,500 shares

He sold 10,000 Pollock plc shares on 18 January 1999.

Show how the shares sold are matched.

5.4   Solution

Order of matching

(a)   Shares acquired in the following 30 days

3 February 1999 purchase	1,500

(b)   Shares acquired since 6 April 1998 (LIFO)

7 August 1998 purchase	1,000	
Add 1 for 5 bonus	200	
	———	1,200
5 May 1998 purchase	4,000	
Add 1 for 5 bonus	800	
	———	4,800

(c)   Shares in the pool (as increased by bonus issue)

Balance at 6 April 1998	2,500	
Add 1 for 5 bonus	500	
	———	
	3,000	
Number to complete sale	2,500	
	———	2,500
Balance remaining in pool	500	
	———	
Shares sold		10,000
		———

5.5   Example

Blackburn had the following transactions in the shares of Gray plc.

October 1976	purchased 1,000 shares for £1,500
November 1980	purchased 1,200 shares for £1,900
April 1984	purchased 600 shares for £1,100
January 1989	purchased 700 shares for £1,350
February 1991	bonus issue of one for five
September 1998	sold 2,000 shares for £8,000

The price of Gray plc shares on 31 March 1982 (as adjusted for the bonus issue) was £1.50. Gray plc shares are not 'business assets' for taper relief purposes.

Calculate the chargeable gain or allowable loss arising on the sale in September 1998.

5.6   Solution

Calculation of chargeable gain

(a)   Shares matched against the FA 1985 pool

	£
Proceeds (1,560 shares (W1)) $\frac{1,560}{2,000} \times £8,000$	6,240
Less: Cost (W1)	2,450
	———
Unindexed gain	3,790
Less: Indexation allowance (3,960 − 2,450)	1,510
	———
Chargeable gain	2,280
	———

(b)   Shares matched against the 1982 holding

	Cost	31.3.82 value £
Proceeds (2,000 − 1,560 = 440)		
$\frac{440}{2,000} \times £8,000$	1,760	1,760
Less: Cost/March 1982 value		
£567 (W2)/£1.50 × 440	567	660
Unindexed gain	1,193	1,100
Less: Indexation allowance (to April 1998)		
$\frac{161.2 - 79.44}{79.44}$ (= 1.029) × £660	679	679
Chargeable gain	514	421

The smaller gain is taken, £421.

Total gain on disposal is thus £2,701 (2,280 + 421).

Workings - construction of pool costs

The disposal must be worked through in the order prescribed by the new matching rules. Since there were no acquisitions since 6 April 1998 the first matching is against shares held in the pool.

(W1)   Shares held in the FA 1985 pool

	Shares	Unindexed cost £	Indexed cost £
April 1984			
purchase	600	1,100	1,100
attributable bonus shares (1 for 5)	120	-	-
	720	1,100	1,100
indexation allowance to April 1985			
$\frac{94.78 - 88.64}{88.64}$ (= 0.069) × £1,100			76
			1,176
January 1989			
indexed rise (April 1985 to January 1989)			
$\frac{111.0 - 94.78}{94.78} \times £1,176$			201
purchase	700	1,350	1,350
attributable bonus shares (1 for 5)	140		-
	1,560	2,450	2,727
September 1998			
indexed rise (January 1989 to April 1998)			
$\frac{161.2 - 111.0}{111.0} \times £2,727$			1,233
			3,960
sale	1,560	2,450	3,960

(W2)	Shares in 1982 holding	*Shares*	*Cost* £
	October 1976		
	purchase	1,000	1,500
	attributable bonus shares (1 for 5)	200	-
	November 1980		
	purchase	1,200	1,900
	attributable bonus shares (1 for 5)	240	-
		2,640	3,400
	September 1998		
	sale (2,000 – 1,560 (W1))	440	*567
		2,200	2,833

$$\text{* Cost of shares sold is } \frac{440}{2,640} \times £3,400 = £567.$$

5.7 Rights issues

Rights issues have an essential feature in common with bonus issues; new shares are acquired as a result of an existing holding (and the number of new shares acquired is proportionate to the existing holding). Accordingly the same rule applies for rights issues as bonus issues; the new shares are deemed to have been acquired at the same time as the original shares.

But in contrast with bonus issues, the shareholder has to subscribe new money to acquire them. Subscribing new money has potentially three important consequences for capital gains tax:

(a) the cost of the total shareholding is increased by the amount subscribed for the rights shares;

(b) the shareholder obtains additional indexation allowances, based on the amount of new expenditure (provided, in the case of individual shareholders, the new expenditure is incurred before April 1998); and

(c) the shareholder (if an individual) becomes entitled to taper relief based on the period of ownership of the original shares (and the gain attributable to them on sale).

Care is needed in dealing with (b) above. Although for matching purposes the rights issue shares are deemed to have been acquired at the same time as the original shares, the indexation allowance is computed from the time they were actually issued. To do otherwise would be illogical as the shareholder would be receiving indexation allowance for a period before he made his investment in the rights issue shares.

5.8 Example

Carmichael had the following transactions in the shares of Rudderham plc.

October 1979	purchased 600 shares for £1,200
November 1982	purchased 1,200 shares for £1,700
January 1987	purchased 900 shares for £1,500
February 1990	took up 1 for 3 rights issues at £2.30 per share
August 1998	sold 3,200 shares for £15,750

As 31 March 1982 the value of Rudderham plc shares (as adjusted for the rights issue) was £1.55.

Calculate the chargeable gains or allowable loss on the disposal in August 1998.

5.9   Solution

Calculation of chargeable gain

(a)   Shares matched against the pool

	£
Proceeds £15,750 × $\frac{2,800}{3,200}$ (W1)	13,781
Less: Unindexed cost (W1)	4,810
Unindexed gain	8,971
Less: Indexation allowance (7,894 − 4,810)	3,084
Chargeable gain	5,887

(b)   Shares matched against 1982 holding

	Cost £	31.3.82 value £
Proceeds (15,750 − 13,781)	1,969	1,969
Less: Cost (W2)/31.3.82 value	830	
£1.55 × 400		620
	1,139	1,349
Less: Indexation allowance		
(i) On original cost		
$\frac{161.2 - 79.44}{79.44}$ (= 1.029) × 1,200 × $\frac{300}{600}$	617	617
(ii) On cost of rights shares		
$\frac{161.2 - 120.2}{120.2}$ (= 0.341) × 460 × $\frac{100}{200}$	78	78
	444	654

The smaller gain of £444 is taken. The total gain is thus £6,331 (£5,887 + £444).

WORKINGS

(W1)   Shares pool

	Shares	Unindexed cost £	Indexed cost £
November 1982 purchase	1,200	1,700	1,700
Indexation allowance to April 1985			
$\frac{94.78 - 82.66}{82.66}$ (= 0.147) × £1,700			250
	1,200	1,700	1,950

January 1987 purchase
Indexed rise

$$\frac{100.0 - 94.78}{94.78} \times £1,950 \qquad\qquad 107$$

Acquisition	900	1,500	1,500
	2,100	3,200	3,557

February 1990 rights issue
Indexed rise

$$\frac{120.2 - 100.0}{100.0} \times £3,557 \qquad\qquad 719$$

			4,276
Issue of shares (1 for 3)	700	1,610	1,610
	2,800	4,810	5,886

August 1998 disposal
Indexed rise (to April 1998)

$$\frac{161.2 - 120.2}{120.2} \times £5,886 \qquad\qquad 2,008$$

			7,894
Disposal	2,800	4,810	7,894

(W2)	1982 holding		*Shares*	*Cost*
				£
October 1979	purchase		600	1,200
February 1990	rights issue (1 for 3)		200	460
			800	1,660
August 1998	disposal (3,200 − 2,800 (W1))		400	830
			400	830

5.10   Sale of rights nil paid

Where a shareholder does not take up his rights but instead sells the rights ('nil paid') to a third party the proceeds are treated as a capital distribution. This means that the proceeds will be dealt with

- under the part disposal rules; or
- as a reduction of original cost (if proceeds are 'small').

It is only possible to treat them as a reduction of original cost if the proceeds are not more than the greater of £3,000 and 5% of the value of the shareholding giving rise to the disposal.

The overriding £3,000 limit for 'small' was only announced as Revenue Practice from February 1997 and you should assume that for earlier disposals only the 5% test applied.

5.11   Adjusting March 1982 values for bonus and rights issues

When a rights or bonus issue has occurred after 31 March 1982 the value of shares quoted on that day will not reflect it. Nevertheless when making a comparison of cost and March 1982 calculations for disposals matched against the 1982 holding, an adjusted value is needed to make the comparison valid.

In the examples set out earlier in this section the March 1982 values were adjusted for the subsequent alteration in share capital. The examiner may provide adjusted or unadjusted figures. Clearly, if it is already adjusted, it can be used immediately. But if it is unadjusted, a further calculation is needed.

5.12   Example

Kennedy purchased 800 shares in O'Leary plc for £1,200 on 1 September 1978. On 31 March 1982 O'Leary shares were valued at £2.50 per share. In February 1986 Kennedy took up a 1 for 4 rights issue, the shares being issued at £2.75 each.

Calculate the adjusted 31 March 1982 value of O'Leary plc shares.

5.13   Solution

	Shares	31.3.82 value £
September 1978		
purchase	800	
value at 31 March 1982		2,000
February 1986		
rights issue (1 for 4)	200	
rights subscription (200 × £2.75)		550
	1,000	2,550

The adjusted 31 March 1982 value is thus $\dfrac{£2,550}{1,000}$ = £2.55 per share.

6   REORGANISATIONS AND TAKEOVERS

6.1   Reorganisations

A reorganisation involves the exchange of existing shares and securities for others of another class. No CGT is charged until the replacement shares or securities are disposed of, unless the reorganisation involves a cash payout to shareholders.

The key aspect of reorganisations is attributing the cost of the original holding to the different component parts of the new holding. The rules differ according to whether the shares are quoted or unquoted. For quoted shares the apportionment of cost is made according to the relative values of the replacement shares and securities on the first day of quotation. For unquoted shares the apportionment is based on the relative values of the replacement shares and securities at the time the first disposal is made from them.

In many cases shareholders do not have to provide new consideration at the time of a reorganisation. If this is so the indexation allowance is calculated from the time the original holding was acquired (or 31 March 1982 if appropriate). Where new consideration is subscribed, however, the same principle applies as in rights issues; indexation allowance on the new consideration is calculated from the time it was subscribed (but not beyond April 1998 in the case of subscribers who are individuals).

6.2 Example

Major purchased 2,000 ordinary shares in Blue plc (a quoted company) for £5,000 in June 1990. In July 1991 Blue plc underwent a reorganisation and Major received 2 'A' ordinary shares and 1 preference share for each ordinary share. Immediately after the reorganisation 'A' ordinary shares were quoted at £2 and preference shares at £0.50. In December 1998 Major sold all his holding of 'A' ordinary shares for £8,000.

Calculate the chargeable gain or allowable loss arising on the disposal in December 1997.

6.3 Solution

	£
Disposal proceeds	8,000
Less: Cost (W)	4,444
Unindexed gain	3,556
Less: Indexation allowance (to April 1998)	
$\dfrac{161.2 - 126.7}{126.7} \times £4,444$	1,210
Indexed gain	2,346

Working - cost of 'A' ordinary shares

Major received:

        4,000 'A' ordinary shares, valued at 4,000 × £2 = £8,000
        2,000 preference shares, valued at 2,000 × £0.50 = £1,000

Cost attributable to the 'A' ordinary shares is thus:

$$£5,000 \times \frac{8,000}{9,000} = £4,444$$

6.4 Takeovers

Where a takeover is a 'paper for paper' transaction shareholders of the company taken over acquire shares in the acquiring company. This does not constitute a disposal for capital gains tax purposes provided that:

(a)   the acquiring company obtains more than 25% of the target company's ordinary share capital as a result of the offer; or

(b)   there is a general offer to members of the target company which would give control to the acquirer if accepted; or

(c)   the acquirer can exercise more than 50% of the voting power in the target company.

In all cases there is a condition that the transaction must be for bona fide commercial reasons and not have tax avoidance as one of its main purposes. Advance clearance may be sought from the Revenue that this condition is not breached.

The new shares are deemed to have been acquired at the same time and at the same cost as the original shares, provided that there is no substantial cash element in the consideration given by the acquiring company. If there is a cash element there are two possibilities:

(a)   the cash is either £3,000 or less or represents 5% or less of the value of the holding, in which case the cash is deducted from the allowable cost of the holding for future disposals; or

(b)   in other cases, there is a part disposal and the gain relating to the cash element must be calculated. In these circumstances the part of the cost of the original holding apportioned to the cash is calculated as:

$$\frac{\text{Cash received}}{\text{Cash received} + \text{market value of new shares}} \times \text{original cost}$$

A feature of takeover transactions in recent years has been that the price paid by the acquirer has been partly dependent on the financial performance of the target company after the takeover (an 'earn-out'). Where any additional consideration resulting from an earn-out is satisfied by the issue of more shares, no CGT liability arises from it immediately. This additional consideration is taken into account when the shares are eventually disposed of.

6.5   Example

Patrick bought 1,000 shares in Target plc in September 1991 for £20,000. On 3 November 1998 the entire share capital of Target plc was acquired by Bidder plc. Target plc shareholders received 2 Bidder plc shares and £5.00 cash for each share held. Bidder plc shares were quoted at £12.50.

Calculate the chargeable gain or allowable loss, if any, accruing to Patrick as a result of the takeover in November 1998.

6.6   Solution

The total consideration provided by Bidder plc is:

	£
Shares (2,000 @ 12.50)	25,000
Cash (1,000 × £5.00)	5,000
	30,000

As the cash Patrick has received exceeds both £3,000 and 5% of the total (£30,000) he has made a part disposal.

	£
Disposal proceeds (cash)	5,000
Less: Original cost:	
$\dfrac{5,000}{30,000} \times £20,000$	3,333
Unindexed gain	1,667
Less: Indexation allowance (to April 1998)	
$\dfrac{161.2 - 134.6}{134.6} \times £3,333$	659
Chargeable gain	1,008

If the shares in Target plc had been 'business assets', taper relief of 7.5% would be available.

Patrick's allowable cost on the future disposal of his shares in Bidder plc will be £16,667 (20,000-3,333). He will be treated as having held the shares on 17 March 1998 for taper relief purposes.

7   QUALIFYING CORPORATE BONDS AND LISTED GOVERNMENT SECURITIES

7.1   Introduction

It was mentioned earlier in the chapter that securities are subject to the same capital gains tax rules as shares. Listed government securities (gilt edged securities or gilts) and qualifying corporate bonds are the exception to this rule. They are not subject to capital gains tax and thus no chargeable gains or allowable losses arise on their disposal.

7.2   Scope of qualifying corporate bonds

A qualifying corporate bond is one which:

(a)   represents a normal commercial loan;

(b)   is expressed in sterling and has no provision for either conversion into, or redemption in, any other currency; and

(c)   was issued after 13 March 1984 or was acquired by the disposer after that date (whenever it was issued).

The term 'corporate bond' is also extended to permanent interest-bearing shares in building societies, provided they meet the condition set out in (b) above.

8   CHAPTER SUMMARY

8.1   Introduction

Shares and securities present a special problem in the context of capital gains tax because one is indistinguishable from another (if they are of the same class in the same company). The capital gains tax system gets around this problem by inventing a procedure, known as the matching rules, for identifying the shares involved in any particular sale.

8.2   Share pools

Provided that shares are retained for ten days, they enter a pool. The share pool contains all shares acquired from 6 April 1982 to 5 April 1998 (for individuals) or from 1 April 1982 onwards (for companies). Unlike other assets, for which an indexation allowance is calculated on sale, shares in the share pool have the indexation allowance added to cost each time there is an operative event. Operative events are mostly purchases and sales but include any transaction that affects the total cost of shareholder's investment.

The 1982 holding (also effectively a share pool) contains shares acquired between 6 April 1965, the date capital gains tax was introduced, and the start of the share pool in 1982. No new shares are added to it; it continues in existence until such time as the shares held in 1982 are deemed to have been disposed of under the matching rules.

8.3   Changes occasioned by taper relief

Shares acquired by individuals after 5 April 1998 are not pooled but are identified as separate assets. Disposals by individuals after 5 April 1998 require 'new' matching rules. These effectively give a LIFO matching order first using post 5 April 1998 acquisitions, then the pool and then the 1982 pool. There is a rule designed to defeat 'bed and breakfasting' which gives matching priority to shares acquired in the 30 days after the disposal. The new matching rules are needed to fit in with the way taper relief is given.

Note that for the present, for exam purposes the old and the new matching rules are both likely to be required knowledge.

8.4   Alterations to share capital

Rights and bonus issues present different problems for capital gains tax but there is a common theme. In each case the shares resulting from the new issue are deemed to have been acquired at the time the shareholding giving rise to them was acquired. In the case of rights issues the indexation allowance complicates the picture because it is calculated from the time the new investment was made (not the time of the original acquisition).

Where there is a reorganisation or takeover the problem is to apportion the cost of the original shares among whatever shares and securities replace them. For quoted shares this is done on the basis of the market values of the new shares and securities immediately afterwards. For unquoted shares no apportionment of cost is done until a disposal is made from the replacement holding and it is then based on the relative market values at that time.

8.5   Gilts and qualifying corporate bonds

Dealing with gilts and qualifying corporate bonds is easy for capital gains tax. Both are exempt and so no chargeable gains or allowable losses arise.

9   SELF-TEST QUESTIONS

9.1   Why are the matching rules necessary? (2.1)

9.2   What is the new matching order? (2.2)

9.3   Do shares sold within ten days of acquisition rank for indexation allowance (where the old matching rules apply)? (2.6)

9.4   From what date are shares aggregated in the share pool? (3.2)

9.5   How is the calculation of the indexed rise for a share pool different from normal indexation allowance calculation? (3.6)

9.6   What calculation is required to ascertain the indexed cost of a parcel of shares sold from the share pool? (3.9)

9.7   The 1982 holding contains shares acquired between certain dates. What are the dates? (4.1)

9.8   How do the matching rules apply to bonus issues? (5.2)

9.9   In what two ways does the treatment of a rights issue differ from that of a bonus issue? (5.5)

9.10   What is a qualifying corporate bond? (7.2)

10   EXAMINATION TYPE QUESTIONS

10.1   Gore and Blood

The details of Gore's holdings of £1 ordinary shares of Blood plc are as follows:

		Shares	Cost or MV 31.3.82	Cost or MV 31.3.82 Indexed to 5.4.98
The 1982 pool at 5.4.98		500	850	1,725
The 1985 pool at 5.4.98		1,000	5,000	8,430
7 May 1998	Purchased	500	3,050	
20 December 1998	Purchased	280	2,060	

Gore has elected for market value 31 March 1982 basis to be applied to all his chargeable assets held on that date.

On 11 December 1998 Gore sold 1,980 shares for £11,484.

Calculate the chargeable gain or allowable loss on the disposal in 1998/99.

10.2   Jasper

Jasper had the following transactions in securities during the year 1998/99

(1)   Sold all of his 2,085 25p ordinary shares in Carrot plc on 19 November 1998 for net sale proceeds of £8,379.

His previous dealings in these shares were as follows

		Shares	Cost or MV 31.3.82	Cost or MV 31.3.82 Indexed to 5.4.98
The 1982 pool at 5.4.98		1,200	1,750	3,551
The 1985 pool at 5.4.98		300	600	1,042
11 August 1998	Purchased	585	2,160	

(2)   Sold 400 £1 ordinary shares in Grasp plc for £3,600 on 30 September 1998. Jasper had acquired these Grasp plc shares as a result of a successful takeover bid by Grasp plc of Cawte plc on 5 June 1998. Prior to the takeover Jasper had owned 12,000 £1 ordinary shares in Cawte plc, which he had acquired for £14,000 on 3 May 1983. The indexed cost of these shares to April 1998 was £26,700. The terms of the take-over bid were

- one £1 ordinary share in Grasp plc, plus
- two 10% preference shares in Grasp plc, plus
- 40p in cash

for every £1 ordinary share in Cawte plc.

The following are the quoted prices for the shares of Grasp plc at 5 June 1998

£1 ordinary shares	350p
10% preference shares	110p

(3)   Sold £1 ordinary shares in Disney plc as follows

    11 September 1998   His provisional allotment of 500 rights issue shares 'nil paid' for £500

    12 November 1998   2500 shares for £6,075

    His holding of Disney plc shares was acquired

    8 May 1998   4000 shares for £6,300

The Disney plc shares were quoted at 220p on 11 September 1998 (immediately before the rights issue)

(4)   On 29 September 1998 received a distribution of 45p per share on each of his 9,000 unquoted shares in Quicksand Ltd. These shares had been acquired for 180p each on 6 October 1969. On 1 July 1998 the company was put into liquidation and it is unlikely that the winding up will be completed before December 2000, the liquidator estimates a final distribution of 15p per share. The market value of the shares on 31 March 1982 was 75p per share.

Jasper has elected for the market value basis of computation to be used for disposals of all assets held on 31 March 1982. None of the above assets qualify as 'business assets' for taper relief purposes

You are required to calculate the chargeable gains and allowable losses arising in respect of the disposals in 1998/99.

11   ANSWERS TO EXAMINATION TYPE QUESTIONS

11.1   Gore and Blood

The disposal of 1980 shares is matched as follows:

(i)   280 shares acquired on 20.12.98 (within 30 days after the disposal)
(ii)   500 shares acquired on 7.5.98
(iii)   1,000 shares from the 1985 pool
(iv)   200 shares from the 1982 pool

Computations

		Gain/(loss)	
		£	£
(i)	Sale proceeds $11,484 \times \dfrac{280}{1,980}$	1,624	
	Less: Cost	(2,060)	
	Allowable loss	(436)	
			(436)
(ii)	Sale proceeds $11,484 \times \dfrac{500}{1,980}$	2,900	
	Less: Cost	(3,050)	
	Allowable loss	(150)	
			(150)

(iii)   Sale proceeds $11,484 \times \dfrac{1,000}{1,980}$ 5,800

          Less: Cost   (5,000)

          Unindexed gain   800
          Less: Indexation allowance (8,430 - 5,000), restricted to   (800)

          Nil result   -

(iv)   Sale proceeds $11,484 \times \dfrac{200}{1,980}$ 1,160

          Less: MV 31.3.82   (850)

          Unindexed gain   310
          Less: Indexation allowance (1,725 - 850)
            restricted to   (310)

          Nil result   -

                                                      -

          Total allowable loss   (586)

11.2   Jasper

Capital gains computation 1998/99

(1)   **Shares in Carrot plc**

			Gain/(loss)
		£	£

(i)   11 August 1998 acquisition

          Sale proceeds $\dfrac{585}{2,085} \times £8,379$ 2,350

          Less: Cost   2,160

          Gain   190
                                                        190

(ii)   1985 pool

          Sale proceeds $\dfrac{300}{2,085} \times £8,379$ 1,206

          Less: Cost   (600)

          Unindexed gain   606
          Less: Indexation allowance (1,042 - 600)   442

          Gain   164
                                                        164

(iii)   1982 pool

Sale proceeds $\dfrac{1,200}{2,085} \times £8,379$	4,823
Less: MV 31.3.82	(1,750)
Unindexed gain	3,073
Less: Indexation allowance (3,551 - 1,750)	1,801
Gain	1,272

	1,272
Total gain on disposal of 2,085 shares	1,626

(2)   **Grasp plc**

Apportionment of cost of Cawte plc securities
to new securities and cash

	5.6.98 Purchase consideration £	Cost £	Cost indexed to April '98 £
For 12,000 Cawte plc ordinary shares:			
12,000 Grasp £1 ordinary shares at 350p	42,000	8,033	15,320
24,000 Grasp 10% preference shares at 110p	26,400	5,049	9,630
Cash – 12,000 × 40p	4,800	918	1,750
	73,200	14,000	26,700

5% of £73,200 = £3,660

As cash exceeds this figure (and is not less than £3,000), roll-over relief does not apply

Disposal for cash on 5 June 1998	Indexed cost £	b/f 1,626
1985 pool		
Deemed cost, indexed to April 1998	1,750	
Cash received	4,800	
Chargeable gain	3,050	3,050

	Indexed cost £	
Disposal on 30 September 1998		
Deemed cost of 12,000 shares, indexed to April 1998	15,320	
Sold on Sep'98 400/12,000	(511)	(511)
Proceeds	3,600	
Chargeable gain	3,089	3,089
		7,765
Pool cost (indexed to April 1998) c/f	14,809	

(3)   **Disney plc**   b/f 7,765

    (a)   **Sale of rights 'nil paid'**

            11 September 1998 Cash received   500
            Less: Cash rolled-over   500
                                              Nil

        Although proceeds >5% × (4,000 @ 220p + £500), they are less than £3,000 and so 'small'

    (b)   **Sale of shares**   £
            12 November 1998 Proceeds
            2,500 shares   6,075
        Less: Cost £6,300 × 2,500/4,000   3,937
               Cash rolled-over:
               £500 × 2,500/4,000   (312)   3,625

        Gain   2,450
                                                  2,450

                                            10,215

(4)   **Liquidation of Quicksand Ltd**

        Since liquidation not expected within
        2 years of 29.9.98 distribution assessable
        in 1998/99
        Distribution received: 9,000 × 45p   4,050
        Less: MV 31.3.82 £6,750 × $\dfrac{4,050}{4,050+(9,000\times 15p)}$ 5,063

        No indexation allowance available to increase a loss
        Unindexed loss   (1,013)   (1,013)

    Net gains for the year 1998/99   9,202

18 CHATTELS AND WASTING ASSETS

INTRODUCTION

This chapter covers chattels and wasting assets. Special attention should be paid to the more straightforward aspects of chattels, especially marginal relief, as these are the areas that tend to be examined.

When you have studied this chapter you should have learned the following:

- The definition of chattels and wasting assets.
- The scope of the exemption for chattels.
- How to calculate marginal relief and losses for chattels.
- To distinguish between wasting assets with different CGT treatments.
- The calculation for reducing the allowable cost of a wasting asset when it is sold.
- To distinguish between disposal of different kinds of leases and their CGT treatments.
- How to deal with compensation receipts for damaged assets.
- How to deal with assets that are lost or wholly destroyed.

---

1 CHATTELS

1.1 Chattel exemption

Chattels are defined as tangible, movable property. Paintings, furniture and jewellery are examples of chattels. Note the requirement that a chattel is tangible; therefore shares and leases are not chattels.

Chattels (which are defined as tangible movable property), do **not** have a general exemption from capital gains tax. There is, however, an exemption where a chattel is sold at a gain for a consideration (proceeds or market value, as appropriate) of £6,000 or less. The limit of £6,000 applies to the gross consideration (ie, before deducting disposal expenses).

Remember that cars have a separate specific exemption and are thus not chargeable assets, whatever their value.

2 MARGINAL RELIEF AND LOSS RELIEF

2.1 Marginal relief

Where a chattel is sold for more than £6,000 a marginal relief is available. In these circumstances the gain is **limited** to

$$5/3 \times (\text{gross disposal consideration} - £6,000)$$

Thus two calculations are needed, one using the marginal relief formula and the other computed in the normal way. Provided that both results produce a gain, the lower one is taken. Where the ordinary CGT computation produces a loss different rules apply.

The relief helps the taxpayer on the disposal of low value chattels. Just where it ceases to be advantageous depends on the levels of disposal consideration and allowable expenditure.

2.2   Activity

Andrew sells a picture on 1 February 1999 for £6,600 that he acquired on 1 March 1990 for £3,200.

Calculate the chargeable gain arising, if any.

2.3   Activity solution

	£
Disposal proceeds	6,600
Less: Cost	3,200
Unindexed gain	3,400
Less: Indexation allowance (to April 1998)	
$\frac{161.2 - 121.4}{121.4}$ (= 0.328) × £3,200	1,050
Indexed gain	2,350

Marginal relief imposes a limit on the gain of:
$$5/3 \times (6,600 - 6,000) = £1,000$$

2.4   Loss relief

Where a chattel is sold for £6,000 or more at a loss, the loss is computed in the normal way. However, if it is sold for less than £6,000 the allowable loss is restricted. This is achieved by substituting notional proceeds of £6,000 for the actual, lower, proceeds.

The substitution of £6,000 for actual proceeds is not allowed to turn a loss into a gain. If the calculation produces an apparent gain the result is no gain/no loss.

2.5   Activity

Brian bought an antique table for £6,500 in September 1990 and sold it for £5,600 in December 1998. He incurred £250 to advertise it for sale.

Calculate the allowable loss arising, if any.

2.6   Activity solution

	£
Notional sale proceeds	6,000
Less: Cost	6,500
Expenses of sale	250
Unindexed loss	750

The unindexed loss is the allowable loss, as an indexation allowance is not available to increase a loss.

3   WASTING ASSETS

3.1   Introduction

> *Definition*   A wasting asset is an asset with a predictable life not exceeding 50 years. 'Life' means the asset's useful life, having regard to the purpose for which the disposer acquired it.

In addition to the general definition, the legislation deals with two specific cases, as follows.

(a)   Freehold land is **never** a wasting asset (irrespective of its nature or that of any buildings on it).

(b)   Plant and machinery is **always** a wasting asset.

The importance of the definition of a wasting asset lies in two points. Firstly certain wasting assets are exempt from capital gains tax. Secondly non-exempt wasting assets have a modified calculation of the gain or loss on disposal which reflects the fact that their relatively short life causes them generally to decline in value.

What distinguishes the treatment of wasting assets for capital gains tax is firstly whether the wasting asset is also a chattel (a 'wasting chattel') and secondly whether capital allowances may be claimed on it. From this three categories of wasting asset may be identified, with differing CGT treatments. These are:

(a)   wasting chattels on which capital allowances could **not** be claimed by the disposer;

(b)   wasting assets and chattels on which capital allowances could be claimed by the disposer; and

(c)   wasting assets that are not chattels and have no entitlement to capital allowances.

The first category is easily dealt with as wasting chattels on which capital allowances could not be claimed are exempt.

The Revenue have recently clarified the position as far as plant and machinery is concerned. It was stated above that plant and machinery is always a wasting asset, and therefore, is exempt when owned privately. The word 'machinery' is not defined in statute so the normal meaning is given. The Revenue have said that a machine is any apparatus which applies mechanical power. They accept that antique clocks and watches fall into this category and are therefore exempt.

3.2   Wasting assets and chattels with capital allowances

This category includes both wasting assets and chattels on which capital allowances have been claimed and those on which capital allowances could have been claimed (but, in fact, they have not been).

Where the disposal is of a chattel and gives rise to a gain it is computed in the normal way for chattels, with the benefit of the £6,000 exemption described earlier in the chapter.

Capital allowances may be ignored when the asset is disposed of at a gain as they are clawed back. However, if a loss is suffered, some or all of the loss may be disallowed because relief has been given under the capital allowances system.

Where net capital allowances are made (ie, net of balancing charges on disposal) they are deducted from the asset's allowable expenditure.

3.3   Example - reduction in value relieved by capital allowances

Fred bought some machinery for use in his trade for £35,000 in April 1992. In October 1998 he decides to replace it and sells the old machinery for £26,500.

Calculate the chargeable gain or allowable loss arising on the disposal in October 1998.

3.4   Solution

Fred obtains net capital allowances of £8,500 (35,000 - 26,500) during his ownership of the machinery.

	£	£
Disposal proceeds		26,500
Less: Cost	35,000	
Less: Net capital allowances	8,500	
		26,500
Allowable loss		Nil

Notes:

(1)   It sometimes happens that the net allowances given are more than the drop in value of the asset between purchase and sale prices. Where this occurs the calculation results in an unindexed gain. An indexation allowance is then available, although it may not create a loss.

(2)   The indexation allowance is calculated on the allowable expenditure **after** deducting the net capital allowances.

3.5   Wasting assets (not qualifying for capital allowances)

The special point about wasting assets which are not chattels and which do not qualify for capital allowances is that the allowable expenditure is deemed to waste away over the life of the asset. Consequently, when a disposal is made, the allowable expenditure is restricted to take account of the asset's natural fall in value. Otherwise allowable losses could be accumulated merely by holding wasting assets (irrespective of financial and commercial conditions).

The depreciation of most wasting assets is deemed to occur on a straight line basis over its predictable life (the exception being leases of land, which are considered later in the chapter). Total depreciation over a wasting asset's entire life is cost minus scrap value (if any). The part of this depreciation that is attributable to the disposer's period of ownership is then:

$$\frac{P}{L} \times (C - S)$$

where: P is the disposer's period of ownership;
         L is the asset's predictable life;
         C is the cost of the asset; and
         S is any residual or scrap value at the end of the asset's predictable life.

3.6   Example

On 1 February 1991 Ian bought a wasting asset at a cost of £25,000. It had an estimated useful life of 30 years and an estimated scrap value of £1,000. He sold the asset for £38,000 on 1 February 1999.

Calculate the chargeable gain or allowable loss arising from the disposal in February 1999.

3.7   Solution

	£	£
Disposal proceeds		38,000
Less: Purchase cost	25,000	
Less: Wasting asset depreciation		
$\frac{8}{30} \times (25,000 - 1,000)$	6,400	
Allowable element of acquisition cost		18,600
Unindexed gain		19,400
Less: Indexation allowance (to April 1998):		
$\frac{161.2 - 130.9}{130.9} \ (= 0.231) \times £18,600$		4,297
Indexed gain		15,103

3.8   Impact of rebasing provisions

Where a wasting asset was held at 31 March 1982 it is deemed to have been sold and immediately reacquired at market value. Consequently, for the purposes of calculating a gain or loss based on the 31 March 1982 value, the predictable life is that remaining at 31 March 1982 and the disposer's period of ownership is calculated from 1 April 1982 to the date of disposal.

4   LEASES OF LAND

4.1   Introduction

Leases of land are considered separately here because in some cases, even where they have less than 50 years to expiry (and so count as wasting assets) the capital gains tax computation is different to other wasting assets.

There are essentially two different situations to consider:

(a)   assignment of a lease with more than 50 years to expiry (a 'long' lease); and
(b)   assignment of a lease with less than or exactly 50 years to expiry (a 'short' lease);

The duration of a lease is normally obvious. If, however, the landlord has an option to terminate the lease early, the lease is deemed, for CGT purposes, to expire at the first time the landlord can exercise his option.

An assignment occurs when the seller disposes of his lease; it is the disposal of his whole interest.

Where a taxpayer occupies his principal private residence under the terms of a lease, any gain on its disposal qualifies for the principal private residence exemption (see earlier chapter on principal private residence).

4.2   Assignment of a lease with more than 50 years to expiry

This is the most straightforward case. The disposal is of the seller's whole interest and, since the lease has more than 50 years to run, it is not a wasting asset. The calculation of the gain or loss follows the normal capital gains tax rules.

4.3   Assignment of a lease with 50 years or less to expiry

A lease with 50 years or less to expiry is a wasting asset and the capital gains tax calculation reflects this. For most wasting assets, considered earlier in the chapter, depreciation is assumed to occur on a straight line basis. Leases are treated differently; the value assumed to be left in a lease of less than 50 years is given by a table set out in the legislation. It assumes that the lease loses value gradually at first and much more quickly close to the time of expiry.

The deductible part of the original cost (that is the actual cost less the assumed depreciation) is given by the formula

$$\frac{A}{B} \times \text{original cost (or 31 March 1982 value if appropriate)}$$

where: A is the table percentage for the number of years left to expiry at the time of disposal; and

B is the table percentage for the number of years left to expiry at the time of acquisition (or 31 March 1982 if appropriate)

If the dates of disposal or acquisition do not fall conveniently to make whole years, the calculation is done to the nearest month. One twelfth of the difference between the percentages for the years either side of the actual duration is added for each extra month. Fourteen or more days count as a month.

4.4   Example

Geoffrey purchased a lease with 48 years to run on 1 September 1994 for £62,000. On 28 January 1999 he sold the lease for £75,000.

Calculate the chargeable gain or allowable loss arising on the sale.

4.5   Solution

	£
Disposal proceeds	75,000
Less: Cost (W)	60,815
Unindexed gain	14,185
Less: Indexation allowance (to April 1998)	
$\frac{161.2-145.0}{145.0}$ (= 0.112) × £60,815	6,811
Indexed gain	7,374

Working - deductible lease cost

Years to run at acquisition	48 years
Years to run at disposal	43 years 7 months

Thus percentage for 43 years 7 months is:

$$97.107 + (97.595 - 97.107) \times 7/12 = 97.392$$

Deductible cost is thus $\frac{97.392}{99.289} \times £62,000 = £60,815$

Note that as for other wasting assets, the indexation allowance is based on the cost after depreciation, not the whole original cost.

5   COMPENSATION AND INSURANCE RECEIPTS

5.1   Introduction

In most circumstances a capital transaction has two parties, a buyer and a seller. For capital gains tax, the seller takes the agreed price into his disposal calculation as proceeds and the buyer has normally incurred allowable expenditure that will be used to calculate any gain or loss when he eventually disposes of the asset.

However, when an asset is damaged or destroyed, and the asset's owner receives compensation (either from the perpetrator or an insurance company) the position is different. The owner has received a capital sum without disposing of the asset and the payer has received nothing in return. Consequently a separate set of rules is required.

The rules vary according to whether the asset has been completely destroyed or merely damaged. In the former case the owner may (or may not) choose to restore the asset. In the latter case the choice is whether or not to replace the asset.

5.2   Treatment of damaged assets

(a)   The basic position is that where the owner of the asset receives compensation he has made a part disposal of it; the extent is determined by the degree of damage. The part disposal is deemed to occur when the owner receives the compensation money (not the date the damage was incurred, which might be in an earlier tax year). Allowable cost for the part disposal calculation is calculated using the normal formula:

$$\frac{\text{Value of part disposal of}}{\text{Value of part disposed of + value of part retained}}$$

If the compensation money is not used in restoration work, the value of the part retained is the value of the asset in its damaged condition.

Often, however, the owner uses some or all of the compensation money to restore the asset. In these circumstances the receipt of the compensation is **not** treated as a part disposal provided that the taxpayer claims for the receipt to be rolled over and:

- it is wholly applied in restoring the asset; or
- only a small part of it is not used for restoration (5% or less); or
- it is a small percentage (5% or less) of the value of the asset.

In the second of these cases there is also a requirement that the remaining, unused amount of the compensation money was not reasonably required for the restoration.

If, on the basis of the tests set out above, there is no part disposal the compensation money is simply deducted from allowable costs when the asset is eventually sold (ie, rolled over).

For February 1997 onwards it is Revenue Practice to treat amounts as small if they are less than £3,000 whether or not they fail the '5%' test.

(b)   Where the receipt of compensation is substantial and more than 5% of it is not used for restoration, the part not used is treated as a part disposal.

Two points arise that need care. Firstly, the part disposal fraction has to be applied to both the original cost and the part of the compensation used for restoration. Secondly, the indexation allowance has to be calculated separately for the deductible part of the original cost and the deductible part of the restoration cost. Indexation on the part of the original cost is calculated from the date of acquisition to the date of receipt of the compensation. On the part of the restoration cost it is calculated from the date the restoration expenditure was incurred to the date of the receipt of the compensation.

5.3   Example

Shoesmith purchased an office block for £500,000 in April 1985. In September 1997 it was damaged by fire. Restoration expenditure of £70,000 was incurred in February 1998 and Shoesmith's insurance company paid compensation of £150,000 in June 1998. After restoration, the office block had a market value of £1,075,000.

5.4   Solution

	£	£
Disposal proceeds		
(compensation not used for restoration)		80,000
Less: Proportion of original cost		
$\dfrac{80,000}{80,000+1,075,000} \times £500,000$	34,632	
proportion of restoration cost		
$\dfrac{80,000}{80,000+1,075,000} \times £70,000$	4,848	
		39,480
Unindexed gain		40,520
Less: Indexation allowance		
(i) on original cost (to April 1998)		
$\dfrac{161.2-94.78}{94.78} (= 0.701) \times £34,632$	24,277	
(ii) on restoration cost (to April 1998)		
$\dfrac{161.2-160.3}{160.3} (= 0.006) \times £4,848$	29	
		24,306
		16,214

Note that the date of disposal is June 1998 (when the insurance compensation was received, **not** September 1997 when the damage took place).

5.5   Assets lost or destroyed

Where assets are simply damaged there is a part disposal if all (or almost all) of any compensation is not applied in restoration. If there is no compensation (for example where the owner was uninsured) there is no disposal at all.

The situation differs for assets lost or wholly destroyed. In this case, whether or not there is any compensation, there is a deemed disposal of the asset.

(a)   If no compensation is received the capital gains tax calculation proceeds in the normal way. Disposal proceeds are nil (or any small scrap value from the asset). Deduction of allowable expenditure and any indexation allowance crystallises a loss subject to the normal loss restriction for indexation allowance.

(b)   Where the asset's owner receives compensation that is all used to buy a replacement asset within 12 months, the taxpayer can claim that the loss or destruction of the original asset should be treated as a no gain/no loss disposal. In these circumstances, if the compensation received (plus any scrap value) is greater than the deemed disposal value of the original asset on a no gain/no loss basis, the excess is deducted from the replacement asset's allowable expenditure.

Note that neither this relief (nor the parallel one for damaged assets) applies to wasting assets.

(c)   As no gain is chargeable on the compensation proceeds if no gain/no loss treatment is claimed there can be no taper relief at that point. When the replacement asset is sold, any taper relief is given solely by reference to the period of ownership of the replacement asset. The earlier period of ownership of the original asset is ignored. It seems unfair that taper relief entitlement on the original asset is lost but this is a common feature of deferral reliefs which operate by effectively reducing the base cost of a new asset (see chapters 20 and 21 for further examples).

5.6   Example - replacement of lost or destroyed asset

Bill purchased an asset for £25,000 on 1 October 1989 which was destroyed by fire on 30 September 1998. He received scrap proceeds of £1,000 and compensation of £35,000 from his insurance company on 1 January 1999 and purchased a replacement asset for £40,000 on 1 February 1999.

Assuming that Bill claims the loss by fire to be a no gain/no loss disposal, calculate the allowable expenditure (base cost) for the replacement asset.

5.7   Solution

		£	£
Cost of replacement asset			40,000
Less:	Compensation	35,000	
	Scrap proceeds	1,000	
		36,000	
	Less: Deemed disposal proceeds of old asset (W)	34,300	
			1,700
Replacement asset base cost			38,300

Working - deemed disposal proceeds

Since the disposal of the old asset is assumed to be on a no gain/no loss basis, the disposal proceeds are the allowable cost plus indexation allowance.

	£
Allowable cost	25,000
Indexation allowance (to April 1998) $\dfrac{161.2-117.5}{117.5}\ (=0.372) \times £25,000$	9,300
Deemed disposal proceeds	34,300

Note:

(1)   This is a form of rollover relief. The allowable expenditure on the new asset is restricted only to the extent that the receipts from the old asset are greater than its cost plus indexation. Were it not for this special treatment, which the taxpayer must claim, the receipt of the compensation money and scrap proceeds would be treated as a disposal (and any excess over the indexed cost of the original asset ie, £1,700 - taxed immediately).

(2)   Had the £1,700 become chargeable, taper relief may have been due thereon. However, by rolling it over any such entitlement to taper relief is lost. When the replacement asset is sold, any taper relief will be based solely on the ownership period from 1 February 1999.

6   CHAPTER SUMMARY

(a)   Chattels (tangible movable property) are exempt when they are sold at a gain for £6,000 or less. The limit of £6,000 applies to the gross consideration (before taking into account any disposal expenses).

(b)   Gains on chattels sold for more than £6,000 are restricted to 5/3 x (disposal consideration - £6,000) if this is less than the gain calculated using normal CGT principles.

(c)   Losses on chattels sold for less than £6,000 are restricted (by substituting £6,000 for the actual sale proceeds).

(d)   Wasting assets (assets with predictable lives of not more than 50 years) have a deduction made from allowable cost to reflect their depreciation during the disposer's period of ownership. Indexation allowance is based on cost less the depreciation deduction.

(e)   Wasting assets that are also chattels are exempt (unless they have, or could have, capital allowances claimed on them).

(f)   Disposal of leases of more than 50 years to expiry are treated like any other asset. Other leases (commonly known as short leases) are wasting assets. These have a separate treatment. The depreciation deduction is based on a table set out in the legislation (rather than assuming the straight line depreciation used for other wasting assets).

(g)   Compensation and insurance receipts are treated under a special regime because there is no disposal in the normal sense of the word. Receipts for assets that are merely damaged may be rolled over (deducted from allowable expenditure) against the asset's eventual disposal, provided that all, or nearly all, of the compensation is applied in restoring the asset. Otherwise there is a deemed part disposal at the time the compensation is received.

(h)   When an asset is lost or wholly destroyed there is a deemed disposal of it. If compensation is received and all applied in acquiring a replacement asset, any accrued gain can be rolled over into the replacement asset. However, this removes any potential for taper relief on the rolled over gain. Taper relief on disposal of the replacement asset takes no account of the ownership of the original asset.

7   SELF TEST QUESTIONS

7.1   What are chattels? (1.1)

7.2   How are gains on chattels sold for more than £6,000 restricted? (2.1)

7.3   How are losses restricted for disposals of chattels for less than £6,000? (2.4)

7.4   What is a wasting asset? (3.1)

7.5   When are wasting assets exempt from CGT? (3.2)

7.6   In what way is allowable expenditure on a wasting asset (other than a lease) restricted when it is sold? (3.3)

7.7   In what circumstances can compensation receipts for a damaged asset be rolled over until the asset's eventual disposal? (5.2)

7.8   How long does a taxpayer have to acquire a replacement asset when he wishes to treat the destruction of the original as no gain/no loss? (5.5)

8   EXAMINATION TYPE QUESTION

8.1   Mr and Mrs Steel

Mr and Mrs Steel had the following transactions in assets in the year ended 5 April 1999

Mr Steel

(a)   A house, which had been bought for £4,000 on 3 April 1983 and let to tenants thereafter, was sold on 1 July 1998. On 2 April 1984 an extension costing £2,000 was built, and on 12 June 1986 the loft was converted into a bedroom at a cost of £3,000. The net proceeds of sale were £62,750.

(b)   Sold a piece of sculpture for £6,500 on 30 August 1998 which he had bought for £3,900. Indexation factor is 0.424 to April 1998.

(c)   Sold a one-tenth share in a racehorse on 31 August 1998 for £6,200. The interest had cost £1,340 in November 1989.

(d)   Sold a vintage Alfa Romeo motor car for £76,500 on 19 December 1998. The car had cost £17,400 on 31 March 1983. During his period of ownership Steel had never actually used the car on the road.

Mrs Steel

(e)   Sold a rare Russian icon on 24 May 1998 for £5,600 which had cost £6,300. Indexation factor is 0.618 to April 1998.

(f)   Sold three acres out of a twelve acre plot of land on 14 December 1998 for £8,000. The whole plot had been purchased for £2,000. On 14 December 1998 the unsold acres had an agreed market value of £20,000. Indexation factor is 0.682 to April 1998.

(g)   Sold a piece of Chinese jade for £13,800 on 1 September 1998. This was purchased at auction in May 1970 for £4,100. The market value on 31 March 1982 was £6,500.

Mr Steel had capital losses brought forward at 6 April 1998 of £3,024. His taxable income for 1998/99 is £22,400. Mrs Steel has no income. None of the above assets qualify as 'business' assets for taper relief purposes.

You are required:

(a)   to calculate Mr Steel's tax liability on chargeable gains for 1998/99 if any.
(b)   to calculate Mrs Steel's tax liability on chargeable gains for 1998/99 if any.

9   ANSWER TO EXAMINATION TYPE QUESTION

9.1   Mr and Mrs Steel

Mr Steel

(a)   **House**

	£	£	*Gain/(loss)* £
Net sale proceeds (1.7.98)		62,750	
Cost (3.4.83)	4,000		
Extension (2.4.84)	2,000		
Loft (12.6.86)	3,000		
		(9,000)	
Unindexed gain		53,750	

Less: Indexation allowance

Cost $4,000 \times \dfrac{161.2 - 84.28}{84.28}$ (0.913)
 (Apr 1983 – Apr 1998)   3,652

Extension $2,000 \times \dfrac{161.2 - 88.64}{88.64}$ (0.819)
 (Apr 1984 – Apr 1998)   1,638

Loft $3,000 \times \dfrac{161.2 - 97.79}{97.79}$ (0.648)
 (Jun 1986 – Apr 1998)   1,944

	£	£	Gain/(loss) £
		(7,234)	
Chargeable gain		46,516	46,516

(b)   **Sculpture**

	£
Sale proceeds	6,500
Less: Cost	3,900
Unindexed gain	2,600
Less: Indexation allowance $3,900 \times 0.424$	1,654
	946

Gain cannot exceed $(6,500 - 6,000) \times \frac{5}{3}$ 833

(c)   **One-tenth interest in racehorse**

Exempt as a chattel which is also a wasting asset   -

(d)   **Alfa-Romeo vintage car**

Exempt asset   -

Net gains   47,349

Mrs Steel

(e)   **Icon**

	£	£	£
Deemed sale proceeds		6,000	
Cost		6,300	
Allowable loss		(300)	(300)

(f)   **Plot of land**

	£
Sale proceeds of 3 acres (>20% × 28,000)	8,000
Less: Cost of 3 acres	

$$2,000 \times \frac{8,000}{8,000+20,000}$$ 571

	£	£
Unindexed gain	7,429	
Less: Indexation allowance 571 × 0.682	389	
Chargeable gain	7,040	7,040

(g)   **Jade**

	Cost basis £	31.3.82 basis £	
Sale proceeds	13,800	13,800	
Less: Cost/MV 31.3.82	4,100	6,500	
Unindexed gain	9,700	7,300	
Less: IA (Mar 1982 – Apr 1998) Use higher MV 31.3.82			

$$6,500 \times \frac{161.2-79.44}{79.44} \ (1.029)$$ (6,688)   (6,688)

Lower gain applies	3,012	612	612
Net gains			7,352

	Mr Steel £		Mrs Steel £
Net gains for 1998/99	47,349		7,352
Less: Losses b/f	(3,024)		-
	44,325		7,352
Less: Annual exemption	(6,800)		(6,800)
Taxable amount	37,525		552

		£	£	£	£
Tax	4,700 × 23%		1,081	552 × 20%	110
	32,825 × 40%		13,130		
	37,525		14,211		

19 RETIREMENT RELIEF

INTRODUCTION & LEARNING OBJECTIVES

This relief applies to the gains realised on the transfer of a business, or shares in a personal company. Earlier in the text it was explained that capital gains tax reliefs either exempt the gain or defer it; retirement relief exempts gains made on the transfer of a business or shares in a personal company. It is frequently examined and should be studied carefully.

When you have studied this chapter you should have learned the following:

- The purpose and scope of retirement relief.

- The monetary limits and the circumstances in which these are scaled down.

- The interaction with taper relief.

- The conditions applying to sole traders.

- The additional conditions applying to certain shareholders of personal companies.

- The conditions that must be met by assets to qualify for relief.

- The definition of a personal company.

- The restriction for non-business assets owned by a personal company.

- When two periods of business ownership may be aggregated to calculate the qualifying period.

- The circumstances in which retirement relief is extended to associated disposals.

When an individual disposes of a business, or shares in a trading company retirement relief may be available.

This exempts the gain.

Other reliefs that may be available:

- gift relief

- reinvestment relief

- rollover relief (for disposal of a business only)

---

1 INTRODUCTION

1.1 Purpose of retirement relief

For many years the Conserative Government in power up to 1997 thought it right to provide generous relief from capital gains tax for people retiring from business towards the end of their careers. Broadly it applies only to chargeable gains realised by people actively involved in the business; generally gains realised by passive investors do not qualify for retirement relief.

It is particularly valuable in assisting families to pass businesses on from one generation to the next. Such transfers are often made by gift. Although there is a separate relief for gifts of business assets, it is not so comprehensive as retirement relief. Since market value is substituted for disposal proceeds when a gift is made, if it were not for retirement relief the disposer would often find himself paying a large tax bill without having received any cash.

The New Labour Government has decided to phase out retirement relief for disposals after 5 April 1999 arguing that taper relief, particularly at the higher rates for business assets, is a sufficient exchange. However, as gains up to £250,000 are fully exempt under retirement relief but taper relief can only exempt up to 75% of business gains many taxpayers will, in fact, be worse off once phasing out of retirement relief starts.

1.2   Scope of retirement relief

The most important groups of people covered by the retirement relief rules are:

(a)   sole traders; and
(b)   certain shareholders of personal companies.

Each group has its own set of conditions which must be met before retirement relief is available.

For both groups, however, the size of the eligible gain that can be relieved is the same. The first £250,000 is entirely exempt and, if the gain is large enough, an additional £750,000 attracts relief at 50%. Thus a total of £1,000,000 chargeable gains may be wholly or partly sheltered. The relief is deducted from the indexed gain.

1.3   Activity

Griffiths made indexed gains of £1,200,000 on the disposal of his business on 1 February 1999. He met all the conditions for retirement relief in full.

Calculate the chargeable gain after retirement relief.

1.4   Activity solution

	£	£
Gain before retirement relief		1,200,000
Less: Retirement relief		
(i) first £250,000	250,000	
(ii) (£1,000,000 − £250,000) × 50%	375,000	
		625,000
Chargeable gain after retirement relief		575,000

A gain remaining after retirement relief will attract taper relief in the normal way. Thus, if the above £575,000 remains chargeable, it will be reduced by taper relief at 7.5%.

1.5   Phasing out of retirement relief

Between 6 April 1999 and 5 April 2003 the £250,000 and £1,000,000 limits are being phased out in annual steps of £50,000 and £200,000 respectively. For example, a qualifying disposal in 1999/00 will be fully exempt on the first £200,000 and 50% exempt on gains between £200,000 and £800,000.

2   SOLE TRADERS

2.1   Conditions applying to the individual

The normal rule is that an individual must have reached 50 years of age (at the time of the disposal) for retirement relief to be available. Oddly, however, there is no need for the individual actually to retire. Afterwards he may engage in another business or take up employment if he wishes to do so.

To avoid unfairness, the age limit does not apply to those who retire due to ill-health. In these circumstances the age of the disposer is irrelevant.

For those aged 50 or more, retirement relief is automatic (ie, it does not need to be claimed). When the ill-health provisions are used, however, a claim does have to be made, backed up with the appropriate medical evidence.

The condition that the disposer must be at least 50 years old or be retiring due to ill-health is absolute. If it is not met there is no relief.

In contrast, there is a condition that the disposer must have owned the business for at least ten years to obtain full retirement relief. If he has owned it for a shorter period his entitlement to relief is scaled down proportionately (provided that he has owned it for an absolute minimum period of one year). For instance, an individual who had owned a business for four years at the time of retirement would qualify for complete exemption on the first £100,000 of gains (4/10 × £250,000) and 50% exemption on the next £300,000 (4/10 × £750,000). Note that it is the retirement relief limits that are scaled down, not the gain.

2.2   Conditions applying to the assets producing a chargeable gain

To qualify for relief the disposal must be a 'material disposal of business assets'. In the context of a disposal by a sole trader, business assets are:

(a)   a disposal of the whole or part of a business; and

(b)   a disposal of one or more assets which, at the time the business ceased to be carried on, were in use for the purposes of that business.

Assets can thus be disposed of by way of a going concern or piecemeal after it has ceased. Importantly, however, if the disposal is made while the individual remains in business, it must be of a business unit ('the whole or part of a business'). Disposing of single assets or a group of assets which could not be run as a business does not qualify for relief.

2.3   Chargeable business assets

Gains eligible for retirement relief are restricted to those on chargeable business assets. Chargeable business assets are those used for the purposes of the taxpayer's trade or profession (including goodwill but excluding shares, securities and other assets held as investments).

An asset cannot be a chargeable business asset where a gain that might arise on its disposal would not be a chargeable gain. This provision rules out exempt assets but not those that could produce a gain on disposal but currently stand at a loss.

2.4   Activity

Which of the following constitute chargeable business assets for retirement relief purposes?

(a)   an item of plant, purchased originally for £10,000 and now valued at £4,000
(b)   bank balance of £3,000
(c)   stock, valued at £25,000
(d)   current creditors of £15,000
(e)   goodwill, valued at £60,000
(f)   trade debtors of £18,000
(g)   shares in a supplier with a market value of £9,000
(h)   freehold premises, valued at £45,000

2.5   Activity solution

(a), (e) and (h) count as chargeable business assets. As for the others:

(b) -   cash is not normally an asset subject to capital gains tax

(c) -   any profit on disposal of stock is subject to income tax (and thus not to CGT)

(d) -   creditors are not an asset at all

(f) -   trade debts are not subject to CGT

(g) -   although a gain might arise on the disposal of these shares, shares are specifically excluded from the definition of chargeable business assets.

2.6   Example

Joe Smith purchased a steel stockholding business on 1 February 1992. As part of the purchase he acquired freehold premises, valued at £200,000, stock of £150,000 and goodwill of £80,000. On 31 January 1999, when he was 52 years old, he sold the business. The assets sold were valued as follows:

(i)   freehold premises   £480,000
(ii)   stock   £175,000
(iii)   shares in a supplier   £40,000   (acquired for £20,000 in January 1993)
(iv)   goodwill   £655,000

Calculate:

(a)   the retirement relief due to Joe Smith; and
(b)   the chargeable gain arising on the disposal of his business.

2.7   Solution

		£	£
Premises			
	Proceeds		480,000
	Less: Purchase price		200,000
	Unindexed gain		280,000
	Less: Indexation allowance (to April 1998)		
	$\frac{161.2-136.3}{136.3}$ $(=0.183) \times £200,000$		36,600
			243,400

Goodwill

Proceeds		655,000
Less: Purchase price		80,000
Unindexed gain		575,000
Less: Indexation allowance (to April 1998)		
$0.183 \times £80,000$		14,640
		560,360

Gains qualifying for retirement relief		803,760
Less: Retirement relief		
(i) first £250,000 × 7/10	175,000	
(ii) next ((1,000,000 × 7/10) – 175,000) × 50%	262,500	
		437,500
Chargeable gains after retirement relief		366,260

Shares

Proceeds		40,000
Less: Purchase price		20,000
Unindexed gain		20,000
Less: Indexation allowance (to April 1998)		
$\dfrac{161.2 - 137.9}{137.9} \times £20,000$		3,379
		16,621
Total chargeable gains		382,881

Notes:

(1)   Where there are several assets to be dealt with, only some of which qualify for retirement relief, it is simpler to deal first with all the qualifying assets. This approach makes it easier to deal with the limits for retirement relief.

(2)   In this case Joe Smith has owned the business for only seven years and so he is entitled only to reduced retirement relief. Remember this is calculated by scaling down the retirement relief limits (by the fraction 7/10) **not** the gains. Thus his upper limit is £700,000.

(3)   The shares, purchased in January 1993, are held in a share pool. Thus the indexation factor is **not** rounded to three decimal places.

(4)   Taper relief at 7.5% will be available on the £366,260 of business asset gains net of retirement relief as they have been held on 17 March 1998 and qualify for a bonus year. The shares in the supplier company would only count as a business asset for taper relief if, inter alia, they represented at least 25% of the voting rights.

(5)   It is presumed that where there is more than one qualifying business asset, retirement relief can be allocated to maximise any available taper relief.

(6)   The conditions for business asset rate taper relief are more generous than the asset conditions for retirement relief. For example, retirement relief requires the disposal of the whole or part of a business - even though gains are calculated asset by asset. Business asset taper relief would apply to the disposal of a single business asset without any requirement for the sale of the business.

(7)   Similarly, shares only attract retirement relief where the shareholder is a full time working officer or employee of the company (see below) whereas taper relief at the business asset rate can apply on shares if they represent at least 25% of the voting rights regardless of working for the company.

3   RELIEF FOR DISPOSALS OF SHARES IN A PERSONAL COMPANY

3.1   Introduction

Retirement relief applies to the owners of both unincorporated and incorporated businesses. Broadly, the conditions examined earlier in the chapter relating to disposals by sole traders are mirrored for shareholders in personal companies. The rules ensure, however, that retirement relief for shareholders is given only where the individual has both an ownership stake in the company and is intimately concerned with its management. How this is achieved is looked at below.

3.2   Conditions applying to the individual

The same basic conditions apply to a shareholder as to the owner of an unincorporated business. At the time of disposal the individual must be at least 50 years old (or be retiring due to ill-health). Unless this condition is met no retirement relief is available. Again mirroring the position for unincorporated business, maximum relief is available for ownership of ten years or more and is scaled down proportionately for shorter periods (with an absolute minimum ownership period of one year).

There are other conditions, however, that apply only to shareholders. These are:-

(a)   the shares disposed of must be in the individual's personal company. A company qualifies as an individual's personal company if not less than 5% of the voting rights are exercised by the individual.

(b)   The individual must be a full-time officer or employee of the company, working in a technical or managerial capacity.

The qualifying period (from a minimum of one year to a maximum of ten) applies not only to the individual's shares qualifying his holding as a personal company but also to his acting as a full-time working officer or employee. Consequently, if either (or both) periods are less than ten years, the shorter period is the qualifying period for retirement.

3.3   Activity

In each of the following cases would the disposal of the shares mentioned below qualify for retirement relief? If so, what is the qualifying period? Assume that all shares carry the same voting rights and the conditions stated are satisfied up to the date of any disposal.

(a)   Mr A has owned 10% of A Ltd for 8 years and been a full-time working director for 11 years.

(b)   Mr B has owned 6% of B Ltd for 10 years and has been a full-time working manager for the same period.

(c)   Mr C has owned 30% of C Ltd for 7 years and has been a full-time working director for 5 years.

(d)   Mr D owns 7% of D Ltd. He purchased the shareholding 9 months ago and has been a full-time working director for 11 years.

3.4   Activity solution

(a)   Restricted retirement relief available. Mr A has owned more than the 5% threshold for a qualifying period of 8 years.

(b)   Full retirement relief available (ie, qualifying period of 10 years). Mr B has owned a stake of at least 5% and has been a full-time working employee in a managerial capacity for more than 10 years.

(c)   Restricted retirement relief available. He owns more than 5% of the company. Relief is restricted to 50% (qualifying period of 5 years) because he has been a full-time working officer for only 5 years.

(d)   No retirement relief available. The shares have been owned for less than the absolute minimum period of one year.

3.5   Restrictions of relief for non-business assets

Where the qualifying disposal is of specific assets (in the case of sole traders) dealing with non-business assets is straightforward. It was seen earlier in the chapter that they are simply not taken into account when quantifying the amount of retirement relief available.

In the case of a disposal of shares in a personal company the position is different. The gain on the shares automatically reflects gains attributable to business and non-business assets alike. Consequently a restriction is needed to ensure that non-business assets do not attract retirement relief by being sheltered in a personal company. The gain on which retirement relief is given is:

$$\text{Total indexed gain on share disposal} \times \frac{\text{Chargeable business assets}}{\text{Chargeable assets}}$$

If either all chargeable assets are chargeable business assets or alternatively the company has no chargeable assets at all (perhaps a service company in rented accommodation) there is no restriction on retirement relief.

3.6   Example

Fred owned 35% of his family company, Fred Ltd, of which he had been managing director since 1975. On 20 February 1999, his sixtieth birthday, he sold his shares, which he had owned for the past 19 years. At the time of disposal Fred Ltd owned the following assets.

	Value at disposal
	£
Freehold trading premises	400,000
Goodwill	150,000
Plant and equipment (see note)	64,000
Investments	88,000
Stock and work in progress	75,000
Debtors	105,000
Cash	28,000
	910,000

Note: Plant and equipment contained one item valued at £8,000 (original cost £18,000 in 1988). All other items were worth less than £6,000.

Fred purchased his shares in 1980 for £41,000. On 31 March 1982 they were worth £43,500 and he sold them on 20 February 1999 for £308,000.

Calculate the chargeable gain arising on the disposal, after retirement relief (if any) but before taper relief.

3.7   Solution

	£
Sale proceeds	308,000
Less: March 1982 value (see note)	43,500
Unindexed gain	264,500
Less: Indexed allowance (to April 1998)	
$\dfrac{161.2 - 79.44}{79.44}$ $(= 1.029) \times £43,500$	44,761
Indexed gain	219,739
Less: Retirement relief (W)	189,806
Chargeable gain	29,933

Note:

(1)   in this case both cost and March 1982 value clearly produce gains and the lower is that found by using the March 1982 value.

(2)   Oddly, the taper relief rules appear to allow business asset taper rates to apply to the part of the gain on the shares not qualifying for retirement relief.

Working - retirement relief

It is first necessary to categorise Fred Ltd's assets into assets not subject to CGT, chargeable assets and chargeable business assets.

	Non-chargeable assets	Chargeable assets	Chargeable business assets
	£	£	£
Freehold trading premises		400,000	400,000
Goodwill		150,000	150,000
Plant and equipment	56,000	8,000	8,000
Investments		88,000	
Stock and WIP	75,000		
Debtors	105,000		
Cash	28,000		
	264,000	646,000	558,000

Fred has fulfilled the conditions for retirement relief for more than ten years and is thus entitled to full relief. His modest gain falls wholly within the wholly relieved first £250,000 but is restricted due to the investment portfolio of Fred Ltd.

Relief is thus £219,739 $\times \dfrac{558}{646} = £189,806$.

4   AGGREGATION OF QUALIFYING PERIODS

4.1   Introduction

Suppose a businessman, aged 49, sold the business he had owned for 15 years and immediately purchased another business. Two years later he decided finally to retire and sold the second business, realising a substantial capital gain. On the basis of the rules set out above, it would appear that the retirement relief limits would be scaled down to 20% of the norm.

4.2   Recognition of ownership of a previous business

This position is recognised as unfair by the retirement relief legislation, since, had the businessman simply retained his earlier business he would have been entitled to full retirement relief.

Ownership of a previous business within ten years of the disposal of the current one counts towards an individual's qualifying period, provided that the 'gap' between the disposal of the earlier business and the acquisition of the later one is not more than two years. Note, however, that the gap period itself does not count as part of the qualifying period.

Retirement relief can be given on more than on disposal. However, if it is given on an earlier disposal it must be taken into account on a later qualifying disposal. The qualifying gains on the earlier disposal are aggregated as part of the qualifying gains on the later disposal to compute the amount of relief based on the qualifying period for the later disposal. The relief given on the earlier disposal is then deducted.

4.3   Activity

Charles set up a business on 1 May 1989. On 30 April 1993 he sold the business but purchased another on 1 November 1994. He sold the second business and retired, aged 57, on 30 April 1998.

How long is Charles's retirement relief qualifying period for the disposal on 30 April 1998?

4.4   Activity solution

Charles's qualifying period for his second business runs from 1 November 1994 to 30 April 1998 (ie, 3.5 years). The qualifying period for his earlier business (falling in the 10 years up to 30 April 1998) began on 1 May 1989 and ended on 30 April 1993 (ie, 4.0 years).

His total qualifying period is thus 7.5 years

4.5   Transfer of a business between spouses.

Where an individual makes a disposal of business assets (including shares in a personal company) that were acquired from his or her spouse less than ten years before the disposal, the spouse's period can be the aggregate of:

(a)   his or her own qualifying period; and

(b)   the period of ownership of the transferor spouse that falls within the ten-year period before the disposal.

For this extension of the qualifying period to apply, the transfer between the spouses must occur either as a lifetime gift (not sale) or on the transferor spouse's death. Whichever of these circumstances applies, the couple must have been living together during the tax year in which the transfer took place.

4.6   Activity

Suzie owns 35% of S Ltd, which she sells on 1 February 1999, her sixtieth birthday. She acquired the shares from her husband on his death on 31 January 1996. He had acquired them on 1 August 1990. Both had been managing director of S Ltd while they owned the shares in the company.

What is Suzie's qualifying period for retirement relief on the disposal of the shares?

4.7   Activity solution

Suzie's qualifying period is the aggregate of:

(i)   her own period of ownership (3.0 years); and

(ii)   her husband's period of ownership within the last ten years (4.5 years).

Her total qualifying period is thus 7.5 years.

5   ASSOCIATED DISPOSALS

5.1   Introduction

Where an individual carries on a business through the vehicle of a personal company it is sometimes useful to own assets personally and allow their use by the company. Disposal of such assets also qualifies for retirement relief, subject to meeting the conditions set out below. Such disposals are known as 'associated disposals'.

5.2   Conditions for associated disposals

For retirement relief to be a available, the following conditions must be fulfilled.

(a)   The normal age or ill-health criteria must be met.

(b)   The asset in question must have been in use in the personal company's trade immediately before the disposal (or when trade ceased, if appropriate). If the business paid the individual any consideration for the asset's use (such as rent for premises) the Inland Revenue have discretion to restrict relief.

(c)   The asset must be a chargeable business asset in the normal way.

(d)   The disposal must be part of the individual's withdrawal from his business.

(e)   The individual making the disposal must qualify for retirement relief on disposing of his interest in the personal company.

(f)   Normally full relief or restricted relief is given on the same basis as for the principal disposal that attracts retirement relief (which is dependent on the length of time the individual has met the necessary conditions). But where the asset was used in the owner's period for only part of individual's ownership, or where the asset was used but the individual was not concerned in the running of the business, relief may be restricted by the Inland Revenue.

6 CHAPTER SUMMARY

Retirement relief is available to both:

(a)   sole traders; and
(b)   certain shareholders of personal companies.

Where an officer or employee of a personal company is withdrawing from his business, assets which he or she owned personally and were used in the business's trade may also qualify for relief. These are known as associated disposals.

Sole traders obtain relief on the gains that arise on the sale of their chargeable business assets. Non-business assets are not covered by the relief. Shareholders obtain relief on the gain realised on the shares in their personal company. Where the company owns chargeable assets that are not business assets the gain eligible for retirement relief is scaled down by the fraction:

$$\frac{\text{Chargeable business assets}}{\text{Chargeable assets}}$$

Relief may be obtained only where the disposal is a 'material disposal of business assets'. In relation to a sole trader this is normally the whole or part of the business. For a shareholder of a personal company it is the whole or part of his shareholding.

Owners of both incorporated and unincorporated businesses must be at least 50 years old to benefit from retirement relief (or their retirement must be caused by ill-health if they are younger). To be eligible for full retirement relief the business (for sole traders) or the shares (for owners of personal companies) must have been owned throughout a qualifying period of ten years ending at the time of disposal. Ownership between one year and ten years entitles the disposer to partial relief; the normal retirement relief limits are scaled down arithmetically. There is no relief for ownership of less than one year.

In addition to the age and period of ownership requirements, shareholders are subjected to two further hurdles before they qualify for retirement relief. The company must count as their personal company (the individual must own not less than 5% of the voting power) and he must be a full-time working officer or employee.

Where an individual previously owned a business (or personal company shares) during the ten years before the disposal of the one he is selling, the period of ownership of that first business can count towards the qualifying period of retirement relief on the disposal of the second one. Similarly, where one spouse makes a gift of his or her interest in a business (or personal company) to the other, the transferor spouse's period of ownership can count towards the qualifying period of the transferee spouse on a disposal that is eligible for retirement relief.

Taper relief applies to the gain after deducting retirement relief. For businesses/shares owned on 5 April 1998 taper relief increases incrementally on every 6 April but retirement relief is phasing down in annual steps also on 6 April.

7 SELF TEST QUESTIONS

7.1   What groups of people may be eligible for retirement relief? (1.2)

7.2   What are the normal monetary limits for retirement relief? (1.2)

7.3   When is a claim for retirement relief necessary? (2.1)

7.4   How is retirement relief restricted when an individual's qualifying period is less than ten years long? (2.1)

7.5   What are chargeable business assets in the context of retirement relief? (2.3)

7.6   What additional conditions apply to owners of incorporated businesses? (3.2)

7.7   How are gains on the disposal of personal company shares restricted for non-business assets? (3.5)

7.8   What conditions apply to the extension of the qualifying period when a business has been given by one spouse to the other? (4.5)

7.9   What are associated disposals? (5.1)

7.10   What conditions must be met for retirement relief to be available on an associated disposal? (5.2)

8   EXAMINATION TYPE QUESTIONS

8.1   Roy

The following is the balance sheet of a sole trader as at 31 December 1998 the date on which the owner, Roy, sold his business, which he had started and run continuously since 1 January 1969.

The sale consideration was £494,000.

Net assets	£
Freehold land and buildings at cost	10,000
Stock-in-trade	23,000
Debtors	12,000
Balance at bank	6,000
	51,000
Less: Current liabilities	10,000
	41,000
Financed by capital account of	41,000

The following valuations are relevant

		Valuations at	
		31.3.82	31.12.98
		£	£
(i)	Goodwill – all created	25,000	81,000
(ii)	Freehold land and buildings	60,000	388,000

The plant and machinery is all leased and there is no entitlement to any capital allowances.

At 31 December 1998 Roy was 48 years old. The sale of his business had been precipitated by Roy's serious illness in 1997. The Inland Revenue have accepted that his retirement is due to ill health.

Roy has elected that all of his assets held on 31 March 1982 are deemed acquired at their MV on that date.

Compute the chargeable gains, if any, in respect of which Roy will be assessable for 1998/99 assuming any available taper relief is not restricted by loss relief etc.

8.2   Robert

Robert sold his 30% shareholding in his personal trading company on 30 June 1998 giving rise to an indexed gain, before retirement relief of £272,500. He was aged 62 at the date of disposal and had at that time been a full time working director of the company for the last 8 years.

On 30 June 1998 the open market values of relevant assets held by the company were as follows:

	£	£
Goodwill		50,000
Freehold land and buildings		315,000
Plant and machinery:		
Movable items whose individual values do not exceed £6,000	28,000	
Motor cars	42,000	
Fixed plant	50,000	
		120,000
Investments		50,000
Net current assets		105,000
		640,000

Calculate the chargeable gain assessable on Robert on the sale of the shares in 1998/99 assuming taper relief is not restricted by loss relief etc.

9   ANSWERS TO EXAMINATION TYPE QUESTIONS

9.1   Roy

Gains and losses on chargeable assets of the business

Goodwill

	£	Gains/ (losses) £
Deemed sale proceeds	81,000	
Less: MV 31.3.82	25,000	
	56,000	
Unindexed gains		
Less: IA (March 1982 – April 1998)		
$\frac{161.2 - 79.44}{79.44}$ (= 1.029) × £25,000	(25,725)	
	30,275	30,275

Freehold land and buildings

	£	
Deemed sale proceeds	388,000	
Less: MV 31.3.82	60,000	
Unindexed gains	328,000	
Less: IA (March 1982 – April 1998)		
£60,000 × 1.029 (as above)	(61,740)	
	266,260	266,260

Gains on chargeable business assets (available for relief)		296,535

Less: Retirement relief (claim submitted for premature
retirement on grounds of ill-health) – maximum
qualifying period of 10 years achieved:

Full relief		250,000	
50% relief: $\frac{1}{2}$ (£296,535 – 250,000)		23,267	
			273,267

Chargeable gain	23,268
Less: Taper relief @ 7½%	(1,745)
Final chargeable gain	21,523

9.2   Robert

	£	£	£
Chargeable gain before retirement relief			272,500

Retirement relief will be the *lower* of

(a)   Maximum relievable gain attributable to chargeable
business assets

$£272,500 \times \dfrac{415,000}{465,000}$ (Note 1)   243,199

(b)   Full: £250,000 × 80%   200,000

Additional:	(a) £243,199 – 200,000 =	43,199
	(b) 80% × £750,000 =	600,000

$\frac{1}{2}$ × £43,199   21,600

221,600

221,600

Chargeable gain	50,900
Less: Taper relief @ 7½%	(3,817)
Final chargeable gain	47,083

Notes:

(1)   Chargeable business asset value at 30 June 1998 comprises

	£
Goodwill	50,000
Freehold land and buildings	315,000
Plant and machinery except attributable exempt value (see note 2)	50,000
	415,000

Chargeable asset value is chargeable business assets +
value of investments £415,000 + £50,000 =   465,000

(2)   The market value of plant and machinery included in the value of chargeable business
assets and chargeable assets is £120,000 less the value of the specifically exempt assets (ie,
the value covered by the £6,000 chattels exemption and that attributable to motor cars).

(3)   Taper relief does not appear to take account of non-business chargeable assets held by the
company (unlike retirement relief).

20 ROLLOVER RELIEFS

INTRODUCTION & LEARNING OBJECTIVES

This chapter covers two roll-over reliefs; one allows the gain realised on the disposal of business assets to be rolled over when the proceeds are reinvested in business assets; the second is a rollover relief which is available for any chargeable disposal where the proceeds are reinvested in 'qualifying investments'. Notice that these reliefs do not exempt the gain, but defer it by rolling over the gain and reducing the base cost of the new asset.

When you have studied this chapter you should have learned the following:

- The purpose and basic form of rollover relief.
- The time limit for claiming the relief.
- The categories of asset that qualify.
- The time period during which reinvestment must occur.
- The restriction on rollover relief when not all of the proceeds of sale are reinvested.
- The way relief is restricted when only part of the asset is used for trade, or the asset is used for trade for only part of the period of ownership.
- The interaction of rollover relief and taper relief.
- How the modified relief, hold over relief, is applied when reinvestment is made in depreciating assets.
- The definition of depreciating assets.
- The 50% rebasing relief.
- The rollover relief available on the sale of any of an individual's assets where the proceeds are reinvested in a subscription for qualifying shares.

Rollover relief is available when an individual or a company disposes of a qualifying business asset. The gain is deferred and rolled over into the base cost of a new business asset.

Reinvestment relief is available to an individual when he disposes of any asset and subscribes for qualifying shares. The gain on the disposal of the asset is deferred until some future event such as the disposal of the qualifying shares.

---

1 PURPOSE AND FORM OF THE RELIEF FOR REPLACEMENT OF BUSINESS ASSETS

1.1 Introduction

The first relief we study is the relief allowing the gain on the disposal of business assets to be rolled over when the proceeds are reinvested in business assets. This relief is covered in paragraphs 1 - 5. The relief, commonly known as rollover relief, exists to allow taxpayers to update and improve assets used in their trade without incurring an immediate liability to capital gains tax.

There are a number of conditions and restrictions, which are considered in this chapter but the essentials of rollover relief are straightforward. Where a taxpayer disposes of a qualifying chargeable asset used in his trade at a gain, and reinvests the proceeds in another asset, the gain is not taxed immediately but is deferred until he eventually makes a disposal of the replacement asset without reinvesting.

The deferral is achieved by deducting the gain made on the old asset from the cost of the new one. The old asset qualifies for indexation allowance up to the date of sale (or, if earlier, April 1998 where the owner is an individual) and the new asset from the date of purchase (unless, for an individual, this is after April 1998). For the new asset, indexation allowance is calculated on the cost as reduced by the rolled over gain.

This treatment is not automatic. The taxpayer must make a claim within five years of the 31 January following end of the tax year in which the disposal occurred (six years following the end of the accounting period for companies).

Where the old asset is disposed of after 5 April 1998 by an individual, any gain rolled over cannot be reduced by taper relief. When the replacement asset is sold (without further replacement) taper relief is given on the resulting gain appropriate to the period for which the replacement asset was held.

1.2   Example

Smith purchased an asset qualifying for rollover relief in January 1987 for £100,000. In May 1998 he sold the asset for £180,000 and spent £200,000 in August 1998 on a new qualifying asset.

The new asset is sold without replacement in December 2003 for £360,000.

Calculate the gain net of taper relief arising when the new asset is sold.

1.3   Solution

	£
Cost of new asset	200,000
Less: Gain on old asset (W)	18,800
Deductible cost of new asset	181,200
Sale proceeds of new asset (Dec 2003)	360,000
Less: Cost (Aug 1998)	181,200
Gain before taper relief	178,800
Less: Taper relief - 5 years and business asset - @ 37.5%	67,050
Gain finally chargeable	111,750

Working - gain on old asset

	£
Disposal proceeds	180,000
Less: Cost	100,000
Unindexed gain	80,000
Less: Indexation allowance	
$\dfrac{161.2 - 100.0}{100.0}$ (= 0.612) × £100,000	61,200
Indexed gain rolled over	18,800

2   REINVESTMENT: QUALIFYING ASSETS AND TIME PERIOD

2.1   Qualifying assets

Not all assets qualify for rollover relief, even if they are chargeable assets used for trading purposes.

The following are qualifying assets:

(a)   land and buildings that are both occupied and used for trading purposes;

(b)   fixed plant and machinery;

(In this context 'fixed' means immovable)

(c)   goodwill;

(d)   satellites, space stations, spacecraft, ships, aircraft and hovercraft;

(e)   milk and potato quotas.

(f)   ewe and suckler cow premium quotas.

The first three categories are the most important for exam purposes. To benefit from rollover relief the taxpayer's old and new assets must fall within one of the categories set out above (but not necessarily the same one). Thus a taxpayer could sell a factory and reinvest in an aircraft. It's not even necessary that the assets should be used in the **same** trade, because rollover relief treats all trades carried on by a taxpayer as one.

2.2   Time period for reinvestment

The acquisition of the replacement asset must occur during a period that begins one year **before** the sale of the old asset and ends three years after the sale.

3   PARTIAL REINVESTMENT OF PROCEEDS

3.1   Introduction

The purpose of rollover relief is to allow reinvestment in capital assets without the trader or company facing a tax bill. In part this is because if the proceeds are reinvested the transaction will not have generated cash with which to pay any tax. This is not true, however, where only part of the sale proceeds are used to purchase a new asset and thus, when this occurs, some immediate tax liability may arise. Any part of the gain remaining chargeable attracts taper relief in the normal way.

3.2   Restriction where partial reinvestment

Where the disposal proceeds of the old asset are not fully reinvested, the surplus retained reduces the gain allowed to be rolled over. Thus if the surplus proceeds are greater than the gain there is no rollover relief at all.

3.3   Example

Jarvis bought a factory in September 1986 for £400,000. In December 1998, wishing to move to a more convenient location, he sold the factory for £750,000. He moved into a rented factory until March 1999 when he purchased and moved into a new factory.

What is the base cost of the new factory if it was purchased for

(a)   £700,000; or

(b)   £650,000.

3.4 Solution

	£
Disposal proceeds (old factory)	750,000
Less: Cost	400,000
Unindexed gain	350,000

Less: Indexation allowance (to April 1998)

$$\frac{161.2 - 98.30}{98.30} \ (= 0.640) \times £400,000 \qquad\qquad 256,000$$

Indexed gain   94,000

(a) New factory purchased for £700,000.

Not all proceeds reinvested, thus restricted rollover relief.

	£	£
Purchase cost of new factory		700,000
Less: Gain on old factory	94,000	
Less: Restriction on rollover		
(750,000 – 700,000)	50,000	
Gain rolled over		44,000
Base cost of new factory		656,000

(b) New factory purchased for £650,000

In this case the amount of proceeds not reinvested of £100,000 (750,000 - 650,000) exceeds the gain made on the old factory. Thus none of the gain is eligible to be rolled over and so there is no adjustment to the base cost of the new factory. It remains at the purchase price of £650,000.

Note in case (a) the gain remaining chargeable of £50,000 attracts taper relief of 7.5%. The £44,000 gain rolled is effectively assessable when the replacement asset is sold but the taper relief then takes no account of the period of ownership of the original asset.

In case (b) all the gain is chargeable therefore taper relief of 7.5% on the £94,000 of gain is available.

4 NON-BUSINESS USE

4.1 Introduction

Full rollover relief is only available where the asset being replaced (the old asset) was used entirely for business purposes throughout the trader's period of ownership. Where this condition is not met rollover relief is still available but is scaled down in proportion to the non-business use. Periods before 1 April 1982 are ignored.

The rollover relief rules achieve this effect by assuming that the asset is in fact two assets, one that qualifies for relief (the part wholly used in the trade) and another that does not. Normally proceeds and costs of the old asset for the qualifying and non-qualifying parts are in the same proportion and thus the same scaling down factor may be used.

4.2 Example

Hadley purchased a factory in November 1987 for £350,000. Not needing all the space, he let out 15% of it. In August 1998 he sold the factory for £560,000 and bought another in October 1998 for £600,000.

Calculate:

(a)   the chargeable gain or allowable loss, if any, arising on the disposal in August 1998; and

(b)   the allowable expenditure (base cost) of the new factory.

4.3 Solution

(a)   First, split the old factory into qualifying and non-qualifying parts and compute the gains on them separately.

	Qualifying	Non-qualifying
	£	£
Disposal proceeds (85%/15%)	476,000	84,000
Less: Cost	297,500	52,500
Unindexed gain	178,500	31,500
Less: Indexation allowance		
$\dfrac{161.2 - 103.4}{103.4}$ (= 0.559) × £297,500/£52,500	166,302	29,347
Indexed gain	12,198	2,153

The gain of £2,153 is taxable immediately, as it does not qualify for rollover relief.

(b)   The base cost of the new factory is reduced by the amount of the gain rolled over. It is thus:

	£
Purchase cost	600,000
Less: Gain rolled over	12,198
	587,802

Note:

(1)   If a question asks only for the base cost of the replacement asset (and not the gain taxable immediately) there is no need to calculate the gain arising on the non-qualifying part.

(2)   As 15% of the building has been used for a non-business purpose for the period 5 April 1998 to the date of sale, 15% of the gain is treated for taper relief purposes as arising on a non-business asset. Thus the £2,153 of gain remaining chargeable cannot be tapered as it arises on a non-business asset held for less than three years post 5 April 1998.

5   REINVESTMENT IN DEPRECIATING ASSETS

5.1   Introduction

Rollover relief is modified where the new asset purchased is a 'depreciating asset'.

Definition   a depreciating asset is one which is either:

(a)   a wasting asset (ie, having a predictable life of not more than 50 years); or

(b)   will become a wasting asset within 10 years.

Thus any asset with a predictable life of not more than 60 years is a depreciating asset.

The purpose of the modification to rollover relief where the new asset is a depreciating asset is to ensure that any gain accrued on the old asset does not escape tax because the new one loses value over a short life. In practice, it mostly occurs when the new asset is either fixed plant and machinery or a short lease.

5.2   Treatment of gain on reinvestment in a depreciating asset

The gain on the old asset is normally rolled over against the cost of the new asset. This does not happen when the new asset is a depreciating one. In these circumstances it is simply deferred (held over) until the **earliest** of three events. These are:

(a)   the disposal of the depreciating asset;

(b)   the depreciating asset ceases to be used for trading purposes; or

(c)   10 years has elapsed since the depreciating asset was acquired.

At this time the gain on the old asset simply becomes taxable. It is not deducted from the cost of the depreciating asset, even where the event that triggers the charge is its sale.

When the gain on the old asset becomes taxable, taper relief is available by reference to the post - 5 April 1998 period of ownership of the old asset.

As with rollover relief proper, if only part of the proceeds are reinvested, or the asset was not wholly used for the trade, an element of the gain becomes taxable immediately.

5.3   Example

Cooper purchased a freehold factory in June 1985 for £250,000. In May 1992 he sold it for £420,000 and in June 1992 bought fixed plant and machinery. In December 1998 he sold the fixed plant and machinery for £550,000.

Calculate the chargeable gains or allowable losses arising in December 1998 if Cooper bought the fixed plant and machinery for:

(a)   £450,000;

(b)   £400,000.

5.4   Solution

(a)   Purchase for £450,000

	£
Disposal proceeds	550,000
Less: Cost	450,000
Unindexed gain	100,000
Less: Indexation allowance	
$\dfrac{161.2 - 139.3}{139.3}$ (= 0.157) × £450,000	70,650
Chargeable gain (subject potentially to 7.5% taper relief)	29,350

The held over gain on the sale of the factory in May 1992 also becomes chargeable, because the depreciating asset has been sold. This is £55,000 (see working below). No taper relief is available as period of ownership only prior to 6 April 1998.

Working - gain on sale of factory in May 1992

	£
Disposal proceeds	420,000
Less: Cost	250,000
Unindexed gain	170,000
Less: Indexation allowance	
$\dfrac{139.3-95.41}{95.41}$ (= 0.460) × £250,000	115,000
Chargeable gain held over	55,000

(b)   Purchase for £400,000

In this case not all the disposal proceeds of the factory (£420,000) have been reinvested in the depreciating asset. The amount not reinvested, £20,000 (420,000 – 400,000), becomes chargeable to tax in May 1992. The remainder of the gain on the factory, £35,000 (55,000 – 20,000) is held over until the disposal of the fixed plant and machinery in December 1998.

The gain on the disposal of the plant and machinery is calculated as follows.

	£
Disposal proceeds	550,000
Less: Cost	400,000
Unindexed gain	150,000
Less: Indexation allowance	
0.157 × £400,000	62,800
Chargeable gain	87,200

Note that the held over gain (£35,000) is not deducted from the cost of the plant and machinery. Taper relief at 7.5% is potentially available against the gain of £87,200.

5.5   Acquisition of a new non-depreciating asset

The held over gain normally becomes chargeable after 10 years, when the depreciating asset is sold or when it ceases to be used in the trade, whichever is the earliest. If, before this happens, a new non-depreciating asset is acquired rollover relief can be reinstated. The gain on the original asset is then rolled over into the new non-depreciating asset and the depreciating asset is, effectively, ignored. One can think of the impact of the depreciating asset as simply giving the taxpayer an extended period for reinvestment.

If the whole of the proceeds of the original asset are not reinvested in the new, non-depreciating asset, the excess is still treated as being held over. This is still an improvement on the 'basic' rollover relief position, since the existence of the depreciating asset prevents the excess proceeds from being taxable immediately.

5.6   Example

Smith purchased a factory in February 1988 for £295,000. In May 1990 he sold it for £380,000 and acquired a lease of commercial property (with 55 years to expiry) in June 1990 for £385,000. In November 1992 he purchased a new factory for £370,000 and he sold the lease for £430,000 in December 1992. In March 1999 he sold the second factory for £490,000.

Calculate the chargeable gain or allowable loss on:

(a)   the disposal of the first factory:

(b)   the disposal of the lease; and

(c)   the disposal of the second factory.

5.7   Solution

(a)   Gain on first factory - disposal in May 1990

		£
Disposal proceeds		380,000
Less: Cost		295,000
Unindexed gain		85,000
Less: Indexation allowance		
$\frac{126.2 - 103.7}{103.7}$ (= 0.217) × £295,000		64,015
Gain available for hold over relief		20,985

(b)   Disposal of the lease - December 1992

		£
Disposal proceeds		430,000
Less: Allowable expenditure (see note)		385,000
Unindexed gain		45,000
Less: Indexation allowance		
$\frac{139.2 - 126.7}{126.7}$ (= 0.099) × £385,000		38,115
		6,885

(c)   Disposal of second factory - March 1999

	£	£
Disposal proceeds		490,000
Less: Cost	370,000	
Less: Rolled over gain (W)	10,985	
		359,015
Unindexed gain		130,985
Less: Indexation allowance (to April 1998)		
$\frac{161.2 - 139.7}{139.7}$ (= 0.154) × £359,015		55,288
Chargeable gain (potentially qualifying for 7.5% taper relief)		75,697

Working - rolled over gain

The rolled over gain is the gain on the sale of the first factory minus the sale proceeds of the first factory not reinvested in the second factory.

	£
Gain on sale of first factory (part (a))	20,985
Less: Proceeds not reinvested (380,000 – 370,000)	10,000
Gain rolled over	10,985

Notes:

(1)   The lease, although a depreciating asset for rollover relief purposes, is not a wasting asset because it had more than 50 years to expiry when it was sold. Its cost is therefore not scaled down when computing the gain or loss on disposal.

(2)   Because Smith reinvested the proceeds of the first factory in a depreciating asset (the lease) the gain on the first factory is held over. Smith then purchased another non-depreciating asset (the second factory) before the depreciating asset was sold. He could therefore rollover the gain on the first factory into the second (except for the element of proceeds not reinvested (£10,000), which became chargeable when the lease was sold in December 1992).

6   RELIEF FOR REBASING

6.1   Introduction

Rebasing CGT to March 1982 was introduced for disposals made after 5 April 1988 with the intention of relieving gains accruing before 31 March 1982.

To relieve pre-March 1982 gains a special relief is needed where:

(a)   A replacement asset is sold after 5 April 1988; and

(b)   The replacement asset had been acquired after 31 March 1982; and

(c)   A gain is rolled over onto the replacement asset from the disposal of an asset which had been acquired before 31 March 1982.

In this situation, only 50% of the rolled over gain is deducted from the base cost of the replacement asset.

6.2   Example

George sells a factory in October 1998 for £280,000 having acquired it for £130,000 in June 1985. In May 1985 he had sold a warehouse for £120,000 having purchased it in October 1977 for £76,000. The March 1982 value of the warehouse was £98,000. George had claimed roll over relief.

6.3   Solution

Gain on warehouse (1985/86)

	£
Proceeds (May 1985)	120,000
Less: Cost	(76,000)
	44,000
Less: Indexation allowance (on March 1982 MV) $\left(£98,000 \times \left(\dfrac{95.21 - 79.44}{79.44}\right) 0.199\right)$	(19,502)
Gain rolled over	24,498

Gain on factory (1998/99)

	£	£
Proceeds (October 1998)		280,000
Less: Cost (June 1985)	130,000	
Half gain rolled over 24,498 × 50%	(12,249)	
		(117,751)
		162,249
Less: Indexation allowance (to April 1998) $117,751 \times \left(\dfrac{161.2 - 95.41}{95.41}\right) 0.690$		(81,248)
Gain (prior to taper relief)		81,001

Note: Prior to 6 April 1988 gains were based on cost (not 31 March 1982 MV) but for disposals after 5 April 1985 the indexation allowance was allowed on the 31 March 1982 MV.

The fairest way to exclude pre 31 March 1982 gains would have been to recalculate the rolled over gain as if rebasing had been available. This was deemed to be too complicated so a 'rough and ready' '50% - off' rule is used.

6.4   Depreciating assets

If the replacement asset in the above situation is a depreciating asset, when a gain crystallises (having accrued partly before 31 March 1982) only half of it is chargeable.

6.5   Example

Fred acquires fixed plant and machinery in February 1990 thereby deferring a gain of £50,000 on a factory sold in November 1987 (ie, within 3 years of the disposal). The factory had been acquired in 1975 and the plant and machinery ceased to be used in Fred's trade in January 1999.

6.6   Solution

On the event of ceasing to use the plant, the deferred gain from the factory becomes chargeable. Because the relevant conditions have been met, only half the gain (£25,000) becomes chargeable.

7   ROLLOVER RELIEF ON REINVESTMENT

7.1   Introduction

The second relief we study in this chapter is now covered in paragraph 7.

As we have just seen when a taxpayer disposes of a business asset and reinvests the proceeds in another business asset, the gain is deferred. A further form of rollover relief is available so that, broadly, an individual may now, subject to certain conditions being fulfilled, dispose of **any** asset (whether a business asset or not) and defer the gain provided he reinvests the proceeds in new shares a 'qualifying investment'.

With effect from 6 April 1998 the FA98 has taken the 'reinvestment relief' and a relief called the 'Enterprise Investment Scheme' (EIS) - which was excluded from the paper 7 syllabus - and created a new relief, (unfortunately named 'new EIS'), which combines features of both of the old reliefs. As old EIS was not examinable and we are only concerned here with the capital gains aspects of 'new EIS' the following sections only cover the reinvestment relief aspects in their post 5 April 1998 form. We continue to use the old label 'reinvestment relief' as it accurately describes its effect even though it is renamed in statute as EIS.

7.2   The relief available

Deferral relief is available where:

*   an individual makes a disposal of any asset; and
*   the individual subsribes for shares in a qualifying investment wholly in cash at any time in the qualifying period.

The qualifying period is defined as the period beginning 12 months before and ending three years after the original disposal.

There is no limit on the amount of reinvested gains which can be deferred by investing in eligible shares.

The relief is similar to deferred relief for the replacement of business assets where a depreciating asset is acquired, but there are some provisions peculiar to reinvestment relief.

7.3   Qualifying investment

Deferral relief is available when an individual acquires a qualifying investment. An individual is regarded as acquiring a qualifying investment if it satisfies the following conditions:

*   The investment must be in newly issued eligible shares (basically fully paid up ordinary shares with no preference rights) in an unquoted company;

*   The shares must be in a qualifying company (ie, a company which carries on a qualifying trade) or be the holding company of a qualifying subsidiary.

*   The qualifying company must not be the same company, or in the same group as the company, whose shares were the subject of the original disposal.

*   To be a qualifying company, the company must have less than £15 million of gross assets before the investment and not more than £16 million after it.

Note:

(1)   There is no requirement that the individual has any active involvement in the new company.

(2)   There is no requirement that the company be incorporated in the UK nor that it is resident in the UK but the qualifying trade must be carried on wholly or mainly in the UK.

(3)   A qualifying trade excludes most 'safe' property-backed activities such as farming, property development and operating hotels or residential care homes.

7.4   Details of the deferral

(a)   The amount of chargeable gain that can be deferred is the lower of:
- the chargeable gains; and
- the amount subscribed for the new qualifying investment.

Therefore full deferral is available by reinvesting only the amount of the gain.

(b)   The amount to be deferred can be restricted in the claim so that, for example, the CGT annual exemption is not wasted or use is made of available losses.

(c)   The relief is applied before retirement relief and before taper relief.

7.5   Example: deferral relief on reinvestment

Guy, age 25 bought 4,000 ordinary £1 shares in Workhorse Ltd for £80,000 in March 1982.

He sold his entire holding in December 1998 for £250,000, and subscribed £200,000 for shares in a qualifying company, Jackass Ltd, on 1 March 1999.

You may assume that Guy's disposal qualifies for reinvestment relief.

His entire holding of Jackass Ltd shares were sold on 1 August 2003 for £350,000.

Both companies were qualifying companies for the purposes of taper relief.

You are required to calculate

(a)   How much deferral relief Guy will claim
(b)   The chargeable gains arising on the sale of the Jackass Ltd shares.

Guy made no other capital disposals in 1998/99.

7.6   Solution

		£
(a)	Disposal proceeds	250,000
	Less: Cost	(80,000)
	Less: Indexation allowance	
	$80,000 \times \dfrac{161.2 - 79.44}{79.44}$ (1.029)	(82,320)
	Gain	87,680

The amount that can be deferred is the lower of

(a)   the chargeable gain (£87,680) and

(b)   the subscription cost of the qualifying investment (£200,000)

The gain deferred can be restricted so that the CGT annual exemption is not wasted. Guy would therefore defer £80,329, leaving £7,351 to be taxed in 1998/99. After 7.5% taper relief, the chargeable gain would be £6,800, which is covered by the annual exemption.

		£	
(b)	Deferred gain on Workhorse shares becomes chargeable		80,880
	Deduct taper relief (held 17 March 1998 - one bonus year) @ 7.5%		6,066
			74,814
	Disposal of Jackass shares		
	Proceeds	350,000	
	Less: Cost	200,000	
		150,000	
	Less: Taper relief (4 years) @ 30%	45,000	105,000
	Chargeable gains (before annual exemption)		179,814

7.7   Clawback of relief

The relief is clawed back if the shares ever cease to be eligible shares eg, the company ceases to be a qualifying company

A clawback also applies if the individual becomes non resident in the UK during the five years after the issue of the qualifying shares.

Conclusion   This relief allows a person to realise capital from assets, and use the proceeds to subscribe for shares in a qualifying company, thereby postponing the capital gains tax liability he would otherwise suffer.

8   CHAPTER SUMMARY

Relief for replacement of business assets

(a)   Rollover relief is designed to help taxpayers renew and update assets without incurring an immediate chargeable gain. It achieves this, provided the various conditions for the relief are met, by assuming that the disposal of an old asset occurred at no gain/no loss and deducting the indexed gain actually made from the allowable expenditure incurred on the replacement asset. Rollover relief must be claimed within five years of 31 January following the end of the tax year in which the original disposal occurred (six years following the end of the accounting period for companies) .

(b)   Only assets that fall within certain classes qualify for rollover relief. The most common ones are land and buildings, fixed plant and machinery and goodwill. Both the original and the replacement asset must be qualifying assets, but not necessarily of the same class.

(c)   Reinvestment in a qualifying asset must normally take place within a period that begins one year before and ends three years after the disposal of the original asset.

(d)   Rollover relief is restricted where the taxpayer fails to reinvest all of the proceeds of sale of the original asset in a replacement one. In these circumstances the proceeds not reinvested are taxable immediately (ie, at the time of the original asset's disposal) unless they are larger than the gain itself (in which case the whole of the gain is taxable immediately and there is no rollover relief). If the proceeds not reinvested are smaller than the gain, the balance of the gain may be rolled over.

(e)   Rollover relief is similarly restricted when either:

   • only part of the asset was used for the trade (such as a factory partly let out); or

   • the asset was used for the purposes of the trade for only part of the taxpayer's period of ownership.

The restriction is applied in either of these circumstances by treating the asset as two separate parts, one which qualifies for rollover relief and one which does not. The gains on each are calculated separately. The 'non-qualifying' asset's gain is taxable immediately but the gain on the qualifying part may be rolled over (subject to the other conditions for relief being met).

(f)   If the reinvestment is in a depreciating asset (one with a predictable life of not more than 60 years) rollover relief does not apply. The gain on the original asset is 'held over' (ie, put to one side) until the earliest of the dates when:

   • the depreciating asset is sold; or
   • the depreciating asset is no longer used in the trade; or
   • 10 years have elapsed since the depreciating asset was acquired.

When the first of these three events occurs, the gain held over on the original asset becomes taxable.

(g)   If, before a held over gain crystallises, the taxpayer makes a further investment in a non-depreciating asset, the gain on the original asset that was held over can be rolled over into the new, non-depreciating asset.

(h)   The new asset, depreciating or non-depreciating, attracts taper relief appropriate to its own period of ownership as you might expect. Hence, a gain rolled over against a non-depreciating asset effectively receives taper relief by reference to the new assets period of ownership, whilst a gain deferred using a depreciating replacement asset attracts taper relief (when it eventually becomes chargeable), by reference to the ownership period of the original asset.

Rollover relief on reinvestment

(a)   A form of rollover relief (better described as deferral relief) is also available where individuals dispose of any assets and reinvest by subscribing for shares in a qualifying company.

(b)   The reinvestment must be within the period beginning 12 months before and ending 3 years after the disposal.

(c)   Full deferral relief is available by reinvesting the amount of the gain.

(d)   As this is a deferral relief, taper relief will be available when the deferred gain eventually becomes chargeable, by reference to the period of ownership of the original asset.

9   **SELF TEST QUESTIONS**

9.1   How does roll over relief work? (1.1)

9.2   On what figure is the indexation allowance for a replacement asset based? (1.1)

9.3   What is the time limit for making a rollover relief claim? (1.1)

9.4   What are the classes of assets qualifying for rollover relief? (2.1)

9.5   What is the period during which acquisition of the replacement asset must occur? (2.2)

9.6   How is rollover relief restricted when only part of the disposal proceeds of the original asset are reinvested? (3.2)

9.7   How is rollover relief restricted when only part of the original asset was used for the purposes of the trade? (4.1)

9.8   What is a depreciating asset ? (5.1)

9.9   How is relief given when reinvestment is in a depreciating asset ? (5.2)

9.10   What are the three circumstances that bring a held over gain into charge? (5.2)

9.11   How does taper relief on the original gain work for reinvestment in a depreciating asset? (5.2)

9.12   When may an individual claim reinvestment relief? (7.2)

9.13   What is a qualifying investment? (7.4)

9.14   What is the maximum amount that may be deferred under reinvestment relief? (7.5)

10   **EXAMINATION TYPE QUESTION**

10.1   **Spanner**

Spanner is the sole proprietor of a small country garage. In June 1998 he sold a hydraulic vehicle lift for £35,000, net of expenses. The lift had cost £18,000 in June 1985. In May 1998 some adjacent freehold land was bought, to extend forecourt parking, for £60,000. Spanner claims roll-over relief.

You are required:

(a)   to calculate the chargeable gain, if any, on the disposal of the hydraulic lift;

(b)   to calculate the cost of the new land for future capital gains tax purposes; and

(c)   to explain the position if the proceeds had instead been used for purchase of a new hydraulic lift.

11   ANSWER TO EXAMINATION TYPE QUESTION

11.1   Spanner

      £

(a)   **1998/99**

Disposal of hydraulic lift:

	£
Net sale proceeds	35,000
Less: Cost	18,000
	17,000

Less: IA (April 1998 – June 1985):

$$\frac{161.2 - 95.41}{95.41} \ (=0.690) \times £18,000 \qquad (12,420)$$

	£
	4,580
Less: Roll-over relief (all proceeds reinvested)	4,580
Chargeable gain	Nil

(b)   The cost of the new land for future capital gains purposes is

	£
Purchase price	60,000
Less: gain rolled-over	4,580
Allowable cost	55,420

(c)   The position is that a claim should still be made, since the lift is fixed plant and machinery.

The chargeable gain on disposal is £4,580.

Since the replacement asset is a depreciating asset, the gain is **not** rolled-over and deducted from the cost of the replacement but is, instead, **deferred** until the earliest of

(a)   May 2008 (10th anniversary of acquisition of lift)

(b)   the date of disposal of the lift

(c)   the date the lift ceases to be used in any of Spanner's businesses.

At that point, taper relief of 7.5% on the gain crystallising of £4,580 will be available.

21 OTHER RELIEFS

INTRODUCTION & LEARNING OBJECTIVES

This chapter deals with the relief for gifts of business assets, and the relief available on the transfer of a business to a limited company. Although these capital gains tax reliefs are not examined as frequently as reliefs covered earlier in the text, they are still of relevance to the exam.

When you have studied this chapter you should have learned the following:

- The purpose and nature of the relief for gifts of business assets.
- Who may claim relief for gifts of business assets and the time limit for claims.
- What assets are qualifying assets for the relief.
- How the relief is computed, for both gifts and sales at undervalue.
- The restriction on relief that applies when assets are not wholly used for trading purposes.
- How retirement relief interacts with relief for gifts of business assets.
- The purpose of, and conditions that apply to, the relief on transfer of a business to a company.
- How the relief for transfer of a business to a company operates.
- How the relief interacts with retirement relief.
- The purpose and scope of the relief for irrecoverable loans to traders.
- The conditions for the relief.
- How it operates and how relief is withdrawn where the loan is later repaid.

Gift relief is available for individuals when a business asset is gifted or sold at undervalue. The gain is deferred, and rolled over into the base cost of the asset gifted.

Incorporation relief is available when an individual (or a partnership) incorporates a business. When a business is incorporated, the individual business assets are treated as having been sold. Any gain on these assets can be deferred and rolled over into the base cost of the shares that the owner of the business received on incorporation.

---

1 RELIEF FOR GIFTS OF BUSINESS ASSETS

1.1 Introduction

There is a general problem with gifts for capital gains tax. A gift is an occasion of charge (except when it occurs on death) and so tax may be payable. The donor, however, has received no funds with which to meet his tax bill. For many gifts the problem is unresolved but for gifts of certain business assets there is a deferral of tax until a future disposal.

1.2   Nature of the relief

The relief works by treating the disposal by way of gift as though it occurred at a value giving no gain and no loss to the donor. At the same time, the donee is treated as having paid the donor the market value of the asset but has the actual gain accruing to the donor deducted from his allowable expenditure.

1.3   Activity

Jones bought an asset for £25,000 in September 1988. In June 1998 he gifted it to Smith, when its market value was £40,000. The asset qualified for relief for gifts of business assets.

Show Jones's capital gains tax position on the gift to Smith and calculate Smith's allowable expenditure.

1.4   Activity solution

Jones has made a disposal in June 1998 as follows:

	£
Market value of asset	40,000
Less: Cost	25,000
Unindexed gain	15,000
Less: Indexation allowance (to April 1998)	
$\dfrac{161.2 - 108.4}{108.4}$ (= 0.487) × £25,000	12,175
Indexed gain	2,825
Less: Hold over relief for business assets	2,825
Chargeable gain	Nil

Smith has allowable expenditure to set against a future disposal, calculated as follows.

	£
Market value of asset acquired	40,000
Less: Rolled over gain	2,825
	37,175

Note that taper relief cannot apply to the gain realised in June 1998 because none of it remained chargeable. Smith will be entitled to taper relief when he eventually sells the asset but only by reference to his own period of ownership (ie, from June 1998).

1.5   Who may claim the relief

The relief is available to individuals, not companies. Both the donor and donee must claim and this must be done within five years of 31 January following the end of the year in which the gift was made. Although, for the sake of simplicity, the relief is described as a relief for gifts, it also applies to sales made below market value (ie, where there is an element of gift).

1.6   Qualifying assets

An individual may only claim the relief where the gift is of a qualifying asset. The following are the principal categories of qualifying asset.

(a)   Assets used in the trade of:

   •   the donor (ie, where he is a sole trader); or

   •   the donor's personal company; or

   •   a company in a trading group, of which the holding company is the donor's personal company.

The second and third of these cases extend the relief to assets owned by the individual but not used by him **directly** for trading purposes.

(b)   Shares and securities of trading companies (or the holding companies of trading groups) provided that one of the following conditions apply.

   •   The shares or securities gifted are those of the individual's personal company.

   •   The shares or securities are not quoted on either a recognised stock exchange or the unlisted securities market.

An individual's personal company is defined in the same way as for retirement relief.

1.7   Computation of the relief

The basic form of the relief works in the way shown earlier in the chapter. If, however, the disposal is by way of a sale at undervalue, rather than a straight gift, the computation is adjusted to reflect this. In these circumstances any proceeds received over and above original cost are chargeable to tax immediately. The rolled over gain is reduced by this amount (and thus so is the deduction from allowable expenditure for the donee).

1.8   Example

Webster purchased shares in an unquoted trading company in November 1989 for £50,000. In January 1999 he sold them to his grandson for £70,000 when their value was £165,000. Webster and his grandson claimed relief for a gift of business assets.

Calculate:

(a)   the chargeable gain, if any, incurred by Webster assuming taper relief is available as for busines assets; and

(b)   the allowable expenditure incurred by Webster's grandson.

1.9   Solution

(a)   Webster - gain on shares sold in January 1999

		£	£
Market value of shares in January 1999			165,000
Less: Cost			50,000
Unindexed gain			115,000
Less: Indexation allowance (to April 1998)			
$\dfrac{161.2 - 118.5}{118.5} \times £50,000$			18,017
Indexed gain			96,983
Less: Gain rolled over			
Indexed gain		96,983	
Less: Proceeds received - cost			
(70,000 − 50,000)		20,000	
Gain rolled over			76,983
Chargeable gain			20,000
Less: Taper relief @ 7½%			1,500
Final chargeable gain			18,500

(b)   Webster's grandson - allowable cost

	£
Market value of shares, January 1999	165,000
Less: Gain rolled over	76,983
Allowable expenditure	88,017

1.10   Assets not wholly used for trading purposes

Where only part of an asset (such as a building) is used for trading purposes the relief is restricted. There is a similar restriction where an asset (such as plant and machinery) has been used for trading purposes for only part of the donor's period of ownership.

The gain eligible for relief is scaled down arithmetically. So where an asset owned for ten years has been used in the trade for only six years, 60% of the chargeable gain is eligible for relief. The other 40% is chargeable to tax immediately.

As with retirement relief, the way of reducing the eligible gain described above applies only to individual trading assets. When the subject of the gift is shares in a company, the position is different. Unless the donor has a significant stake in the company, there is no restriction. But if, in a 12-month period before the disposal takes place the company has qualified as the donor's personal company then the gain on the shares eligible for relief is scaled down by the following fraction.

$$\frac{\text{Market value of company's chargeable business assets}}{\text{Market value of company's chargeable assets}}$$

1.11   Interaction of retirement relief and gift relief

The interaction works to the taxpayer's advantage. First the indexed gain on the disposal is calculated. From that retirement relief is deducted and any balance that qualifies for gift relief is then rolled over.

1.12 Example

Willis gave his business to his son in December 1998 when he was 58 years old. Chargeable gains of £250,000 and £150,000 arose on the disposal in respect of premises and goodwill respectively. Willis had owned the business since 1980.

Calculate:

(a)   the gain or loss accruing to Willis on the disposal, if any, and

(b)   the allowable expenditure available to Willis's son.

Assume that any available claims are made.

1.13 Solution

(a)   Disposal by Willis - December 1998

		£	£
Gain on premises			250,000
Gain on goodwill			150,000
			400,000
Less:	Retirement relief		
	Limit for full relief	250,000	
	50% on gains over £250,000		
	(400,000 – 250,000)	75,000	
			325,000
Gain eligible for gift relief			75,000
Less:	Rollover relief		75,000
Chargeable gain			Nil

(b)   Allowable expenditure - Willis's son

	£
Total expenditure	400,000
Less: Rollover relief	75,000
Allowable expenditure	325,000

1.14 Indexation allowance and taper relief

Where the donee receives assets subject to gift relief his base cost is reduced. When he eventually sells the assets himself the indexation allowance is based on their deemed acquisition cost, as reduced by the relief. The donee's indexation entitlement will run from the date of the gift. Of course, in the above example Willis's son will have no indexation entitlement as the gift was made after April 1998. He will be entitled to taper relief by reference to his period of ownership (ie, since December 1998) and whether it qualified as a business asset in his hands.

1.15 The 50% rebasing relief

For disposals prior to 14 March 1989 gift relief was available on a gift of any asset - not just business assets.

If an asset was gifted before 6 April 1988 having been acquired before 31 March 1982 the gain had to be based on cost - the 31 March 1982 MV (rebasing) was not available.

If the gifted asset is subsequently sold after 5 April 1988, only one half of the rolled over gain is deducted from the base cost.

2   TRANSFER OF A BUSINESS TO A COMPANY

2.1   Introduction

If an individual wishes to incorporate his business a capital gains tax liability can arise because the transfer is deemed to take place at market value irrespective of the consideration actually paid.

As a consequence, to avoid creating disincentives to incorporation, there is a rollover relief (a deferral of the gain) when a business is transferred to a company. The relief is automatic so no claim for it is required.

2.2   Conditions for the relief

There are three types of condition. These concern the transferor, the assets transferred, and the consideration given by the company for the transfer.

Any transferor other than a company is eligible to benefit from the relief. Principally the relief is for sole traders.

The assets transferred have to meet two conditions. Firstly, all the assets of the business (other than cash) must be transferred. Secondly, the transfer must be of a business as a going concern.

The form of the consideration given by the acquiring company is also important. To qualify for the relief it must be wholly or partly shares issued to the transferor (not someone else). Whereas the conditions relating to the transferor and the assets transferred are absolute (ie, if not met in full there is no relief) the condition concerning the consideration received may be relaxed. To the extent that consideration for the transfer is not in the form of shares, the potential relief is scaled down.

2.3   Operation of the relief

The relief is a deferral of tax and operates by rolling over the gain accruing to the transferor and deducting it from the allowable cost of the shares he acquires in exchange.

Initially, one calculates the gains accruing on the assets to be transferred (as reduced by losses where appropriate). If the exchange is wholly for shares the whole gain may be held over, provided that the value of the shares received in exchange is high enough. Where a company takes over significant liabilities as well as assets, the value of the shares will be reduced and this may prevent the whole of the gain being held over.

Where some of the consideration given by the company for the assets is not shares (for example debentures or cash) the gain eligible for hold over relief is calculated by the formula:

$$\text{Gain} \times \frac{\text{Value of shares issued}}{\text{Total consideration}}$$

It may be possible for the non eligible part of the gain to be rolled over using reinvestment relief if the appropriate conditions are satisfied. This would require shares to be subscribed for in cash and might be difficult to achieve in practice.

2.4   Example

Smithers started a retail business in 1984. On 1 January 1990 he transferred his business to a company, Smithers Ltd. The assets transferred are set out below. In exchange he received 4,000 £1 ordinary shares (fully paid), valued at £80,000 and £20,000 cash. On 1 February 1999 Smithers sold his entire holding in Smithers Ltd for £150,000.

Calculate:

(a)   Smithers' gains realised in January 1990 after holdover relief; and

(b)   the chargeable gain arising on the disposal of the shares in Smithers Ltd in February 1999.

Assets transferred	Market value at 1.1.90 £	Chargeable gain £
Freehold premises	35,000	25,000
Furniture and fittings	8,000	-
Plant and machinery	14,000	-
Stock	25,000	-
Goodwill	18,000	18,000

2.5   Solution

(a)   Gain - January 1990

	£
Total chargeable gain (25,000 + 18,000)	43,000
Less: Gain rolled over	
$\dfrac{80,000}{80,000+20,000} \times 43,000$	34,400
Chargeable gain on Smithers (1989/90)	8,600

(b)   Disposal of shares - February 1999

	£	£
Disposal proceeds		150,000
Less: Cost	80,000	
Less: Rolled over gain	34,400	
		45,600
Unindexed gain		104,400
Less: Indexation allowance (to April 1998)		
$\dfrac{161.2-119.5}{119.5} \times £45,600$		15,912
Chargeable gain (before taper relief)		88,488

As is the case with other rollover reliefs, the indexation allowance on a subsequent disposal is based on the cost as reduced by the deferred gain.

2.6   Interaction with retirement relief

The interaction of this relief with retirement relief operates to the taxpayer's advantage. Retirement relief is deducted first, making any restrictions necessary. The gain that is left is then available for rollover relief. If rollover relief is also restricted (because part of the consideration given by the transferee company is not in the form of shares) the restricting fraction is applied to the gain left in charge after retirement relief (not the full gains accrued on the transferred assets).

2.7 Example

Embleton started a manufacturing business in November 1992. On 30 November 1998, when he was aged 62, he transferred all the assets of his business to Embleton Ltd, making (indexed) gains on the disposal of £350,000. Embleton Ltd issued shares valued at £500,000 and paid £100,000 cash in consideration for the transfer. All the assets transferred qualified for retirement relief.

Calculate the chargeable gain on Embleton arising from the disposal on 30 November 1998.

2.8 Solution

			£	£
Total chargeable gains				350,000
Less:	Retirement relief			
	(i)	6/10 × £250,000	150,000	
	(ii)	(£350,000 − £150,000) × 50%	100,000	
				250,000
				100,000
Less:	Rollover relief			
	$\dfrac{500,000}{500,000+100,000} \times £100,000$			83,333
Chargeable gain (before taper relief)				16,667

Note: retirement relief limits are restricted as Embleton owned the business for only six years. The upper retirement relief limit of £600,000 (£1,000,000 × 6/10) is higher than the gains actually realised of £350,000.

3 RELIEF FOR IRRECOVERABLE LOANS TO TRADERS

3.1 Introduction

Debts, other than debts on a security and foreign currency bank accounts, are exempt from capital gains tax. Nevertheless, there are specific provisions that allow both lenders to traders and guarantors of traders' debts to claim CGT loss relief if their debt becomes irrecoverable (or the guarantee has to be fulfilled).

3.2 Conditions for the relief

These are the following.

(a) The loan that has proved irrecoverable must have been used for the purposes of the borrower's trade (or for setting up that trade).

(b) The borrower must be UK resident.

(c) For the relief to lenders (but not for guarantors) the debt must not be a debt on a security. (Otherwise it would be a chargeable asset anyway and these special rules would be unnecessary.)

If these conditions are fulfilled the loan is a 'qualifying loan'.

In addition to satisfying the Inspector that the loan is a qualifying loan, the creditor or guarantor must be able to meet certain conditions. In the case of a creditor these are:

(a)   that all or part of the loan is irrecoverable;

(b)   that the creditor has not assigned his right to receive repayment; and

(c)   that the creditor and borrower were (at no time since the loan was made) neither spouses living together nor companies in the same group.

Essentially the same conditions apply to guarantors.

3.3   Operation of the relief and its withdrawal

Provided the lender or guarantor can satisfy the Inspector that the conditions set out above are met (there is a right of appeal if agreement cannot be reached) the lender or guarantor is treated as incurring an allowable loss for capital gains tax purposes. It is treated as a loss of the tax year specified in the claim, provided that the claim is made within two years of the end of the tax year (and that the loan was irrecoverable at that time). In the case of a guarantee, the claim must be made within five years of 31 January following the year of assessment in which the payment was made.

The relief is withdrawn if all or part of the loan thought to be irrecoverable is repaid, to the extent of the repayment. It is withdrawn by deeming the lender or guarantor to have made a capital gain equal to the repayment, at the time the repayment was made.

4   CHAPTER SUMMARY

(a)   Because a gift or sale at undervalue is not made at arm's length, market value is substituted for proceeds in the CGT computation. The disposer may thus incur a CGT liability without receiving funds to pay it. To overcome this problem, in some cases, there is a relief for gifts of business assets. It is available to individuals, not companies, and must be claimed jointly by the donor and donee within five years of 31 January following the end of the tax year in which the gift was made.

(b)   Relief for gifts of business assets works by treating the donor as though he made neither gain nor loss on the gift. The actual indexed gain is deducted from the allowable expenditure of the donee. The donee is treated as having paid market value for the asset. When the donee eventually sells the asset the gain that had accrued to the donor automatically becomes taxable as a result of the reduction in the donee's allowable expenditure.

(c)   Only certain assets qualify for the relief. Broadly speaking, these are assets used for trading purposes by a business run by the donor. Shares and securities of a company also qualify, provided they are shares or securities of an unquoted trading company or of the donor's personal company.

(d)   Relief is restricted (and so part of the gain is immediately chargeable on the donor) where the qualifying assets have not been wholly used for business purposes or have not been so used throughout the donor's period of ownership.

(e)   Where relief for gifts of business assets and retirement both apply to a disposal, retirement relief is deducted first and only the balance is eligible for rollover relief.

(f)   Relief is also given when an unincorporated business is taken over by a company. In these circumstances too a CGT bill could be payable by the transferor, without his having funds to meet it, were it not for a specific relief.

(g) Individuals, but not companies, may obtain relief for transfer of a business to a company. No formal claim is necessary and thus the relief is automatic where the conditions are met.

(h) All assets other than cash must be transferred to the company. Full relief is obtained where the consideration given by the company to the owner of the unincorporated business is in the form of shares. Relief is scaled down proportionately where consideration is provided in other forms (for example cash or debentures). The gains not eligible for relief are taxable immediately on the transferor.

(i) The relief is provided by deducting the accrued gains on the assets transferred from the allowable expenditure incurred on the shares (which is normally their market value at the time of issue).

(j) Where retirement relief also applies to the disposal it is deducted first.

(k) Relief is given to lenders or guarantors where a loan has become irrecoverable or a guarantee payment has had to be made. The relief applies to qualifying loans. Broadly, a qualifying loan is one which was made to a UK resident trader and used for trading purposes. The irrecoverable loan or guarantee payment is treated as a capital loss. If any part is subsequently repaid it is treated as a capital gain.

5 SELF TEST QUESTIONS

5.1 How does relief for gifts of business assets work? (1.2)

5.2 Who may claim relief for gifts of business assets? (1.5)

5.3 What is the time limit for making a claim for relief of business assets? (1.5)

5.4 What assets qualify for relief of business assets? (1.6)

5.5 How is relief restricted when a disposal is a sale at undervalue rather than an outright gift? (1.7)

5.6 Where a disposal qualifies for both gifts of business assets and retirement relief, which takes priority? (1.11)

5.7 What are the conditions that must be met for relief on transfer of a business to a company? (3.2)

5.8 How is relief restricted when some of the consideration received from the acquiring company is not in the form of shares? (3.3)

5.9 What is a qualifying loan for the purposes of the relief given for irrecoverable loans to traders? (4.2)

5.10 What form does the relief take? (4.3)

6 EXAMINATION TYPE QUESTION

6.1 Gold

On 5 October 1998 Gold, who was then aged 65, gave his 75% shareholding in Montreux Ltd, a TV film company, to his sister Rose. The market value of the shares was £249,000. The shares had cost £30,000 (including expenses) in 1977. Gold has elected for the 31 March 1982 basis to be applied to all his assets held on that date.

The value of the chargeable assets of Montreux Ltd on 5 October 1998 was £700,000 of which £10,000 were trade investments. The market value of Gold's shares on 31 March 1982 has been agreed at £76,000.

Gold has been a full-time working director of the company since 1977.

A joint claim will be made for relief for gifts of business assets if appropriate.

On 8 January 1999 Rose sold her shares to a merchant bank for £300,125 (net).

Calculate

(a)   the chargeable gain, if any, assessable on Gold for 1998/99 (ignore taper relief),

(b)   the chargeable gain assessable on Rose for 1998/99, and

(c)   the chargeable gain assessable on Gold for 1998/99 if the market value of the shares had, instead, been £475,000 (again ignoring taper relief).

(d)   the chargeable gain assessable on Rose for 1998/99, if (c) applied, and Rose's sale proceeds had instead been £500,125.

7   ANSWER TO EXAMINATION TYPE QUESTION

7.1   Gold

1998/99

(a)   **Gold (1982 Pool)**

	£	£
Deemed proceeds = MV 5.10.98		249,000
Less: MV 31.3.82 (by election)		(76,000)
		173,000
Less: IA (April 1998 – March 1982):		
$£76,000 \dfrac{161.2 - 79.44}{79.44} (1.029)$		(78,204)
		94,796

Less: Retirement relief:

(i)	Attributable to business assets:			
	$94,796 \times \dfrac{690}{700} =$		93,442	(93,442)
(ii)	Full band:	250,000		
	(No excess over £250,000)			
Chargeable gain (before taper relief)				1,354

Note: the whole of the 'appropriate proportion' of the gain (£93,442) is relieved by retirement relief (limited to £93,442) therefore no part of the remaining gain (£1,354) can be held-over.

(b) **Rose** (separate holding acquired post 5 April 1998)

		£	£
Net sale proceeds			300,125
Less:	MV on acquisition	249,000	
	Less: Held-over gain	Nil	
			(249,000)
Chargeable gain			51,125

(c) **1998/99**

			£	£
Gold (1982 Pool)				
Deemed proceeds = MV 5.10.98				475,000
Less: MV 31.3.82				(76,000)
				399,000
Less: IA (April 1998 - March 1982) as above				(78,204)
				320,796
Less: Retirement relief				
	(i)	320,796 × 690/700	316,213	
	(ii)	Full band	250,000	
		Excess ½ (316,213 – 250,000)	33,106	
			283,106	283,106
				37,690

Since the gain attributable to chargeable business
assets (£316,213) is not wholly relieved by retirement
relief, a claim for holdover relief is admissible ie,

Gain heldover is £316,213 − 283,106		33,107
Chargeable gain (before taper relief)		4,583

(d) **Rose** (separate holding acquired post 5 April 1998)

		£	£
Net sale proceeds			500,125
Less:	MV on acquisition	475,000	
	Less: Held-over gain	33,107	
			(441,893)
Chargeable gain			58,232

22 OUTLINE OF CORPORATION TAX

INTRODUCTION & LEARNING OBJECTIVES

Companies earn different types of income and incur different sorts of expenditure. This chapter explains how these items are dealt with in arriving at the profits chargeable to corporation tax and how the corporation tax liability is calculated.

A thorough understanding of this chapter is essential as

- these matters are frequently examined as a long computation question; and

- this chapter is a building block towards an understanding of more advanced aspects of corporation tax.

When you have studied this chapter you should have learned the following:

- The scope of corporation tax;
- How to determine the residence of a company;
- The basis of assessment to corporation tax;
- How profits chargeable to corporation tax are computed;
- How to deal with a period of account longer than 12 months;
- The rates of corporation tax;
- When the small companies' rate of tax applies; and
- When corporation tax is due.

1 THE CHARGE TO TAX

Corporation tax is charged on the **profits** of **companies resident** in the UK by reference to the **total profits** arising in each **accounting period**.

Definition A company is any body corporate, limited or unlimited, or unincorporated association. This does not include a partnership, a local authority or a local authority association.

2 COMPANY RESIDENCE

2.1 Determination of company residence

There are two criteria important in determining the residence of a company:

- the country in which the company is incorporated; and
- the country in which the company is centrally managed and controlled.

A company incorporated in the UK is resident here for corporation tax purposes irrespective of where it is centrally managed and controlled.

If a company is incorporated elsewhere, it is regarded as resident in the UK if it is centrally managed and controlled here.

In deciding where a company is centrally managed and controlled the courts have held that the country where the directors regularly meet and the place where decisions are made is of great importance.

2.2   Examples

(a)   X Ltd is incorporated in the UK. The directors hold monthly board meetings in France where major policy decisions are made.

X Ltd is regarded as resident in the UK. If a company is incorporated in the UK it is immaterial where meetings are held and decisions are made.

(b)   Y Ltd is incorporated in Holland. The directors hold frequent board meetings in London, where the managing director is based.

Y Ltd would probably be regarded as resident in the UK for corporation tax purposes. Although not incorporated in the UK, it would appear that the company is centrally managed and controlled here.

(c)   Z Ltd is incorporated in Germany. The directors hold weekly meetings in Germany, and quarterly meetings in London where the non-executive directors are based.

Z Ltd would probably be regarded as resident in Germany. The company is not incorporated in the UK, and it appears to be centrally managed and controlled in Germany.

3   THE BASIS OF ASSESSMENT

3.1   Introduction

Having discussed the meaning of the word 'company' and 'residence' it is now necessary to look at how the profits are assessed. Earlier in the text it was stated that corporation tax is charged by reference to the total profits arising in each accounting period. It is essential to differentiate between an 'accounting period' and a 'period of account'.

Definition   A period of account is any period for which a company prepares accounts. It is usually 12 months in length, but may be shorter or longer than this.

Definition   An accounting period is the period for which a charge to corporation tax is made. It may never be longer than 12 months.

3.2   Accounting period

(a)   An accounting period begins when:

- a company starts to trade, or when the profits of a company first become liable to corporation tax; or

- the previous accounting period ends, providing that the company is still liable to corporation tax.

(b)   An accounting period ends on the earliest of:

- 12 months after the beginning of the accounting period;
- the end of the company's period of account;
- the company beginning or ceasing to trade
- the company beginning or ceasing to be resident in the UK;
- the company ceasing to be liable to corporation tax; or
- the commencement of the winding up of the company.

(c)   As an accounting period must not exceed 12 months, if a company has a period of account longer than 12 months, this must be split into two accounting periods, the first of 12 months and the second of the remainder of the accounting period. Note that the period of account **must** be split in this way.

3.3   Activity

A Ltd prepares accounts for the 15 month period from 1 October 1997 to 31 December 1998. What are the accounting periods of A Ltd?

3.4   Activity solution

(a)   12 months from 1 October 1997 to 30 September 1998

(b)   3 months from 1 October 1998 to 31 December 1998.

3.5   Companies and Individuals

Notice the difference between the way a company is assessed to corporation tax and the way an individual is assessed to tax:

COMPANY	INDIVIDUAL
• Companies are assessed on profits arising in an accounting periods.	• Individuals are assessed on income and gains arising in tax years.
• Chargeable gains are assessed to corporation tax.	• Chargeable gains are assessed to capital gains tax.
• There are no personal allowances.	• Personal allowances are available for income.
• Indexation allowance is available in full (but not taper relief)	• Indexation allowance applies up to April 1998 with taper relief thereafter.
• There is no annual exemption for capital gains.	• An annual exemption is available for capital gains.

Conclusion   The profits of companies resident in the UK are charged to corporation tax by reference to the total profits arising in each accounting period. The accounting period must not exceed 12 months.

4   RATES OF CORPORATION TAX

The rate of corporation tax is fixed by reference to financial years.

Definition   A financial year runs from 1 April to the following 31 March and is identified by the calendar year in which it begins.

The year commencing 1 April 1998 is the financial year 1998 (FY 1998). Financial years should not be confused with fiscal years, the tax years for income tax which run from 6 April to the following 5 April.

The full rate of corporation tax for the current financial year (FY 1998) is 31%. It was also 31% for FY97. For FY 1996 and earlier years it was 33%. A reduced rate of 21% known as the small companies rate applies to companies with lower profits. (The small companies rate was 21% for FY97, 24% for FY 1996 and 25% for earlier years.)

The full rate and the small company rate for FY99 will be 30% and 20% respectively.

5   PROFITS CHARGEABLE TO CORPORATION TAX

5.1   Introduction

A corporation tax computation is necessary to calculate the amount of profits that are charged to corporation tax for an accounting period. Included in the computation are the world-wide income of a company plus any chargeable gains. Note that dividends received from a company resident in the UK are not included.

5.2   Layout of a corporation tax computation

X Ltd corporation tax computation for the 12 months ended 31 March 1999

	£
Schedule D Case I (eg, profits of trade)	X
Schedule D Case III (eg, bank/building society/debenture interest)	X
Schedule D Case V (eg, foreign dividends)	X
Schedule D Case VI (eg, sundry commissions)	X
Schedule A (eg, rent from property)	X
Taxed income (gross) (eg, patent royalties received)	X
Chargeable gains (eg, sale of shares at a profit)	X
	X
Less: Charges on income (gross) (eg, patent royalties paid)	(X)
Profits chargeable to corporation tax (PCTCT)	X

(a)   The use of this layout is essential in any corporation tax exam question. The company and the chargeable accounting period should be identified. Each separate source of income should be identified by Schedule or otherwise.

(b)   Any amounts received or paid net such as taxed income and charges on income, should be grossed-up for inclusion in the computation. This is an area where special care is needed. Although in company accounts these figures are usually included at the gross amount, you may find that the examiner gives the amount actually received or paid. In this case, the amount must be grossed up. Taxed interest must be grossed up by 100/80 (100/75 before 6 April 1996) and charges on income must be grossed up by 100/77 (100/76 for 1996/97 and 100/75 before 6 April 1996).

Remember the **lower** rate of deduction applies to savings income (eg, most interest other than bank or building society interest) whereas charges (eg, patent royalties and gift aid) are paid net of **basic** rate tax.

If a company's accounts show the following amounts received and paid in an accounting period:

£

Interest received on debenture stock (amount received)   1,600
Patent royalties paid (amount paid)   2,695

They must be grossed-up before being included in the PCTCT computation as follows:

£

Interest on debenture stock (1,600 × $^{100}/_{80}$)   2,000
Patent royalties paid (2,695 × $^{100}/_{77}$)   3,500

(c)   The different types of profits are dealt with separately according to the different Schedules or other category. Income assessed under a particular Schedule must be included according to the rules of that Schedule. Other income and charges must be included according to the rules given later in this chapter. They are then totalled to give the total profits chargeable to corporation tax.

(d)   The Schedules used in the corporation tax computation are broadly the same as those you are familiar with from income tax although there are some computational differences and some categories of income are assessed under different Schedules or Cases, as follows:

Rents: For a company, prior to 1 April 1998 rents from unfurnished UK property were assessed under Schedule A using rules which differed significantly from those applying for individuals. Similarly rents from furnished properties were assessed under Schedule D Case VI.

Interest: All interest received by a company - whether received net or gross or whether from a UK or foreign source - is assessable under Schedule D Case III. Note that while grossed up taxed interest might be shown in the layout as 'taxed income', it is technically Schedule D Case III income.

(e)   Care is also needed to include certain payments or receipts such as grossed up amounts (as calculated in (b) above) in the correct accounting period. The following is a useful summary of items that give particular problems:

-   Interest paid on borrowings for a trading purpose (eg, to provide working capital or buy plant) should be charged as a trading expense in the company accounts on an 'accruals' basis. No tax adjustment is needed whether the interest was paid net (eg, on a debenture) or gross (eg, on a UK bank loan or overdraft).

-   Interest received (net or gross) is usually credited in the company accounts on an 'accruals' basis. In which case no adjustment is needed for tax purposes.

-   Charges on income (eg, patent royalties or gift aid payments) have to be included in PCTCT on a paid basis regardless of whether the company accounts show them debited on a paid or accruals basis. Note that interest (whether paid net or gross) is never a charge on income. Instead, if it is for a trading purpose it is a trading expense. However, if it is for a non-trading purpose (eg, on a loan to buy commercial letting property) it is deducted from interest received (if any) or relieved under special loss relief rules.

5.3   Schedule D Case I: adjustment of accounting profit

(a)   As with Schedule D Case I adjustment of profits for an individual, the Revenue will look closely at the information supplied by a company and will identify and investigate any areas that cause concern.

(b)   The net profit disclosed by a company's profit and loss account will need adjustment to arrive at the net trading profit for Schedule D I purposes. The adjustments necessary can be classified, **as for income tax,** under the following headings:

		£	£
Net profits per accounts			X
Add:	Expenditure not allowable for taxation purposes	X	
	Income not credited in the accounts but taxable under Schedule D Case I	X	
			X
			X
Less:	Income credited in the accounts but not taxable under Schedule D Case I	X	
	Expenditure not charged in the accounts but allowable for the purposes of taxation	X	
	Capital allowances	X	
			X
Schedule D Case I			X

The following points should be noted:

- The accounting profit is adjusted for corporation tax in the same way that business profits are adjusted for income tax purposes (see the income tax chapter).

- Capital allowances are treated as a trading expense of the company. The Schedule D Case I figure is the adjusted trading profit after capital allowances. This is dealt with in more detail below.

- Interest payable on borrowings for a trading purpose are allowed as a trading expense (on an accruals basis) regardless of whether it is payable net (on a debenture) or gross (to a UK bank).

(c)   The rules regarding expenditure in the accounts not allowed for corporation tax purposes are basically the same as those for income tax, covered earlier in the study text. However, the following points should be noted:

- When adjusting profits for corporation tax purposes, no adjustment is necessary for private expenses. Thus where a car is provided for an employee and the company pays all the expenses, for both business and private use, the full amount is deductible. The employee is **then** taxed under Schedule E on any benefit he has received.

- Appropriations of profit are not allowable expenditure. The sort of appropriations a company may make are payment of dividends, transfers to reserves and general provisions.

- Any costs incurred directly by a company in obtaining long term finance are allowable, but not apparently if the loan finance is not eventually obtained. The sort of costs allowed are fees, commission, legal expenses and advertising, but any indirect costs such as stamp duty are excluded. The costs are allowed as a trading expense if the loan is such that the interest is a trading expense.

- Any revenue expenditure incurred in the seven years before a company commences to trade is treated as an expense on the day that the company starts trading. For example if a company which started to trade on 1 April 1998 had spent £6,000 in the previous six months advertising the fact that it was about to trade, this expenditure would be treated as if it had been incurred on 1 April 1998.

- Payments to Employee Share Ownership Trusts (ESOTs) and other approved arrangements for providing benefits to employees in the form of shares in the company are allowable trading expenses.

(d) Certain items of income may be included in the accounts, but are not taxable under Schedule D Case I. The main items are as follows:

- Income taxed under another Schedule or Case such as interest, taxed under Schedule D Case III, and rent, taxed under Schedule A. Note that rents may be included in the profits figure on an accruals basis, but prior to 1 April 1998 rents were taxed on the amount receivable during the accounting period.

- Taxed income such as interest on most government securities and patent royalties and interest received gross from banks and building societies. Remember all interest whether received net or gross is assessed under Schedule D Case III. Interest on 3½% War Loan was always paid gross and interest on government stocks is now generally paid gross if the stocks are acquired after 5 April 1998. An election can be made for gross payment where stocks were acquired before 6 April 1998.

- Capital receipts, which are taxed as chargeable gains.

- Items which are exempt, such as profits on the sale of capital items which are exempt (motor cars), dividends from UK companies and repayment supplements from the Revenue.

5.4 Capital allowances

It was explained earlier in this chapter that capital allowances are treated as a trading expense for corporation tax purposes just as they are for individual traders where the current year basis applies. The rules for capital allowances have been dealt with in detail earlier in the study text.

Capital allowances are computed as follows for companies:

- Allowances are given for accounting periods by reference to acquisitions and disposals in that accounting period.

- If the accounting period is less than 12 months the writing down allowance is proportionately reduced.

- Where there is private use of an asset, there is no reduction in the writing down allowance.

5.5 Example: Capital allowances for companies

(a) Conifer Ltd prepared accounts for the nine month period ended 31 March 1999. On 1 November 1998 a car costing £10,000 was bought for the managing director, who used the car 80% for business purposes.

(b)   Mr Bramble commenced trading on 1 April 1997, preparing accounts to 31 March. On 1 November 1998 he bought a car for £10,000 which was used 80% for business purposes.

You are required to calculate the capital allowance in each of the above situations.

5.6   Solution

(a)   **Conifer Ltd**

Capital allowances for the nine month period to 31.3.99
$£10,000 \times 25\% \times \frac{9}{12} =$ £1,875

(b)   **Mr Bramble**

Capital allowances for year ended 31.3.99

$£10,000 \times 25\% \times 80\% =$ £2,000

5.7   Schedule D Case V

Where a company trades abroad they do so either with an overseas branch or an overseas subsidiary.

Profits of an overseas branch are included in the Schedule D Case I figure. Where a company has an overseas subsidiary any dividends received are not exempt, (only dividends from a UK company are exempt) the gross amount is taxable under Schedule D Case V.

6   SCHEDULE A

6.1   Introduction

The rules for computing the income taxable under Schedule A for companies changed on 1 April 1998, and are now aligned with the income tax rules.

6.2   Property letting business

The taxable property income is calculated as if all property letting formed a single business, ie, with income and expenses being dealt with on an accruals basis. This applies both to unfurnished and furnished lettings (furnished lettings were previously taxed under Schedule D Case VI).

Premiums on short leases are also taxed under Schedule A, as for income tax.

6.3   Interest paid

In contrast to the income tax treatment of interest paid in connection with let property (treated as an expense), interest paid by companies is not an expense of the property letting business. Instead it is deducted from interest received taxable under Schedule D Case III (non-trading interest).

6.4   Losses

Schedule A losses are deducted from the company's total income of the same accounting period. Any excess is carried forward and offset against total income in succeeding accounting periods.

6.5   Example

ABC Ltd owns two properties, K and L. K is let at an annual rent of £5,000, and L at an annual rent of £3,000 until 29 September 1998 when the rent was increased to £4,000 pa. Rents are payable quarterly in advance on the normal quarter days.

Expenses paid in the year to 31 March 1999 are:

	K	L
	£	£
Insurance	800	750
Agents fees	500	375
Repairs	1,000	2,900

The repairs on property K related to a redecoration of the building, whilst those on property L related to refelting the roof and replacing broken tiles.

Compute the income taxable under Schedule A for the year to 31 March 1999.

6.6   Solution

Accounting period to 31.3.99

	K	L
	£	£
Rent accrued for year	5,000	
$3,000 \times \frac{6}{12} + 4,000 \times \frac{6}{12}$		3,500
Expenses		
Insurance	800	750
Agents fees	500	375
Repairs	1,000	2,900
	2,300	4,025
	1,700	(525)
Taxable under Schedule A (1,700 - 525)		1,175

7   OTHER INCOME

7.1   Taxed income

(a)   Examples of taxed income which a company may receive and which must be included in the computation of profits calculation are:

- interest on gilt edged securities (received net of lower rate tax);

- interest received from another UK company, for example debenture or loan stock interest (received net of lower rate tax);

- patent royalties (received net of basic rate tax).

(b)   The interest received is grossed-up by 100/80, so that if a company receives £8,000 (net) the gross equivalent to include in chargeable profits is £10,000. The £2,000 of income tax suffered at source is recoverable by the company (see the following chapter). Remember, the grossed-up interest is included in chargeable profits for an accounting period on an *accruals* basis. Interest received is always assessable under Schedule D Case III whether it is received gross or net.

(c)   Patent royalties received are grossed up at 100/77 (100/76 for 1996/97 and 100/75 pre 6 April 1996) and are chargeable on a received basis. Thus, if a company receives £10,780 (net) of patent royalties on 10 April 1998 in respect of the usage of a patent during its accounting period to 31 March 1998, it has income of £14,000 (£10,780 × 100/77) for its year to 31 March 1999 (year of receipt). The accruals basis does not apply to taxed income other than interest.

(d)   Remember:

   •   dividends received from UK companies are **not** included in the profits calculation (see below).

   •   bank interest and building society is received gross by companies, and is taxed under Schedule D Case III.

   •   UK government stock interest is only received net after 6 April 1998 if the stock was purchased before that date and the company has not elected for gross payment.

7.2   Franked investment income

(a)   It has already been mentioned that dividends received from UK companies are not included in the profits calculation. Such dividends are paid out of post-tax profits of the company paying them, and are not subject to further tax. Note that although a company is not liable to tax on UK dividends, an individual is.

(b)   Dividends received from UK companies are treated as a net amount, and carry a deemed tax credit. The amount of the credit is:

   •   for dividends paid before 6 April 1999, 20% of the gross amount, ie, $\frac{20}{80}$ ths of the net dividend, and

   •   for dividends paid after 5 April 1999, 10% of the gross amount, ie, $\frac{10}{90}$ ths of the net dividend.

Definition   Dividends received from UK companies plus the associated tax credit are known as franked investment income.

(c)   It is only dividends paid out of profits which have suffered UK corporation tax that are treated in this way. If dividends are received from foreign companies, they are taxed under Schedule D Case V.

7.3   Chargeable gains

(a)   When a company disposes of a capital asset, the chargeable gain is calculated in the same way as for individuals (generally disposal proceeds less allowable deductions). Individuals, however, are entitled to indexation allowance only up to April 1998 with taper relief thereafter. Companies are entitled to indexation allowance up to the month of disposal but not taper relief. This was covered in detail in the chapters on capital gains tax in the study text.

(b)   Companies do not pay capital gains tax as individuals do, instead their chargeable gains form part of their profits chargeable to corporation tax for an accounting period and are taxed at the rate of corporation tax applying to the company's profits figure.

(c)   Companies do not have an annual exemption as individuals do.

7.4   Charges on income

(a)   Companies may make payments which are charges on income: these are deducted from the total of profits from all sources to arrive at the profits chargeable to corporation tax figure.

The payments are made net of basic rate income tax, and the company accounts to the Revenue for the amount deducted. This is dealt with in more detail in the following chapter.

Note that it is the gross amount, before deduction of tax, that is included in the profits chargeable to corporation tax computation.

Examples of payments which are treated as charges on income are:

•   patent royalties;

•   charitable deeds of covenants; and

•   one off donations to charities under the Gift Aid Scheme. These are dealt with below.

The accounts of the company will have been prepared on the accruals basis, and will include amounts due but not yet paid. For corporation tax purposes, the gross amount of charges actually paid in the chargeable accounting period must be included in the profits computation.

For example, a company may show patent royalties of £23,300 (gross) in the accounts for the year ended 31 March 1999 made up as follows:

	£
Amount paid December 1998	23,000
Accrual 31 March 1999	2,100
Less: accrual 1 April 1998	(1,800)
	23,300

The amount to be included as a charge in the profits computation is £23,000.

Note that although a company usually pays loan or debenture interest net of (lower rate) tax it is not a charge on income. The gross amount of interest is generally allowed as a trading expense charged on an accruals basis. Thus if the amounts in the above example had been loan interest the trading deduction of £23,300 would not be adjusted.

(b)   The Gift Aid Scheme allows companies to make one off payments to charities which are treated as charges on income and thus qualify for tax relief. The company must deduct basic rate income tax from the payments and account for the deduction via the quarterly accounting system (see next chapter).

There is no upper limit for relief under the Gift Aid Scheme. There is a minimum limit for certain companies (close companies) of a net payment of £250.

7.5   Dividends paid

(a)   Dividends paid are appropriations of profit, and are not deducted in the computation of profits chargeable to corporation tax.

(b)   Prior to 6 April 1999, when a company paid a dividend it had to account for tax, known as advance corporation tax (ACT), at the rate of $^{20}/_{80}$ ths of the net dividend.

(c)   As its name implies, ACT was an advance payment, and so could be deducted from the corporation tax payable for the accounting period in which the dividend was paid. There were limits on the amount that could be deducted, any excess (surplus ACT) could either be carried back for deduction in earlier years, or carried forward for deduction in later years.

(d)   ACT will not be paid in respect of any dividend paid after 5 April 1999, and there are complicated rules to allow a company to continue to deduct surplus ACT brought forward at 5 April 1999.

(e)   In view of the abolition of ACT, the examiner has stated that ACT is no longer examinable.

Conclusion   When given the results of a company it is necessary to adjust them according to the proforma given above in order to arrive at the profits chargeable to corporation tax figure.

7.6   Activity

The following information relates to Holly Ltd for the year ended 31 March 1999.

	£
Trading profit (adjusted for taxation purposes other than capital allowances and interest payable)	1,500,000
Capital allowances	60,000
Bank interest receivable	25,000
Dividend received from overseas subsidiary (gross amount)	15,000
Dividend received from UK subsidiary (gross amount)	20,000
Interest on gilts (net amount receivable)	44,800
Debenture interest payable (gross amount)	35,000
Patent royalties payable (gross amount)	32,000

The amount of net patent royalties actually paid in the year ended 31 March 1999 amounted to £29,260.

You are required to calculate the profits chargeable to corporation tax.

7.7   Activity solution

Holly Ltd: Profits chargeable to corporation tax for the year ended 31 March 1999.

	£
Adjusted trading profit	1,500,000
Less: Capital allowances	(60,000)
Debenture interest payable	(35,000)
Schedule D Case I	1,405,000
Schedule D Case III - bank interest	25,000
- taxed interest (£44,800 × 100/80)	56,000
Schedule D Case V	15,000
	1,501,000
Less: Patent royalties paid (£29,260 × 100/77)	(38,000)
Profits chargeable to corporation tax	1,463,000

7.8   Example: calculation of PCTCT

The following is a summary of the profit and loss account of Ash Ltd for the year ended 31 March 1999.

	£	£
Gross trading profit		319,760
Loan interest receivable from UK company (gross)		60,000
Patent royalties (amount received)		18,480
3½% War Loan interest (amount receivable)		1,000
Building society interest (amount receivable)		2,800
Dividends from UK companies (gross)		8,400
		410,440
Less: Trade expenses (all allowable)	89,000	
Debenture interest payable (gross)	6,800	
Payment to charity (net)	3,192	(98,992)
Net profit per accounts		311,448

Capital allowances for the year have been agreed at £7,920. All amounts shown for interest (paid or received) have been calculated on an accruals basis.

A capital asset was disposed of in January 1999 giving rise to a chargeable gain of £3,920. The payment to charity qualifies as a payment under the Gift Aid provisions. You are required to calculate the profits chargeable to corporation tax.

7.9   Solution

Step 1   The net profit per accounts must be adjusted for tax purposes, the capital allowances must then be deducted to arrive at the Schedule D Case I figure.

	£	£
Net profit per accounts		311,448
Less: Loan interest receivable	60,000	
Patent royalties received	18,480	
3½% War Loan interest receivable	1,000	
Building society interest receivable	2,800	
UK Dividends received	8,400	
		(90,680)
		220,768
Add: Payment to charity		3,192
		223,960
Less: Capital allowances		(7,920)
Schedule D Case I		216,040

Step 2   The profits chargeable to corporation tax can now be computed using the layout given earlier in this chapter.

Remember:

- payments made and income received net of basic rate tax must be included gross.

- dividends received from UK companies are not included.

Ash Ltd: profits chargeable to corporation tax for the year ended 31 March 1999

		£
Schedule D Case I		216,040
Schedule D Case III (1,000 + 2,800 + 60,000)		63,800
Taxed income: Patent royalties (18,480 × 100/77)		24,000
Chargeable gain		3,920
		307,760
Less: Charges paid: Charitable payment (3,192 × 100/77)		(4,145)
Profits chargeable to corporation tax (PCTCT)		303,615

7.10   Example: calculation of PCTCT with capital allowances computation

Superscoff plc is a trading company operating a fast food retailing business. The profit and loss account for the 12 months to 31 March 1999 shows the following.

	£		£
Salaries and wages	146,323	Gross profit	1,489,055
Rates, light and heat	11,650	Bank deposit interest	1,200
Travelling expenses	13,200	Dividends from UK	
Entertaining	6,000	companies	
Advertising	18,600	(received June 1997)	6,000
Depreciation	27,800	Rent (net of expenses)	1,460
Director's remuneration	40,000	Gain on investments	798
General expenses	3,150		
Debenture interest paid	8,800		
Dividend paid (March 1999)	31,950		
Net profit	1,191,040		
	1,498,513		1,498,513

The following information is also relevant.

(a)   The entertaining expenses comprise £4,750 cost of entertaining customers, and £1,250 for the staff Christmas party.

(b)   Advertising includes the cost of 500 calendars, bearing the company's name, at a cost of £2 each.

(c)   General expenses comprise

	£
Subscriptions to BHRCA, the trade association	40
Donation to Oxfam (net) 1 January 1999	500
Fine for breach of hygiene regulations	250
Allowable expenses	2,360
	3,150

(d)   The debenture interest is on £88,000 10% Debentures issued in 1985. The interest is payable half-yearly on 30 September and 31 March.

(e)   The gain on the investments arises on the sale of 5,000 shares in Finefish Ltd, purchased and sold, in May 1998 and is equal to the chargeable gain.

(f)   The rent received is in respect of the adjacent shop premises let under a tenant's insuring and repairing lease at £4,000 per annum, payable on the normal quarter days. The rent due on 25 March 1999 had not been received by 31 March 1999. The company incurred expenses of £250 on administration, £40 on agents' fees, and £1,250 being part of the cost shared with the tenant of installing a new shop front.

(g)   The written down value of the plant and machinery, for capital allowances purposes, on 1 April 1998 was as follows.

	£
General pool	200
General car pool	11,200
Car costing £18,750 used 60% privately by managing director	6,750

During the year ended 31 March 1999 the following transactions took place

1 August 1998   Sold the MD's car for £6,350 and purchased a replacement for £18,000. Private use remains at 60%.

1 March 1999   Sold a cold food display cabinet for £1,200 (cost £2,500).

You are required to compute the total profits liable to corporation tax for the 12 months ended 31 March 1999.

7.11   Solution

Superscoff plc

Corporation tax computation: 12 months ended 31 March 1999.

	£
Schedule D Case I trading profit (W1)	1,241,632
Schedule D Case III - bank deposit interest	1,200
Schedule A rent receivable (W3)	3,710
Chargeable gain	798
	1,247,340
Less: Charges on income (gross):	
Gift aid payment (gross) £500 × $\frac{100}{77}$	(649)
Profits chargeable to corporation tax	1,246,691

WORKINGS

(W1) Schedule D Case I profit

		£	£
Net profit per accounts			1,191,040
Add:	Entertaining customers		4,750
	General expenses:		
	Gift aid payment	500	
	Fine	250	
	Depreciation	27,800	
	Dividend paid	31,950	
			1,265,090
Less:	Bank deposit interest	1,200	
	Dividend received	6,000	
	Rent received	1,460	
	Profit on investments	798	
			(9,458)
			1,246,832
Less:	Capital allowances (W2)		(6,200)
Add:	Balancing charge (W2)		1,000
	Schedule D Case I profit		1,241,632

(W2) Capital allowances: Plant and machinery

	General pool £	Car pool £	Car over £12,000 £	Allowances £
WDV b/f 1 April 1998	200	11,200	6,750	
Sale proceeds (1.8.98 + 1.3.99)	(1,200)		(6,350)	
Balancing charge	(1,000)			(1,000)
Balancing allowance			400	400

			Car over £12,000 £	
Cost of new car (1.8.98)			18,000	
WDA 25%		(2,800)	(3,000) (max)	5,800
				6,200
WDV c/f at 31 March 1999	Nil	8,400	15,000	

(W3) **Schedule A income**

	£	£
Rent (on accruals basis)		4,000
Less: Letting expenses	250	
Agent's fee	40	290
		3,710

Notes:

(1) Pay particular attention to the format of the answer, with the working schedules supporting the main computation, which should be kept as clear as possible. This is the standard of presentation the examiner hopes to see.

(2) The Schedule A assessment is computed under the new rules applying for companies, based on the rent receivable using business principles of measurement.

8 LONG PERIODS OF ACCOUNT

8.1 Introduction

Where a company prepares accounts for a period of more than 12 months, this must be split into two chargeable accounting periods of the first 12 months and the remainder of the period of account, as was explained earlier in this chapter.

A problem arises over how to allocate profits and charges between the two chargeable accounting periods.

The following rules apply:

	Method of allocation
• Trading profits before capital allowances.	Adjust profit for period of account for tax purposes and then apportion on a time basis.
• Capital allowances and balancing charges.	Separate calculation for each chargeable accounting period. (WDAs will be restricted if accounting period less than 12 months).
• Schedule A income (eg rent).	Allocated on an accruals basis.
• Interest receivable.	Allocated on an accruals basis.
• Schedule D Case VI income.	Apportioned on a time basis.
• Chargeable gains.	Dealt with in accounting period in which disposal takes place.
• Charges on income.	Deducted from profits of the accounting period in which they are paid.

Conclusion Where a period of account is longer than 12 months, it must be split into two chargeable accounting periods. Profits and charges must be allocated between the two accounting periods. There are then two separate calculations for profits chargeable to corporation tax.

8.2   Activity

Oak Ltd prepared accounts for the 15 month period to 30 June 1999, with results as follows:

	£
Trading profit (adjusted for tax purposes)	383,880
Bank interest (received 31 December 1998)	22,000
Schedule A (receivable 1 April 1999)	10,000
Schedule D Case VI income (received 1 June 1998)	30,000
Chargeable gain (asset disposed of 1 June 1999)	16,000
Debenture interest (amount actually paid, interest due 1 May each year)	38,400
Patent royalties (net amount paid 1 February 1999)	18,480
Dividends received from UK companies (amount received)	
1 November 1998	15,000
1 February 1999	12,800

Bank interest accrued was as follows:	
At 1 April 1998	£5,200
At 1 April 1999	£4,100
At 30 June 1999	£9,780

The company bought plant costing £120,000 on 1 May 1998. It had made no previous acquisitions qualifying for capital allowances.

The rent was in respect of the year from 1 April 1999 paid in advance.

You are required to calculate the profits chargeable to corporation tax.

8.3   Activity solution

Oak Ltd: profits chargeable to corporation tax for the

	Year ended 31.3.99 £	3 months ended 30.6.99 £
Trading profit (12:3)	307,104	76,776
Less: Capital allowances		
£120,000 × 50%	(60,000)	
£60,000 × 25% × 3/12		(3,750)
Debenture interest payable		
£19,200 × 100/80	(24,000)	
£19,200 × 100/80 × 3/12		(6,000)
Schedule D Case I	223,104	67,026
Schedule D Case III - (22,000 − 5,200 + 4,100)	20,900	–
- (9,780 − 4,100)	-	5,680
Schedule A 10,000 × 3/12		2,500
Schedule D Case VI (12 : 3)	24,000	6,000
Chargeable gain		16,000
	268,004	97,206
Less: Patent royalties paid (£18,480 × 100/77)	(24,000)	–
Profits chargeable to corporation tax	244,004	97,206

9   THE SMALL COMPANIES' RATE

9.1   Introduction

The full rate of corporation tax is 31% for FY 1998 and FY 1997, and was 33% for FY 1996 and earlier. For companies with 'profits' of £300,000 or less for FY 1998, a reduced rate of corporation tax known as the small companies' rate applies to their profits chargeable to corporation tax. This rate is 21% for FY 1998 and FY 1997 (24% for FY 1996 and 25% for FY1995 and before).

> **Definition**   'Profits' are defined as profits chargeable to corporation tax plus franked investment income excluding any dividends from companies in the same group.

> **Definition**   Franked investment income is the grossed up amount of dividends received from UK companies.

9.2   Example: calculation of corporation tax

Beach Ltd had the following results for the year ended 31 March 1999:

	£
Schedule D Case I	169,000
Dividend from UK company (amount received)	4,800

Compute the corporation tax payable.

9.3   Solution

	£
PCTCT	169,000
FII (£4,800 × 100/80)	6,000
'Profits'	175,000

The 'profits' are below £300,000, so the small companies' rate applies.

Corporation tax payable

£169,000 × 21%	£35,490

Note: the FII is included to arrive at the 'profits' figure. The 'profits' determine what corporation tax rate applies. Corporation tax is, of course, payable on the PCTCT figure (and **not** the 'profits' figure).

Dividends received between 6 April 1993 and 5 April 1994 are grossed up by 100/80 to arrive at FII needed to compute 'profits', despite the fact that ACT of $^{22.5}/_{77.5}$ will have been paid.

9.4   Marginal relief

If the 'profits' of an accounting period are more than £300,000 but less than £1,500,000 a year, then marginal relief applies (sometimes called taper relief). The profits chargeable to corporation tax are first charged at the full rate of tax. From that amount, the following is deducted:

$$\text{Marginal relief fraction} \times (\text{Upper limit} - \text{Profits}) \times \frac{\text{PCTCT}}{\text{Profits}}$$

Where Profits = PCTCT plus franked investment income (see above).

For FY 1998

Marginal relief fraction = 1/40

Upper limit = £1,500,000

Conclusion   Where 'profits' are at least £1,500,000 a year, the full rate of corporation tax applies (FY 1998: 31%). Where 'profits' are £300,000 or less a year, the small companies rate applies (FY 1998: 21%).

Where 'profits' are between the two limits, PCTCT are first charged at the full rate of corporation tax which is then reduced by the marginal relief calculated:

$$\text{Marginal relief fraction} \times (\text{Upper limit} - \text{'Profits'}) \times \frac{\text{PCTCT}}{\text{'Profits'}}$$

9.5   Activity

Sycamore Ltd has the following results for the year ended 31 March 1999.

	£
Schedule D Case I	320,000
Chargeable gain	10,000
Dividends from UK companies (amount received)	16,000

You are required to calculate the corporation tax liability.

9.6   Activity solution

	£
Schedule D Case I	320,000
Chargeable gain	10,000
	————
PCTCT	330,000
FII (£16,000 × 100/80)	20,000
	————
'Profits'	350,000
	————

Marginal relief applies as 'profits' are above £300,000 but below £1,500,000.

	£
Corporation tax on PCTCT £330,000 × 31%	102,300
Less: Marginal relief $1/40 \times (1,500,000 - 350,000) \times \dfrac{330,000}{350,000}$	(27,107)
	————
	75,193
	————

9.7   Accounting period straddling 31 March

When a company's chargeable accounting period falls into two financial years, then the corporation tax liability must be calculated in two parts if either the corporation tax rate changes or the limits for small companies relief changes between the two financial years. For example, the full rate of corporation tax was reduced from 33% (FY96) to 31% (FY97), the small companies rate went from 24% (FY96) to 21% (FY97) and there was an accompanying change in the marginal relief fraction. However, there were no changes between FY 1997 and FY 1998.

Note: it is only the corporation tax liability that is affected: the profits chargeable to corporation tax calculation remains unchanged.

9.8   **Example: corporation tax liability with change in rates**

Oak Ltd has the following results for the year ended 31 December 1997:

	£
Schedule D Case I	170,000
Schedule D Case III	70,000
Patent royalties paid (gross)	10,000
Dividends from UK companies (amount received 1 November 1997)	64,000

The rates, limits and fraction for FY 1996 and FY 1997 are as follows:

	FY 1996	*FY 1997*
Full rate of corporation tax	33%	31%
Small companies rate	24%	21%
Lower limit	£300,000	£300,000
Upper limit	£1,500,000	£1,500,000
Marginal relief fraction	9/400	1/40

You are required to calculate the corporation tax liability for the year.

9.9   **Solution**

Step 1   Calculate the PCTCT and 'profits' for the year.

	£
Schedule D Case I	170,000
Schedule D Case III	70,000
	240,000
Less: Charges paid	(10,000)
PCTCT	230,000
FII (£64,000 × 100/80)	80,000
'Profits'	310,000

Step 2   The 'profits' figure falls between the upper and lower limits, therefore marginal relief applies.

Step 3   The chargeable accounting period is the year ended 31 December 1997; three months falls into FY 1996, and nine months into FY 1997.

Step 4   Calculate the corporation tax payable

	£
FY 1996 (3 months)	
Corporation tax at 33% on £230,000 × 3/12	18,975
Less: Marginal relief 9/400 × (£1,500,000 – 310,000)	
$\times \dfrac{230,000}{310,000} \times 3/12$	(4,966)
	14,009
FY 1997 (9 months)	
Corporation tax at 31% on £230,000 × 9/12	53,475
Less: Marginal relief 1/40 × (1,500,000 – 310,000)	
$\times \dfrac{230,000}{310,000} \times 9/12$	(16,554)
Corporation tax payable	50,930

9.10   Short accounting periods

The upper and lower limits of £1,500,000 and £300,000 apply for an accounting period of 12 months.   If the accounting period is for less than 12 months, the limits must be reduced proportionately.

9.11   Associated companies

If a company has any associated companies, then the upper and lower limits are divided by the number of companies associated with each other.

Definition   Companies are associated with each other for small companies rate purposes if either

-    one company controls the other; or
-    they are both under common control.

In the second situation the companies may be controlled by an individual, a partnership or another company.

When determining if companies are associated, the following applies.

- control is established by holding:

    - over 50% of the share capital; or
    - over 50% of the voting rights; or
    - being entitled to over 50% of the distributable income, or net assets on a winding up.

- both UK resident and companies resident overseas are included.

- dormant companies are excluded.

- companies which have only been associated for part of an accounting period are deemed to have been associated for all of the accounting period for those purposes.

9.12 Activity

Chestnut Ltd prepared accounts for the nine months to 31 December 1998. The company acquired a subsidiary in 1997 which is resident in France, and a further subsidiary, on 1 July 1998 which is resident in the UK. You are required to calculate the upper limit for small companies rate purposes for the period to 31 December 1998.

9.13 Activity solution

The upper limit must be divided by the number of companies associated with each other

£1,500,000 × 1/3 = £500,000

Note: Companies are associated even when

- they are resident overseas;
- they have not been associated for the entire accounting period.

The upper limit must be further reduced because the accounting period is only nine months long.

£500,000 × 9/12 = £375,000.

9.14 Example: corporation tax liability, upper and lower limits restricted

Chestnut Ltd, in the activity above, had PCTCT of £140,000 for the period to 31 December 1998 and received franked investment income of £10,000. None of the dividends were received from the subsidiary companies. You are required to calculate the corporation tax payable.

9.15 Solution

Step 1 Calculate 'profits'

	£
PCTCT	140,000
FII	10,000
'Profits'	150,000

Step 2 Restrict the upper and lower limits to account for the associated companies and short accounting period.

Lower limit: £300,000 × 1/3 × 9/12 = £75,000.

Upper limit: £375,000 (as above).

Step 3 Determine where the 'profits' figure lies in relation to the restricted limits.

£150,000 lies between £75,000 and £375,000, therefore marginal relief applies.

Step 4 Calculate the corporation tax payable

	£
£140,000 × 31%	43,400
Less: Marginal relief 1/40 (£375,000 − 150,000) × $\frac{140,000}{150,000}$	(5,250)
	38,150

10   PAYMENT OF CORPORATION TAX

10.1   Corporation tax

Corporation tax (CT) is due for payment nine months after the end of the chargeable accounting period to which it relates.

10.2   Payment by instalments

For accounting periods ending on or after 1 July 1999 companies with profits above the £1,500,000 large company limit will pay CT in four quarterly instalments on the basis of their estimated tax liability for the accounting period.

The first two instalments fall in the period in months 7 and 10 and the second two instalments fall in months 1 and 4 of the next accounting period. Instalments are due on the 14th day of the month. Thus the CT for the year to 31 December 2005 will be due in 4 equal instalments on 14 July 2005, 14 October 2005, 14 January 2006 and 14 April 2006.

The switch for large companies from paying CT nine months after the period end to paying on earlier quarterly paydays is being phased in over 4 years as follows:

Period ending on or after 1 July 1999	%age of CT payable by instalments	%age of CT payable 9 months after period
1st	60	40
2nd	72	28
3rd	88	12
4th	100	-

Large companies will have to estimate their CT for each period as the first two instalments are due even before the period has ended. Interest will be charged on underpayments but such interest will be tax deductible. Similarly overpayments will attract interest payable by the Revenue but this will be taxable.

A large company is not liable to pay tax by instalments for an accounting period if it was not 'large' (ie, profits < £1.5 million) in the previous period and its taxable profits for the current accounting period do not exceed £10 million.

11   CHAPTER SUMMARY

This chapter has dealt with the basics of corporation tax. The following areas were covered:

- The charge to tax. Corporation tax is charged on the total profits of UK companies arising in each accounting period.

- Company residence. A company is resident in the UK if incorporated here or centrally managed and controlled here.

- The basis of assessment. Remember that a chargeable accounting period can never exceed 12 months.

- The computation of profits chargeable to corporation tax. Remember that figures in the company accounts may need adjusting and that all figures in the computation are gross.

- Long period of account. If a period of account is longer than 12 months, it must be split into two accounting periods of the first 12 months and the remainder. Profits and charges must be allocated between the two accounting periods in accordance with the rules given in the chapter.

- The rates of corporation tax. Remember that the rates are fixed by reference to financial years. The full rate for FY98 and FY97 is 31%, and was 33% for earlier years.

- Small companies' rate. Companies with 'profits' of £300,000 or less pay corporation tax of 21% on PCTCT. (The small companies rate was 24% from 1 April 1996 to 31 March 1997.) If 'profits' are £1,500,000 or more the company pays corporation tax of 31%.

  If 'profits' are between the two limits, the company pays corporation tax at 31% reduced by marginal relief fraction $\times$ (upper limit $-$ 'profits') $\times \dfrac{\text{PCTCT}}{\text{'profits'}}$.

- Payment of corporation tax. Payment is generally due within nine months of the end of the chargeable accounting period although large companies are being switched to paying quarterly.

12   SELF-TEST QUESTIONS

12.1   How is a company's residence determined? (2.1)

12.2   What is the definition of an accounting period? (3.2)

12.3   What is a financial year? (4)

12.4   What adjustments are needed for the net profit per the company's accounts to arrive at the Schedule D Case I figure (5.3)

12.5   What are the differences between how capital allowances are computed for companies and for individuals? (5.4)

12.6   What is the basis of assessment under Schedule A for companies after 1 April 1998? (6)

12.7   When a company prepares accounts for a period that exceeds 12 months, what will be the company's chargeable accounting periods? (8.1)

12.8   How will trading profits be allocated when the period of account exceeds 12 months? (8.1)

12.9   When does the small companies' rate apply? (9.1)

12.10   When does marginal relief apply? (9.4)

12.11   When are the upper and lower limits for small companies' rate reduced? (9.10, 9.11)

13   EXAMINATION TYPE QUESTION

13.1   Springvale Ltd

Springvale Ltd has been carrying on a manufacturing business since 1970 and the following is a summary of the profit and loss account for the year to 31 March 1999.

	£		£
Director's remuneration	37,840	Trading profit	162,372
Depreciation	44,400	Debenture interest (gross)	
Loan stock interest payable (gross)	480	(31 March 1999)	1,200
Entertaining expenses (all customers)	420	Bank deposit interest	359
Gift aid paid to charity (net)	3,800	Dividend from UK trade	
Patent royalty paid (gross)	350	investment (including tax credit)	400
Salaries and wages	16,460		
Rent and business rates	1,650		
Audit fee	350		
Trade expenses	15,418		
Net profit before taxation	43,163		
	164,331		164,331

Of the loan stock interest payable of £480, £80 was accrued at 31 March 1999. Debenture interest is receivable annually on 31 March.

The trade expenses include the following items

		£
Christmas gifts		
	Wines and spirits for UK customers	280
	5,000 ball-point pens with company's name	250
Legal costs		
	Re long-term loan finance secured by a floating charge	500
	Re loan to employee	40
	Re staff service agreements	90

The written down value on 1 April 1998 of plant and machinery was £24,220.

On 10 July 1998 the company purchased a new lathe for £1,200 and second-hand plant for £2,000. On 1 December 1998 plant that had cost £11,000 was sold for £1,500. On 1 February 1999 plant costing £5,200 and a motor car costing £13,000 were purchased (the private use of this car by the sales director was agreed at one-third).

During the year the company made a chargeable gain after indexation of £51,160.

Recent dividends (cash amounts) paid by the company have been as follows:

		£
12 May 1998	Final y/e 31 March 1998	39,760
10 September 1998	Interim for y/e 31 March 1999	19,000

You are required to compute the profits chargeable to corporation tax for the year ended 31 March 1999. (Ignore VAT)

(15 marks)

14   ANSWER TO EXAMINATION TYPE QUESTION

14.1   Springvale Ltd

Computation of profit chargeable to corporation tax (PCTCT)

Commence the answer with WORKINGS, as follows

WORKINGS

(W1)   **Schedule DI profit**

	£ –	£ +
Net profit per accounts		43,163
Depreciation		44,400
Entertaining		420
Gift aid to charity (paid net)		3,800
Patent royalty (paid net)		350
Trade expenses		
Gifts of alcohol		280
Employee loan expenses		40
Debenture interest received	1,200	
Bank deposit interest received	359	
Dividend (FII) received	400	
c/f	1,959	92,453

The capital allowances must now be computed and inserted in the above computation.

(W2)   **Capital allowances**

		General pool £	Car costing £12,000 £	Total £
Plant and machinery				
1.4.98 WDV b/f		24,220		
1.2.99 Purchase			13,000	
1.12.98 Sale		(1,500)		
		22,720		
WDA 25%/restricted		(5,680)	(3,000)	8,680
		17,040	10,000	
10.7.98 Purchases				
(1,200 + 2,000)	3,200			
1.2.99 Purchase	5,200			
	8,400			
FYA 40%	(3,360)			
		5,040		3,360
WDV c/f at 31.3.99		22,080	10,000	12,040

Now complete working (1) as follows

		£	£
		−	+
	b/f	1,959	92,453
Capital allowances (W2)		12,040	
		13,999	92,453
			13,999
Schedule D Case I profits			78,454

The 'above the line' computation is now completed and this will form the answer to the question, supported by the above workings.

Springvale Ltd
Corporation tax computation for year ended 31 March 1999

	£	£
Schedule D Case I (W1)		78,454
Schedule D Case III (bank deposit interest)		359
(debenture interest receivable)		1,200
Chargeable gain		51,160
		131,173
Less: Charges on income		
Gift aid (gross) 3,800 × 100/77	4,935	
Patent royalty paid	350	
		5,285
PCTCT		125,888

Notes:

(1)   The private use of a car has no effect on capital allowances. If the user is a director or £8,500 + employee the private use is assessed as a benefit-in-kind.

(2)   The gross dividend received (FII) is not liable to CT.

(3)   The deduction of income tax at source does not apply to bank deposit accounts held by companies. It is assumed that the bank interest figure is the amount accruing for the year.

(4)   Interest paid is allowed on an accruals basis as a trading expense (if the loan has a trading purpose).

(5)   Dividends paid are not an allowable deduction.

23 INCOME TAX

INTRODUCTION & LEARNING OBJECTIVES

This chapter covers income tax. It explains how a company has to retain income tax on certain payments and how it suffers income tax on certain income. The way to account for this income tax is dealt with and the manner in which it is either paid over to the Inland Revenue, or alternatively, how it is set-off against the corporation tax liability.

A thorough understanding of income tax is necessary to deal with basic corporation tax questions.

When you have studied this chapter you should have learned the following:

- How to account for income tax.

---

1 INCOME TAX

1.1 Introduction

In earlier chapters in this manual it has been explained that the Inland Revenue prefer, where possible, to collect income tax by deduction at source. In particular this applies to interest paid by companies, such as debenture (although not to interest paid by companies to banks).

The mechanism by which the Revenue collect such tax deducted at source is the quarterly accounting system.

The system has to recognise not only the fact that companies must deduct income tax from certain payments made, but also the fact that the company may receive income from which tax has been deducted.

1.2 Income tax suffered

A company may receive income which has suffered basic rate or lower rate income tax. This is known as taxed income or unfranked investment income. Examples of such income were given in the previous chapter. This income is part of a company's chargeable profits and the gross amount must be included in the PCTCT computation. As the company only receives the net amount of income, the income tax suffered is deducted from the corporation tax liability, to avoid the company being charged to tax twice.

1.3 Charges paid

When a company pays charges on income, the gross amount is deducted in the PCTCT computation. Charges are generally paid net of basic rate tax, for example gift aid payments and patent royalties (both net of basic rate). The company deducts basic rate income tax and must account for it to the Revenue.

1.4   Interest paid

When a company pays interest it is generally required to deduct lower rate income tax and account for it to the Revenue. The main exception to tax deduction at source is where the company pays interest to a UK bank. Interest paid on loans taken out for trading purposes is deducted as a trading expense. Interest paid on non-trading loans is usually netted off against any interest assessed under Schedule D Case III. Special 'loss' relief rules apply where there is an excess of non-trading interest paid. Interest is never a charge on income.

1.5   Net income tax deducted or suffered

When a company both pays charges on income or interest where basic rate or lower rate income tax has been retained and receives income which has suffered basic rate or lower rate income tax, the two amounts of tax can be netted off and the company only has to account to the Revenue where the income tax on charges or interest paid exceeds the income tax on income received.

The company accounts for the income tax on form CT61 through the quarterly accounting system.

If a company's income tax suffered on income exceeds the income tax retained on charges on income and interest, then the net amount of income tax will be repaid. The repayment can be made through the quarterly accounting system, (this is restricted to the amount of income tax already paid in the same accounting period) or by deduction from the corporation tax liability. If the income tax is greater than the corporation tax liability, then the balance is repaid.

Payments or receipts subject to deduction are always dealt with through the quarterly accounting system on a paid basis. Thus, the amounts of charges on income and taxed income (other than interest) used in calculating PCTCT for an accounting period are the same amounts dealt with under quarterly accounting for that accounting period. This is because the paid basis is used for both purposes. However, as shown in the following examples, interest paid or received net of income tax is dealt with on a paid basis for quarterly accounting but on an accruals basis for constructing PCTCT. Extra care must be taken over interest to use the correct basis.

1.6   Activity

A company had a corporation tax liability of nil for the year ended 31 March 1999. During the year it had suffered income tax on taxed income received. How may the income tax be relieved?

1.7   Activity solution

Income tax

As there is no corporation tax liability for the year, the income tax suffered will be repaid.

2   QUARTERLY ACCOUNTING

2.1   Introduction

Quarterly accounting is the system under which companies account to the Revenue for income tax deducted, after taking into account income tax suffered.

2.2   Forms CT61 and quarterly accounting dates

(a)   Companies must account to the Revenue for income tax on a quarterly basis on Form CT61. Returns are made for each of the quarters ended 31 March, 30 June, 30 September and 31 December. If the company's accounting date does not coincide with one of these dates, the company must make an additional return for the period which ends on its accounting date.

(b)   A company which makes up accounts to 31 August each year will have the following returns for the year to 31 August 1998.

1 month ended	30 September 1997
Quarter ended	31 December 1997
Quarter ended	31 March 1998
Quarter ended	30 June 1998
2 months ended	31 August 1998

(c)   The quarterly return shows the amount of income tax deducted, the amount of income tax suffered, and the net amount payable or recoverable.

(d)   The net income tax is payable 14 days after the end of the return period in which the tax is deducted.

2.3   Example

Wood Limited has the following taxed income, charges and interest paid for the year ended 31 March 1999.

		£	£
1.5.98	Patent royalties paid (net)	15,200	
1.7.98	Interest on gilts received (net)*		28,000
1.11.98	Debenture interest paid (net)	20,000	
2.2.99	Interest on gilts (net)		52,000

*   The gilts had been held for many years and Wood Limited had not elected to receive the interest gross.

The company had PCTCT of £360,000 for the year ended 31 March 1999. The company has no associated companies. You are required to calculate the company's corporation tax liability and the amounts of tax payable to the Collector under the quarterly accounting system.

2.4   Solution

Step 1   First, the CT61 income tax return must be completed. The quarterly returns for income tax are completed in terms of the tax suffered or deducted. As the income and charges are given in net terms, they must be multiplied by 20/80 (for interest on gilts and debenture interest) and 23/77 (for patent royalties) to arrive at the tax suffered or deducted.

Return period ended	Tax deducted on charges £	Tax suffered on income received £	Cumulative net £	IT paid/ (repaid) £	Due date
30.6.98	4,540		4,540	4,540	14.7.98
30.9.98		(7,000)	(7,000)	(4,540)	
			(2,460)		
31.12.98	5,000		5,000		
			2,540	2,540	14.1.99
31.3.99		(13,000)	(13,000)	(2,540)	
Net income tax suffered			(10,460)		

Notes:

(1)   The repayment for the quarter ended 30 September 1998 is restricted to the income tax already paid in the same accounting period.

(2)   The repayment for the quarter ended 31 March 1999 is restricted in the same way.

(3)   The net income tax suffered of £10,460 can be set against the company's corporation tax liability. If there is insufficient liability to set the £10,460 against, the balance will be repaid.

Step 2   The corporation tax can now be calculated.

Wood Limited: calculation of corporation tax liability for the year ended 31 March 1999

	£	£
Corporation tax at 31% on £360,000		111,600
Less: marginal relief 1/40 (1,500,000 – 360,000)		(28,500)
		83,100
Less: Income tax suffered (net)		(10,460)
CT payable		72,640

2.5   Activity

Plastics Ltd has PCTCT of £20,000 for the year ended 31 March 1999. The net amount of income tax suffered by the company was £6,000. You are required to calculate the company's corporation tax liability or income tax repayable.

2.6   Activity solution

Plastics Ltd: calculation of corporation tax liability for the year ended 31 March 1999.

	£	£
Corporation tax at 21% on £20,000		4,200
Less income tax suffered (net)		(6,000)
Income tax repayable		(1,800)

Conclusion   Where a company receives taxed income and pays charges the income tax suffered and deducted is accounted for via the quarterly accounting system on form CT61. If the income tax suffered exceeds income tax deducted there will be a net amount of income tax suffered which is set against the company's corporation tax liability. In the absence of any corporation tax liability, the income tax suffered is repaid.

2.7   Activity

In the example of Wood Ltd above the company had an accrual for gross gilt interest of £13,600 at 1 April 1998 and of £7,200 at 31 March 1999. The same amount of debenture interest (£25,000 gross) is paid every year on 1 November. You are required to reconstruct Wood Ltd's PCTCT of £360,000 for the year to 31 March 1999 assuming that the only other income is trading profits.

2.8   Activity solution

	£	£
Schedule D Case I (balancing figure)		286,140
Schedule D Case III		
Received (28,000 + 52,000) × 100/80	100,000	
Deduct opening accrual	(13,600)	
Add: Closing accrual	7,200	
		93,600
		379,740
Less: Charges paid 15,200 × 100/77		(19,740)
PCTCT		360,000

Notes:

(1)   Although relief is given for tax suffered on £100,000 of taxed interest (partly through the quarterly accounting system and partly against MCT), the gross amount of taxed interest included in PCTCT is only £93,600. This highlights the care needed to include interest on an accruals basis for PCTCT but on a paid basis for quarterly accounting.

(2)   The £25,000 (gross) of debenture interest paid has been deducted as a trading expense in arriving at the Schedule D Case I figure. As the same amount of interest is paid each year the paid basis (for quarterly accounting) and the accruals basis (as a trading expense) produce the same figure.

(3)   Charges are included on a paid basis for both PCTCT and quarterly accounting purposes.

3   CHAPTER SUMMARY

This chapter has dealt with income tax. The following areas were covered.

•   **Accounting for income tax**. Where a company receives taxed income and pays charges net of basic rate income tax or interest net of lower rate tax it must account to the Revenue for the income tax through the quarterly accounting system on form CT61.

•   **Set off of income tax suffered**. When income tax suffered exceeds income tax retained in an accounting period, the net income tax suffered may be used to reduce the corporation tax liability. In the absence of sufficient corporation tax, the balance will be repaid.

4   SELF TEST QUESTIONS

4.1   How does a company account for income tax suffered on income and income tax deducted from charges? (1.5)

4.2   When a company suffers income tax on taxed income in excess of income tax retained on charges paid earlier in the accounting period, how much of the income tax repayment may be made through the quarterly accounting system? (1.5)

4.3   When a company suffers tax on taxed income that cannot be repaid through the quarterly accounting system, what relief is available for the company? (1.5)

4.4   When must income tax due under the quarterly accounting system be paid? (2.2)

5   EXAMINATION TYPE QUESTION

5.1   Drew plc

Drew plc prepares accounts to 31 March annually. During the year ended 31 March 1999 the company had the following receipts and payments.

1998		£
15 April	Loan interest paid (gross)	5,000
17 June	Royalties received (gross)	6,800 ✓
31 July	Debenture interest paid (gross)	1,500
15 September	Loan interest paid (gross)	5,500
23 December	Royalties received (gross)	7,500 ✓
1999		
31 January	Debenture interest paid (gross)	1,500

You are required to:

(a)   Prepare the quarterly returns for IT for the year ended 31 March 1999.

(b)   Calculate the mainstream corporation tax payable for the year ended 31 March 1999, assuming that the adjusted trading profit was £531,250, and a chargeable gain of £1,000 was realised. Bank deposit interest of £2,000 was received during the year with an opening accrual of £640 and a closing accrual of £890.

6   ANSWER TO EXAMINATION TYPE QUESTION

6.1   Drew plc

Quarterly accounting for income tax

Income tax

Return period	Income tax deducted £	Income tax suffered £	Cumulative £	IT paid/ (repaid) £
30.6.98	1,000		1,000	
		1,564	(1,564)	
			(564)	
30.9.98	300		300	
	1,100		1,100	
			836	836
31.12.98		1,725	(1,725)	(836)
			(889)	
31.3.99	300		300	

Income tax to be offset against MCT liability of year end 31.3.99.   (589)

Corporation tax computation - year ended 31.3.99

	£	£
Schedule D Case I		531,250
Taxed income (6,800 + 7,500)		14,300
Bank deposit interest receivable (2,000 − 640 + 890)		2,250
Chargeable gain		1,000
PCTCT		548,800
CT liability (W1)		
On 548,800 @ 31%		170,128
Less: 1/40 (1,500,000 - 553,400) × $\dfrac{548,800}{553,400}$		(23,468)
		146,660
Less: income tax suffered (net)		(589)
CT payable		146,071

(handwritten: 946,600   0.99168)

WORKING

	£
PCTCT	548,800
Add: FII (800 + 2,880) × 100/80	4,600
'Profits'	553,400

Therefore, marginal relief applies.

Note: Any interest paid is assumed to have been correctly charged (on an accruals basis) in arriving at the adjusted trading profit figure advised in the question.

24 CORPORATION TAX LOSSES

INTRODUCTION & LEARNING OBJECTIVES

This chapter deals with the different ways that companies which incur trading losses can obtain relief. Earlier chapters have dealt with the basic computation of profits chargeable to corporation tax and the calculation of corporation tax liability, with how to account for ACT and income tax and how these amounts are set-off. Exam questions will require a thorough understanding of these topics. The examiner will also expect detailed knowledge of the various loss reliefs that are available.

In this chapter you should learn:

- Carry forward of trading losses (S393(1) ICTA 1988) where the loss is carried forward and set against future trading income.

- Loss relief against total profits (S393A ICTA 1988) where the loss is set off against current profits and may be carried back and set against earlier profits.

- Unrelieved charges on income paid (S393(9) ICTA 1988) where unrelieved trade charges are carried forward and set against future trading income.

- Unrelieved interest on non-trading loans set first against current profits.

- The effect of loss relief on ACT set off.

---

1 INTRODUCTION

1.1 Loss reliefs available

This chapter deals primarily with trading losses incurred by a company. However, trading losses are not the only losses that a company can incur, and it would be useful at this point to discuss how relief for other types of losses is obtained.

1.2 Capital losses

Where a company disposes of a capital asset and incurs a loss, this capital loss can only be set off against current chargeable gains, or where none are available, future chargeable gains.

Note: that

- a capital loss may never be carried back and relieved against chargeable gains for earlier periods; and

- capital losses may not be set against income.

An exam question may give a company's results in columnar form, and include a capital loss. When transferring these figures across into a computation of PCTCT, never include the capital loss, unless there are current chargeable gains to set it against.

1.3   Schedule A losses

Schedule A losses arising after 31 March 1998 are

- first set-off against non-Schedule A income and gains of the current period; and
- any excess can be carried forward for set-off against future income of any type

Prior to 1 April 1998, Schedule A losses could be set against current or future Schedule A income. There were restrictions for tenant's repairing leases and leases at a nominal rent.

1.4   Schedule D Case VI losses

Where a Schedule D Case VI loss is incurred it may be set-off against other Schedule D Case VI income in the same accounting period. In the absence of such income in the current accounting period, the loss may be carried forward and set against future Schedule D Case VI income.

Note: that in this instance the set-off is not limited to profits of the same source; the loss can be relieved against any source of Schedule D Case VI income.

1.5   Schedule D Case III losses

Interest and other costs payable on loans taken out for a non-trading purpose are automatically set off against interest receivable which is assessable under Schedule D Case III. There are special rules (explained below in section 5) for obtaining relief where interest payable exceeds interest receivable.

2   CARRY FORWARD OF TRADING LOSSES; S393(1) ICTA 1988

2.1   Details of the relief

- Where a company incurs a trading loss, it may carry the loss forward and set it off against profits from the same trade in future accounting periods.

- The loss can be carried forward indefinitely, there is no time limit for obtaining relief, but it must be set-off against the first available trading profits.

- A claim to establish the amount of the loss available to carry forward should be made within six years of the end of the loss making accounting period.

2.2   Computation of the loss

A company's trading loss is computed in the same way as a company's trading profit ie, after deducting capital allowances and interest payable on loans etc taken out for the purposes of the trade.

2.3   Example: carry forward of trading losses

Rose Ltd has the following results for the two years to 31 August 1999.

	Year ended	
	31.8.98	*31.8.99*
	£	£
Trading profit/(loss)	(20,000)	18,000
Schedule D Case III income	6,000	9,000
Capital loss	(2,000)	
Chargeable gains		7,000
Patent royalties paid (gross)	(1,000)	(1,000)

You are required to calculate the profits chargeable to corporation tax for the two periods, assuming that the loss is relieved under S393(1) showing any losses carried forward at 1 September 1999.

2.4   Solution

Under S393(1) trading losses are relieved against the first available trading profits.

Capital losses can only be set against current or future chargeable gains.

Rose Ltd: profits chargeable to corporation tax for the two years ended 31 August 1999.

	Year ended	
	31.8.98	*31.8.99*
	£	£
Schedule D Case I	-	18,000
Less: S393(1) loss relief		(18,000)
		Nil
Schedule D Case III	6,000	9,000
Chargeable gains (£7,000 – £2,000)		5,000
	6,000	14,000
Less charges paid	(1,000)	(1,000)
PCTCT	5,000	13,000
Loss carried forward under S393(1) (£20,000 – £18,000)		£2,000

Conclusion	Where a company incurs a trading loss, in the absence of any other relief being claimed, the loss is carried forward and set against the first available trading profits of the same trade.

3   LOSS RELIEF AGAINST TOTAL PROFITS: S393A ICTA 1988

3.1   Introduction

Where a company incurs a trading loss it may claim to set the loss against total profits (before all charges) of the accounting period producing the loss.

Any trading loss remaining unrelieved may then be carried back and set against total profits (this time before non-trading charges) of earlier accounting periods. This means that when a loss is carried back, the set-off is restricted so that trade charges do not become unrelieved.

Definition	Trade charges are payments made wholly and exclusively for the purposes of the trade (for example patent royalties).

Definition	Non-trading charges are payments not made wholly and exclusively for the purposes of the trade (for example deed of covenant to charity).

3.2   Relief available

(a)   When a trading loss is incurred, the company may claim to set the loss against total profits (before all charges) of the accounting period producing the loss.

When relief is claimed for a trading loss against total profits of the current accounting period, trade charges may become unrelieved. They may be relieved under S393(9) (see later in this chapter) and carried forward and set against the first available trading profits of the same trade.

(b)   A trading loss may also be carried back and set against total profits (this time before non-trade charges) of the twelve months preceding the loss making accounting period.

This means that when a loss is carried back, the set off is restricted so that trade charges do not become unrelieved.

(c)   The loss of the twelve months prior to the cessation of trade may be carried back for three years. Where the final twelve months do not coincide with an accounting period(s), the loss will be calculated by time apportionment. The loss of the final twelve months is usually referred to as the 'terminal loss'.

(d)   If a company has prepared accounts for a period other than 12 months in the twelve months preceding the loss making accounting period, then the results of the accounting period which falls partly outside the carry back period are apportioned, and loss relief is limited to the proportion of profits (before all charges) which falls within the carry back period.

(e)   A claim must be made to relieve the loss against profits arising in the loss making period before a claim can be made to carry the loss back to preceding periods.

(f)   A company may claim to relieve the loss against current year profits and not claim to carry the loss back against earlier profits. However, if the loss is carried back, it must be relieved as far as is possible within the carry back period.

(g)   If a claim is made to carry back the loss, the set off is against later periods before earlier periods. This is relevant where there is a < 12 month accounting period immediately before the loss making period.

(h)   Losses must be dealt with in the order that they arise. Thus a loss in 1998 must be relieved, either against total profits, or carried forward and relieved against future trading income, before a loss arising in later years, say 2000, can be carried back.

(i)   Any loss remaining unrelieved after a S393A claim is carried forward under S393(1) and relieved against future trading profits of the same trade.

(j)   If in the accounting period in which trade ceases a trading loss is incurred, and a claim is made under S393A to relieve the loss against total profits, any unrelieved trade charges in the final accounting period may be added to the loss claimed under S393A.

(k)   A claim for loss relief under S393A (either against current year profits, or by carry back) must be made within two years of the end of the loss making accounting period.

(l)   A claim under S393A must be for the whole loss, including capital allowances. The amount of the loss may be reduced by not claiming the full amount of capital allowances available. A company may claim any amount of capital allowances, up to the full amount; a reduced claim would leave a higher tax written down value on which to claim allowances next year.

3.3   Example: Loss relieved against total profits

Clover Ltd has the following results for the accounting periods ended 31 August 1998 and 31 March 1999:

	Year to *31.8.98* £	*7 months to* *31.3.99* £
Trading profit/(loss)	60,000	(49,000)
Schedule A	2,000	1,500
Non-trade charges	500	500
Trade charges	1,000	700

You are required to calculate the profits chargeable to corporation tax for both periods, assuming that relief under S393A is claimed for the loss in the period ended 31 March 1999. Show any losses available to carry forward at 1 April 1999.

3.4   Solution

First prepare a PCTCT computation for both periods. The loss may be carried back against the profits of the twelve months to 31 August 1998.

Underneath the PCTCT computation prepare a loss memorandum, to show how the loss is relieved and any amounts carried forward at 1 April 1999.

Clover Ltd: PCTCT computation for the two periods ending 31 March 1999

	Year to 31.8.98 £	7 months to 31.3.99 £
Schedule D Case I	60,000	-
Schedule A	2,000	1,500
	62,000	1,500
Less: S393A relief	(47,500)	(1,500)
	14,500	-
Less: Trade charges	(1,000)	-
Non-trade charges	(500)	-
PCTCT	13,000	Nil
Unrelieved non-trade charges		500

Loss memorandum	£
Loss for 7 months ended 31.3.99	49,000
Less: S393A relief: 7 months to 31.3.99	(1,500)
y/e 31.8.98	(47,500)
	-
Unrelieved trade charges carried forward	700

4   UNRELIEVED CHARGES ON INCOME PAID: S393(9) ICTA 1988

4.1   Introduction

Charges on income paid are usually relieved against total profits in computing the profits chargeable to corporation tax. Both trade charges and non trade charges are relieved in this way. For a definition of trade and non-trade charges see earlier in this chapter.

4.2   Details of the relief

- Where there are insufficient profits in an accounting period to relieve all charges paid, non-trade charges are set against profits before trade charges.

- Where trade charges are unrelieved in an accounting period, relief is available under S393(9). The unrelieved trade charges are carried forward and set against the first available trading profits of the same trade in the same way as a S393(1) loss.

  This relief is not available for non-trade charges.

- When relief for a trading loss is claimed under S393A against total profits of the accounting period producing the loss, trade charges may become unrelieved. Relief is available for these unrelieved trade charges under S393(9) and they may be carried forward and set against the first available trading profits of the same trade.

- When a trading loss is incurred in the accounting period in which trade ceases, and a claim is made under S393A to relieve the loss against total profits, any unrelieved trade charges in the final accounting period may be added to the loss to be claimed under S393A.

4.3   Activity

A company paid the following charges on income.

Charitable deed of covenant.

Patent royalties.

Gift aid.

Which of these payments are trade charges?

4.4   Activity solution

Patent royalties.

4.5   Example: unrelieved trade charges

Aster Ltd has the following results for the three years ended 31 March 2001.

	Year ended		
	31.3.99	31.3.00	31.3.01
	£	£	£
Trading profit/(loss)	(10,000)	12,000	1,200
Charitable covenant (gross)	500	500	500
Patent royalties paid (gross)	1,000	1,000	1,000

Calculate the profits chargeable to corporation tax for all three years, assuming that loss relief is claimed as early as possible.

4.6   Solution

The trading loss is relieved against future trading profits of the same trade.

Non-trade charges are set-off in priority to trade charges. Unrelieved trade charges can be carried forward and relieved against future trading profits of the same trade.

There is no relief available for unrelieved non-trade charges.

	Year ended		
	31.3.99	*31.3.00*	*31.3.01*
	£	£	£
Schedule D Case I	-	12,000	1,200
Less: S393(1) & (9) loss relief	-	(11,000)	(500)
	-	1,000	700
Less: Charitable covenant	-	(500)	(500)
Patent royalties	-	(500)	(200)
PCTCT	Nil	Nil	Nil
Unrelieved non-trade charges	500		

Loss memorandum	£
Loss for y/e 31.3.99	10,000
Unrelieved trade charges y/e 31.3.99	1,000
	11,000
Less: S393(1) & (9) relief y/e 31.3.00	(11,000)
	-
Unrelieved trade charges y/e 31.3.00	500
Less: S393(1) & (9) relief y/e 31.3.01	500
	-
Unrelieved trade charges y/e 31.3.01	800
Loss carried forward under S393(1) & (9)	800

4.7   Activity

Iris Ltd ceased trading on 31 December 1998. The results for the final period were:

	£
Trading loss	(20,000)
Schedule D Case III	1,000
Patent royalties paid (gross)	3,000
Charitable deed of covenant (gross)	750

The company claims to relieve the loss under S393A against current and previous years' profits. What is the amount of the loss available for relief under S393A?

4.8   Activity solution

	£
Trading loss	20,000
Unrelieved trade charges	3,000
Loss claimed under S393A	23,000

Note: relief under S393A against current profits, is against total profits before all charges. This relieves the £1,000 of Schedule D Case III income and leaves the deed of covenant payment of £750 unrelieved. Any trade charges which become unrelieved in the accounting period in which trade ceases can be added to the amount of the loss claimed under S393A but surplus non-trading charges are wasted.

4.9 Example: losses in final period of trading

Daisy Ltd made up accounts to 30 September each year but ceased to trade on 31 March 1999.

Results have been as follows:

	Year ended 30.9.96 £	30.9.97 £	30.9.98 £	Period ended 31.3.99 £
Trading profits/(loss)	6,200	5,700	4,200	(30,000)
Schedule A	2,000	1,800	1,900	500
Schedule D Case III	750	900	840	400
Chargeable gains	3,000	-	2,000	
Charges on income:				
Patent royalties (gross)	1,000	1,000	1,000	500
Charitable covenant (gross)	300	300	300	300

Show the profits chargeable to corporation tax for all years, assuming that the loss is relieved under S393A.

4.10 Solution

Step 1 Set out the PCTCT proforma, and fill in all the income.

Step 2 Prepare a loss memorandum.

Remember that unrelieved trade charges in the accounting period in which a trade ceases can be added to the loss. When the loss is carried back, trade charges in earlier periods must remain relieved. Terminal losses can be carried back for up to three years.

	Year ended 30.9.96 £	30.9.97 £	30.9.98 £	Period ended 31.3.99 £
Schedule D Case I	6,200	5,700	4,200	-
Schedule A	2,000	1,800	1,900	500
Schedule D Case III	750	900	840	400
Chargeable gains	3,000	-	2,000	
Less: S393A relief	(10,950)	(7,400)	(7,940)	(900)
	1,000	1,000	1,000	-
Less: Patent royalties	(1,000)	(1,000)	(1,000)	-
Charitable covenant	-	-	-	
PCTCT	Nil	Nil	Nil	Nil
Unrelieved non-trade charges	£300	£300	£300	£300

Loss memorandum	£
Loss incurred in 6 months to 31.3.99	30,000
Unrelieved trade charges 6 months to 31.3.99	500
	30,500
Less: S393A 6 months to 31.3.99	(900)
y/e 30.9.98	(7,940)
y/e 30.9.97	(7,400)
y/e 30.9.96	(10,950)
Loss remaining unrelieved	3,310

No relief is available for the £300 charitable covenants paid in the last four accounting periods, nor is relief available for the remaining loss of £3,310.

Note: corporation tax questions involving losses may seem daunting at first. The key to answering them successfully is to adopt a systematic approach as follows.

(1)   Prepare a PCTCT proforma for the relevant accounting periods. In the proforma, enter relief under S393(1) and S393A in the appropriate place as follows:

PCTCT proforma	£
Schedule D Case I	X
Less: S393(1) relief	(X)
	X
Schedule A; Schedule D Case III etc	X
Net chargeable gains	X
	X
Less: S393A relief	(X)
	X
Less: Trade charges	(X)
Non-trade charges	(X)
PCTCT	X

(2)   The various amounts of income are then entered into the proforma.

(3)   Identify the losses.

Where there is more than one loss, deal with the earliest loss first, claiming relief in the appropriate place in the proforma.

(4)   Remember that normally losses may only be carried back for twelve months, but terminal losses may be carried back for three years.

(5)   As the losses are relieved, complete a loss memorandum, detailing how the loss has been relieved.

5   UNRELIEVED INTEREST ON NON-TRADING LOANS

5.1   Introduction

If interest is paid on a trading loan (ie, one taken out for a trading purpose) it is deductible (on an accruals basis) as a trading expense. If this creates or increases a trading loss, trading loss reliefs, as described earlier in this chapter, are available.

However, interest paid on a non-trading loan (eg, a loan taken out to buy commercial letting property) is relieved against interest assessable under Schedule D Case III. If there is insufficient income assessed under Schedule D Case III relief for the surplus is given as follows.

5.2   Relief for surplus non-trading interest

Interest is relieved as follows:

(a)   against any profits of whatever description of the same accounting period;

(b)   by carry back against Schedule D Case III income of the previous twelve months.

(c)   against any future profits of the company (other than trading profits) as soon as they arise.

Relief is given under (a) above after relieving any trading loss brought forward but before relieving any trading loss arising in the same period or carried back from a future period.

Relief under (a) for the excess interest of the current period takes priority over a claim under (b) where future excess interest is being carried back.

Interestingly, relief for excess non-trading interest can be taken in whole or in part under either (a) or (b) provided that the same amount of excess interest is not relieved more than once (ie, partial claims are allowed).

Claims under (a) or (b) must be made within two years of the end of the accounting period in which the excess interest arose.

Note that it is not particularly likely in practice or in an exam that a trading company would pay non-trading interest let alone so much interest that it could not be relieved in the same period firstly against interest receivable and then against any other profits.

6   CHAPTER SUMMARY

This chapter has dealt with corporation tax losses. The following areas were covered:

- Carry forward of trading losses: S393(1) ICTA 1988. A trading loss may be carried forward and relieved against future trading losses of the same trade.

- Loss relief against total profits: S393A ICTA 1988. A trading loss may be relieved against total profits (before all charges) of the loss making accounting period. Any unrelieved loss may be carried back and relieved against total profits of earlier periods (trade charges may not become unrelieved). The carry back period is normally twelve months but it is three years for terminal losses. Any remaining loss is carried forward under S393(1).

- Unrelieved charges on income paid S393(9) ICTA 1988. Unrelieved trade charges may be carried forward and set against the first available trading profits of the same trade.

- Unrelieved non-trading interest can be set against any profits of the same period or against Schedule D Case III income of earlier periods with any remaining amount set against future profits other than trading profits. The carry back period is twelve months.

7   SELF-TEST QUESTIONS

7.1   If a company cannot relieve a trading loss against current profits, or profits from earlier periods, how is relief for the loss obtained? (2.1)

7.2   When a company relieves a trading loss under S393A in the loss making accounting period, what is the loss relieved against? (3.1)

7.3   When a company relieves a trading loss under S393A in the accounting period(s) preceding the loss making accounting period, what is the loss relieved against? (3.1)

7.4   What is the definition of a trade charge? (3.1)

7.5   What is the definition of a non-trade charge? (3.1)

7.6   May a company claim to carry back a trading loss if it has not claimed to relieve the loss in the period in which the loss was incurred? (3.2)

7.7   If a company claims to relieve a trading loss against the current year's profits, must any remaining loss be carried back and relieved against earlier profits? (3.2)

7.8   When a company carries back a trading loss, what is the order of set-off? (3.2)

7.9   If there are insufficient profits in an accounting period to relieve trade charges, how may they be relieved? (4.2)

8   EXAMINATION TYPE QUESTIONS

8.1   Swanee Ltd

Swanee Ltd, which trades from rented premises, has the following results for the year ended 31 March 1999

	£
Trading loss before capital allowances (Note (c))	(96,000)
Schedule D Case III - bank deposit interest (gross)	3,500
Chargeable gain	14,500
Net loss	(78,000)

Notes:

(a)   The trading loss is after charging

	£
Depreciation	10,800
Entertaining customers	1,200

(b)   All other expenses are allowable for corporation tax.

(c)   The balance on the capital allowances' pool of plant and machinery on 1 April 1998 was £16,000. There were no purchases or sales during the year ended 31 March 1999.

(d)   Swanee Ltd has the following results for the previous year.

	Year ending 31 March 1998 £
Schedule D Case I profits	40,000
Bank deposit interest	2,000
Chargeable gain	-
	42,000

You are required:

(a)   to compute the Schedule D Case I trading loss for the year ended 31 March 1999.

(b)   to compute the profits chargeable to corporation tax, assuming no claims are made to relieve the loss for the year ended 31 March 1999.

(c)   to show how the trading loss is relieved.

8.2   Flounder Ltd

Flounder Ltd has the following results up to its date of ceasing to trade.

	Trading profit/ (loss) before CAs £	Capital allowances £	Taxed interest received (gross) £	Patent royalties paid (gross) £
12 m/e 31.3.95	20,000	3,800	900	1,500
12 m/e 31.3.96	30,000	7,200	1,000	3,000
12 m/e 31.3.97	33,000	5,400	1,200	3,000
9 m/e 31.12.97	16,500	4,050	1,300	3,000
12 m/e 31.12.98	(75,000)	6,600	1,400	3,000

Assume that the amount of taxed interest received is also the amount accruing for the period.

You are required to show how the trading loss is relieved.

9   ANSWERS TO EXAMINATION TYPE QUESTIONS

9.1   Swanee Ltd

Year ended 31 March

	1998 £	1999 £
Schedule D I	40,000	-
Schedule D III	2,000	3,500
Chargeable gain		14,500
	42,000	18,000
Less: S393A relief	(42,000)	(18,000)
PCTCT	Nil	Nil

Loss memorandum

	£
Loss y/e 31.3.99 (W)	(88,000)
Less: Relief under S393 A y/e 31.3.99	18,000
y/e 31.3.98	42,000
Loss carried forward under S393(1)	28,000

WORKING

Computation of DI loss y/e 31.3.99

	£	£
Trading loss per accounts		(96,000)
Add: Depreciation	10,800	
Entertaining	1,200	
		12,000
		(84,000)
Add: Capital allowances £16,000 × 25%		(4,000)
Schedule DI loss		(88,000)

9.2   Flounder Ltd

	Year to 31.3.95 £	Year to 31.3.96 £	Year to 31.3.97 £	9 months 31.12.97 £	Year to 31.12.98 £
Trading profit	20,000	30,000	33,000	16,500	
Less: capital allowances	(3,800)	(7,200)	(5,400)	(4,050)	
Schedule D I	16,200	22,800	27,600	12,450	
Taxed interest	900	1,000	1,200	1,300	1,400
	17,100	23,800	28,800	13,750	1,400
Less: S393A	(4,275)	(20,800)	(25,800)	(10,750)	(1,400)
	12,825	3,000	3,000	3,000	-
Less: patent royalties	(1,500)	(3,000)	(3,000)	(3,000)	-
PCTCT	11,325	Nil	Nil	Nil	Nil

Loss memorandum

		£
Trading loss y/e 31.12.98		(75,000)
Add: capital allowances		(6,600)
		(81,600)
Less: Relief under S393A	y/e 31.12.98	1,400
Add: Unrelieved trade charges	y/e 31.12.98	(3,000)
		(80,200)
	9m ended 31.12.97	10,750
	y/e 31.3.97	25,800
	y/e 31.3.96	20,800
	y/e 31.3.95	4,275
	$(17,100 \times {}^3\!/_{12} = 4,275)$	
Loss remaining unrelieved		(21,575)

25 VAT

INTRODUCTION & LEARNING OBJECTIVES

Value added tax (VAT) is a tax on goods and services consumed in the UK. It is levied on goods and services produced in the UK and on imports into the UK. The basic principle of VAT is that it is a tax borne by the final consumer.

It is a tax that is easily overlooked, but is of considerable importance in the exam.

When you have studied this chapter you should have learned the following:

- The scope of VAT: taxable transactions and taxable persons;
- Definition of supply, and the various sorts of supply;
- Registration;
- Output and input tax;
- The tax point;
- The detail required in a tax invoice;
- Bad debt relief; and
- Partial exemption.

---

1 BACKGROUND OF VALUE ADDED TAX

1.1 Introduction

Value added tax (VAT) came into force in the UK with effect from 1 April 1973. It is a tax on consumer expenditure, and is thus classified as an indirect tax along with customs duties, excise duties, betting duty, vehicle licence duty, air passenger duty and a host of similar taxes and duties.

VAT is the common consumer tax adopted by EC member states. Its main features are set out in a series of Directives made by the EC Council of Ministers, which have been translated into statutes and statutory instruments made by Parliament.

VAT is administered by the Commissioners of Customs and Excise partly through a centralised computer centre at Southend (VAT Central Unit) and partly through a network of local VAT Offices situated in most major towns (the 'outfield'). The division of responsibilities broadly results in VAT Central Unit dealing with tax returns and payments and repayments of tax while the outfield deals with the registration and deregistration of traders and the carrying out of tax audits known as 'control visits'. This latter function arises from the fact that VAT is a self-assessed tax.

The Commissioners of Customs & Excise are referred to in the legislation - and in this chapter - as 'the Commissioners'. In practice, their functions are largely carried out by customs officers based at VAT Central Unit and the local VAT Offices.

VAT is charged on the supply of goods and services in the UK where the supply is a **taxable supply** by a **taxable person** in the course or furtherance of a business **carried on by him.** VAT is also charged on **imported goods** and **acquisitions** of goods from another EC member state.

The meaning of these terms is discussed below.

1.2   Taxable transactions

It has already been said that VAT is a tax on consumer expenditure. To be more specific, it is a tax on three different classes of transaction, each of which has its own collection procedures:

(a)   **Supplies of goods and services.** VAT is charged on supplies of goods and services made in the UK by traders known as 'taxable persons'. Tax is charged by the taxable person who makes the supply and he periodically pays the amounts so charged to the Commissioners. This tax is known as 'output tax'.

(b)   **Imported goods.** VAT is charged when goods are imported into the UK from a country other than another EC member state. In broad terms, the importer pays any tax due direct to the Commissioners. He pays any import duties arising at the same time.

(c)   **Acquisitions**. If a UK registered trader imports goods from another EC member state - an 'acquisition' - he has to account for VAT as if he had sold the goods (to himself). The actual sale was zero rated in the seller's member state, being to another member state. The deemed sale in the purchaser's member state enables the VAT rules of the purchaser's state to apply. When VAT rules and rates have been harmonised throughout the EC this device will be no longer necessary.

The transactions which comprise a supply of goods and services and the manner in which output tax is calculated is described later.

1.3   Taxable persons

It will be noted that taxable persons play an important role in the administration of VAT in that it is they who collect output tax on behalf of the Commissioners. In practice, they act as unpaid tax collectors as do employers collecting PAYE on behalf of the Inland Revenue.

The economic purpose of VAT is to tax personal (not business) consumption of goods and services and it is therefore necessary to ensure that VAT does not enter into the business costs. This is done by providing taxable persons with a credit mechanism whereby (subject to certain exceptions) they are able to recover the VAT which they have paid. This is known as 'input tax', and represents:

(a)   tax chargeable on goods and services supplied to them by taxable persons;
(b)   tax paid to the Commissioners on the goods which they import; and
(c)   tax chargeable on acquisitions from other EC member states.

Since taxable persons collect output tax from their customers and recover their input tax from the Commissioners, VAT has (in theory) a neutral effect on business costs.

Not all traders are taxable persons. The manner in which traders are identified as taxable persons and the manner in which input tax is recovered from the Commissioners is described later.

1.4   Legislation

The main structure of VAT is set out in VATA 1994. Many of the detailed provisions concerning the operation of VAT are contained in orders, rules and regulations made by statutory instrument under enabling provisions contained in VATA 1994. Statutory instruments are made at irregular intervals throughout the year and are frequently amended and consolidated.

2   SUPPLIES

2.1   Introduction

VAT is charged on supplies of goods and services made in the UK. This part of the chapter defines what is meant by a 'supply', sets out the conditions to be met before a supply is within the scope of the tax, describes the manner in which supplies of goods are distinguished from supplies of services, and shows how supplies which are charged to tax are segregated from those which are not.

2.2   Definition of supply

'Supply' is the all embracing term given to the infinite variety of transactions met in the commercial world. In broad terms it may be said to comprise 'the passing of possession of goods pursuant to an agreement' and anything else done for consideration.

A number of events are treated as a supply for tax purposes:

(a)   **Goods held at deregistration.** Stock in trade, plant and other assets held by a taxable person when he deregisters are deemed to be supplied by him at that time.

(b)   **Services received from abroad.** Certain services received from overseas suppliers are deemed to be supplied by the trader who receives them. This is known as a 'reverse charge'.

(c)   **Motor cars.** Garages which appropriate a car held for resale to some other use (eg, as a demonstration car) are deemed to supply it to themselves.

(d)   **Stationery.** Certain traders producing stationery for internal use are deemed to supply it to themselves.

2.3   Chargeable supplies

A supply within the foregoing definition must meet four conditions before it is within the scope of VAT:
- it must be made by a taxable person;
- it must be made for a consideration;
- it must be made in the UK; and
- it must be made in the course or furtherance of business.

(a)   **Supplies made by a taxable person**

VAT is charged on supplies made by taxable persons, and it follows that supplies made by traders who are not taxable persons are outside the scope of VAT. The manner in which a trader is identified as a taxable person is described later.

(b)   **Supplies made for a consideration**

The consideration made for a supply may comprise money, something other than money (eg, a barter transaction) or a combination of both (eg, a part exchange deal).

The general rule is that all transactions must be made for a consideration before they are treated as a supply. There are two exceptions. Goods are supplies whether or not there is a consideration if:

- they form part of the assets of a business and are transferred or disposed of in accordance with the trader's directions so as to no longer form part of those assets. This would include, for example, a gift to anyone or an appropriation for the proprietor's personal use; or

- they are held or used for the purposes of a business and are used for a private or non-business purpose in accordance with the trader's directions. This would include, for example, private use of a business motor car by the proprietor or one of the employees.

The following gifts of goods are outside the scope of VAT:

- goods which cost the trader £15 or less and do not form part of a series of gifts;

- industrial or commercial samples unless the recipient is given more than one sample of the same item;

- a motor car which did not give rise to input tax credit when acquired by the donor.

(c)   **Supplies made in the UK**

VAT is charged on supplies made in the UK and it follows that supplies made outside the UK are outside the scope of VAT. Different rules apply to goods and services in determining whether they are supplies in the UK.

Goods are supplied in the UK if they are located here and either removed to another place in the UK or exported. Thus, a motor car manufactured in Birmingham is supplied in the UK whether the manufacturer delivers it to a customer in Bristol or a customer in Zurich.

Services are supplied in the country where the trader belongs and the place where they are actually performed is irrelevant. Three situations can arise:

- **The trader's only business establishment is situated in the UK**. The trader belongs in the UK.

- **The trader has business establishments both in the UK and abroad**. Where the establishment most directly concerned with the supply is situated in the UK, the trader belongs in the UK in relation to that supply.

- **The trader does not have a business establishment.** The trader belongs in the UK if his usual place of residence is in the UK. A company is resident in the UK if it is incorporated in the UK.

(d)   **Supplies made in the course or furtherance of business**

VAT is charged on supplies made in the course or furtherance of any business carried on by the trader who supplies them.

The term 'business' has been widely construed by the courts to include any occupation or function actively pursued with reasonable continuity, regardless of profit motive, unless it is carried on solely for pleasure and social enjoyment. The term includes, among other things, the following activities:

- carrying on a trade, profession or vocation;

- facilities or advantages provided to members for a consideration (eg, a subscription) by a club, association or organisation;

- admitting people at any premises for a consideration (eg, a cinema).

Once an activity has been identified as a business, any supply made while carrying it on is likely to be made in the course or furtherance of business. No distinction is made between revenue and capital, so the sale of surplus plant is just as much a supply as the sale of trading stock. Similarly, no distinction is made between trading and investment, so rent and interest received can amount to the consideration for a supply made in the course or furtherance of business.

2.4   Supplies of goods and services

Supplies which meet the foregoing conditions are divided into supplies of goods, supplies of services, and supplies of neither goods nor services. VAT is charged on supplies of goods and supplies of services. Supplies of neither goods nor services are outside the scope of VAT.

(a)   Supply of goods

The following supplies amount to a 'supply of goods':

- Transferring the ownership and possession of goods, either immediately (eg, on a sale of goods) or at a specified future time (eg, under a hire purchase agreement where ownership passes when the goods are fully paid for).

- Applying a treatment or process to another person's goods.

- Supplying any form of power, heat, refrigeration or ventilation.

- Granting a freehold interest in land or a lease for a term exceeding twenty-one years.

(b)   Supply of services

Anything done for a consideration which is not a supply of goods is a supply of services. This includes the grant, assignment or surrender of any right. The hire, lease and rental of goods amounts to a supply of services.

(c)   Supply of neither goods nor services.

The following supplies are specifically excluded from the scope of VAT by treating them as neither a supply of goods nor a supply of services.

- The assets of a business, or part of a business, transferred as a going concern.

- Goods and services supplied by one group company to another if both companies are included in the same group registration.

- Goods stored in a bonded warehouse. Goods are charged to tax only when they are removed from bond.

2.5   Exempt and taxable supplies

VAT is charged on taxable supplies.

> **Definition**   A taxable supply is a supply of goods or a supply of services as defined above which is not an exempt supply.

From this definition it will be seen that it is necessary to divide supplies of goods and services between exempt supplies on one hand and taxable supplies on the other in order to determine whether tax should be charged.

(a)   **Exempt supplies**

A supply of goods or services is an exempt supply if it is of a description for the time being specified in VATA 1994, Sch 9. The goods and services included therein are briefly described later.

The position of an exempt supply in the scheme of VAT is as follows.:

- **No** tax is charged on it.
- It is **not** taken into account in determining whether a trader is a taxable person.
- Input tax attributable to it is not normally available for credit.

As regards the last item, therefore, the position of an exempt supply is significantly different from a supply of neither goods nor services, which is merely ignored for all VAT purposes.

(b)   **Taxable supplies**

> **Definition**   Any supply of goods or services which is not an exempt supply is a taxable supply, and it is with this category that VAT is primarily concerned.

2.6   The rate of tax

Taxable supplies are charged to tax at one or other of two rates: the zero-rate and the standard rate.

(a)   **The zero-rate**

The zero-rate is a tax rate of nil. Thus, although no tax is charged on a supply taxed at the zero rate, it is in all other respects treated as a taxable supply. It is therefore taken into account in determining whether a trader is a taxable person, and input tax attributable to it is available for credit. In these two respects it has the opposite effect to an exempt supply. The zero-rate applies to goods and services specified in VATA 1994, Sch 8. These are generally items which can be regarded as necessities. It also applies to goods supplied for export regardless of whether or not they are specified in VATA 1994, Sch 8.

Where a supply appears to be both zero-rated and exempt, zero-rating takes precedence.

(b)   **The standard rate**

The standard rate is a tax rate of 17.5% based on the tax **exclusive** value of the goods or services supplies. This is equivalent to 7/47 of the tax **inclusive** value (ie, consideration) of the goods or services supplied. This fraction is known as the 'VAT fraction'.

Any taxable supply which is not charged to tax at the zero-rate is charged to tax at the standard rate.

There are two exceptions. A supply of fuel and power (eg, electricity) for domestic or charity use bears a VAT rate of 5%. From 1 July 1998 a VAT rate of 5% (previously 17½%) applies on the domestic installation of energy saving materials funded by certain Government grant schemes.

Conclusion A taxable supply is a supply of goods or services (other than an exempt supply) made in the UK.

A taxable supply is either

- standard rated (taxed at 17½%); or
- zero rated (taxed at 0%); or
- in the case of domestic fuel and power and certain Government funded insulation costs, taxed at 5%.

An exempt supply is not chargeable to tax.

3 TAXABLE PERSONS

3.1 Introduction

A taxable person is someone who is, or is required to be registered for the purposes of VAT. A trader is liable to be registered if the value of his **taxable** supplies exceeds the statutory limits, but he may be voluntarily registered in other circumstances if he so requests.

A person is entitled to be registered only once, and his registration includes **all** the businesses he carries on, however diverse they may be. Separate businesses carried on by the same partners, even though they may have separate partnership agreements, will have a single registration. A 'person' for this purpose is either:

(a)   a natural person ie, an individual;

(b)   a body corporate eg, a company registered under the Companies Act 1985; or

(c)   an unincorporated association eg, a partnership, or club. Strictly, it is the group of individuals who are registered because the association itself is not a person.

This section sets out the circumstances when a trader may be registered or deregistered for the purposes of VAT, the tax consequences of deregistration, the notifications which taxable persons are required to make, and the special registration provisions applicable to groups of companies and partnerships.

3.2 Registration by reference to historical turnover

Unregistered traders are required to keep a continual eye on their taxable turnover. At the end of every month they must calculate their taxable turnover for the year then ended. A trader is required to register if his taxable turnover for the year then ended exceeds £50,000 (£49,000 prior to 1 April 1998).

A trader can claim exemption from registration if the Commissioners are satisfied that his turnover in the following year will not exceed £48,000 (£47,000 prior to 1 April 1998).

Taxable turnover for a period comprises:

(a)   Amounts received or receivable in respect of taxable supplies made in the period, other than supplies of capital assets (eg, surplus plant sold).

(b)   Value of supplies of services received from abroad deemed to have been supplies by the trader in the period.

A trader liable to registration may claim exemption from registration if his taxable turnover largely comprises zero-rated supplies. Exemption is given if this does not prejudice VAT revenue ie, if the trader would regularly receive repayments of tax if he were to be registered.

A trader liable to registration must notify the Commissioners not later than thirty days after the end of the month in which taxable turnover in the previous year exceeds the statutory limit. He is registered from the end of the month following the month in which turnover exceeded the limit, or an earlier agreed date. Notifications are made on form VAT1. Claims for exemption from registration are made by completing the appropriate parts of the form.

3.3   Example

Harry commenced trading on 1 January 1998. His monthly taxable supplies were as follows:

	1998 £	1999 £
January	2,700	3,590
February	2,800	3,660
March	2,900	4,730
April	3,000	4,800
May	3,040	4,970
June	3,110	5,040
July	3,180	5,010
August	3,250	4,780
September	3,320	4,840
October	3,390	4,910
November	3,450	4,980
December	3,530	5,150

In addition, in October 1998 he sold surplus plant for £1,100, and in February 1999, Jean (a French lawyer) charged him £1,950 for supplies of legal services.

From what date is Harry liable to register for VAT?

3.4   Solution

At the end of July 1999 his taxable turnover for the past year is:

	£
Value of supplies for registration purposes:	
Supplies to customers	48,740
Supply of plant (disregarded)	-
Deemed supply of legal services (note)	1,950
	50,690

Harry is thus liable to register, and must notify the Commissioners by 30 August 1999. He will be registered from 1 September 1999, or such earlier date as may jointly be agreed.

Note: certain services received from overseas suppliers are deemed to be supplied by the trader who receives them. The legal services received from a French lawyer are deemed to be supplied by Harry.

3.5   Registration by reference to future turnover

The historical turnover limits described above are subject to an overriding provision. If at any time, a trader who makes taxable supplies has reason to believe that his taxable turnover for a future thirty day period is likely to exceed £50,000 (£49,000 prior to 1 April 1998), he must notify the Commissioners no later than the end of that period and is normally registered with effect from the start of that period. Thus, if a trader starts a new business with reasonable expectations, or an established trader expands his business, this provision could well require him to register immediately.

3.6   Activity

Charles leaves his job on 31 December 1998, signs a lease for new business premises on 1 January 1999 and opens for business on 20 June 1999. He estimates, from the outset, that taxable supplies will be in the region of £60,000 per month.

When, if at all, is Charles liable to register?

3.7   Activity solution

Charles is liable to registration because supplies for the thirty days to 19 July 1999 will exceed £50,000. He must notify the Commissioners of his liability to registration by 19 July 1999 and is registered with effect from 20 June 1999.

Note: Charles does not make taxable supplies during the period 1 January 1999 to 19 June 1999. The future limit does not apply to such traders so that a liability to registration cannot arise during this period. However, Charles could apply for intending trader registration (see later in this chapter) at any time during this period if he so wished eg, to accelerate claims for input tax credit.

3.8   Disaggregation

There is a provision to prevent a business from being artificially split into small units thereby avoiding VAT registration because one or more units fell below the turnover limits.

Where the Commissioners are satisfied that persons are carrying on separate activities which could properly be regarded as part of a single business, and that the main purpose of carrying on the activities as separate units is to avoid liability for registration, then they will issue a direction.

The direction will state that the persons named therein are carrying on activities listed together, ie, a partnership is deemed to exist. However, a direction cannot have retrospective effect.

For example, if a husband and wife run a pub together, but the wife operates the pub catering separately, both activities will be considered as one business if a direction is made. The turnover from both activities will be taken into account for the registration limits.

Finance Act 1997 enhances these provisions in that the Commissioners may now issue a direction to separate businesses which are closely bound to each other by financial, economic and organisational links to be treated as one, without needing to show that the purpose of separate operations was VAT avoidance.

3.9   Registration certificate

VAT Central Unit maintains a central computerised register of taxable persons. Traders are required to notify the Commissioners within thirty days of any change in the name, constitution or ownership of the business and of any other event which gives rise to the variation or cancellation of a registration.

3.10   Deregistration

A registered trader ceases to be liable to registration when he ceases to make taxable supplies. He must notify the Commissioners of this event within thirty days and is then deregistered from the date of cessation or a mutually agreed later date. For example, if James closes down his business on 10 January 1999, he must notify the Commissioners on or before 9 February 1999 and is then deregistered from 10 January 1999 or an agreed later date.

A trader is eligible for **voluntary** deregistration if the value of his anticipated taxable turnover for the ensuing year does not exceed £48,000 (£47,000 prior to 1 April 1998). The twelve month period is measured at any time and the onus is on the trader to satisfy the Commissioners that he qualifies under this provision. The trader is deregistered from the date of his request or a mutually agreed later date. Thus, if Edward reckons that taxable turnover for the year to 31 December 1999 will be £40,000, and applies for deregistration on 1 January 1999, he is deregistered with effect from 1 January 1999 or an agreed later date.

Where a trader disposes of his business as a going concern, and thereby ceases to make taxable supplies, he is liable to be deregistered under the foregoing provisions. However, instead of doing so, both the transferor and the transferee may make a joint election for the transferor's registration to be transferred to the transferee. Where this done, the transferee assumes all rights and obligations in respect of the registration including the liability to pay any outstanding tax.

3.11   Tax consequences of deregistration

Traders are deemed to supply their business assets (eg, plant and trading stock) when they cease to be a taxable person. The deemed supply is valued at cost and output tax must be paid on this value. There are two principal exemptions:

(a)   Individual items are not deemed to be supplied if (broadly) they did not qualify for input tax credit when acquired;

(b)   If output tax on the remaining items would not exceed £250, they are not deemed to be supplies.

For example, Frank ceases business on 1 December 1998. Trading stock (valued at cost) was £1,250 and the only unsold assets was a car which cost £2,750 in 1990. Input tax credit is disallowed on motor cars, so this asset is ignored for the purposes of the deemed supply. Output tax on trading stock would be £1,250 @ 17.5% = £218.75. Since this is less than £250 it is not deemed to be supplied.

In principle, the disposal of a business as a going concern is a supply made in the course or furtherance of business. It follows, therefore, that the assets concerned are charged to tax. However, two reliefs are available:

(a)   If the purchaser is a taxable person who intends to carry on the same kind of business, the supply is outside the scope of tax. This exemption applies if the business is transferred before the transferor's registration is cancelled.

(b)   If the business is sold to a taxable person the deemed supply of business assets at the date of deregistration is cancelled.

3.12 Voluntary registration

(a) Actual traders

A trader who **makes** taxable supplies, but is not currently liable to registration under the historical or future registration provision, is eligible for voluntary registration. The Commissioners will register him, if he so request, from the date of his request or a mutually agreed earlier date.

The deregistration provisions given above apply to such a trader whether his turnover remains below the current registration limits or subsequently exceed them. He is not required to notify the Commissioners if his turnover subsequently exceeds the current registration limits.

(b) Intending traders

A trader who carries on a business and **intends** to make taxable supplies in the course or furtherance of that business is not liable to registration under the future registration provisions while his intention is unfulfilled. He is, however, eligible for voluntary registration. The Commissioners will register him, if he so requests from the date of his request or a mutually agreed earlier date.

The deregistration provisions given above apply to such a trader once he has begun making taxable supplies. Until that time, however, special deregistration provisions apply:

- If he ceases to intend making taxable supplies, he must notify the Commissioners of that fact within thirty days. The Commissioners will cancel his registration from the date on which he gave up his intention to make taxable supplies or a mutually agreed later date.

- If he no longer wishes to be registered, he may request to be deregistered. The Commissioners will deregister him if they are satisfied that he is not liable to registration under the historical or future registration provisions. Deregistration takes effect from the date of the request or a mutually agreed later date.

(c) Representative offices

A special form of registration is available for overseas traders who maintain an office in the UK, but do not supply goods and services here.

3.13 Partnerships

A partnership registration continues when a partner retires or a new partner is admitted provided that the firm continues to exist. However, the dissolution of a partnership will result in a deregistration, even if a former partner carries on the business as a sole trader. The former partner is required to register in his own name, although a joint election could be made for the partnership registration to be transferred to him. Admissions and retirements must be notified to the Commissioners.

Partners are jointly liable for partnership debts. A retired partner is jointly liable for the firm's VAT liabilities arising between the date of his retirement and the date it is notified to the Commissioners. He should therefore make the required notification as a matter of urgency on retirement.

3.14   Transfer of a business as a going concern

Where a business carried on by a taxable person is transferred as a going concern this is not treated as a supply of goods or services, but rather as a change in the taxable person carrying on the business. The transferee can even apply to retain the VAT registration number if the transferor ceases business entirely. However in this case the transferee would also inherit any liability for VAT unpaid by the transferor.

If the transferee was not registered for VAT, but his taxable turnover for the year prior to the date of transfer exceeded £50,000 (£49,000 for transfers before 1 April 1998) the transferee must notify the Commissioners of his liability for VAT unpaid by the transferor.

As regards his liability to become registered after the transfer (if he was not then liable), the supplies made by the business before the date of transfer are treated as if they had been made by the transferee.

| Conclusion | A trader may be required to register by reference to his historical turnover or his future turnover. Traders may also register voluntarily. A registered trader ceases to be liable to registration when he ceases to be make taxable supplies. A registered trader may deregister voluntarily if the value of his anticipated taxable turnover for the next year does not exceed £48,000. |

4   OUTPUT TAX

4.1   Introduction

Output tax is the tax charged on supplies made by a taxable person. This section deals with two matters:

(a)   The manner in which the tax due on an individual supply is calculated; and

(b)   The manner in which the tax due to the Commissioners for a prescribed accounting period is calculated.

4.2   Value

Tax is charged on the value of the goods or services supplied. Where the consideration for a supply is paid in money, value represents the trader's tax-exclusive selling price less the amount of any cash discount offered. Thus if Anthony's tax-exclusive selling price is £1,000, and he offers a cash discount of 3.75% for payment within seven days, VAT is charged on £962.50 (ie, £1,000 less 3.75% thereof = £37.50). This is **not** amended if the customer fails to qualify for discount and has to pay the higher net amount of £1,000.

Open market value is the tax-exclusive amount which a customer would pay if the price is not influenced by any commercial, financial or other relationship between himself and the seller. VAT is charged on open market value in the following circumstances:

(a)   The supply is made for a consideration which comprises something other than money eg, a barter transaction whereby chickens are exchanged for petrol:

(b)   The supply is made for a consideration which comprises partly money and partly something other than money eg, a new car is sold for £1,000 plus a used car taken in part exchange.

(c)   The supply is made to a connected person for a consideration below market value and the Commissioners issue a direction that VAT is to be accounted for on future supplies by reference to open market value'

Open market value does not apply where an employer supplies catering facilities (eg, works canteen) or accommodation to employees. If the employee pays nothing for such goods or services the value is taken as nil. If the consideration is wholly or partly in money the value is taken as the money element alone.

4.3   The time of supply (the tax point)

Tax is charged in accordance with the legislation in force at the time when goods and services are treated as being supplied. As a general principle, goods are treated as supplied when they are collected, delivered or made available to a customer and services are treated as supplied when they are performed. This is known as the basic tax point.

The basic tax point is amended in two situations:

(a)   **A tax invoice is issued or a payment is received before the basic tax point.** In these circumstances the date of issue or date of payment is the time when the supply is treated as taking place.

(b)   **A tax invoice is issued within fourteen days after the basic tax point.** In these circumstances the date of issue of the invoice is the time when the supply is treated as taking place. The fourteen day period can be extended in a particular case if the Commissioners so agree.

An invoice is 'issued' when it is sent or given to a customer. Thus, preparing an invoice does not by itself create a tax point until something positive is done with it, such as posting it to the customer. In principle, a tax invoice need be issued only in respect of a supply charged to tax at the standard rate. An invoice issued in respect of a zero-rated supply is not a tax invoice and does not create a tax point.

A payment must be unconditional before it creates a tax point.

When the rate of tax changes, or when a particular class of supply is moved from one tax category to another (eg, zero-rate to standard rate), traders may elect that the time of supply is governed by the basic tax point alone if the basic tax point falls on one side of the change and an event in (a) or (b) falls on the other side of the change.

The legislation sets out special rules for certain supplies of goods which do not fit naturally into the above scheme. In particular:

(a)   **Goods on sale or return.** The time of supply is the earlier of the date when the sale is adopted by the customer, twelve months after dispatch of the goods or the date of a tax invoice being issued and a payment received.

(b)   **Continuous supplies.** Supplies such as electricity (goods) and tax advice (services) do not have a basic tax point. The time of supply is the earlier of a tax invoice being issued and a payment received.

   If the supplier wishes he may issue a tax invoice once a year in advance showing the periodical payments and their due dates. In this case there is a separate tax point for every amount due being the earlier of the due date and the date on which payment is received.

(c)   **Periodical payments.** Payments under long term contracts such as leases and royalty agreements do not have a basic tax point. In brief, the time of supply is the earlier of the time when a tax invoice is issued or a payment is received.

(d)   **Sales under hire purchase.** A hire purchase contract gives rise to three supplies: the goods (which may be taxed at the standard or zero -rate, and may or may not attract relief under the used goods schemes); the interest charges thereon (exempt when disclosed as a separate amount); and the option fee (exempt when under £10). Each supply has its own time of supply.

(e)   **Fuel for private use.** Fuel for private use is supplied at the date it is put into the tank of the vehicle.

These rules are generally important when a change of rate applies, eg, when the standard tax rate increased from 15% to 17.5% from April 1991 or when the scope of VAT is increased eg, when supplies of domestic fuel (gas/electricity) ceased to be zero-rated on 1 April 1994.

4.4   Activity

On 30 November 1998, Oak Ltd ordered a new felling machine, and on 16 December 1998, paid a deposit of £25,000. The machine was despatched to Oak Ltd on 31 December 1998. On 12 January 1999 an invoice was issued to Oak Ltd for the balance due of £75,000. This was paid on 20 January 1999.

What is the tax point for

(a)   £25,000 deposit; and
(b)   the balance of £75,000.

4.5   Activity solution

(a)   **£25,000 deposit**

The basic tax point is the date of despatch, 31 December 1998. As the deposit was paid before the date of despatch, this is the actual tax point ie, 16 December 1998.

(b)   **The balance of £75,000**

As an invoice was issued within 14 days of the basic tax point, this is the actual tax point ie, 12 January 1999.

4.6   Tax invoices

Registered taxable persons making supplies to other taxable persons are required to issue a document known as a tax invoice not later than thirty days after the time when a taxable supply of goods or services is treated as being made. The original tax invoice is sent to the customer and forms his evidence of input tax; a copy must be kept by the supplier to support his calculations of output tax. A tax invoice need not be issued if the supplies are zero-rated or if the customer is not a taxable person. A tax invoice is a normal commercial invoice which contains the following particulars:

(a)   an identifying number;

(b)   the date of supply (see above);

(c)   the supplier's name and address and registration number;

(d)   the customer's name and address;

(e)   the type of supply made ie, sale, hire purchase, loan, exchange, hire, making goods from the customer's material, sale on commission, or sale or return;

(f)   a description which identifies the goods or services supplied;

(g)   the value (expressed in sterling) and rate of tax for each supply;

(h)   the total tax-exclusive amount expressed in sterling;

(i)   the rate of any cash discount offered; and

(j)   the amount of tax payable (expressed in sterling).

The Commissioners have the power to approve as tax invoices self-billing arrangements under which a taxable person who is a customer may make out tax invoices on behalf of his supplier who is himself a taxable person. A taxable person who wishes to self bill must get the consent of his supplier. He should then write to the Commissioners to obtain approval. Clearly the supplier must not himself also raise a tax invoice for the same transaction.

4.7   Accounting for output tax

The output tax due from a customer is shown on the tax invoice issued to him. The supplier must account to the Commissioners for all such tax charged during a prescribed accounting period. The following provisions apply when a customer fails to pay a supplier:

(a)   If there is a good commercial reason (eg, goods damaged in transit), the supplier may issue a credit note reducing the value of the supply and tax due thereon to an amount agreed with the customer. The tax so credited is deducted from the amount due to the Commissioners.

(b)   If the customer is bankrupt or insolvent, and thus unable to pay, the supplier may claim bad debt relief, (see below).

(c)   If non-payment arises for any other reason (eg, the customer disappears), relief is available. This is discussed below.

An alternative form of accounting is available for traders satisfying certain conditions. Such traders continue to issue tax invoices in accordance with the normal rules, but output tax for a prescribed accounting period represents the total amount of VAT included in payments received from customers in the period. Similarly, input tax is the total amount of VAT included in payments made by the trader. This is known as cash accounting and is described in detail later in this chapter.

4.8   Bad debt relief

The relief is claimed by including the amount to recover in the total of input tax on the VAT return.

Relief is given where:

(a)   a supply of goods and services has been made; and
(b)   output tax has been accounted for and paid by the supplier; and
(c)   the whole or part of the debt has been written off as bad in the supplier's books; and
(d)   at least 6 months has elapsed since the date the payment was due.

If there has been a series of supplies any payments made by the customer must be allocated on a FIFO basis unless the customer allocated a payment to a particular supply **and** paid in full.

On a claim by the supplier, relief will be given for the VAT chargeable by reference to the outstanding amount. The outstanding amount is simply the amount of the debt that has been written off as bad, less any amount subsequently received in respect of that bad debt. The outstanding amount must be restricted by any amounts owing to the customer by the claimant for which there is right of set-off.

The supplier must notify the customer of any bad debt relief claimed. If the customer has claimed credit for the input tax, this must be repaid to Customs and Excise (by adjusting the next VAT return).

4.9   Retailers

In broad terms, a retailer is someone who supplies goods and services to the general public rather than to other traders. He is not necessarily a shopkeeper. Thus, a hairdresser is just as much a retailer as a newsagent or garage proprietor.

Retailers are not required to calculate the VAT content of individual supplies and do not have to issue a tax invoice unless a taxable person requests one. Their output tax liabilities are calculated by a three stage process.

(a)   **Gross takings.** The first stage is to calculate gross takings for a prescribed accounting period. This is the sales (including any credit sales) made during the period.

Note that credit sales are recorded separately and cash received from credit customers is excluded from cash sales. VAT on the credit sales is then calculated at the rate in force on the date of sale - not the date of payment.

(b)   **Retail scheme.** The second stage is to allocate gross takings between standard rate and zero-rate supplies. This is done by applying the rules set out in the retail scheme adopted by the retailer. There are several different retail schemes available. Where a retailer is using technology which identify and records every individual sale (eg, bar code readers) the Commissioners will not allow the use of a retail scheme.

(c)   **Output tax.** Standard rate takings calculated in (b) represent a tax-inclusive sum. The tax element is 7/47 of this sum.

Retailers may issue a less detailed tax invoice if the consideration for a supply is £100 or less. This must show the following information:

(a)   the retailer's name, address and VAT registration number;
(b)   the date of supply;
(c)   a description of the goods or services supplied;
(d)   the consideration for the supply; and
(e)   the rate of tax in force at the time of supply.

4.10   Secondhand goods

Retailers who sell virtually any kind of second-hand goods are entitled to calculate their output tax on what is referred to as the margin (ie, sale price of the goods less cost price of the goods) rather than the sale price.

The records which retailers are required to keep may be summarised as follows:

(a)   **Stock book.** This contains detailed information identifying individual goods; the person from whom they were bought; the person to whom they were sold; the cost and sale prices; the margin; the output tax due.

(b)   **Sales invoice.** This sets out specified information and a certificate signed by both the retailer and his customer.

(c)   **Purchase invoice.** This sets out specified information and a certificate signed by both the retailer and the person from whom the goods were purchased.

The following points should be noted:

(a)   Goods may **not** be sold under the scheme if a **tax invoice** is received in respect of the purchase or issued in respect of the sale.

(b)   Expenses incurred in respect of the goods are not taken into account in calculating the margin. Thus, if Anthony buys a used car for £1,250, spends £225 in putting it into a saleable condition, and sells if for £2,100, the margin is £2,100 – £1,250 = £850.

(c)   Output tax is calculated by applying the current VAT fraction to the margin. Thus, Anthony must account to the Commissioners for 7/47 × £850 = £126.60.

(d)   If cost exceeds the sale price, no output tax is due. Thus if Bernard buys a used car for £1,400 and sells it for £1,250, he is not required to account to the Commissioners for output tax.

(e)   A system of 'global' accounting is available for businesses dealing in low value margin scheme goods (eg, postage stamps). Rather than accounting for output tax item by item, traders can account on the basis of total purchases and sales in each tax period.

4.11   Deemed supplies

It will be recalled that the following events are treated as a supply for tax purposes:

(a)   Goods supplied without consideration eg, gifts of goods and goods consumed privately by a sole proprietor.

(b)   Business assets used for private or non-business purposes eg, using a business car for non business travelling.

(c)   Motor cars self-supplied by motor dealers.

(d)   Fuel provided for private use for an employee, sole trader, or partner, at less than the original cost to, or manufacturing cost to, the taxable person.

The value of the supply is:

- cost for items (a) and (c);
- full cost of providing the service for (b); and
- scale rate for (d) as follows:

	Three month period		One month period	
	Scale charge	VAT	Scale charge	VAT
	£	£	£	£
Diesel engine				
2,000 cc or less	196	29.19	65	9.68
More than 2,000 cc	248	36.93	82	12.21
Petrol engine				
1,400 cc or less	212	31.57	70	10.42
1,401 cc to 2,000 cc	268	39.91	89	13.25
More than 2,000 cc	396	58.97	132	19.65

Conclusion Output tax is charged on the value of goods or services supplied by a taxable person. The critical areas of VAT for examination purposes from this section are:

- the time of supply
- the rules on and importance of tax invoices; and
- accounting for output tax.

5 INPUT TAX

5.1 Introduction

Input tax is the VAT paid by a taxable person on goods and services supplied to him and on goods which he imports. Input tax is recoverable from the Commissioners provided certain conditions are met. This section describes the conditions to be met.

In general, VAT paid by anyone other than a taxable person is not recoverable from the Commissioners. There are a number of exceptions to this general rule and the principal exception is described in this section.

5.2 Conditions for obtaining input tax credit

The strict wording of the legislation, and case law derived from it, indicate that a number of conditions must be met before VAT is available for credit as input tax:

(a) **The claimant must be a taxable person when the VAT was incurred.** The following exceptions are subject to numerous conditions which are strictly enforced.   Credit is available in respect of:

- goods acquired before registration or before a company is incorporated and held in stock at that date:

- services acquired in the six months before registration or before a company is incorporated; and

- services relating to a registration period supplied after a taxable person has been deregistered.

(b) **The supply must be to the taxable person making the claim.** There is an exception for business use petrol purchased by the employee of a taxable person where the employee is reimbursed.   Businesses are allowed to recover the agreed VAT element in mileage allowance paid to employees even though the VAT-able supply was made to the employee, not the claimant.

(c)   **The supply or importation must be supported by evidence. The following documentary evidence is required:**

- a tax invoice, in respect of supplies from a taxable person;
- an invoice, in respect of supplies of international services received from abroad;
- a customs entry, in respect of goods imported or withdrawn from bond.

In the case of taxable inputs under £25 purchased through coin operated equipment (eg, telephone boxes, parking meters) a deduction is allowed for the VAT suffered without production of a tax invoice.

(d)   **The tax must comprise UK or Isle of Man VAT.**

(e)   **The claimant must use the goods or services for business purposes.** Thus, personal expenses cannot be eligible for input tax credit. An apportionment is made where goods and services are acquired partly for business purposes and partly for private purposes.

Where goods or services supplied to a company are used by that company in connection with the provision of domestic accommodation to a director of that company, the goods or services will not be treated as supplied for business purposes. The input tax will, therefore, not be available for credit.

A director includes any person who acts as a director, and the exclusion extends to domestic accommodation provided to people connected with a director (ie, spouse, relatives, spouse's relatives, and their spouses).

(f)   **The amount due for credit is the tax properly chargeable on the supply**. Thus, if A charges VAT of £100 on an invoice issued to B, and the amount due is only £50, B can obtain input tax credit for £50. If he has paid £100, he must recover the amount overpaid from A.

(g)   **The tax must not be excluded from credit.** See below.

5.3   Input tax excluded from credit.

Input tax on the following goods and services is excluded from credit:

(a)   **Business entertainment.** This means hospitality of any kind eg, food, drink, accommodation or recreational facilities. There are two exceptions. Input tax credit is allowed for expenses incurred in entertaining:

- Directors and employees (but not their guests) eg, a staff party.
- Other persons under a reciprocal arrangement.

Irrecoverable input tax on entertaining cannot be deducted for income or corporation tax purposes

(b)   **Goods installed in new dwellings.** Input tax credit is restricted to the following goods:
- Materials ie, materials normally used for building purposes.
- Builders' hardware eg, door hinges.
- Sanitary ware eg, a bathroom suite.
- Articles of a kind ordinarily installed by builders as fixtures.

These categories do not include fitted or prefabricated furniture (other than for kitchens), carpets and gas or electrical appliances (other than for space and/or water heating).

(c)   **Motor cars.** Input tax credit is generally allowed **only** when new cars are acquired for resale by a motor dealer, for hire in certain circumstances to disabled person, or to be converted into vehicles which are not motor cars.

The general rule, therefore, is that input tax on the purchase of a motor car is not recoverable. However, taxi firms, self-drive hire firms, and driving schools are able to recover input tax on the purchase of cars used for those purposes: but

- on sale of the car output tax must be accounted for on the full selling price;
- if the car is put to a non-qualifying use this will be treated as a self-supply.

The rule is also relaxed for cars bought wholly for business use. In practice this only enables input tax on cars purchased by leasing companies for leasing to be recovered. Where a business leases a car which it uses partly for private motoring, only 50% of the input tax on the leasing charge is recoverable.

Input tax remains irrecoverable on the purchase of all other business cars where there is any private use.

5.4   Partial exemption

Traders who make both taxable and exempt supplies are given credit for only part of the input tax they incur. The amount available for credit is calculated by one or other of the following methods:

(a)   **Standard method**

This works by analysing input tax under the following three headings:

- Input tax on goods and services wholly used for the purpose of making taxable supplies. This tax is wholly available for credit.

- Input tax on goods and services used wholly for making exempt supplies. This tax is wholly disallowed.

- The remainder eg, non-attributable input tax on overheads. The amount available for credit is found by apportionment.

The non-attributable input tax available for credit is found by using the fraction:

$$\frac{\text{Total taxable supplies}}{\text{Total supplies}}$$

In calculating this proportion:

- exclude supplies made on capital goods
- exclude self-supply
- exclude, *inter alia* the following supplies made where these are incidental

    - sale of freehold, or grant of lease for more than 21 years, by a constructor
    - sale/letting of land and buildings
    - supply of exempt financial services.

The ratio is computed as a percentage and, if not a whole number, rounded up to the next whole number.

If input tax wholly or partly attributed to exempt supplies is below the following *de minimis* limit, all such tax is available for credit. This tax is known as exempt input tax. The limit is an amount not exceeding £625 per month on average for any VAT account period.

Also, in order to reclaim all input tax, the exempt input tax must not be more than 50% of the input tax incurred on all purchases. This provision was introduced to prevent traders who make exempt supplies (eg, dentists) from selling items such as toothbrushes, in order to create taxable supplies, thus enabling them to reclaim all their input tax.

(b)   **Special method**

Any other method may be adopted with the Commissioners' agreement.

Traders are required to rework their input tax credits on an annual basis. Any under or over-declaration is then accounted to the Commissioners or reclaimed from them. A tax year for this purpose is generally to 31 March, 30 April or 31 May according to the trader's registration stagger group.

5.5   Input tax credit and cash accounting

The normal rule is that input tax on supplies and importations is available for credit in the prescribed accounting period in which the tax became chargeable.

However, an alternative form of accounting, cash accounting, is available for traders approved by the Commissioners. Such traders are entitled to credit for the total amount for VAT included in payments made to suppliers in a prescribed accounting period. However, VAT in respect of goods purchased on hire purchase terms and VAT on imported goods continues to be credited in accordance with the normal rules.

For a trader to be eligible to use the cash accounting scheme his taxable turnover must not exceed £350,000 p.a., all his returns due to date must have been submitted, if any tax remains outstanding he has agreed with the Commissioners to pay it by specified instalments and for the past year he must not have been convicted of a VAT offence nor been subject to a VAT penalty for conduct involving dishonesty.

A trader must leave the scheme if his taxable turnover exceeds £350,000 by at least 25%, or is expected to do so in the next year. A person may leave the scheme at the end of a prescribed accounting period if he derives no benefit from it or if his accounting records are unsuitable for cash accounting. It is not necessary for the trader to maintain detailed sales and purchase records in addition to an analysed cash book (or similar).

5.6   Interaction with capital allowances

With the exception of motor cars (see above) there are no special rules applicable to a trader's plant and machinery as opposed to his trading stock.

Thus VAT paid on purchases of capital items such as plant and equipment is available for credit as input tax except where used for the purposes of a business making only exempt supplies. When capital goods are sold second hand by a taxable person VAT is chargeable on the sale as on any other supply.

Where capital goods are used by a taxable person the VAT charged on them can be recovered and capital allowances are calculated on the net cost to the business ie, the tax-exclusive price. Where the capital goods are used by the business which is not registered for VAT or whose supplies are exempt no tax can be recovered and capital allowances are calculated on the tax-inclusive price. This is also the position for business cars. Where supplies of a business are partially exempt, then only part of the tax will be recovered and the tax not recovered can be added to the tax-exclusive price to arrive at the cost for capital allowances.

Tax charged on the sale of capital goods is ignored for capital allowances purposes - only the net proceeds are deducted from tax written down value. It will be recalled that output tax on most secondhand assets is calculated on the 'margin' and that no tax arises where sale proceeds are below cost (see above). A certain amount of care is required to ensure that the correct VAT-exclusive amount is brought into the computation.

5.7   Imports

VAT is charged on imported goods from countries outside the EC as if it were a duty of customs. As a general principle, therefore, it is collected at a port or airport at the same time as customs duties, excise duties and other import levies. It follows, therefore, that the Commissioners collect VAT direct from the importer.

The system of immediate payment of tax can cause serious inconvenience to importers dealing with a large volume of individual consignments. Two reliefs are available:

(a)   **Duty deferment system.** Approved traders pay tax arising in a calendar month by direct debit on the fifteenth day of the following month.

(b)   **Postponed accounting system.** Taxable persons importing goods valued below £1,300 by post may account for tax by making an entry in their tax return for the prescribed accounting period in which the goods are imported.

Where imported goods are immediately removed to a bonded warehouse or free zone, payment of VAT is broadly postponed until the goods are removed from bond or the free zone.

Goods may be brought in to the UK without payment of tax provided they are exported within stated time limits. The goods remain under strict customs control while they remain the UK.

> **Conclusion**   Input tax, which is the VAT paid by a taxable person on goods and services supplied to him and on goods which he imports is recoverable provided certain conditions are met.
>
> The most important areas from this section, for examination purposes are:
> * the conditions for obtaining input tax credit;
> * non-deductible input tax;
> * the cash accounting scheme.

6   CHAPTER SUMMARY

This is the first chapter on VAT.

The following areas were covered:

* the scope of VAT   -   taxable transactions and taxable persons;
* supplies   -   chargeable supplies
                       -    supplies of goods and services
                       -    exempt and taxable supplies

- taxable persons
  - registration
  - deregistration
- output tax
  - the tax point
  - tax invoices
  - accounting for output tax
  - bad debt relief
- input tax
  - conditions for obtaining input tax credit
  - non-deductible input tax
  - partial exemption
  - cash accounting scheme

7   SELF TEST QUESTIONS

7.1   What is a chargeable supply? (2.3)

7.2   What is the consequence of making an exempt supply? (2.5)

7.3   What are the consequences of deregistration? (3.11)

7.4   In what situations may a trader register for VAT voluntarily? (3.12)

7.5   In what situations is the basic tax point amended? (4.3)

7.6   What particulars must a tax invoice contain? (4.6)

7.7   How can relief be obtained for the VAT element of a bad debt? (4.8)

7.8   What are the conditions for obtaining input tax credit? (5.2)

7.9   What is the standard method for working out the input tax credit when both taxable and exempt supplies are made? (5.4)

7.10   How does a registered trader making only taxable supplies obtain relief for input tax on cars purchased for his salesmen? (5.6)

8   EXAMINATION TYPE QUESTION

8.1   Ken

(a)   Ken has a market stall, and sells mostly fruit and vegetables and a small amount of other food.

He started trading on 1 September 1998, and anticipates his turnover will be as follows:

	£
One month ended 30 September 1998	20,000
Quarter ended 31 December 1998	46,000
Quarter ended 31 March 1999	48,000
Quarter ended 30 June 1999	51,000

Assume that the amounts accrue evenly.

You are required to advise Ken if he should register for VAT, and if so, when the Commissioners should be notified.

(b)   Toby's input tax and supplies made in the quarter to 31 December 1998 is analysed as follows:

		£
(a)	Input tax wholly re-taxable supplies	23,250
(b)	Input tax wholly re-exempt supplies	14,000
(c)	Non-attributable input tax	28,000
(d)	Value (excluding VAT) of taxable supplies	250,000
(e)	Value of exempt supplies	100,000

Calculate the deductible input tax assuming that Toby uses the standard method of attributing input tax.

9   ANSWER TO EXAMINATION TYPE QUESTION

9.1   Ken

(a)   Traders become liable to register for VAT at the end of any month if the value of taxable supplies in the previous 12 months exceeded £50,000.

Ken will therefore be liable to register for VAT from 30 November 1998, and he must notify the Commissioners by 30 December 1998. Ken will be registered from 1 January 1999.

As all of Ken's sales are likely to be zero-rated he may request exemption from registration. If a small proportion of the other foodstuffs are standard rated, the Commissioners may allow exemption from registration, provided Ken would normally receive re-payment of VAT if registered.

(b)   Deductible input tax

	£
Attributable input tax	23,250

Non-attributable input tax $\times \dfrac{\text{Value of taxable supplies}}{\text{Value of total supplies}}$

	£
$£28,000 \times \dfrac{250,000}{250,000 + 100,000}$ (72%)	20,160
Deductible input tax	43,410

The exempt input tax is £21,840 (28,000 − 20,160 + 14,000) and as this amounts to more than £625 per month on average it is all non-deductible.

26 VAT

INTRODUCTION & LEARNING OBJECTIVES

This is the second of two chapters on Value Added Tax. It deals with the administrative aspects of VAT and the important groups of zero rated and exempt supplies.

When you have studied this chapter you should have learned the following:

- VAT returns and records;
- Assessments and appeals;
- Penalties;
- Zero-rated supplies; and
- Exempt supplies.

1 TAX RETURNS AND RECORDS

1.1 Normal accounting system

Taxable persons account for tax by reference to prescribed accounting periods. Traders who pay tax normally have a prescribed accounting period of three months, while traders who normally receive repayment of tax have prescribed accounting periods of one month.

To ensure that the flow of VAT returns is spread evenly over the year, the three-month tax periods are staggered. The Commissioners do this by allocating tax periods according to the class of trade being carried on. There are three trade groups and registered persons within each group are given three-month tax periods ending on the last days of the following months.

First group	Second group	Third group
June	July	August
September	October	November
December	January	February
March	April	May

A trader may apply for tax periods which fit in with his own financial year, even where this is not based on calendar months. Applications should be made to the Commissioners when notifying liability to, or applying for, registration.

The trader's first prescribed accounting period starts on the effective date of registration and his final period ends on the date this registration is cancelled.

Tax returns are issued by VAT Central Unit. Returns must be completed and returned to VAT Central Unit together with any tax shown to be due within thirty days after the end of a prescribed accounting period. Any tax shown to be repayable to a trader is repaid to him by VAT Central Unit, normally within fourteen days or so. Delayed repayments of tax attract repayment supplement.

The Commissioners are not liable to repay VAT which had been paid to them more than three years before the date of the repayment claim.

Furthermore the Commissioners can deny claims for overpaid tax to be refunded if it would 'unjustly enrich' the claimant. For example, this might apply where the refund cannot practically be passed on to the claimant's customers who have been charged tax incorrectly.

On the other hand, a trader has a statutory right to claim interest from the Commissioners, where, as a result of an error on the part of Customs, too much VAT was paid or underclaimed or where he was prevented from recovering VAT at the proper time.

1.2 Annual accounting system

An alternative accounting system is available for traders approved by the Commissioners. In brief, traders have a prescribed accounting period (described as an accounting year) of twelve months which may be expected to coincide with the financial year for accounting purposes. A return for an accounting year must be furnished within two calendar months after it has ended. Nine payments on account are made at the end of the months 4-12 inclusive of the financial year and a balancing payment when the return is furnished. Each payment on account represents 10% of the estimated tax due for the financial year. Annual accounting is only available to traders with an annual turnover not exceeding £300,000.

Traders with an annual turnover not exceeding £100,000 are entitled under the annual accounting scheme instead to make three quarterly payments each of 20% of the previous years net VAT liability. In addition, if the annual liability is below £2,000 the trader can choose not to make interim payments but pay the full actual liability for a year two months after the year end.

1.3 Example: annual accounting

John's financial year ends on 31 December 1998 and his annual turnover is about £140,000. He applies to adopt the annual accounting scheme and approval is given. The Commissioners estimate his tax liability for the year at £3,600. In the event, his liability is £3,821.

What returns and payments must he make for the year?

1.4 Solution

He must furnish a return no later than 28 February 1999. Payments are made as follows:

		£
Monthly payments commencing 30 April 1998	9 @ £360	3,240
Final payment no later than 28 February 1999	£(3,821 – 3,240)	581
		3,821

1.5 Failure to furnish returns or pay tax

Failure to submit a return or pay tax gives rise to a liability to either civil penalties or default surcharge. It may also lead to the issue of an estimated assessment against which there is no right of appeal. Any tax repaid in error by VAT Central Unit may also be recovered by way of an assessment, but in this case a right of appeal is given.

1.6 Records and accounts

Records and accounts must be kept of all goods and services received and supplied in the course of a business. No particular form is specified but they must be sufficient to allow the VAT return to be completed and to allow the Commissioners to check the return. Records must be kept up to date and must be preserved for six years. In practice the main records which must be kept are as follows:

(a)   Copies of all tax invoices issued.
(b)   A record of all outputs eg, a sales day book.
(c)   Evidence supporting claims for input tax credit.
(d)   A record of all inputs eg, a purchases day book.
(e)   VAT account.

Where a purchases day book is not kept inputs are sometimes based on payments made to suppliers as recorded in a suitable analysed cash book.

| Conclusion | Traders generally account for VAT by reference to three month tax periods, though certain traders may have a twelve month tax period instead. VAT is a self-assessed tax and a taxable person must keep sufficient records and accounts to allow the VAT return to be completed and to allow the Commissioners to check the return. |

2   ASSESSMENTS AND APPEALS

2.1   Control visits

VAT is a self-assessed tax, and it is not unnatural that the Commissioners should wish to conduct spot checks to ensure that traders are properly carrying out the obligations placed upon them by the legislation. These spot checks are known as control visits. From the Commissioner's point of view their principal purpose is to provide an opportunity for officers to verify the accuracy of tax returns rendered by reference to the prime records available. They also serve as a deterrent to fraud. From a trader's point of view, control visits provide an ideal opportunity to sort out any difficulties which have arisen in practice.

The Commissioners have power to enter business premises, inspect documents, including profit and loss accounts and balance sheets, take samples, and inspect computers and gaming machines. As a reserve power, they may search premises when authorised to do so by a warrant granted by a Justice of the Peace, and may obtain documents from a third party when authorised by a production order granted by a Justice of the Peace.

2.2   Assessments

An officer may find that a tax return is incomplete or incorrect. If so, he can issue an assessment to collect the tax which has been underpaid by the trader or overpaid to him.

An assessment must be made to the officer's best judgement.

An assessment must be made within two years from the end of the prescribed accounting period to which it relates, or if later, within one year after the necessary evidence came into the officer's possession. This is subject to an over-riding three year time limit. However, an assessment may not be made more than three years after a person's death. The general three year time limit is increased to twenty years where tax has been lost due to fraud or dishonest conduct (eg, a criminal conviction or a civil default). However, where a person dies, if an assessment under the twenty year limit would have been in time at the date of death, it may be made at any time in the three years thereafter.

Interest may be charged in certain cases (see below).

2.3   Appeals

VAT has a very high incidence. It requires a local first tier court to resolve the treatment of borderline cases and protect the interest of both the Commissioners and the taxpayer. Appeals in connection with VAT are made to an independent tribunal - the VAT Tribunal - which has centres in London, Manchester, Edinburgh and Belfast.

An appeal cannot be entertained unless the trader has rendered all the returns he is due to make and has paid the tax thereon.

The normal time limit for appealing is thirty days, but where a taxpayer has asked Customs and Excise to reconsider a matter they will usually notify him within the thirty day period that the time to appeal will be extended to twenty one days after review of the case has been completed.

If a taxpayer is unable to resolve the matter with the Customs and Excise, he should complete and sign a notice of appeal and send it to the appropriate tribunal centre within the specified time limits.

VAT Tribunals have a statutory constitution and their rules of procedure are formulated by statutory instrument (the **Value Added Tax Tribunal Rules 1986).** A tribunal consists of a chairman sitting either with two other members (majority decision necessary) or with one other member (chairman has casting vote) or alone. Exceptionally a tribunal may sit in private eg, if a public hearing would defeat natural justice. The hearing may proceed even though one party has failed to attend. Clearly his chance of success would be minimal. A hearing may be postponed by the Chairman, normally with the agreement of both parties. Adequate notice should be given.

Costs may be awarded against the unsuccessful party to an appeal unless the winning party's conduct makes this inappropriate.

An unsuccessful party to an appeal may appeal to the High Court (Queen's Bench Division) on a matter or law, and thereafter the Court of Appeal and House of Lords. The Queen's Bench Division may allow a leap frog appeal direct to the House of Lords. The parties may consent for certain appeals to leapfrog from a tribunal direct to the Court of Appeal.

An appeal may be withdrawn by an oral or written notification to the Commissioners. Similarly, both parties may come to an oral or written agreement that the appeal should be determined in agreed terms. In either case, the appellant may resile from the agreement if he changes his mind within thirty days.

3   PENALTIES AND INTEREST

3.1   Criminal penalties

Offence	Maximum penalty
Fraudulent evasion of VAT.	Unlimited fine and/or 7 years' imprisonment.
Provision of false information with intent to deceive.	Unlimited fine and/or 7 years' imprisonment.
Making false statements.	Unlimited fine and/or 7 years' imprisonment.
Where a person deals in goods where he has reason to believe that VAT will be avoided on the supply.	3 × Tax evaded or £2,000 if greater
Obstructing inspection of a computer	£1,000

3.2   Civil penalties

FA 1985 introduced a system of civil penalties to punish the defaults set out in the table below, some of which were previously criminal offences. Civil penalties are assessed.

Default	Penalty	Notes
Any action or omission involving dishonesty for the purpose of evading VAT	100% of VAT evaded	2
Serious misdeclaration or neglect resulting in the understatement of liability (or overstatement of repayment) on a return, or in not notifying the Commissioners of an understatement of an assessment (more detail given later in text)	Up to 15% of tax understated	1, 2
Failure to notify liability to registration	Greater of £50 or 15% of relevant tax	1, 2, 4
Tax invoice issued by unregistered person	Greater of £50 or 15% of relevant tax	1, 2
Removing distrained goods subject to a walking possession agreement	50% of tax recoverable by distraint	1
Failure to notify that taxable supplies are no longer made	Daily penalty	1,3
Failure to keep records, furnish information or produce documents	Daily penalty	1,3
Failure to comply with regulations	Daily penalty	1,3
Failure to furnish tax returns or pay tax due thereon	Daily penalty	1
Failure to preserve records	£500	1
Providing an incorrect certificate regarding zero-rating or exemption of supplies of fuel or land or buildings	100% of VAT which would apply if certificate correct	1

Notes:

(1)   No penalty arises if there is a reasonable excuse for the conduct concerned. An insufficiency of funds is not a reasonable excuse. Nor is dilatoriness or inaccuracy by an agent (eg, an accountant preparing tax returns for a client).

(2)   This penalty may be mitigated (ie, reduced) up to 100% if appropriate (eg, where the person co-operated in the investigation of his tax affairs).

(3)   The daily penalty depends upon the number of previous failures in the previous two years, thus: no previous failures (£5), one failure (£10) and two or more failures (£15).

Maximum penalty: 100 days at the appropriate daily rate. Minimum penalty: £50.

(4)   The minimum penalty for failure to register on time is £50.

The maximum penalty is a percentage of the tax due (depending on the period of delay between the date when the trader should have been registered and the date the Commissioners were notified).

Delay period	%
Registration up to 9 months late	5
Registration over 9 months up to 18 months late	10
Registration over 18 months late	15

3.3   Interest

A charge to interest will arise if:

- the Commissioners find that VAT has been underdeclared or overclaimed on previous VAT returns; or

- an assessment has been paid which is later found to be too low; or

- under declarations or overclaims from previous returns are notified as voluntary disclosures by declaring them to the VAT office.

Note that interest is not charged if an under declaration or overclaim, which does not exceed £2,000 (net), is adjusted in the following return or is the subject of a voluntary disclosure.

Interest is charged from the date outstanding VAT should first have been paid to the date shown on the Notice of Assessment or Notice of Voluntary Disclosure. Where a repayment claim has been made and then it is found that VAT has been overclaimed, interest is calculated from seven days after the date the Commissioners authorised the repayment.

Any interest charged by the Commissioners will be limited to a maximum of 3 years prior to the date shown on the Notice of Assessment or Voluntary Disclosure.

3.4   Default surcharge

A default occurs if a return is not submitted on time or a payment is made late. On the first default, the Commissioners serve a surcharge liability notice on the taxpayer. The notice specifies a surcharge period, starting on the date of the notice and ending on the anniversary of the default.

If a trader defaults in the surcharge period, there are two consequences:

- the taxpayer is subject to a surcharge penalty if a payment is made late; and
- the surcharge period is extended to the anniversary of the new default.

The surcharge depends on the number of defaults in the surcharge period:

Default in the surcharge period	Surcharge as a percentage of the tax unpaid at the due date
First	2%
Second	5%
Third	10%
Fourth or more	15%

Surcharge assessments at rates below 10% will not be issued for amounts less than £200.

Where the rate of surcharge is 10% or more, an assessment will be issued for either £30 or the actual amount of the calculated surcharge, whichever is the greater.

In order to escape a surcharge liability notice the taxpayer must submit four consecutive quarterly returns on time accompanied by the full amounts of VAT due.

3.5   Example: default surcharge

Mark's return for 30 June 1998 is late, and the tax of £14,500 is not paid until 16 August 1998. His return for the following period is submitted late and the tax of £16,200 not paid until 9 November 1998.

What are the default surcharge consequences for Mark?

3.6   Solution

Return period ended 30.6.98.

First default: surcharge liability notice issued.

Return period ended 30.9.98.

First default within the surcharge period.

Penalty of £16,200 × 2% = £324 becomes payable.

The surchargeable period is extended to 30.9.99.

3.7   Activity

Jane accounted for VAT as follows:

Return period ended	VAT £	Date paid
30.6.98	11,500	18.11.98
30.9.98	12,200	18.11.98
31.12.98	10,800	29.1.99
31.3.99	8,900	10.5.99

What surcharge penalties will Jane be liable to?

3.8   Activity solution

Period ended 30.6.98.

VAT is paid late: a surcharge liability notice is served.

Period ended 30.9.98.

VAT is paid late: surcharge penalty of £12,200 × 2% = £244 is due.

Surcharge period extended to 30.9.99

Period ended 31.12.98.

VAT paid on time.

Period ended 31.3.99.

VAT is paid late; surcharge penalty of £8,900 × 5% = £445 is due.

Surcharge period extended to 31.3.00

3.9 Misdeclaration penalty

(a) Misdeclaration penalty is imposed whenever there has been a significant or repeated lack of care in preparing VAT returns. The penalty rate is 15% of the tax that would have been lost if the error had not been discovered.

(b) Penalty is considered when large or repeated misdeclarations are discovered **by the Commissioners.** A misdeclaration means

- a trader has claimed a repayment which is too large on a VAT return; or

- a trader has failed to tell the Commissioners within 30 days that a centrally issued assessment is too low.

Note: there is no penalty if an error is disclosed voluntarily.

(c) Errors will normally be measured against the trader's **gross amount of tax,** or 'GAT'.

Definition GAT is the sum of output tax and input tax that should have been declared on the return.

(d) A penalty will normally result if an error:

- equals or exceeds 30% of the GAT; or
- equals or exceeds £1 million; or
- is one of a series of errors.

(e) A penalty for repeated errors will never be issued without first issuing a warning notice, known as a penalty liability notice (PLN)

A PLN is issued if a misdeclaration is assessed which:

- equals or exceeds 10% of GAT; or
- equals or exceeds £500,000

A penalty will only be issued if all the following conditions are met.

- The Commissioners have issued a PLN

- Two or more errors have been made on separate VAT returns in the eight VAT periods following the issue of the PLN. This includes the period in which the PLN is issued.

- Each of the qualifying errors must exceed the 10% of GAT or £½ million test.

A penalty of 15% of the tax that would have been lost may then be issued.

(f)   There is no penalty if a trader discloses an error before the Commissioners begin enquiries into his VAT affairs.

A trader should deal with errors that he discovers as follows:

- If the net errors discovered in a period are £2,000 or less, he can note them in his VAT account and correct the error on his current VAT return:

- If the net errors exceed £2,000 he must advise his local VAT office.

(g)   No penalty is charged if the trader can convince the Commissioners, or a VAT Tribunal that he has a reasonable excuse.

3.10   Repayment supplement

If a trader is entitled to a VAT repayment because his input tax for a period exceeds his output tax for a VAT period and the repayment is delayed, a supplement of the greater of 5% of the repayment and £50 will be paid to him.

The following conditions must be satisfied.

(a)   the Commissioners must receive the VAT return on or before the due date:

(b)   the Commissioners must authorise repayment at least thirty days after receiving the VAT return; and

(c)   if the tax is overstated on the VAT return the error must not exceed the greater of 5% of the refund and £250.

> **Conclusion**   There are various penalties and surcharges that are imposed on taxpayers; of these, the most important for exam purposes are:
> - late notification of liability to register;
> - default surcharge; and
> - misdeclaration penalty

4   ZERO RATING

4.1   VATA 1994, Schedule 8

This schedule is divided into 16 groups, most of which are sub-divided into a number of items. The notes to each group extend or restrict the general provisions of individual items. The goods and services in each group are briefly described below.

Group 1: Food. Food of a kind used for human consumption is generally zero-rated except luxury items such as alcohol and confectionery.

Animal foodstuffs other than pet food, seeds producing edible crops and livestock are also zero-rated.

Group 2: Sewerage services and water

Group 3: Books and other printed matter. This group zero-rates a wide range of reading material (eg, newspapers, books, maps and sheet music).

Group 4: Talking books for the disabled and wireless sets for certain charities

Group 5: Construction of dwellings, etc. New buildings for residential or charitable use are zero rated.

Group 6: Protected buildings. Alterations to listed buildings where used for residential or charitable use are zero rated.

Group 7: International services. There is no general zero rating for the export of services as there is for the export of goods.

Group 8: Transport. Transporting passengers by road, rail and sea or air is generally zero-rated provided the vehicle or ship is designed to carry over eleven passengers (eg, not taxis). Most services and port handling charges.

Group 9: Caravans and houseboats. The sale or hire of caravans and houseboats is zero-rated. However, accommodation provided in them is excluded from zero-rating.

Group 10: Gold. Gold held in the UK is zero-rated when supplied between central banks and members of the London Gold Market.

Group 11: Bank notes.

Group 12: Drugs, medicines and appliances supplied on prescription by a chemist are zero rated.

Group 13: Imports and exports.

Group 14: Tax free shops.

Group 15: Charities. Gifts to, and supplies by, certain charities are zero-rated.

Group 16: Clothing and footwear. Young children's clothing and footwear are zero-rated provided they are unsuitable for older persons.

4.2   Exported goods

Goods removed from a place in the UK to a destination outside the UK may be zero-rated in certain circumstances, and this applies regardless of whether or not they fall within VATA 1994 Sch8. Such exports fall into three categories:

(a)   goods exported by the person who supplied them;
(b)   goods used as ships' stores and duty free merchandise; and
(c)   goods taken abroad by the person who buys them

5   EXEMPTION

5.1   VATA 1994 Schedule 9

This schedule is divided into twelve groups.

Group 1: Land. This group exempts the grant, assignment or surrender of an interest in land, a right over land or a licence to occupy land. However the freehold sale of a new (or uncompleted) building unless designed solely for a relevant residential or charitable use is standard rated.

Group 2: Insurance

Group 3: Postal services

Group 4: Betting, gaming and lotteries

Group 5: Finance

Group 6: Education. This group exempts education provided on a non-profit making basis.

Group 7: Health. This group exempts the health services.

Group 8: Burial and cremation

Group 9: Trade unions and professional bodies. This group exempts subscriptions charged by non-profit making trade unions, professional bodies.

Group 10: Sports. Entry fees to sports competitions used to provide prizes or charged by non-profit making sporting bodies.

Group 11: Works of art.

Group 12: Fund raising events by charities.

<u>Conclusion</u> It is important to differentiate between zero-rated and exempt supplies. A taxable supplier making only exempt supplies is not able to recover VAT on purchases.

Again, try to remember the main exempt categories ie,

- Land - grant assignment or surrender of an interest in land. But sale of a new freehold building for non-residential/charitable use is standard rated;

- Insurance;

- Postal services supplied by the Post office;

- Financial services eg, loans, brokerage, banking services, interest etc; and

- Education and health.

6   SPECIAL SCHEME FOR FARMERS

If farmers choose to join a special scheme taxable supplies made in the farmer's farming business are ignored in determining whether or not the farmer needs to register for VAT.

If a farmer is not registered for VAT, and makes a supply to a registered trader:

- he may issue an invoice showing a flat rate addition (FRA) to the price;
- the registered trader may treat FRA as input tax;
- the farmer may keep FRA and need not account for it to the Commissioners;
- FRA is 4% of the net price charged.

7   CHAPTER SUMMARY

This is the concluding chapter on VAT. The following areas were covered:

- accounting for VAT;
- the annual accounting system;
- records and accounts;
- assessments and appeals;
- criminal and civil penalties;
- the default surcharge;

- the misdeclaration penalty;
- zero-rated supplies; and
- exempt supplies

8   SELF TEST QUESTIONS

8.1   What is the purpose of a control visit? (2.1)

8.2   Within what time limits must assessment to VAT be made? (2.2)

8.3   How are VAT appeals dealt with? (2.3)

8.4   On which defaults do civil penalties arise? (3.2)

8.5   What are the principal occasions when a charge to interest will arise? (3.3)

8.6   How does the default surcharge operate? (3.4)

8.7   When is a trader entitled to a repayment supplement? (3.10)

8.8   What are the main categories of zero-rated supplies? (4.1)

8.9   What are the main categories of exempt supplies? (5.1)

9   EXAMINATION TYPE QUESTION

9.1   Alan and Roger

Alan and Roger commenced in partnership as chartered architects on 1 February 1998 and the values of their supplies were as follows.

Month	Fees for services invoiced £	Sales of unsuitable office equipment £
1998		
February	2,750	
March	6,000	
April	3,700	
May	3,500	
June	3,100	
July	2,000	
August	1,900	
September	6,200	1,500
October	3,200	
November	6,300	
December	12,400	
1999		
January	-	
February	35,700	
March	29,400	

Alan and Roger informed the Commissioners of their liability to register by telephone on 12 October 1999 and submitted VAT form 1 on 28 November 1999.

You are required:

(a) to discuss when Alan and Roger are liable to be registered for VAT.

(10 marks)

(b) to detail from what date they will be deemed to have registered and explain how any penalties would be computed

(5 marks)

(Total: 15 marks)

10 ANSWER TO EXAMINATION TYPE QUESTION

10.1 Alan and Roger

(a) **Date of liability to register for VAT**

Year	Month	Fees invoiced £	Annual cumulation £
1998	February	2,750	2,750
	March	6,000	8,750
	April	3,700	12,450
	May	3,500	15,950
	June	3,100	19,050
	July	2,000	21,050
	August	1,900	22,950
	September	6,200	29,150
	October	3,200	32,350
	November	6,300	38,650
	December	12,400	51,050
1999	January	-	51,050
	February	35,700	84,000
	March	29,400	107,400

The statutory tests for liability to register for VAT are based on taxable turnover.

However, capital assets of the business are disregarded for the turnover tests even though they are supplied in the course or furtherance of the business.

The statutory tests for registration liability are set out as follows:

(i) If, at the end of any month, the value of taxable supplies in the period of one year ending exceeds £50,000, liability to register applies.

(ii) If, at any time, there are reasonable grounds for believing that the value of taxable supplies in the period of 30 days then beginning will exceed £50,000, liability to register applies.

Under (i) above liability can be avoided if the Commissioners are satisfied that for the period of one year just beginning the limit of £48,000 will not be exceeded ie, the turnover has been uncharacteristically high.

If (i) above applies the trader must notify the Commissioners within 30 days of the end of the relevant month and is registered from the end of the month following the relevant month or from an earlier date if agreed. The relevant month is the month at the end of which the trader became liable to be registered.

If (ii) above applies the trader must notify the Commissioners before the end of the 30-day period in which his taxable supplies are likely to exceed £50,000. He will then be registered from the start of the 30 days.

Applying these test to Alan and Roger it is clear that they should be registered following the year to 31 December 1998. Registration would then be due from 1 February 1999.

(b)   **Penalties for late registration**

As explained in part (a) above registration was required by 1 February 1999.

There is a minimum penalty of £50 for failure to register on time. The maximum penalty depends on the period of delay between the date when the trader should have been registered and the date the Commissioners were notified. It is calculated as a percentage of excess of the output tax over the input tax for the period of delay as follows:

Delay period	*Percentage*
9 months or less	5%
Between 9 and 18 months	10%
Over 18 months	15%

The Commissioners are not notified until they receive VAT Form 1 (ie, on 28 November 1999). Thus, a 10% penalty can be imposed.

The penalty can be avoided if there is a reasonable excuse for failing to notify. Any penalty can be mitigated up to 100% if the Commissioners or, on appeal, a VAT tribunal think fit.

27 NATIONAL INSURANCE CONTRIBUTIONS

INTRODUCTION & LEARNING OBJECTIVES

Individuals who are either employed or self employed must pay national insurance contributions in addition to income tax. National insurance contributions are also payable by employers.

This tax is easily overlooked in an exam situation: remember that individuals (either employees, employers or the self-employed) and companies (as employers) pay national insurance contributions.

When you have studied this chapter you should have learned the following:

- The different classes of contribution.
- The operation of Class 1 primary contributions.
- The operation of Class 1 secondary contributions.
- The operation of Class 1A secondary contributions on company cars and private use fuel.
- How Class 1 contributions are calculated.
- Voluntary Class 3 contributions.
- Class 2 contributions.
- The operation of Class 4 contributions.
- An outline of the basic social security benefits

1   INTRODUCTION

1.1   Classes of contribution

The amount a person pays and the statutory rules governing payment of contributions depend upon the class of contribution. These classes are

| Class 1 | **Primary**. A percentage-based contribution payable by employees earnings £64 or more a week (for 1998/99). |
| | **Secondary:** A percentage-based contribution paid by employers of the above employees. |

Class 2   Flat rate weekly contribution payable by a self-employed person whose annual accounting profits (for 1998/99) are £3,590 or more.

Class 3   Flat rate **voluntary** contribution which can be paid by anyone whose contribution record is otherwise insufficient for entitlement to the full range of benefits.

Class 4   A percentage-based contribution payable, in addition to Class 2 contributions, by a self-employed person on taxable profits between £7,310 and £25,220 (for 1998/99).

2   EMPLOYED PERSONS

2.1   Class 1 contributions: employed persons

A liability for Class 1 contributions arises where an individual

(a)   is employed and
(b)   is aged 16 or over and
(c)   has earnings at least as much as the lower earnings limit.

A person holding an office is classed as an employee for this purpose if the emoluments are assessed under Schedule E. Included under this rule are such persons as company directors (where there is no employee's service contract), MPs and local authority councillors.

Exceptions. Primary and secondary contributions are not payable in respect of certain employed persons. The more important of these are persons:

(a)   aged under 16 or
(b)   employed outside the UK or
(c)   earning below the lower earnings limit (£64 per week).

2.2   Primary contributions

(a)   Virtually every employee is liable to pay Class 1 contributions at the **standard rate**.

The contributions are **not** allowable deductions for income tax purposes.

(b)   The standard rate of contribution is a percentage of the employee's weekly or monthly gross earnings up to the upper earnings' limit (£485 per week). There is no liability if gross earnings fall below the lower earnings' limit. Directors may be dealt with somewhat differently (see below).

(c)   Where a person is liable to pay contributions because earnings exceed the lower earnings' limit - the amount of the contribution is calculated on both the earnings below and above the lower limit: earnings above the upper limit are ignored.

(d)   Where the employer provides an occupational pension scheme, or the employee provides his own personal pension scheme, then those employees who are members of such schemes are 'contracted-out' of the State Earnings Related Pension Scheme (SERPS). Contracted out employees pay a lower rate of contributions.

(e)   The earnings on which Class 1 contributions are calculated comprise ANY remuneration derived from employment and paid in MONEY. The calculation is on gross earnings, with no deduction allowed for any income tax payable. Specifically, gross earnings includes

- wages, salary, overtime pay, commission or bonus
- sick pay, including statutory sick pay
- tips and gratuities paid or allocated by the employer
- payment of the cost of travel between home and work
- maternity pay
- amounts set aside throughout the year to be paid in a lump sum at a specified time (treated as earnings when set aside, not when paid)

- remuneration, such as bonuses, made by using financial instruments such as shares, unit-trusts, options, gilts, gold, precious stones, fine wines and 'readily convertible' assets.

The following are DISREGARDED in calculating gross earnings for primary contributions.

- benefits-in-kind (but see above regarding use of financial instruments)
- reimbursement of expenses actually incurred in carrying out the employment
- redundancy payments
- pay in lieu of notice
- payments of any pension.

2.3   Employers' secondary contributions

The full rate of secondary contributions, as shown in your tax tables, is payable by the employer irrespective of the employee's category.

Only where the employee earns below the lower earnings limit or the employment is not within the scope of Class 1 contributions will there be no liability to secondary contributions.

If earnings exceed the lower earnings limit the liability is calculated on ALL earnings; there is no upper earnings limit.

As with primary contributions, the rate payable by the employer depends upon whether or not the employment is contracted-out of SERPS. The rates for secondary contributions depend on whether a contracted out money purchase (COMP) scheme or a contracted out salary related (COSR) scheme is used.

2.4   Company cars and free fuel

Employers are required to pay Class 1A secondary contributions on the tax assessable benefit of cars and free fuel provided for the private use of their employees.

The main details concerning this charge are

(a)   The NICs will be computed using the income tax car benefit and fuel scale benefit.

(b)   No contributions will be levied where employee's earnings are less than £8,500 a year.

(c)   No contributions will be levied if the car is not available for private use, or if the employee makes full reimbursement for private fuel used.

(d)   Contributions are at the main rate (10% for 1998/99) and are collected annually in arrears.

For example, for an 1,800 cc car costing new £16,000 and under 4 years old on 5 April 1999 Class 1A contributions for 1998/99 will be:

	Business mileage		
	2,500 or less	*2,501- 17,999*	*18,000 or more*
	£	£	£
Income tax scale charges:			
Car (£16,000 × 35%)	5,600	5,600	5,600
Less: £5,600 × ⅓/⅔	-	(1,867)	(3,733)
Fuel (petrol)	1,280	1,280	1,280
	6,880	5,013	3,147

NIC at 10%

Car	560.00	373.30	186.70
Fuel	128.00	128.00	128.00
	688.00	501.30	314.70

2.5   Calculation of contributions

(a)   Exact percentage method

This is mainly used for computerised payrolls, and may also be used to calculate contributions on the earnings of company directors.

Under this method the primary and secondary contributions are computed separately (using the % rates shown in the tables) to the nearest penny.

(b)   Table method

This is the usual method of calculating contributions and uses sets of contribution tables prepared by the DSS. These tables are lettered A to W and are supplied to employers according to their needs. The tables most commonly in use are

- Table A: non-contracted-out standard rate contributions
- Table D: contracted-out standard rate contributions (for COSR schemes).
- Table F: contracted out standard rate contributions (for COMP schemes).

2.6   Deduction and payment by the employer

The employer calculates the primary and secondary contributions at each weekly or monthly pay date and records them on the employee's PAYE deductions working sheet.

At the end of each PAYE month (5th) the total primary and secondary contributions become payable to the Collector of Taxes, along with income tax deducted under PAYE, not later than 14 days thereafter (ie by 19th).

2.7   Persons with more than one job

(a)   Liability

A person with more than one job is separately liable for primary contributions in respect of each job falling within the scope of Class 1 contributions and where earnings are £64.00 or more per week. Each employer is also separately liable for secondary contributions.

(b)   Annual maximum

The total Class 1 contributions from all employments is subject to an overall annual maximum. Employees with more than one job can prevent overpayment of contributions by

- applying for deferment of contributions; or
- refund after the end of the fiscal year.

2.8   Company directors

Where a person is a company director at the **beginning** of the fiscal year, he is deemed to have an **annual** earnings' period and the **annual** upper and lower earnings' limits apply. For 1998/99 these are

	£	
Lower	3,328	(52 × £64)
Upper	25,220	(52 × £485)

These amounts apply even if the directorship terminates before the end of the fiscal year.

Where a person is appointed a director during the fiscal year the earnings period is the remaining weeks in the fiscal year, including the week in which the appointment is made. The upper and lower earnings' limits are proportionally reduced.

The above rules apply regardless of whether the director has emoluments under a service contract or only receives fees voted at the company's AGM. If the director receives advances of fees which are subsequently voted at the AGM, these are regarded as earnings when paid (not when later voted). However, where fees are voted which have not already been treated as earnings for contribution purposes, they must be so treated when voted. Finally, should fees be voted to a director in advance, they will become earnings for contribution purposes on the date that the director has an unreserved right to draw them.

2.9   Example: National insurance contributions for directors

Hobbs and Sutcliffe are directors of Scorers Ltd.   The following information is relevant for 1998/99.

Hobbs: His service contract provides for a salary of £960 (gross) per month and a bonus to be voted by the company at the AGM. He actually had drawings of £1,200 per month and the AGM voted a bonus of £6,500 on 30 June 1999.

Sutcliffe: Has no service contract. Had drawings of £1,200 per month. Fees of £15,000 were voted by the AGM on 30 June 1999.

Calculate each director's earnings in 1998/99 for Class 1 contribution purposes.

2.10   Solution

		£
Hobbs:	Monthly salary earnings under normal rules	
	12 × £960	11,520
	Drawings in advance of bonus voted	
	12 × £(1,200 − 960)	2,880
		———
		14,400
		———

Note: the balance of the bonus (£3,620) will be earnings in 1999/00.

		£
Sutcliffe:	Drawings in advance of fees voted	
	12 × £1,200	£14,400
		———

Note: the balance of fees (£600) will be earnings in 1999/00.

2.11   Employees reaching pensionable age

An employee who continues to work after attaining pensionable age (65 for a man, 60 for a woman) has no liability for primary Class 1 contributions. A certificate of age exemption must be claimed from the local DSS office and given to the employer.

The employer is still liable for full secondary contributions.

2.12   Voluntary Class 3 contributions

(a)   **Purpose**

The only purpose of voluntary contributions is to enable a person to maintain a contribution record sufficient for entitlement to basic retirement pension, widow's pension, widowed mother's allowance and widow's payment.

Such contributions are of particular importance, therefore, for individuals who are excluded from paying as employed or self-employed persons, and for those who do not make sufficient contributions under another Class.

(b)   **Entitlement to contribute**

Class 3 contributions are allowed only to enable a person to qualify for benefits, and entitlement to contribute therefore depends upon the level of Class 1, 2 or 3 contributions already attained in the particular fiscal year.

This level is measured by a person's earnings factor calculated by the DSS. Only where the person's earnings factor is less than the qualifying earnings factor (annual lower earnings limit ie, £3,328 for 1998/99) for a fiscal year may voluntary contributions be paid.

3   SELF EMPLOYED PERSONS

3.1   Liability

All self-employed persons over the age of 16 must pay both Class 2 and Class 4 contributions, unless a certificate of exemption is held.

3.2   Class 2 contributions

Class 2 contributions are payable at a weekly flat rate (£6.35 for 1998/99).

Contributions may be paid by means of direct debit from a bank account or by quarterly billing in arrears.

The following persons are not liable to pay Class 2 contributions

(a)   Children under 16 and men aged 65 or over and women aged 60 or over.
(b)   Those with low earnings who obtain certificates of exemption.

The low earnings limit for 1998/99 is £3,590.

Only **one** Class 2 contribution is payable weekly regardless of the number of self-employed occupations; however, the earnings from all such occupations are aggregated to decide whether or not the low earnings limit is exceeded.

3.3   Class 4 contributions

These contributions are, in effect, a form of additional taxation, since they bring no entitlement to any benefits. The contributions are calculated as a percentage of profits assessed to income tax under Schedule D Case I and II within upper and lower limits specified. The calculation is made without any allowance for income tax payable.

The contribution rate for 1998/99 is 6% on earnings between £7,310 and £25,220.

Earnings for this purpose are Schedule D Case I or II profits after capital allowances and losses, plus any balancing charges. Trading charges on income are also deductible.

The liability is paid as part of the two income tax payments on account (due 31 January in the tax year and 31 July following). Each payment is equal to half the Class 4 NIC liability of the previous year with any over or under payment adjusted for on the following 31 January. There is an interest charge for late payment as though the NIC was tax. There is no income tax allowance for Class 4 NIC paid.

3.4   Persons not liable to pay Class 4 contributions

(a)   Children under 16, men aged 65 or over and women aged 60 or over at the start of the tax year.

(b)   Those whose earnings do not exceed the lower Class 4 profits threshold.

(c)   Those whose earnings are not immediately derived from carrying on a trade, profession or vocation (eg, a sleeping partner in a partnership).

3.5   More than one business

Class 4 contributions are payable on the aggregate of all profits from self-employment up to the upper profits limit, irrespective of the number of self-employed occupations.

4   OUTLINE OF SOCIAL SECURITY BENEFITS

4.1   Introduction

The syllabus requires an outline knowledge of the main areas of social security benefit. You will not be required to know the detail concerning eligibility for these benefits and below we simply list the nature of the main benefits with the amounts currently payable.

4.2   Taxable State Benefits

The following benefits are liable to income tax S617 ICTA 1988

Benefit	Annual total (52 weeks) (where appropriate) chargeable to tax 1998-99
Industrial death benefit:	**£**
Widow's pension	
Permanent rate - higher	3,364.40
lower	1,009.32
Invalid care allowance	
Standard rate	2,012.40
Invalidity allowance paid with retirement pension	
Incapacity before age 40	707.20
40 to 49 years of age	447.20
50 to pension age 60	
(men) or 55 (women)	223.60
Non contributory retirement pension	
Standard rate	2,012.40
Age addition (80 years or over)	13.00
Retirement pension	
Standard rate	3,364.40
Age addition (80 years or over)	13.00
Income support	
Means tested	
Jobseekers allowance (contribution based)	
under age 18	1,575.60
18 to 24 years of age	2,072.20
age 25 or over	2,618.20
Jobseekers allowance (non contributory)	
Means tested	
Widow's benefit	
Pension (standard rate)	3,364.40
Widowed mother's allowance	3,364.40
Dependent adults	
with retirement pension	2,012.40
with invalid care allowance	1,203.80
Incapacity benefit*	
Long term	3,364.40
Increased for age: Higher rate	707.20
Lower rate	353.60
Short term higher rate (under pension age)	3,000.40
(over pension age)	3,226.60

*   Short term incapacity benefit is paid at a lower rate for the first 28 weeks, and is not taxable (see beyond).

4.3   State Benefits: Not Taxable

The following benefits are not liable to income tax

	Weekly rate £ from 6 April 1998
Attendance allowance	
Higher rate (day and night)	51.30
Lower rate (day and night)	34.30
Child benefit	
For the eldest qualifying child	11.45
For each other child	9.30
Christmas bonus	
Rate	10.00
Family credit	
The maximum rate is made up of the following:	
Adult credit (for 1 or 2 parents)	48.80
(for claimants working over 30 hours per week)	
30 hour credit	10.80
and for each child aged: under 11	12.35
11-15	20.45
16-17	25.40
18 (if age 18 before 17 October 1997)	35.50
Guardian's allowance	
For eldest qualifying child	9.90
For each other child	11.30
Disability living allowance	
(care component)	
Higher rate	51.30
Middle rate	34.30
Lower rate	13.60
Disability living allowance	
(mobility component)	
Higher rate	35.85
Lower rate	13.60
Severe disablement allowance	
Rate	39.10
There are additions related to the age of becoming	
incapable of work:	
under 40	13.60
under 50	8.60
under 60	4.30
Extra benefit for dependent adult	23.20
Extra benefit for dependent child - eldest child	9.90
- each other child	11.30
Incapacity benefit	
Short term lower rate	
Under pension age	48.80
Over pension age	62.05
Extra benefits for dependants	
Dependent children	
Child for whom higher child benefit rate is payable	9.90
Each other child	11.30

5   CHAPTER SUMMARY

This chapter has dealt with national insurance contributions. The following areas were covered:

- Classes of contribution;
- Primary Class 1 contributions payable by employees;
- Secondary Class 1 contributions payable by employers;
- Class 1A secondary contributions payable by employers on company cars and free fuel;
- The national insurance position for company directors;
- Voluntary Class 3 contributions;
- Class 2 contributions payable by the self-employed; and
- Class 4 contributions payable by the self-employed.

6   SELF TEST QUESTIONS

6.1   What are the four classes of contribution? (1.1)

6.2   When does liability for Class 1 contributions arise for an individual? (2.1)

6.3   What earnings are Class 1 primary contributions calculated on? (2.2)

6.4   What earnings are Class 1 secondary contributions calculated on? (2.3)

6.5   How are Class 1A contributions calculated? (2.4)

6.6   How are national insurance contributions for company directors calculated? (2.8)

6.7   What Class 1 contributions are payable once employees reach pensionable age? (2.13)

6.8   Which people are not liable to pay Class 2 contributions? (3.2)

6.9   What tax relief is available for Class 4 contributions? (3.3)

6.10   What earnings are Class 4 contributions calculated on? (3.3)

7   EXAMINATION TYPE QUESTION

7.1   Mr Mouland

Mr Mouland commenced trading as a forest fencer on 1 April 1996 and prepares accounts to 31 March each year.

Mr Mouland has given you the following information:

(a)   His trading profit for the year ended 31 March 1999 was £18,329.

(b)   Mr Mouland employed Jack and Jill during 1998/99. Their basic wages were £5,200 and £12,480 respectively. Jack also received a bonus of £1,000 which Mr Mouland paid him in the week commencing 1 May 1998 after early completion of a job.

Jack's and Jill's wages and employer's national insurance were included in the profit figure which Mr Mouland has given you.

You are required to calculate the following:

(a)   The total Class 1 contributions which Mr Mouland must pay to the Revenue for 1998/99;
(b)   The Class 2 and Class 4 contributions payable by Mr Mouland for 1998/99.

8   ANSWER TO EXAMINATION TYPE QUESTION

8.1   Mr Mouland

(a)   **Class 1 contributions**

Employees'

		£	£
Jack	£64 × 52 × 2%	66.56	
	£36 × 51 × 10%	183.60	
	£421 × 1 × 10%	42.10	
			292.26
Jill	£64 × 52 × 2%	66.56	
	£176 × 52 × 10%	915.20	
			981.76
			1,274.02

Employer's

		£	£
Jack	£100 × 51 × 3%	153.00	
	£1,100 × 1 × 10%	110.00	
		263.00	
Jill	£240 × 52 × 10%	1,248.00	
			1,511.00
Total Class 1 contributions			2,785.02

(b)   **Class 2 contributions**

52 × £6.35	£330.20

Class 4 contributions

	£
Schedule D Case I (y/e 31.3.99)	18,329
Less: Lower limit	7,310
	11,019
Class 4 contributions £11,019 × 6%	£661.14

Student Questionnaire

Because we believe in listening to our customers, this questionnaire has been designed to discover exactly what you think about us and our materials. We want to know how we can continue improving our customer support and how to make our top class books even better - how do you use our books, what do you like about them and what else would you like to see us do to make them better?

1 Where did you hear about AT Foulks Lynch ACCA Textbooks?

- ☐ Colleague or friend
- ☐ Employer recommendation
- ☐ Lecturer recommendation
- ☐ AT Foulks Lynch mailshot
- ☐ Conference
- ☐ ACCA literature
- ☐ Students Newsletter
- ☐ Pass Magazine
- ☐ Internet
- ☐ Other ....

2 Overall, do you think the AT Foulks Lynch ACCA Textbooks are:

☐ Excellent   ☐ Good   ☐ Average   ☐ Poor   ☐ No opinion

3 Please evaluate AT Foulks Lynch service using the following criteria:

	Excellent	Good	Average	Poor	No opinion
Professional	☐	☐	☐	☐	☐
Polite	☐	☐	☐	☐	☐
Informed	☐	☐	☐	☐	☐
Helpful	☐	☐	☐	☐	☐

4 How did you obtain this book?

- ☐ From a bookshop
- ☐ From your college
- ☐ From us by mail order
- ☐ From us by telephone
- ☐ Internet
- ☐ Other ....

5 How long did it take to receive your materials?   .... days.

☐ Very fast   ☐ Fast   ☐ Satisfactory   ☐ Slow   ☐ No opinion

6 How do you rate the value of these features of the Tax Framework Textbook?

		Excellent	Good	Average	Poor	No opinion
1	Syllabus referenced to chapters	☐	☐	☐	☐	☐
2	Teaching Guide referenced to chapters	☐	☐	☐	☐	☐
3	Step by step approach and solutions	☐	☐	☐	☐	☐
4	Activities throughout the chapters	☐	☐	☐	☐	☐
5	Self test questions	☐	☐	☐	☐	☐
6	Examination type questions	☐	☐	☐	☐	☐
7.	Index	☐	☐	☐	☐	☐

Continued/...

7 Have you purchased any other AT Foulks Lynch ACCA titles?
If so, please specify title(s) and your rating of each below:

Title	Excellent	Good	Average	Poor	No opinion
....	☐	☐	☐	☐	☐
....	☐	☐	☐	☐	☐
....	☐	☐	☐	☐	☐
....	☐	☐	☐	☐	☐

8 Have you used publications other than AT Foulks Lynch ACCA titles?
If so, please specify title(s) and your rating of each below:

Title and Publisher	Excellent	Good	Average	Poor	No opinion
....	☐	☐	☐	☐	☐
....	☐	☐	☐	☐	☐
....	☐	☐	☐	☐	☐
....	☐	☐	☐	☐	☐

9 Will you buy the AT Foulks Lynch ACCA Textbooks again?

☐ Yes   ☐ No   ☐ Not sure

Why? ....

10 Please write here any additional comments you might have on any of the above areas or tell us what you would like us to do to make the books even better:

....

....

....

....

11 Your details: these are for the internal use of the ACCA and AT Foulks Lynch Ltd only and will not be supplied to any outside organisations.

Name
....

Address
....

....

Telephone
....

Do you have your own e-mail address?   ☐ Yes   ☐ No
Do you have access to the World Wide Web?   ☐ Yes   ☐ No
Do you have access to a CD Rom Drive?   ☐ Yes   ☐ No

Please send to:

Quality Feedback Department
FREEPOST 2254
AT Foulks Lynch Ltd, 4 The Griffin Centre, Staines Road, Feltham, Middlesex, TW14 0BR.

Thank you for your time.

ACCA
AT FOULKS LYNCH

HOTLINES
Telephone: 0181 844 0667
Enquiries: 0181 831 9990
Fax: 0181 831 9991

AT FOULKS LYNCH LTD
Number 4, The Griffin Centre
Staines Road, Feltham
Middlesex TW14 0HS

Examination Date:
☐ December 98
☐ June 99

	Publications			Distance Learning	Open Learning
	98 Edition Textbooks	**2/98 Edition Revision Series**	**2/98 Edition Lynchpins**	**Include helpline & marking (except for overseas Open Learning)**	
Module A - Foundation Stage					
1 Accounting Framework	£17.95 ☐UK ☐IAS	£10.95 ☐UK ☐IAS	£5.95 ☐	£85 ☐	£89 ☐
2 Legal Framework	£17.95 ☐	£10.95 ☐	£5.95 ☐	£85 ☐	£89 ☐
Module B					
3 Management Information	£17.95 ☐	£10.95 ☐	£5.95 ☐	£85 ☐	£89 ☐
4 Organisational Framework	£17.95 ☐	£10.95 ☐	£5.95 ☐	£85 ☐	£89 ☐
Module C - Certificate Stage					
5 Information Analysis	£17.95 ☐	£10.95 ☐	£5.95 ☐	£85 ☐	£89 ☐
6 Audit Framework	£17.95 ☐UK ☐IAS	£10.95 ☐UK ☐IAS	£5.95 ☐	£85 ☐	£89 ☐
Module D					
7 Tax Framework FA(2)97 Dec 98	£17.95 ☐	£10.95 ☐	£5.95 ☐	£85 ☐	£89 ☐
7 Tax Framework FA98 Jun 99	£17.95 ☐	£10.95 ☐	£5.95 ☐	£85 ☐	£89 ☐
8 Managerial Finance	£17.95 ☐	£10.95 ☐	£5.95 ☐	£85 ☐	£89 ☐
Module E - Professional Stage					
9 ICDM	£18.95 ☐	£10.95 ☐	£5.95 ☐	£85 ☐	£89 ☐
10 Accounting & Audit Practice	£22.95 ☐UK ☐IAS	£10.95 ☐UK ☐IAS	£5.95 ☐	£85 ☐	£89 ☐
11 Tax Planning FA(2)97 Dec 98	£18.95 ☐	£10.95 ☐	£5.95 ☐	£85 ☐	£89 ☐
11 Tax Planning FA98 Jun 99	£18.95 ☐	£10.95 ☐	£5.95 ☐	£85 ☐	£89 ☐
Module F					
12 Management & Strategy	£18.95 ☐	£10.95 ☐	£5.95 ☐	£85 ☐	£89 ☐
13 Financial Rep Environment	£20.95 ☐UK ☐IAS	£10.95 ☐UK ☐IAS	£5.95 ☐	£85 ☐	£89 ☐
14 Financial Strategy	£19.95 ☐	£10.95 ☐	£5.95 ☐	£85 ☐	£89 ☐
P & P + Delivery UK Mainland	£2.00/book	£1.00/book	£1.00/book	£5.00/subject	£5.00/subject
NI, ROI & EU Countries	£5.00/book	£3.00/book	£3.00/book	£15.00/subject	£15.00/subject
Rest of world standard air service	£10.00/book	£8.00/book	£8.00/book	£25.00/subject	£25.00/subject
Rest of world courier service†	£22.00/book	£20.00/book	£14.00/book	£47.00/subject	£47.00/subject

SINGLE ITEM SUPPLEMENT: If you only order 1 item, INCREASE postage costs by £2.50 for UK, NI & EU Countries or by £10.00 for Rest of World Services

TOTAL		
Sub Total £		
Post & Packing £		
Total £		

Telephone number essential for this service *Payments in Sterling in London* | Order Total £ | |

DELIVERY DETAILS
☐ Mr ☐ Miss ☐ Mrs ☐ Ms Other
Initials   Surname
Address

Postcode
Telephone   Deliver to home ☐
Company name
Address

Postcode
Telephone   Fax
Monthly report to go to employer ☐   Deliver to work ☐

Please Allow:	UK mainland	- 5-10 workdays
	NI, ROI & EU Countries	- 1-3 weeks
	Rest of world standard air service	- up to 6 weeks
	Rest of world courier service	- 10 workdays

PAYMENT OPTIONS
1. I enclose Cheque/PO/Bankers Draft for £_____
   Please make cheques payable to AT Foulks Lynch Ltd.

2. Charge Access/Visa A/c No: Expiry Date 0 1 9 1

   4 9 2 9 7 7 2 1 7 1 1 3 4

Signature   Date

DECLARATION
I agree to pay as indicated on this form and understand that
AT Foulks Lynch Terms and Conditions apply (available on
request). I understand that AT Foulks Lynch Ltd are not liable
for non-delivery if the rest of world standard air service is used.

Signature   Date

Notes: All delivery times subject to stock availability.
Signature required on receipt (except rest of world
standard air service). Please give both addresses for
Distance Learning students where possible.

Form effective from June 98 (ACCATXJ8).   *All details correct at time of printing.*   *Source: ACCATXJ8*